The Writer's Roles

READINGS WITH RHETORIC

Elizabeth Penfield
University of New Orleans

Nancy Wicker
United States Naval Academy

Audience:
Publication:
seperate sheet of paper or on
Acknowledgements

Scott, Foresman and Company
Glenview, Illinois London, England

Acknowledgments for literary selections appear on pp. 487–492, which are an extension of the copyright page.

An Instructor's Manual is available.
It may be obtained through your local Scott, Foresman representative or by writing to the English Editor, College Division, Scott, Foresman and Company, 1900 East Lake Avenue, Glenview, Illinois 60025.

Library of Congress Cataloging in Publication Data

Penfield, Elizabeth, 1939-
The writer's roles.

Includes index.
1. College readers. 2. English language—Rhetoric.
I. Wicker, Nancy, 1949- II. Title.
PE1417.P434 1985 808′.042 84-14069
ISBN 0-673-15859-4

1 2 3 4 5 6–MVN–89 88 87 86 85 84

PREFACE

The approach of this reader with rhetoric is eclectic rather than exclusive. The book provides ample discussion of the traditional modes of narration, description, comparison and contrast, cause and effect, example, analogy, process analysis, and argument. But rather than emphasize these modes as aims in themselves, we have chosen to subordinate them to the more important concerns of rhetorical stance—occasion, audience, purpose, and voice.

Thus this book is first and foremost a text for writers. In each part and chapter, the introduction, the writing assignments, and the description of the writing process emphasize the techniques and methods that writers use. Each chapter's selected readings reinforce those techniques by exemplifying writers, both nonliterary and literary, in their roles of observer, expositor, evaluator, persuader, and speaker. These authors and all the writers represented in the text are writing as professionals, but they are writing to a general, educated audience not to an audience of fellow experts. The writers represented are journalists, reviewers, literary critics, historians, scientists, technical writers, doctors, professors, and military officers.

THE WRITER'S ROLES

The Writer's Roles: Readings with Rhetoric, through explanation and illustration, emphasizes the process of writing, of taking account of one's self, one's world, audience, and purpose. In determining what to say, to whom, and how, a writer chooses a role or a rhetorical stance. Depending upon the relationship among author, subject, and audience, a writer's rhetorical stance relies primarily on observing, explaining, evaluating, or persuading, and in some cases on a combination of those skills. A good book, for instance, can move a writer to record observations in a journal, to write a report explaining the book's contents, to draft a review evaluating the book for a magazine or newspaper, or to persuade people to read the volume. For these reasons, we have divided the book into four roles of the writer—observer, expositor, evaluator, persuader; a fifth section focuses on written forms of spoken discourse, and a sixth includes the writer in multiple roles.

We have sequenced these roles from simplest to most complex, so that one builds upon the other. Though the roles overlap, all good writers choose among them, finding the ones best suited to their purpose, selecting the proper voice, audience, and subject. Thus, for example, observers focus more often on themselves and on their relationship to the world; in contrast, evaluators, though they use the techniques of observing and researching, focus on deriving judgments from carefully weighed information and articulated standards.

Each of the text's six parts is introduced by a discussion of the role under consideration, and each of the twelve chapters opens with a description of the specific rhetorical stance analyzed and concludes with a writing assignment and extended analysis of the writing process. Except for the journal entries in Part 1 and the anthology of readings in Part 6, each selection is introduced by a headnote and is followed first by questions on style and structure and then by ideas for a first draft. Traditional rhetorical terms are discussed in the text and further defined in the Glossary of Rhetorical Terms, where they are cross-referenced to the readings. A comprehensive Index emphasizes various writing techniques, keyed to passages in the text.

READINGS FROM A VARIETY OF DISCIPLINES AND PROFESSIONS

The readings in *The Writer's Roles* are in cases interdisciplinary because we believe that understanding the essential rhetorical principles of each writer's role is basic to the later development of a writer in a given profession. Thus we include, for example, a historian writing about the death of Mary, Queen of Scots, a scientist discussing the proportion of size to weight, and a political analyst evaluating a recent presidential campaign. These authors, however, are writing to a general audience. So, too, the literary figures are chosen because they illustrate particular roles, not because they write literary masterpieces that present the central ideas of the humanities. No matter what the field or discipline, the readings have been selected because they show writers at work, instructing and entertaining, writing with personal and professional concerns for audiences with whom they want to share those same concerns.

THE WRITING PROCESS

After each reading selection, we suggest ideas for a first draft, an assignment that can be turned into a finished paper by turning to the Writing Process at the end of each chapter. There, we discuss how to derive ideas for writing, how to develop and organize those ideas, how to find a voice, how to revise, and how to link one role to another by considering additional contexts for writing. Thus all the assignments lead students through the overlapping stages of the writing process and encourage a variety of rhetorical choices.

INTERDISCIPLINARY WRITING ASSIGNMENTS

In addition to analyzing how to write essays, the writing assignments explain how to carry out research, how to conduct interviews, how to deliver effective oral presentations, and how to work together on group projects. Framed for the world beyond the English classroom and frequently for the world beyond the university, the assignments include the traditional genres of the personal essay, the review, and the argumentative essay; at the same time, the text offers innovative assignments such as a history of a company or product, a scientific analysis of a natural disaster, and a written interview. Whether the form is a diary entry, an autobiography, an argument, an explanation, an analysis, an advertisement, a speech, or a lecture, the writing assignments encourage students to see themselves not only as students writing but as writers writing.

THE WRITER

Upon occasion we read to be moved by the power of language and thought. Other times we read for information or for simple entertainment. This text is based on the belief that before most writers achieve the former, they must practice the latter. To write is to learn; to write effectively is to share that knowledge. Thus *The Writer's Roles* takes its name from its dual focus on the writer's rhetorical stance and on the writing process. It is a book of and about writing, composed for apprentice writers. The text will not necessarily make writing any less arduous, but it will make it more comprehensible, more accessible, more engaging, and more rewarding.

ACKNOWLEDGMENTS

For their support and encouragement, we wish to thank our colleagues at the United States Naval Academy, particularly David O. Tomlinson and Laurence W. Mazzeno, and at the University of New Orleans, particularly Edward M. Socola and David Dillon. Special thanks, as always, go to Betty Wisdom, Harriett Prentiss, and our students, and for their keen editing and proofreading, our particular appreciation goes to Lydia Webster and Lillian R. Wicker. We are also grateful for the advice of the able reviewers of the manuscript: Marilyn Cooper, University of Southern California; Lezlie Laws Couch, University of Missouri—Columbia; Michael Feehan, University of Texas—Arlington; Donald Ross, University of Minnesota; Jack Selzer, Pennsylvania State University; and Stephen Zelnick, Temple University.

Elizabeth Penfield
Nancy Wicker

OVERVIEW

CONTENTS

CHAPTER 3

THE PERSONAL ESSAYIST

PART 6

THE WRITER IN MULTIPLE ROLES
FURTHER READINGS

INTRODUCTION

The skilled writer, like an accomplished actor, can choose from a repertoire of roles and adopt each with ease. But whether observer, expositor, evaluator, persuader, or speaker, the writer strives for clarity, felicity, drama, original thought, style, and, above all, truth.

The significance of writing has been recognized since writer first put stylus to tablet. In "Of Studies," the Renaissance essayist and philosopher Francis Bacon asserts, "Reading maketh a full man, conference a ready man, and writing an exacting man." But writing is more than a skill: it is an essential art, as Francois René de Chateaubriand, nineteenth-century French statesman, declared, "Achilles exists only through Homer. Take away the art of writing from this world, and you will probably take away its glory."

That clear and felicitous writing is difficult to achieve is an understatement. From the conception of an idea to its final written form lies a journey often as exhausting and frustrating as Ghandi's march to the sea. And writers throughout time have commented on the arduous task of writing well. The Jacobean dramatist Ben Jonson notes, "Who casts to write a living line, must sweat," while Richard Brinsley Sheridan, his counterpart in the comedy of manners, reiterates the obverse, "But easy writing's curst hard reading." Writing is indeed an art, one that involves invention, arrangement, and style—one that demands development, revision, countless drafts, further editing, polishing, and proofreading. The eighteenth-century poet and satirist Alexander Pope made this point deftly when he wrote, "True ease in writing comes from art, not chance, / As those move easiest who have learn'd to dance." But "ease in writing" does not come easily, and anyone who struggles with the process can take consolation in the metaphor of novelist F. Scott Fitzgerald: "All good writing is swimming underwater and holding your breath."

The need for clarity and grace is rooted in the soil of daily existence. All who are familiar with bureaucratic correspondence can appreciate lucid communication. A famous admiral once received a memorandum entitled "Technical Strategy Meeting" that announced, among other items:

> Particular emphasis has been placed on developing timelines and in achieving prioritization of technology thrusts. There is much interest in the content of the technology strategies that result from this process and in the workings of the process itself.

The Admiral responded: "I assume from the tone of the memorandum that this meeting must be of great importance. Unfortunately, I cannot understand what it is that I am being asked to discuss and participate in." He concluded his reply with a plea for clarity:

> Those of us who are compelled to work with ordinary people and with real technical problems do not have time to become familiar with rarified and abstruse words such as you have used in your memorandum. Therefore, it would be most helpful if, in future, you write memoranda to me in ordinary English.

Ordinary English is not so ordinary. It requires the same kind of voice, character, and action as does drama. As Robert

Frost avowed, "Everything written is as good as it is dramatic. It need not declare itself in form, but it is drama or nothing." Writers must also be true to their ideas, uncoerced by any political, intellectual, and religious powers that might dominate the age. So thought Sinclair Lewis when he wrote,

> Every compulsion is put upon writers to become safe, polite, obedient, and sterile. In protest, I declined election to the National Institute of Arts and Letters some years ago, and now I must decline the Pulitzer Prize.

In addition to writing dramatically and with freedom, writers strive for style—distinction, originality, and character. No mean feat to be sure. The romantic British poet William Wordsworth explained distinction and originality, "Every great and original writer, in proportion as he is great or original, must himself create the taste by which he is to be relished." The Victorian prose stylist of the same era, Thomas Carlyle, concurred, emphasizing character: in everything a person writes "the character of the writer must lie recorded." The permanence of writing and what it reveals about character should encourage thorough research, comprehensive thought, clarity of expression, and honesty.

Clarity, felicity, drama, original thought, style, and, above all, truth are the heart of all effective writing and the lifeblood of all good writers, whether observers, expositors, evaluators, persuaders, or speakers. Though our most profound, most moving, most artfully crafted writing flows from the pens of literary writers, writing in the modern world has other essential functions. Our thoughts and ideas are shaped and we ourselves are formed by the sea of verbal information that surrounds us—by newspapers, magazines, textbooks, radio, and television, by billboards, box tops, letters, and fliers, by advertisements, reports, analyses, reviews, political tracts, and philosophical treatises, by diaries, sermons, speeches, lectures, comedy routines, screenplays, and essays.

In this book, we have divided this volume of information into the various roles that writers adopt when they write, and we have sequenced the roles from simplest to most complex, so that one builds on the other. Though these roles overlap, all good writers choose among them, finding the ones best suited to their purpose, selecting the proper voice, audience, and subject. Thus observers focus more often on themselves and on their relationship to the world—articulating their own thoughts and ideas. In contrast, expositors focus on informing an audience about the world around them—often taking on the specialized perspective of the historian or scientist. Evaluators focus on deriving judgments; though they use the techniques of observing and researching, they present carefully weighed information, using defined criteria and standards. Persuaders, too, research, evaluate, and judge, but they focus on changing their audience's perceptions or exhorting them to act. Speakers use all of these roles, yet they shape language for the human voice and ear, not for the eye.

Writing itself is done in stages, and though the stages are never as discrete as writers and teachers would like, they do involve the processes identified at the end of chapters 2 through 12:

invention—deriving ideas, perspectives, points of view, forming and shaping a thesis;
organizing and developing—finding or creating logical patterns of organization, fleshing out ideas, and adding supporting information;
finding a voice—developing a sharpened sense of audience and tone;
polishing—refining the thesis, the organization, the body of information, the sense of audience and writer, as well as insuring grammatical and mechanical accuracy and proofreading; and
thinking ahead—making sense out of each experience with writing, noting successes and failures as well as techniques and methods for future use.

Observation, exposition, evaluation, persuasion, and the cadences of the speaking voice come into play in greater or lesser degrees in almost all good writing, as is aptly illustrated by three pieces, one from *Business Week*, one from the *New York Times*, and the other from a broadcast by Edward R. Murrow. *Business Week* is what its title suggests, a weekly periodical offering reports on all aspects of the business world. One recent cover story focuses on Coca-Cola, "Coke's Big Marketing Blitz." A report on the marketing and economics of a large company can be deadly dull, but here Coke adds life, as the introductory paragraph demonstrates:

> An era of tumultuous change has been uncapped in the U.S. soft-drink industry, now coming alive after several years of slow growth and desultory product innovation. Diet and caffeine-free drinks have captured the public's fancy, and retailers' shelves are overcrowded with new entries. But few companies have the resources to finance and distribute a steady stream of new beverages successfully. The result, say industry executives, will be a shakeout during the next few years among producers and bottlers alike. Only one thing is now certain about the industry's future: Coke will still be "it."

The opening sets the scene, establishes the tone, engages the reader, and announces the thesis of Coca-Cola's supremacy. The writer's playful yet serious language, careful word choice, and allusions to the soft-drink industry and its advertising make the reader thirst to read on.

In contrast, consider the *New York Times* the day after a lunar eclipse. The front page ran three pictures of the moon, taken at 2:00 A.M., 2:15 A.M., and 2:35 A.M. The brief caption read: "LUNAR ECLIPSE: The moon early yesterday as the Earth's shadow crept across it. A glance at eclipse watchers, Day by Day, page B4." Turning from this factual, terse, photographic record and its captions to the interpretive story in the "Day by Day" section on page B4, we find a subjective, discursive analysis:

> Most New Yorkers slept while someone turned off the moon for a few hours yesterday. They probably figured there wasn't much they could do about it. But on a gentle night, more than enough of the curious turned out for the longest total lunar eclipse in 123 years.
>
> Romantics took a Staten Island ferryboat from Manhattan at 1:30 A.M. so they could be on the water as the moon started to fade at 1:33. A few missed the boat, but were content with the view from South Ferry. One guy brought his girl in a Mercedes. Two Upper East Siders carried binoculars. Inevitably, a panhandler worked the small crowd. Two young fellows passed a marijuana cigarette back and forth.
>
> "I'm telling you that physics-wise we're no closer to the moon here than we were on 94th Street," one of them said.
>
> "Physics-wise, no," the other replied. "But psychology-wise, yes."
>
> It was all affable, and they freely shared binoculars and in-

> sights, whether about the phases of the moon or the joys of a 1958 Corvette. But New Yorkers can be a demanding bunch. At 2:38, when the moon was in total eclipse, hanging there like a copper dot, restlessness began to set in.
>
> "I thought it would be brighter," a woman complained.
>
> "I thought it would be darker," said another.
>
> "What does it do now?" said one man, sounding like an insistent Broadway agent, the type who would ask Shakespeare what he's written lately.

The observation and analysis here—"turned off the moon," "romantics"—couples with the casual observations of the subjects themselves to create a personal, interpretive view of the event.

Or, finally, consider Edward R. Murrow's broadcast from London on August 30, 1942, in which he combines the writer's multiple roles. Observing, explaining, and evaluating, Murrow uses the cadences of the speaking voice to bring home the poignancy of the war and to persuade us of its horror:

> August 30, 1942
>
> Before this weary week wanders off the calendar and its events become the stuff with which historians work, Britain will have ended three years of war. How long is three years? I don't know. It's long enough for people to marry and have children, long enough for a revolution, long enough for small boys to be able to put their elders to shame when it comes to identifying aircraft. And it's plenty of time for big English breakfasts, thick Devonshire cream, good cigarettes and good wine to be lost in the mists of memory. Three years is long enough for you to forget what it was like to be able to buy and drive a new car, buy a new suit of clothes whenever you wanted it and travel whenever you had the money and the inclination. Three years is long enough for schoolboys to grow up and become soldiers but not long enough to permit you to forget the friends who have died. It's plenty of time for empires to change hands, for the reputation of generals to be made and unmade and for the social, economic and political fabric of nations to be ripped to shreds. More damage can be done in three years than can be measured in dollars. Millions of people can be made into slaves; hundreds of thousands may starve or be butchered. There's plenty of time for a civilization to die but not enough for a new one to be born.

An objective visual record, a subjective narrative account, an expository report, an impressionistic description—within these extremes lies a multiplicity of roles for the writer.

The essentials of writing and the roles a writer can play are perfected by practice, but the demands of writing are so complex that knowing where to begin is difficult. Perhaps the best advice comes from the American historian Samuel Eliot Morison: "First and foremost, *get writing!*"

PART 1

THE WRITER AS OBSERVER

> Wolves have marvelous legs. The first thing one notices about them is how high they are set on their skinny legs, and the instant, blurred gait these can switch into, bicycling away, carrying them as much as forty miles in a day. With brindled coats in smoky shades, brushy tails, light-filled eyes, intense sharp faces which are more focused than an intelligent dog's but also less various, they are electric on first sighting, bending that bushy head around to look back as they run. In captivity when they are quarreling in a cage, the snarls sound guttural and their jaws chop, but scientists watching pet wolves in the woods speak of their flowing joy, of such a delight in running that they melt into the woods like sunlight, like running water.

This vivid and unusual description introduces an essay, "Howling Back at the Wolves." Edward Hoagland, the writer behind the portrayal, is an insightful observer of nature who depicts with drama and sympathy an animal that is often feared and hated.

Writing such an artful paragraph is a complex task. In order to be credible as well as entertaining, the writer in the role of observer has several obligations to the audience: to describe the external world with accuracy while filtering it through the perceptions, sensations, and thoughts of the inner world. Writers must evoke the subject described with startling reality so that their readers—who have only words on the page, memory, and imagination—can recreate the scene before them.

Thus in his portrayal, Hoagland skillfully depicts wolves by incorporating accurate description—"brindled coats in smoky shades, brushy tails, light-filled eyes." At the same time, because the essay suggests mankind's similarity to wolves, he tries to convince his readers that wolves are creatures to be admired. Hoagland achieves his latter goal through a light tone (how can we be fearful of something we laugh at?) and personification (if wolves are viewed in human terms, we must be sympathetic to them). Thus he opens with "Wolves have marvelous legs," an observation that few of his readers will have made and one that makes them expectant about what will follow. When Hoagland personifies wolves as "bicycling away," he creates both a memorable and a humorous image. "Flowing joy" and "delight" further personify wolves, yet the writer reincarnates them as part of nature in the paragraph's close: "they melt into the woods like sunlight, like running water."

Before writing such masterful descriptions, writers must do their homework. They may spend months observing their subjects, and often they record notes—details, images, analogies—in a diary, journal, or notebook. Writers in the role of the observer emphasize their personalities and present the material more subjectively than writers in other roles. The writer as reporter, for example, would present the reader with a more objective description of wolves, like the one in the *Encyclopaedia Britannica*, which begins:

> Wolf *(Canis lupus)*, the common English name for any wild member of the typical section of the genus *Canis* . . . . They present great diversities of size, length and thickness of fur, and coloration . . . . The ordinary colour of the wolf is yellowish or fulvous grey, but almost pure white and entirely black wolves are known.

In contrast, the writer as observer must focus simultaneously on both the external and the internal world. The writer's task is not an easy one. All artists must try to see beyond the stereotypes and conventions imposed upon us since childhood. For example, a little boy, drawing for the first time, may sketch a picture of his father, that to the adult eye is distorted:

Yet when his father bends down to address him, he sees only a big, hairy face; when he stands beside him he sees only a large shoe. As the child grows older, society conditions him to draw his father, not as he really sees him, but as a stereotype that reduces the human body to a stick figure (see below). But who thinks of a person as a stick figure? Shoes and hairy faces are far truer to human experience.

Good writers, like skilled artists, try to break through stereotypes and restructure the complexities before them. Just as Monet's impressionism and Picasso's cubism give us insights into our public and private worlds, so, too, good writers lead us toward perceptions because they are more than careful observers of human beings, environments, and events. As they record elements of the external world, they also formulate and articulate the elements of the internal world of individual responses, emotions, associations, and ideas.

The detail is the heart of all writing, and for writers in the role of the observer, details provide individuality, personality, and life. Ziegler's cartoon (below) from the *New Yorker* emphasizes the skewed view of the observer. Here the obese writer, surrounded by the remains of his obsession, filters the world through his own senses. For him, obviously, the primary sense is taste. As he restructures the world through food, his writing—through his metaphors—reveals his personality, offering original, and of course comic, perceptions to his readers. If we are what we eat, the cartoonist may be emphasizing here, we certainly are what we write.

Perhaps no writer was a better observer than Samuel Clemens, who as Mark Twain rode through the country on stagecoaches and piloted the rivers on riverboats. *The Adventures of Huckleberry Finn*, *Roughing It*, and *Life on the Mississippi* are books filled with descriptions of nineteenth-century America, observations that are comic yet accurate, serious yet evocative.

"The face of the pear-shaped man reminded me of the mashed turnips that Aunt Mildred used to serve alongside the Thanksgiving turkey. As he got out of the strawberry-hued car, his immense fists looked like two slabs of slightly gnawed ham. He waddled over to the counter and snarled at me under his lasagna-laden breath, 'Something, my little bonbon, is fishy in Denmark.' Slowly, I lowered my grilled cheese sandwich . . ."

In *Roughing It,* Clemens provides his Eastern readers with probably their first—and unforgettable—glimpses of the prairie wolf:

> The coyote is a long, slim, sick and sorry-looking skeleton, with a gray wolf-skin stretched over it, a tolerably bushy tail that forever sags down with a despairing expression of forsakenness and misery, a furtive and evil eye, and a long, sharp face, with slightly lifted lip and exposed teeth. He has a general slinking expression all over. The coyote is a living, breathing allegory of Want. He is *always* hungry. He is always poor, out of luck and friendless. The meanest creatures despise him, and even the fleas would desert him for a velocipede.

Anyone who has seen a coyote appreciates the accuracy of the caricature. Like Hoagland, Clemens personifies his wolf, incorporates humor, entertains. We delight in the object being described and in the writer of the description. Our observations are now permanently altered by the world of words.

CHAPTER 1

THE DIARIST

In order to develop powers of careful observation, writers need to be sensitive to their external environments and to their internal worlds. The scream of the wind, the treble of a piccolo on the radio, the tapping of a hammer on a nail, and the discussion of the day's plans are only a few of the simultaneous sounds we can hear. Concurrently we also are surrounded by a multiplicity of sights, smells, and textures. The impressions we receive through our five senses are further compounded by internal sensations—hunger pangs, an itch, a headache—and the emotions that accompany them, such as excitement or anxiety. Add to these sensations multiple layers of conscious thought—fantasy, insights—and it is easy to see how the complexity and fluctuation of these internal and external impressions force us to make choices that limit our conscious perceptions.

How then does one develop the ability to bring order out of sensory and intellectual chaos? Keeping a journal, a diary, or a notebook is one way many writers collect details and explore their external and internal worlds. Journals, diaries, and notebooks are, of course, frequently kept by fiction writers, as the entries included here reveal, but similar records have also been essential to scientists like Charles Darwin, whose *Origin of Species* was the culmination of several sets of diaries; to psychologists like Sigmund Freud, whose case studies were recorded in his journals to help develop his theories; and to political leaders like Harry Truman, whose diaries include a comprehensive record of his professional duties and personal opinions.

The etymological origins of *diary* and *journal* reveal both to be daily records, but often a journal may focus more exclusively on an individual's ideas, emotions, and activities. A notebook, as its name suggests, is a collection of notes, impressionistic and fragmentary, that a writer makes as a source book for the future, but it too can be ordered chronologically and can contain a wide assortment of observations and insights. Notebook, diary, and journal selections follow in this chapter, yet they all share the characteristic of shaping the writer's world.

Such a chronicle allows the writer to observe, to record, to explore, to synthesize, and to articulate experience—to collect details and ideas and then to create order out of the chaos of sensations. The diary, journal, or notebook may serve as a record of the past, as it does for Virginia Woolf; as a storehouse of ideas for future fiction, as it does for Thomas Hardy; as a scientific record of both past and future experiments, as it does for Michael Faraday; or as a detailed account of a private world, as it does for May Sarton.

Notebooks not only allow writers to record information for future use and to explore personal feelings and conflicts, but they also enable writers to practice the craft of writing. The audience for a journal is the writer both at the moment of writing and at some time in the future. Written without revision and often quickly, the author's entries may set out unintentional juxtapositions and change abruptly in subject matter, style, and tone. Notebooks can serve as appropriate places for generating ideas and recording instant impressions. The writer gives less attention than usual to matters of grammar and mechanics and focuses more on sensations, emotions, images, and ideas.

Journals, notebooks, and diaries are like photograph albums—records and explorations of the past, like sketchbooks—experiments with skills in the present, and like blueprints—sources for more complete and comprehensive statements in the future.

THOMAS HARDY

from *The Personal Notebooks*

The English writer Thomas Hardy (1840–1928) first embarked on a career as an architect before turning all his efforts to prose and poetry. Best known today for what he classified as his "novels of character and environment," among which are *Far from the Madding Crowd* (1874), *Tess of the D'Urbervilles* (1891), and *Jude the Obscure* (1896), he was also the author of *The Dynasts,* a verse drama, and seven volumes of lyrics.

Although Hardy destroyed many of his notebooks and letters and further hid himself by ghostwriting his own biography, some of his notebooks survive. Hardy's personal notebooks, "Memoranda" as he called them, illustrate the wide range of details, images, and ideas that caught his eye, ear, and mind. The excerpts that follow are representative, and you will quickly see that they are indeed notes. Sometimes a whole month is skipped or receives at best a sentence while other times an entry for one day may run to several pages. What's memorable, however, is the quality of observation: the quick sketching of a story (October, 1873, the genesis for "The Lady Icenway," written and published in 1890), the construction of an aphorism (February, 1871), the detailing of a scene (May, 1872, and August, 1874), the recording of dialogue (February, 1871), the description of a setting (October 30 and November 9, 1872), and the telling of a family tale (March 22, 1871).

Feb. 7 [1871]. A pedlar came to Miss ——, an old maid, & in asking her to buy some of his wares addressed her as "Mother." She said, "How dare you cast such a scandal upon my character as to call me by that name!"

Feb. Some men waste their time in watching their own existence.

Feb. Nothing is so interesting to a woman as herself.

Though a good deal is too strange to be believed, nothing is too strange to have happened.

March 22. Smuggling, &c. While superintending the church music from 1801 onwards to about 1805, my grandfather used to do a little in smuggling, his house being a lonely one, none of the others in Higher Bockhampton being then built, or only one other. He sometimes had as many as eighty "tubs" in a dark closet (afterwards destroyed in altering staircase) each tub containing 4 gallons. The spirits often smelt all over the house, being proof, & had to be lowered for drinking. The tubs, or little elongated barrels, were of thin staves with wooden hoops; I remember one of them which had been turned into a bucket by knocking out one head, & putting a handle. They were brought at night by men on horseback, "slung," or in carts. A whiplash across the window pane would awake my grandfather at 2 or 3 in the morning, & he would dress & go down. Not a soul was there, but a heap of tubs loomed up in front of the door. He would set to work & stow them away in the dark closet aforesaid, & nothing more would happen till dusk the following evening, when groups of dark long-bearded fellows would arrive, & carry off the tubs in two & fours slung over their shoulders—T.O. The smugglers grew so bold at last that they would come by day, & my grandmother insisted to her husband that he should stop receiving the tubs, which he did about 1805, though not till at a christening of one of their children they "had a washing pan of pale brandy" left them by the smugglers to make merry with. Moreover the smugglers could not be got to leave off depositing the tubs for some while, but they did so when a second house was built about 100 yards off.

Many years later, indeed, I think in my mother's time, a large woman used to call, & ask if any of "it" was wanted cheap. Her hugeness was caused by her having bullocks' bladders slung round her hips, in which she carried the spirits. She was known as "Mother Rogers."

March, contd. Lonely places in the country have each their own peculiar silences.

Apl. 1871. In Church. The sibilants in the responses of the congregation, who bend their heads like pine-trees in a wind.

May 7. My mother remarked today concerning an incident she had witnessed in which a man & woman were the characters, strangers to her: "They were mother & son I supposed, or perhaps man & wife, for they marry in such queer ways nowadays that there's no telling which. Anyhow, there was a partnership of some kind between them."

May 29. The most prosaic man becomes a poem when you stand by his grave at his funeral & think of him.

June. Old Midsummer custom: on old Midsr. eve, at going to bed:

> "I put my shoes in the form of a T,
> And trust my true love for to see."
> Another:

On old Midsr. noon dig a hole in the grass plot, & place your ear thereon precisely at 12. The occupation of your future husband will be revealed by the noises heard.

Another old custom. Allhallows eve. Kill a pigeon: stick its heart full of pins. Roast the heart in the candle flame. Faithless lover will twist & toss with nightmare in his sleep.

1872. May 29. "Well, mind what th'rt about. She can use the corners of her eyes as well as we can use the middle." (Heard in Dorset)

August. At Beeny. The Cliff: green towards the land, blue-black towards the sea . . . Every ledge has a little starved green grass upon it; all vertical parts bare. Seaward, a dark grey ocean beneath a pale green sky, upon which lie branches of red cloud. A lather of foam round the base of each rock. The sea is full of motion internally, but still as a whole. Quiet & silent in the distance, noisy & restless close at hand.

End of Aug. Brentor, nr. Tavistock. Church on the top. Like a volcano. [Page 19]

Sept 11, 1872. In London. Saw a lady who when she smiled smiled too much—over all her face, chin, round to her ears, & up among her hair, so that you were surfeited of smiling, & felt you would never smile any more.

Oct. 30. Returning from D. Wet night. The town, looking back from S. Hill, is circumscribed by a halo like an aurora: up the hill comes a broad band of turnpike road, glazed with moisture, which reflects the lustre of the mist.

Nov. 9. Went to Kingman's early. A still morning: objects were as if at the bottom of a pool.

[1873 Feb] At Melbury Osmond there was a haunted barn. A man coming home drunk entered the barn & fell asleep in a cow's crib that stood within. He awoke at 12, & saw a lady riding round & round on a buck, holding the horns as reins. She was in a white riding-habit, & the wind of her speed blew so strong upon him that he sneezed, when she vanished.

1873 Sept 17. One man is a genius in trifles, a fool in emergencies: another a fool in trifles, a genius in emergencies.

Octr. Some rural person says of Cheapside that "it is a place he should like to retire to & spend his declining days in, being a romantic spot."

A good story or play might run as follows: A certain nobleman, a widower, has one son, a young man now lying at the point of death. The nobleman his father is an old man, in great trouble that there will be no heir in the direct succession. Son dies. Among his papers are found a girl's letter—the letter of a girl whom the son had begged his father to keep from want, as he had seduced her. The father finds that she is going to have a child. He marries her, parting from her at the church door. He obtains an heir of his own blood.

Nov. 3. A sunset. A brazen sun, bristling with a thousand spines, which struck into & tormented my eyes.

August. A scene in Celbridge Place. Middle-aged gentleman talking to handsome buxom lady across the stone parapet of the house opposite, which is just as high as their breasts—she inside, he on pavement. It rains a little, a very mild moisture, which a duck would call nothing, a dog a pleasure, a cat possibly a good deal. He holds his plum-coloured silk umbrella across the parapet over her head, she being without a bonnet, & her black hair done up in a knot behind. She wears a rich brown dress, with a white "modesty piece" of lace (as old writers call it). He has nearly white whiskers, & wears a low felt hat. With the walking stick in his right hand he occasionally points at objects east & west. She gesticulates with her right hand, which frequently touches the gentn's left on the parapet holding the umbrella.

Dec 19. 1874. Long Ditton. Snow on graves. A superfluous piece of cynicism in Nature.

The Revd. Mr Wilkinson (Cornwall) married a handsome actress. She settled down to serve God as unceremoniously as she previously had done to Mammon.

1875. Jan 6. A curate or vicar, disgusted with the smallness of his stipend, or poverty of his living, goes into a remote county & turns cidermaker, dairyman, lime-burner, or what-not.

June 16. Reading Life of Goethe. Schlegel says that "the deepest want & deficiency of all modern art lies in the fact that the artists have no Mythology."

1876. Aug. Rain: like a banner of gauze waved in folds across the scene.

1877. Sept. Rapid riding by night, the moon & stars racing after, & the trees & fields slipping behind.

1878. Nov. The honest Earl. Earl is accidentally shut up in a tower—the Hardy monument, say—with a blacksmith's daughter. Goes to parson next day & says he feels it his duty to marry her. Does so. Finds her not so good as she seemed, & . . . . . .

THE THINKING PROCESS

IDEAS FOR JOURNAL ENTRIES

To sharpen your skills of observation and to record impressions and details that later may be useful in developing a personal essay, find a busy scene: a checkout line in a supermarket, the university cafeteria, an airport ticket counter, a crowded bar, a fast-food restaurant. Select a spot where you can observe the action yet write in a notebook without feeling conspicuous, and then listen and start writing. You may want to look for particular details, or you may find yourself struck by an unusual sight. You may also want to consider one or more of the following ideas:

1. Look for a couple deeply engaged in conversation, perhaps two people of contrasting appearance. Describe each in detail: features, size, clothes, posture, gestures, anything of note. Like Hardy, you may want to add a summarizing epigram.

2. Seek out a line of people, the slower and longer the better. Observe how people caught in the same circumstances act differently, and describe the differences in behavior that you detect. Who is bored? Angry? Resigned? Oblivious? How does each person demonstrate that emotion?

3. Keep your ears open listening for snatches of curious conversation and record them in your journal. Perhaps the words seem inappropriate to the speaker or are startling in and of themselves. F. Scott Fitzgerald, for instance, jotted down a number of overhead comments in his notebooks: " 'Call me Mickey Mouse,' she said suddenly"; " 'Perfectly respectable girl, but only been drinking that day. No matter how long she lives she'll always know she's killed somebody." Provide a context for the dialogue that strikes you as the most interesting, and you will have a character sketch or vignette as a journal entry.

MICHAEL FARADAY

from *The Journals*

Perhaps best known for the physical law of electrodynamics that bears his name, Michael Faraday (1791–1867) recorded much of his scientific study in journals, now collected in seven volumes. Growing up in England, he overcame the limitations of a relatively scant formal education by reading and by attending scientific lectures, most notably those of Sir Humphry Davy, a leading figure in physics and chemistry.

Faraday apprenticed as Davy's assistant at the laboratory of the Royal Institution in London and soon went on to make his own name in science. He discovered the compound benzene, developed the first dynamo, and advanced research in electrolysis.

As the entries that follow show, Faraday's diary is more than a record of his experiments. He not only records his scientific studies in detail, noting both success and failure, but he also applies the same keen powers of observation to the natural world, whether a cloud formation (August 20, 1823) or the flight of gulls (August 3, 1824). Constantly checking, rechecking, cross-referencing, and annotating his entries, Faraday uses his diary to analyze, to find analogies, to draw conclusions, and to ask questions.

1821. March 20th. Put some Lamp black that had previously been heated red into a retort, filled the retort with chlorine, drew out the neck at the blow pipe and sealed it hermetically. Placed on the house top and left there for solar influence. See April 4th, 1822.

25th. Introduced some Ether with chlorine into a dry retort. Much chlorine absorb[ed] and ether became bright yellow colour. Colour disappeared—introduced a little water—much mur. acid gas condensed—let in more chlorine—repeated the introduction of chlorine and left it for a day or two.

29th. Put a little ether into a large dry retort with chlorine and had introduced more chlorine into the retort above; was proceeding with them to the house top and had just got out at the door into bright *cloud* light when inflammation took place in both retorts. The larger one was burst into atoms; mur. acid gas and charcoal were evolved. The smaller (25th) did not burst but became black from charcoal.

March 30th. Put a little ether into a large retort and filled it with chlorine. This done by candle light: a little absorption at first, then left it all night in a dark place. On April 1 examined it; there was very slight expansion of volume. The colour of the chlorine considerably diminished and the substance inside thick and apparently adhesive. Exposed to sun light no further change took place. A little water let in absorbed 26·5 c:i: of mur. acid gas and produced a milky appearance in the retort. The retort was filled with water to remove gas, acid, etc.; an insoluble adhesive substance remained on the glass. The water was poured off and alcohol introduced; it immediately dissolved the substance. The solution tasted piquant, precipitated with water white and very much resembled the substance from Naptha (1820, Oct. 23). Evaporated to dryness got a small quantity of a gummy substance still resembling the other.

1823. Aug. 20th. At Folkestone, the atmosphere clear and a fine view of the cliffs to Dover. Soon after the sun set (the wind being about S.S.W. so as to blow on land) observed a cloud forming just above the brow of Shakespeare cliff. It streamed inwards, increasing in size, but all seemed to pour nearly from the same spot; the air which came from over the sea there taking on a visible form and passing in to the interior as a cloud. By degrees the generation of cloud took place along the whole line of cliff from Dover to Folkestone hill, the wind still carrying the portion formed over the land. We ascended the cliffs about ½ a mile beyond Folkestone hill about an hour after sunset and found all above envelloped in a dense moist mist, so as to deposit water on our cloaths; the temperature also low to the feelings. We walked back towards Folkestone and on descending a little way down the hill by the road emerged from the cloud and found all clear beneath. The cloud now extended a considerable way in land, covering the tops of the hills. Was not this effect produced by the cooling of the surface of these hills after the sunset by radiation into the clear space above, and the consequent cooling of the moist air brought by the wind from the sea below its point of deposition?

We saw a smaller effect of the same kind a few evenings before in similar circumstances at the same place—and also over the land of Romney marsh.

1823. Aug. *Flying of Gulls, hawks, etc.* Folkestone.

At times when the wind has been rather strong I have frequently watched the gulls who were flying over the waves looking for food, and have often seen them move slowly against the wind or remain stationary facing it, balancing themselves on their wings but without flapping them. This has lasted for 1, 2, 3 or more minutes, and I think could not be due to any previously acquired momentum because they would suddenly sweep round, going down with the wind, and then again return against it, all without flapping the wings. I have also remarked hawkes over land advance in a similar manner in similar circumstances, without having been able to detect any motion of the wing calculated to support them. They seemed to remain suspended in the air by an apparent balancing of the body on the wings against the wind.

Sometimes similar appearances were observed in situations where it might be accounted for. Thus I have seen gulls and hawks leave a resting place in a cliff, move in to the free space and poize themselves whilst they examined the ground beneath, and without a single flap of the wing; but the wind has in these cases been blowing on to the land, and being thrown upward against the face of the cliff may have produced a current upwards abundantly sufficient to support the bird. But I have seen the same thing many times with gulls, and once with a hawk, w[h]ere the birds moved out clearly into the horizontal current and where the means they used to support themselves escaped my perception.

Last year when at Swansea and standing on the end of the

pier I noticed a gull coming up across the mouth of the harbour against a westerly wind in this manner, without flapping the wings. On coming to a spot a little beyond me it returned with the wind to the place from where it came up, and again renewed its course towards me; this I remarked done 7 or 8 times, occupying above a quarter of an hour, and with only an occasional flap of the wing now and then.

How do these birds fly? and why may not a man or a machine fly in the same way in the same circumstances?

See notes Aug. 3, 1824.

Sept. 3. Heated diamond with borax, nitre and other fluxes on Platinum wire by blow pipe. No action, or at least a very slight one: no remarkable effects.

1823. Sept. 9th. A plate or band of sheet zinc about 2 feet long, ½ inch wide and $\frac{1}{30}$ thick was coiled together at the two ends so as to form an endless band and put into a jar of strong sul. acid solution as in the figure. When the action was well established there was a deviation of the magnetic needle in the direction of the upper circle. When a rod of zinc was dipped into the acid and made to touch the band at 1 or 1 this deviation was increased, or when a rod of copper touched the band at 2 the same effect was produced; but when the zinc touched at 2 or the copper at 1 or 1 then the deviation was in the direction of the lower circle. [See fig. 4.]

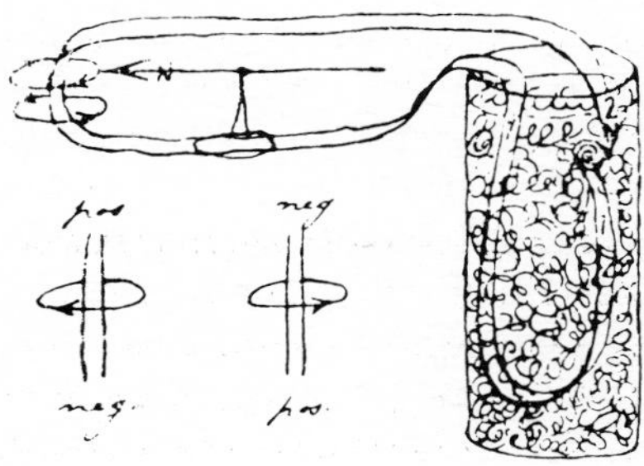

1823. Novr. 14. Muriatic acid added in excess to solution of hydro-sulphuret of ammonia—turbidness appeared and in a short time a strong smell of *sulphurous acid.* The hydrosulphuret contained sulphite of ammonia. There is no action on the pure compound of sul. hydrogen and ammonia except liberation of Sul. hy.

Solution of chlorine added to sol. of Mur. amm. and left a while till Azotane formed; then added Hydro sulphuret of ammonia in excess—a pleasant odorous smell produced, something like chloride of carbon, but no traces of Sulphuret of Nitrogen.

Carbonate of ammonia added in excess to lime water dissolves the carbonate first thrown down and the lime is not then detectable by oxalate of ammonia, ammonia, potash or carb. pot.; but phosphate of soda throws it down. Mur. or other salt of lime with Carb. ammonia—similar effects.

Could not get this to succeed again; see Octr. 1, 1824.

Aug. 3rd, 1824. A creeping ceres growing in a pot has been hung up in a window—several new strong shoots have been thrown out which rise up into the air; all of these shoots have thrown out rootlets and they all proceed from those sides of the shoots which are farthest from the light—the direction of the rootlets is mostly horizontal but some proceed upwards, some downwards, according to their situation—they seem to be uninfluenced by gravity but to respect obscurity.

A scarlet bean was growing in a pot in the same window and was trained on a string running upwards. The bean at first twined closely round the string as usual but on rising so high as to be level with the top of the sash it no longer twined round the string although that proceeded much higher but went off into the air towards the light.

Aug. 3, 1824. See Aug. 20, 1823.

When at Freshwater cliffs had opportunities of again remarking the balancings of the gulls in a strong wind. Many of them would rise together and there seemed to be a sort of emulation among them; all had their heads to the wind which was here parallel to the cliffs, being about E.S.E.; they did not seem to respect the top of the cliff or any upward action of the wind from against it, but floated in the air both over the sea and the land and at various heights above and below the top of the cliffs. They did not seem able to make away against the wind or at least only slowly, but they could readily rise or fall. Sometimes they seemed to lose their balance, or the wind was too strong for them, and then they took a sweep sideways, going down with the wind but soon turning their heads to the wind, recovering their balance and slowly coming up again. All this was done without striking the air with their wings but apparently only by keeping them in a certain position with regard to the current of air.

Perhaps the effect which may sometimes be observed in flying a kite may be connected with this subject. Sometimes a kite when badly rigged will, upon rising, not cease to ascend when the string forms a certain angle with the current of air, but will continue to mount, taking nearly a horizontal position in the air, and that till the string is nearly vertical when the kite generally falls over and comes down.

1826. Jany. 18th. Measurements and weight of a fine sea gull brought here by George from Mr Harding. [See below]

	feet	inches
From tip to tip of wings	4	10
,, beak to tail	2	4
Average width of wings through the 4 ft. 10 i.	0	7½
From tip of tail to setting in of wings . .		9 inches
Width of tail part near wings, i.e., of body there		5 "
,, ,, extremity moderately extended		9
Each wing, length of	2	3
Thickness of body		5
Weight of the bird with all its feathers, etc.	3 lb.	4¼ oz.

or 52¼ ounces avoirdupois.

Jany. 6, 1829. Occasionally fires appear to burn with more than ordinary vigour and this usually taking place in winter is supposed to indicate a frosty air. This cause does not seem sufficient to account for the effect. Query does the air at these times really contain a larger proportion of oxygen, for that is the explanation which most readily arises in the mind of a chemist.

This evening my parlour fires were burning in this bright manner. Collected three bottles full of air from the Laboratory where all was clear and sweet, and leaving a little distilled water in each, put them bye for comparison in an inverted position. The time was 10 P.M.: the Barometer 30.06—thermometer in the Laboratory 46°F. Temperature out of doors just as freezing.

Jany. 8th. Morning. Fires burn in the ordinary way—put by two bottles of air for future comparison.

THE THINKING PROCESS

IDEAS FOR JOURNAL ENTRIES

1. Choose an animal, insect, plant, or person to observe over a short period of activity. Record what you see as accurately as possible, noting any movement, behavior, or physical attributes that you discern. Reread your journal entry to see what questions your observations lead to. Write them down so that together with your notes they can serve as a possible springboard for a personal essay or perhaps a scientific report.

2. If you are taking a laboratory science course, examine one of your recent lab reports, comparing it to one of Faraday's scientific entries. In your journal, list the similarities and differences you discover between the nature of your observations and Faraday's. Later, you might want to use your ideas to develop a paper comparing a lab course to laboratory research or analyzing the role lab sciences play in general education.

3. Think of a situation that you have an opportunity to observe a number of times: a traffic jam at a particular bottleneck, a long cafeteria or checkout line, a series of dissatisfied customers, or the like. Describe the situation and the responses to it. What patterns of behavior can you deduce? Record your conclusions in your journal for possible later use as a report, personal essay, or scientific parody.

VIRGINIA WOOLF

from *The Diaries*

Virginia Woolf (1882–1941), a distinguished British critic and novelist, is probably best known for her widely admired novels *Mrs. Dalloway* (1922) and *To the Lighthouse* (1927) though the contemporary feminist appreciation of *A Room of One's Own* (1929), an extended essay on the difficulties of being a woman and a writer, has led to a renewed interest in her nonfiction.

A prolific diary writer, Virginia Woolf first started her diaries when she was fourteen, but she is best known for those diaries that she kept after her marriage to Leonard Woolf (the L. to whom she refers). Thirty volumes in all, they are a remarkable account of her life—a record of her days, reactions, emotional states, friends, and thoughts.

Woven through her diaries are various reflections on keeping a journal, as the first entry that follows, written in 1919, illustrates. There she ponders upon her diaries—how she writes them and their intended purpose. Several months later in the April 20 entry, she comments on spending Easter in London and on an article she had just finished on the eighteenth-century English novelist Daniel Defoe. Bruce Richmond, whom she mentions, was the editor of the *Times Literary Supplement*, and Dalton, to whom she also refers, was Richmond's major editorial assistant. Virginia Woolf's thoughts, however, soon turn again to her diary, and in rereading it, she gains some insight into its value to her as a writer.

Monday 20th January. I mean to copy this out, when I can buy a book, so I omit the flourishes proper to the New Year. It is not money this time that I lack, but the capacity, after a fortnight in bed, to make the journey to Fleet Street. Even the muscles of my right hand feel as I imagine a servant's hand to feel. Curiously enough, I have the same stiffness in manipulating sentences, though by rights I should be better equipped mentally now than I was a month ago. The fortnight in bed was the result of having a tooth out, & being tired enough to get a headache, a long dreary affair that receded & advanced, much like a mist on a January day. One hour writing daily is my allowance for the next few weeks; & having hoarded it this morning, I may spend part of it now, since L. is out, & I am much behindhand with the month of January. I note, however, that this diary writing does not count as writing; since I have just re-read my years diary, & am much struck by the rapid haphazard gallop at which it swings along, sometimes indeed jerking almost intolerably over the cobbles. Still, if it were not written rather faster than the fastest typewriting, it would never be written at all; & the advantage of the method is that [it] sweeps up accidentally several stray matters that I should exclude if I took thought; & it is these accidents that are the diamonds in the rubbish heap. If Virginia Woolf, at the age of 50, when she sits down to build her memoirs out of these books, is unable to make a phrase as it should be made, I can only condole with her, & remind her of the existence of the fireplace, where she has my leave to burn these pages to so many black films with red eyes. But how I envy her the task I am preparing for her. There is none I should like better. Already my 37th birthday next Saturday is robbed of some of its terrors. Partly for [the] benefit of this elderly lady (no subterfuge will then be possible: 50 is elderly, though, I agree, not old) partly to give the year a solid foundation I intend to spend the evenings of this week of captivity in making out an account of my friendships & their present condition, with some account of my friends characters; & to add an estimate of their work, & a forecast of their future works. The lady of fifty will be able to say how near to the truth I come; but I have written enough for tonight. (Only 15 minutes, I see).

Sunday (Easter) 20 April. We are, for the first time for many years, spending Easter in London. We had arranged to go, but dissolved all our arrangements in 5 minutes; partly to escape what was said to be the worst journey on record; partly that L. may get 10 clear days, which will be possible at the end of the week. I own to some hopes of a wet Easter; but was disappointed. Both Friday & Saturday were of the texture of full summer. We walked along the river & through the park on Good Friday, & the sun made the crowd to swelter unpleasantly. They tramped placidly along, in their coats & skirts & bowler hats, leading their dogs, save for a random terrier who had secured a muzzle. Meanwhile the green of the leaves thrust at least one inch out of the envelopes, & today the tree against the window has some perfectly shaped small leaves, & the tree at the end of the garden is as green as it will be until September. On Saturday Bruce Richmond came in person to fetch my Defoe article; & we had a little talk about mistakes in proofs. He prides himself upon letting none through his fingers;—& charges such as do get through (& I was under the impression they were by no means rare) to Dalton. And then we walked; & I came out in my summer things, shady hat, thin muslin dress, stockings, & cloak on my arm. Today I'm sitting in a jersey & serge over the fire; but the evening repents, & through an open window the birds sing, & the leaves are yellow green in the sun. . . .

In the idleness which succeeds any long article, & Defoe is the 2nd leader this month, I got out this diary, & read as one always does read one's own writing, with a kind of guilty intensity. I confess that the rough & random style of it, often so ungrammatical, & crying for a word altered, afflicted me somewhat. I am trying to tell whichever self it is that reads this hereafter that I can write very much better; & take no time over this; & forbid her to let the eye of man behold it. And now I may add my little compliment to the effect that it has a slapdash & vigour, & sometimes hits an unexpected bulls eye. But what is more to the point is my belief that the habit of writing thus for my own eye only is good practise. It loosens the ligaments. Never mind the misses & the stumbles. Going at such a pace as I do I must make the most direct & instant shots at my object, & thus have to lay hands on words, choose them, & shoot them with no more pause than is needed to put my pen in the ink. I believe that during the past year I can trace some increase of ease in my professional writing which I attribute to my casual half hours after tea. Moreover there looms ahead of me the shadow of some kind of form which a diary might attain to. I might in the course of time learn what it is that one can make of this loose, drifting material of life; finding another use for it than the use I put it to, so much more consciously & scrupulously, in fiction. What sort of diary should I like mine to be? Something loose knit, & yet not slovenly, so elastic that it will embrace any thing, solemn, slight or beautiful that comes into my mind. I should like it to resemble some deep old desk, or capacious hold-all, in which one flings a mass of odds & ends without looking them through. I should like to come back, after a year or two, & find that the collection had sorted itself & refined itself & coalesced, as such deposits so mysteriously do, into a mould, transparent enough to reflect the light of our life, & yet steady, tranquil composed with the aloofness of a work of art. The main requisite, I think on re-reading my old volumes, is not to play the part of censor, but to write as the mood comes or of anything whatever; since I was curious to find how I went for things put in haphazard, & found the significance to lie where I never saw it at the time. But looseness quickly becomes slovenly. A little effort is needed to face a character or an incident which needs to be recorded. Nor can one let the pen write without guidance; for fear of becoming slack & untidy . . . .

THE THINKING PROCESS

IDEAS FOR JOURNAL ENTRIES

1. Rereading her entries for the year, Virginia Woolf likens her writing to a horse's gait and is "much struck by the rapid haphazard gallop at which it swings along, sometimes indeed jerking almost intolerably over the cobbles." Review what you have written so far in your journal. What metaphor fits your writing? To discover the shape of your journal entries, write a few sentences that express the metaphor and then support it with references to specific examples from your journal.

2. As the first sentence of the January 20 entry implies, Virginia Woolf was writing in an improvised notebook and intended to copy the entry into a more permanent diary as soon as she could go to Fleet Street and buy a new exercise book, which she later did. Anne Oliver Bell has edited Virginia Woolf's diaries, and volume 1 of *The Diary of Virginia Woolf* (1977) contains both versions of the January 20 entry. Compare the original version that precedes with the revised one that follows. In your own journal, list the differences, no matter how minute, between the two versions. What else would you have changed and why? Why do you think Virginia Woolf did not make those changes?

> **Monday 20 January** I mean to copy this out when I can buy a book, so I omit the flourishes proper to the new year. It is not money this time that I lack, but the capacity, after a fortnight in bed, to make the journey to Fleet Street. Even the muscles of my right hand feel as I imagine a servants hand to feel. Curiously enough, I have the same stiffness in manipulating sentences, though by rights I should be better equipped mentally now than I was a month ago. The fortnight in bed was the result of having a tooth out, & being tired enough to get a headache—a long dreary affair, that receded & advanced much like a mist on a January day. One hours writing daily is my allowance for the next few weeks; & having hoarded it this morning, I may spend part of it now, since L. is out, & I am much behindhand with the month of January. I note however that this diary writing does not count as writing, since I have just reread my years diary & am much struck by the rapid haphazard gallop at which it swings along, sometimes indeed jerking almost intolerably over the cobbles. Still if it were not written rather faster than the fastest typewriting, if I stopped & took thought, it would never be written at all; & the advantage of the method is that it sweeps up accidentally several stray matters which I should exclude if I hesitated, but which are the diamonds of the dustheap. If Virginia Woolf at the age of 50, when she sits down to build her memoirs out of these books is unable to make a phrase as it should be made, I can only condole with her & remind her of the existence of the fireplace, where she has my leave to burn these pages to so many black films with red eyes in them. But how I envy her the task I am preparing for her! There is none I should like better. Already my 37th birthday next Saturday is robbed of some of its terrors by the thought. Partly for the benefit of this elderly lady (no subterfuge will then be possible: 50 is elderly,

> though I anticipate her protest & agree that it is not old) partly to give the year a solid foundation, I intend to spend the evenings of this week of captivity in making out an account of my friendships & their present conditions, with some account of my friends characters; & to add an estimate of their work, & a forecast of their future works. The lady of 50 will be able to say how near to the truth I come; but I have written enough for tonight (only 15 minutes, I see).

3. After seeing, hearing, reading, or listening to something that impresses you favorably or unfavorably, describe your immediate reaction in your journal, writing as quickly as you can. What emotions are evoked? What else do you associate with these emotions? What else have you seen, heard, read, or listened to that is similar? Different? Put your entry aside for a few days and then reread it to see what it reveals. Virginia Woolf finds that writing "at such a pace," she "must make the most direct and instant shots." What words and phrases in your entry best capture your feelings? How or how not? Upon rereading, like Virginia Woolf, do you find significance where you did not see it before? If so, how do you explain that fact?

MAY SARTON

from *Journal of a Solitude*

The American writer May Sarton was born in 1912. Though her first career was in the theatre—she founded and directed the Associated Actors Theatre—she soon focused on writing, first as a script writer, then as a teacher of writing, and finally as a distinguished poet and novelist. Selections of her poetry appear in her *Collected Poems* (1974). She has written screenplays and various works of fiction, including a fable and a novel for juveniles, as well as several works of nonfiction, most of which are autobiographical.

"September 15th" is the first entry in Sarton's *Journal of a Solitude*, and as such it deals with her expectations as a writer, her "hope to break through into the rough rocky depths, to the matrix itself." As you read the selection, notice the inner conflicts and the importance of the outside world with its "passionate love," its "small pink roses," and its "simplest conversation." *Plant Dreaming Sleep*, which Sarton mentions in paragraph 15, is one of her earlier autobiographical works. If the selection strikes you as polished, keep in mind that although *Journal of Solitude* is indeed a writer's journal, the author has refined her entries for publication.

September 15th. Begin here. It is raining. I look out on the maple, where a few leaves have turned yellow, and listen to Punch, the parrot, talking to himself and to the rain ticking 1 gently against the windows. I am here alone for the first time in weeks, to take up my "real" life again at last. That is what is strange—that friends, even passionate love, are not my real life unless there is time alone in which to explore and to discover what is happening or has happened. Without the interruptions, nourishing and maddening, this life would become arid. Yet I taste it fully only when I am alone here and "the house and I resume old conversations."

On my desk, small pink roses. Strange how often the au- 2
tumn roses look sad, fade quickly, frost-browned at the edges! But these are lovely, bright, singing pink. On the mantel, in the Japanese jar, two sprays of white lilies, recurved, maroon pollen on the stamens, and a branch of peony leaves turned a strange pinkish-brown. It is an elegant bouquet; *shibui,* the Japanese would call it. When I am alone the flowers are really seen; I can pay attention to them. They are felt as presences. Without them I would die. Why do I say that? Partly because they change before my eyes. They live and die in a few days; they keep me closely in touch with process, with growth, and also with dying. I am floated on their moments.

The ambience here is order and beauty. That is what fright- 3
ens me when I am first alone again. I feel inadequate. I have made an open place, a place for meditation. What if I cannot find myself inside it?

I think of these pages as a way of doing that. For a long time 4
now, every meeting with another human being has been a collision. I feel too much, sense too much, am exhausted by the reverberations after even the simplest conversation. But the deep collision is and has been with my unregenerate, tormenting, and tormented self. I have written every poem, every novel, for the same purpose—to find out what I think, to know where I stand. I am unable to become what I see. I feel like an inadequate machine, a machine that breaks down at crucial moments, grinds to a dreadful halt, "won't go," or, even worse, explodes in some innocent person's face.

Plant Dreaming Deep has brought me many friends of the 5
work (and also, harder to respond to, people who think they have found in me an intimate friend). But I have begun to realize that, without my own intention, that book gives a false view. The anguish of my life here—its rages—is hardly mentioned. Now I hope to break through into the rough rocky depths, to

the matrix itself. There is violence there and anger never resolved. I live alone, perhaps for no good reason, for the reason that I am an impossible creature, set apart by a temperament I have never learned to use as it could be used, thrown off by a word, a glance, a rainy day, or one drink too many. My need to be alone is balanced against my fear of what will happen when suddenly I enter the huge empty silence if I cannot find support there. I go up to Heaven and down to Hell in an hour, and keep alive only by imposing upon myself inexorable routines. I write too many letters and too few poems. It may be outwardly silent here but in the back of my mind is a clamor of human voices, too many needs, hopes, fears. I hardly ever sit still without being haunted by the "undone" and the "unsent." I often feel exhausted, but it is not my work that tires (work is a rest); it is the effort of pushing away the lives and needs of others before I can come to the work with any freshness and zest.

THE THINKING PROCESS

IDEAS FOR JOURNAL ENTRIES

1. Sarton sets out the relationship between her public and private lives when she asserts that "friends, even passionate love, are not my real life unless there is time alone in which to explore and to discover what is happening or has happened" (1). Consider the interplay between the time you spend with others and the time you spend by yourself. What is your "real" life? Is it your public one? Your private one? Some combination of the two? To arrive at a clearer understanding of your "real" life, work out your ideas in your journal and see what definition you can derive.

2. "Here" to May Sarton means both the literal house in which she is writing and its more abstract atmosphere: "The ambience here is order and beauty" (3). "Here" is "a place for meditation" (3), a place to center in on what is important, to sort out ideas, to create meaning out of experience. Many people have a similar retreat—a study, a bedroom, a quiet spot in the woods;

others find that certain actions serve the same purpose—driving, fishing, going for a walk. Where is your "place for meditation"? Write a journal entry describing your "here" in such a way that ten years from now, rereading your entry, you can not only see it vividly but also understand its significance.

3. Paragraph 2 describes the flowers in the room, Sarton's emotional attachments to them, and what they signify to her. She states, "Without them I would die." Think about where and how you live. What objects mean a great deal to you? List them and then select one item from your list to focus on in a journal entry. What does the object look like? What do you associate with it? What emotions do you feel toward it? Why does it hold such significance? If it were lost or destroyed, in what sense would you "die"?

THE WRITING PROCESS

PRELIMINARIES

1. Keep a journal for a week and then answer the following questions:

a. Looking back over your entries, do you find that you focus more on the external or internal world? That is, do you write more about people, places, events, and nature or more about your responses to them, your sensations, emotions, and ideas? Do you find that your entries lean toward objective description or subjective response? What reasons can you find for preferring one approach over another? Consider limiting your journal entries for the next week to the type of entry that you find more difficult.

b. Examine the style of your journal entries. Recall Virginia Woolf's comparison of her writing to the gait of a horse and Thomas Hardy's comparison of a church to a volcano. Note several examples of your own images and metaphors in your descriptions. What descriptions do you think are particularly successful?

2. To sharpen your powers of observation and your ear for language, consider writing a journal entry or two as described below.

a. The nineteenth-century British poet Gerard Manley Hopkins was an avid diary and journal keeper. In the selection below, he considers the etymology of the word *horn:*

Horn.

The various lights under which a horn may be looked at have given rise to a vast number of words in language. It may be regarded as a projection, a climax, a badge of strength, power or vigour, a tapering body, a spiral, a wavy object, a

> bow, a vessel to hold withal or to drink from, a smooth hard material not brittle, stony, metallic or wooden, something sprouting up, something to thrust or push with, a sign of honour or pride, an instrument of music, etc. From the shape, *kernel* and *granum, grain, corn*. From the curve of a horn, . . . *corona, crown*. From the spiral *crinis*, meaning ringlets, locks. From its being the highest point comes our *crown* perhaps, in the sense of the top of the head . . . . The tree *cornel*, Latin *cornus* is said to derive its name from the hard horn-like nature of its wood, and the *corns* of the foot perhaps for the same reason. *Corner* is so called from its shape, indeed the Latin is *cornu*. Possibly (though this is rather ingenious than likely, I think) *grin* may mean to curve up the ends of the mouth like horns. Mountains are called *horn* in Switzerland . . . .

Write an entry on an aspect of language that you find striking—analyzing words with long *i* sounds perhaps or words that form associative chains in your mind. For instance whether real or fictional, people's names can summon images: Uriah Heap, Sir Peregrine Pickle, Ernest Worthing, Fidele Armore. If no words or names come to mind, explore a dictionary, a thesaurus, or a telephone book.

b. In his later journal entries, Hopkins studies the particular effects of common occurrences, for example, a boiling pot of hot chocolate. In the selection below he describes what he sees when he holds his hand up against the sky:

> Putting my hand up against the sky whilst we lay on the grass I saw more richness and beauty in the blue than I had known of before, not brilliance but glow and colour. It was not transparent and sapphire-like but turquoise-like, swarming and blushing round the edge of the hand and in the pieces clipped in by the fingers, the flesh being sometimes sunlit, sometimes glassy with reflected light, sometimes lightly shadowed in that violet one makes with cobalt and Indian red.

Select a trivial occurrence that people take for granted—a glass of iced tea on a warm day, a spoon plunged halfway into a bowl of water, the effect of the light shimmering off the chrome of an automobile on a hot day, the actions of a rain drop as it trickles down a window pane. Describe in detail what you see.

CHAPTER 2

THE AUTOBIOGRAPHER

Why do writers choose to write about themselves? And why do readers find these life stories compelling? Autobiographies originate with *The Confessions of St. Augustine*, where St. Augustine celebrates his inner life of sin, conversion, and redemption, encouraging his readers to lead virtuous lives by presenting a moral paradigm. A different style of autobiography was written by Benvenuto Cellini, a renowned Italian Renaissance goldsmith and sculptor. In vivid detail and in dramatic style, Cellini describes his Florentine world and praises his own artistic achievements. In contrast to such acclaim, some twentieth-century autobiographers focus on the struggle of the individual—the difficulties of growing up black (James Baldwin's *Notes of a Native Son*), female (Maxine Hong Kingston's *The Woman Warrior*), Jewish (Alfred Kazin's *A Walker in the City*), or Catholic (Mary McCarthy's *Memoirs of a Catholic Girlhood*).

The autobiographical form allows writers to reflect on their lives as a whole or in part. In a short essay or a full-length book, writers can explore the meaning and purpose of their lives to discover order and destiny. They can inform their readers about their experiences and environments, and they can move their audience to dissolve prejudices or to adopt specific beliefs or actions. The tenor of the autobiography can be moralistic, profound, humorous, nostalgic, or whimsical. The style can be discursive, as in the selection by Charles Darwin, or descriptive, as in the excerpt by Mark Twain, or narrative, as in the passage by Frederick Douglass. The fluid form of autobiography allows the writer to experiment with a variety of tones and styles.

Like journals, autobiographies focus on the self, but unlike journals, they are written for other readers. Autobiographers speak to audiences directly about themselves, and because they are the sole authorities on their material, they may, at times, shape it for dramatic effect. Responsible writers, however, present themselves as truthfully as possible, thus providing insights unavailable to the biographer, who can merely recreate an individual from what Mark Twain calls "acts and deeds." Only the autobiographer can record thoughts, and those, according to Mark Twain, are the writer's "history."

Organization of the autobiography is frequently chronological. Yet autobiography can be organized dramatically or thematically. Mark Twain prescribes a formula with both humor and seriousness:

> Finally in Florence, in 1904, I hit upon the right way to do an Autobiography: Start it at no particular time of your life; wander at your free will over your life; talk only about the thing which interests you for the moment; drop it the moment its interest threatens to pale, and turn your talk upon the new and more interesting thing that has intruded itself into your mind meantime.

The discursive narrative may appear shapeless, but a well-written autobiography, no matter what the length, is artfully structured, as exemplified by Alice Walker's "When the Other Dancer is the Self."

The autobiography is a record of an individual's life filtered through that individual's senses and intellect. In addition to factual information, the autobiography conveys to an audience the writer's perceptions, visions, and fantasies, allowing the writer to practice self-exploration, description, narration, analysis, and persuasion, to evoke humor and sadness, irony and tragedy, and ultimately, empathy. By recreating the self for others, a writer can come to a fuller self-understanding and self-acceptance, crystalizing his or her identity. Furthermore, an autobiographical writer can evoke social awareness and acceptance, not only for the writer as an individual but as a representative of a particular race, religion, or creed.

FREDERICK DOUGLASS

Life As a Slave

Frederick Douglass (1817–1895) was born in Maryland, the son of a black slave, Harriet Bailey, and an unknown white father. After he escaped from slavery in 1838, he took the name of Douglass from the hero in Sir Walter Scott's *The Lady of the Lake.* He learned to read and write while in service at Baltimore and published his *Narrative of the Life of Frederick Douglass* in 1845. Fearing capture as a fugitive slave, Douglass spent several years in Great Britain, returning in 1847 after English friends purchased his freedom. *My Bondage and My Freedom* (1855), from which this excerpt is taken, is one of his three autobiographies.

Throughout his life, Douglass was a political activist and an abolitionist. He established the *North Star,* a newspaper that he edited for seventeen years. During the Civil War, Douglass urged blacks to join the Union ranks. After the war, he held various government posts, serving as secretary of the Santo Domingo Commission, marshal of the District of Columbia, and minister to Haiti.

I was a slave—born a slave—and though the fact was incomprehensible to me, it conveyed to my mind a sense of my entire dependence on the will of *somebody* I had never seen; and, from some cause or other, I had been made to fear this somebody above all else on earth. Born for another's benefit, as the *firstling* of the cabin flock I was soon to be selected as a meet offering to the fearful and inexorable *demigod,* whose huge image on so many occasions haunted my childhood's imagination. When the time of my departure was decided upon, my grandmother, 1 knowing my fears, and in pity for them, kindly kept me ignorant of the dreaded event about to transpire. Up to the morning (a beautiful summer morning) when we were to start, and, indeed, during the whole journey—a journey which, child as I was, I remember as well as if it were yesterday—she kept the sad fact hidden from me. This reserve was necessary; for, could I have known all, I should have given grandmother some trouble in getting me started. As it was, I was helpless, and she—dear woman!—led me along by the hand, resisting, with the reserve and solemnity of a priestess, all my inquiring looks to the last.

The distance from Tuckahoe to Wye River—where my old 2
master lived—was full twelve miles, and the walk was quite a severe test of the endurance of my young legs. The journey would have proved too severe for me, but that my dear old grandmother—blessings on her memory!—afforded occasional relief by "toting" me (as Marylanders have it) on her shoulder. My grandmother, though advanced in years—as was evident from more than one gray hair, which peeped from between the ample and graceful folds of her newly-ironed bandana turban—was yet a woman of power and spirit. She was marvelously straight in figure, elastic, and muscular. I seemed hardly to be a burden to her. She would have "toted" me farther, but that I felt myself too much of a man to allow it, and insisted on walking. Releasing dear grandmamma from carrying me, did not make me altogether independent of her, when we happened to pass through portions of the somber woods which lay between Tuckahoe and Wye river. She often found me increasing the energy of my grip, and holding her clothing, lest something should come out of the woods and eat me up. Several old logs and stumps imposed upon me, and got themselves taken for wild beasts. I could see their legs, eyes, and ears, or I could see something like eyes, legs, and ears, till I got close enough to them to see that the eyes were knots, washed white with rain, and the legs were broken limbs, and the ears, only ears owing to the point from which they were seen. Thus early I learned that the point from which a thing is viewed is of some importance.

As the day advanced the heat increased; and it was not un- 3
til the afternoon that we reached the much dreaded end of the journey. I found myself in the midst of a group of children of many colors; black, brown, copper colored, and nearly white. I had not seen so many children before. Great houses loomed up

in different directions, and a great many men and women were at work in the fields. All this hurry, noise, and singing was very different from the stillness of Tuckahoe. As a new comer, I was an object of special interest; and, after laughing and yelling around me, and playing all sorts of wild tricks, they (the children) asked me to go out and play with them. This I refused to do, preferring to stay with grandmamma. I could not help feeling that our being there boded no good to me. Grandmamma looked sad. She was soon to lose another object of affection, as she had lost many before. I knew she was unhappy, and the shadow fell from her brow on me, though I knew not the cause.

All suspense, however, must have an end; and the end of 4
mine, in this instance, was at hand. Affectionately patting me on the head, and exhorting me to be a good boy, grandmamma told me to go and play with the little children. "They are kin to you," she said; "go and play with them." Among a number of cousins were Phil, Tom, Steve, and Jerry, Nance and Betty.

Grandmother pointed out my brother PERRY, my sister 5
SARAH, and my sister ELIZA, who stood in the group. I had never seen my brother nor my sisters before; and, though I had sometimes heard of them, and felt a curious interest in them, I really did not understand what they were to me, or I to them. We were brothers and sisters, but what of that? Why should they be attached to me, or I to them? Brothers and sisters we were by blood; but *slavery* had made us strangers. I heard the words brother and sisters, and knew they must mean something; but slavery had robbed these terms of their true meaning. The experience through which I was passing, they had passed through before. They had already been initiated into the mysteries of old master's domicile, and they seemed to look upon me with a certain degree of compassion; but my heart clave to my grandmother. Think it not strange, dear reader, that so little sympathy of feeling existed between us. The conditions of brotherly and sisterly feeling were wanting—we had never nestled and played together. My poor mother, like many other slave-women, had *many children*, but NO FAMILY! The domestic hearth, with its holy lessons and precious endearments, is abolished in the case of a slave-mother and her children. "Little children, love one another," are words seldom heard in a slave cabin.

I really wanted to play with my brother and sisters, but they 6
were strangers to me, and I was full of fear that grandmother might leave without taking me with her. Entreated to do so,

however, and that, too, by my dear grandmother, I went to the back part of the house, to play with them and the other children. *Play*, however, I did not, but stood with my back against the wall, witnessing the playing of the others. At last, while standing there, one of the children, who had been in the kitchen, ran up to me, in a sort of roguish glee, exclaiming, "Fed, Fed! grandmammy gone! grandmammy gone!" I could not believe it; yet, fearing the worst, I ran into the kitchen, to see for myself, and found it even so. Grandmammy had indeed gone, and was now far away, "clean" out of sight. I need not tell all that happened now. Almost heart-broken at the discovery, I fell upon the ground, and wept a boy's bitter tears, refusing to be comforted. My brother and sisters came around me, and said, "Don't cry," and gave me peaches and pears, but I flung them away, and refused all their kindly advances. I had never been deceived before; and I felt not only grieved at parting—as I supposed forever—with my grandmother, but indignant that a trick had been played upon me in a matter so serious.

It was now late in the afternoon. The day had been an exciting and wearisome one, and I knew not how or where, but I suppose I sobbed myself to sleep. There is a healing in the angel wing of sleep, even for the slave-boy; and its balm was never more welcome to any wounded soul than it was to mine, the first night I spent at the domicile of old master. The reader may be surprised that I narrate so minutely an incident apparently so trivial, and which must have occurred when I was not more than seven years old; but as I wish to give a faithful history of my experience in slavery, I cannot withhold a circumstance which, at the time, affected me so deeply. Besides, this was, in fact, my first introduction to the realities of slavery. 7

THE THINKING PROCESS

STRUCTURE

1. Does the selection have an explicit thesis? If so, what is it? If not, what sentence comes closest to expressing Douglass' implied thesis? What effect does Douglass achieve by placing the key sentence where he does?

2. Douglass uses a double structure in his autobiography, the adult's knowledgeable point of view and the child's ignorant one. Where do you find examples of each type? What do you gain from the adult's view? From the child's? What are the advantages of this double viewpoint?

3. How does Douglass structure the story—chronologically, dramatically, or a combination of the two? Underline the key phrases that alert the reader to this structure. Are they sufficient to provide a sense of progression? Why or why not?

4. How is paragraph 2 (the description of the journey) a microcosm for the entire piece? Why is it placed where it is in the selection? How does it support Douglass' overall thesis?

STYLE

1. What is your general impression of Douglass' grandmother? Review the passage and underline all of Douglass' descriptions of her. What words and techniques does Douglass use to suggest her character? To suggest his feelings for her?

2. One way that Douglass conveys the horrors of slavery is by playing on his reader's emotions. What elements of childhood does he include in the passage that most children take for granted but are new to him, a child of slavery? What negative effects does he associate with slavery, and what different emotions does he evoke to convey them?

3. Douglass, like Mark Twain in the piece that follows, frequently appeals to the reader's senses. Find images that evoke sight, sound, touch, and taste. How effective are they? What is their function in the autobiography?

IDEAS FOR A FIRST DRAFT

Think of events in your childhood from which you learned a painful truth—perhaps about human relationships, morality in the world at large, or truth versus illusion. Select the event that will convey an essential point that you would like to communicate, the event that you think will most effectively move your readers and engage their sympathy and understanding.

Consider the advantages of an explicit or an implied thesis. If you decide on an explicit assertion, try it out in different positions—at the beginning, middle, or end of your autobiographical sketch—to see where it is the most effective.

Jot down all of your associations with the event, and see how you can best organize them to affect your reader. Try chronological or dramatic order, or perhaps a mixture of the two. As you write your draft, try to recreate the events by using vivid details that appeal to the senses and to the emotions.

CHARLES DARWIN

On My Reading, Writing, and Thinking

Charles Darwin (1809–1882) is the renowned English scientist who established the theory of organic evolution and of natural and sexual selection, elaborately set forth in the monumental *Origin of Species* (1859). Though Darwin studied medicine and theology, his interest in natural history dominated his life. He was the official naturalist aboard the HMS *Beagle* during a five-year voyage where he accumulated the data for his theories, writing his raw findings in his journals. Darwin wrote his autobiography in 1876 after the acceptance of his theories and books, notable among them *The Descent of Man* (1871).

Nora Barlow, the editor of Darwin's autobiography, opens her preface by asserting, "In his old age Charles Darwin wrote down his recollection for his own amusement and the interest of his children and their descendants." The selection reprinted here serves as the conclusion to the autobiography. As you read it, see if you can deduce any other audiences Darwin might have had in mind as he wrote.

I have now mentioned all the books which I have published, and these have been the milestones in my life, so that little remains to be said. I am not conscious of any change in my mind during the last thirty years, excepting in one point presently to be mentioned; nor indeed could any change have been expected unless one of general deterioration. But my father lived to his 1 eighty-third year with his mind as lively as ever it was, and all his faculties undimmed; and I hope that I may die before my mind fails to a sensible extent. I think that I have become a little more skilful in guessing right explanations and in devising experimental tests; but this may probably be the result of mere practice, and of a larger store of knowledge. I have as much difficulty as ever in expressing myself clearly and concisely; and this difficulty has caused me a very great loss of time; but it has had the compensating advantage of forcing me to think long and intently about every sentence, and thus I have been often led to see errors in reasoning and in my own observations or those of others.

There seems to be a sort of fatality in my mind leading me to 2
put at first my statement and proposition in a wrong or awkward form. Formerly I used to think about my sentences before writing them down; but for several years I have found that it saves time to scribble in a vile hand whole pages as quickly as I possibly can, contracting half the words; and then correct deliberately. Sentences thus scribbled down are often better ones than I could have written deliberately.

Having said this much about my manner of writing, I will 3
add that with my larger books I spend a good deal of time over the general arrangement of the matter. I first make the rudest outline in two or three pages, and then a larger one in several pages, a few words or one word standing for a whole discussion or series of facts. Each of these headings is again enlarged and often transformed before I begin to write *in extenso.* As in several of my books facts observed by others have been very extensively used, and as I have always had several quite distinct subjects in hand at the same time, I may mention that I keep from thirty to forty large portfolios, in cabinets with labelled shelves, into which I can at once put a detached reference or memorandum. I have bought many books and at their ends I make an index of all the facts that concern my work; or, if the book is not my own, write out a separate abstract, and of such abstracts I have a large drawer full. Before beginning on any subject I look to all the short indexes and make a general and classified index, and by taking the one or more proper portfolios I have all the information collected during my life ready for use.

I have said that in one respect my mind has changed during 4
the last twenty or thirty years. Up to the age of thirty, or beyond it, poetry of many kinds, such as the works of Milton, Gray,

Byron, Wordsworth, Coleridge, and Shelley, gave me great pleasure, and even as a schoolboy I took intense delight in Shakespeare, especially in the historical plays. I have also said that formerly pictures gave me considerable, and music very great delight. But now for many years I cannot endure to read a line of poetry: I have tried lately to read Shakespeare, and found it so intolerably dull that it nauseated me. I have also almost lost any taste for pictures or music.—Music generally sets me thinking too energetically on what I have been at work on, instead of giving me pleasure. I retain some taste for fine scenery, but it does not cause me the exquisite delight which it formerly did. On the other hand, novels which are works of the imagination, though not of a very high order, have been for years a wonderful relief and pleasure to me, and I often bless all novelists. A surprising number have been read aloud to me, and I like all if moderately good, and if they do not end unhappily—against which a law ought to be passed. A novel, according to my taste, does not come into the first class unless it contains some person whom one can thoroughly love, and if it be a pretty woman all the better.

This curious and lamentable loss of the higher aesthetic 5
tastes is all the odder, as books on history, biographies and travels (independently of any scientific facts which they may contain), and essays on all sorts of subjects interest me as much as ever they did. My mind seems to have become a kind of machine for grinding general laws out of large collections of facts, but why this should have caused the atrophy of that part of the brain alone, on which the higher tastes depend, I cannot conceive. A man with a mind more highly organised or better constituted than mine, would not I suppose have thus suffered; and if I had to live my life again I would have made a rule to read some poetry and listen to some music at least once every week; for perhaps the parts of my brain now atrophied could thus have been kept active through use. The loss of these tastes is a loss of happiness, and may possibly be injurious to the intellect, and more probably to the moral character, by enfeebling the emotional part of our nature.

My books have sold largely in England, have been trans- 6
lated into many languages, and passed through several editions in foreign countries. I have heard it said that the success of a work abroad is the best test of its enduring value. I doubt whether this is at all trustworthy; but judged by this standard

my name ought to last for a few years. Therefore it may be worth while for me to try to analyse the mental qualities and the conditions on which my success has depended; though I am aware that no man can do this correctly.

I have no great quickness of apprehension or wit which is so remarkable in some clever men, for instance Huxley. I am therefore a poor critic: a paper or book, when first read, generally excites my admiration, and it is only after considerable reflection that I perceive the weak points. My power to follow a long and purely abstract train of thought is very limited; I should, moreover, never have succeeded with metaphysics or mathematics. My memory is extensive, yet hazy: it suffices to make me cautious by vaguely telling me that I have observed or read something opposed to the conclusion which I am drawing, or on the other hand in favour of it; and after a time I can generally recollect where to search for my authority. So poor in one sense is my memory, that I have never been able to remember for more than a few days a single date or a line of poetry. 7

Some of my critics have said, "Oh, he is a good observer, but has no power of reasoning." I do not think that this can be true, for the *Origin of Species* is one long argument from the beginning to the end, and it has convinced not a few able men. No one could have written it without having some power of reasoning. I have a fair share of invention and of common sense or judgment, such as every fairly successful lawyer or doctor must have, but not I believe, in any higher degree. 8

On the favourable side of the balance, I think that I am superior to the common run of men in noticing things which easily escape attention, and in observing them carefully. My industry has been nearly as great as it could have been in the observation and collection of facts. What is far more important, my love of natural science has been steady and ardent. This pure love has, however, been much aided by the ambition to be esteemed by my fellow naturalists. From my early youth I have had the strongest desire to understand or explain whatever I observed,—that is, to group all facts under some general laws. These causes combined have given me the patience to reflect or ponder for any number of years over any unexplained problem. As far as I can judge, I am not apt to follow blindly the lead of other men. I have steadily endeavoured to keep my mind free, so as to give up any hypothesis, however much beloved (and I can- 9 not resist forming one on every subject), as soon as facts are shown to be opposed to it. Indeed I have had no choice but to act in this manner, for with the exception of the Coral Reefs, I cannot remember a single first-formed hypothesis which had not after a time to be given up or greatly modified. This has naturally led me to distrust greatly deductive reasoning in the mixed sciences. On the other hand, I am not very sceptical,—a frame of mind which I believe to be injurious to the progress of science; a good deal of scepticism in a scientific man is advisable to avoid much loss of time; for I have met with not a few men, who I feel sure have often thus been deterred from experiment or observations, which would have proved directly or indirectly serviceable. . . .

10 My habits are methodical, and this has been of not a little use for my particular line of work. Lastly, I have had ample leisure from not having to earn my own bread. Even ill-health, though it has annihilated several years of my life, has saved me from the distractions of society and amusement.

11 Therefore, my success as a man of science, whatever this may have amounted to, has been determined, as far as I can judge, by complex and diversified mental qualities and conditions. Of these the most important have been—the love of science—unbounded patience in long reflecting over any subject—industry in observing and collecting facts—and a fair share of invention as well as of common-sense. With such moderate abilities as I possess, it is truly surprising that thus I should have influenced to a considerable extent the beliefs of scientific men on some important points.

THE THINKING PROCESS

STRUCTURE

1. What are Darwin's reasons for including the information that he does in the conclusion to his autobiography? To what extent do those reasons provide an adequate thesis for the passage?

2. The editor of Darwin's autobiography, as the headnote cites, suggests that Darwin wrote "recollections" rather than a tightly structured book. Outline the structure of the selection by grouping together the paragraphs with similar concerns, and provide a descriptive label for each section. Do you find any connections among the groups? If so, what? If not, do you find the selection flawed? Why or why not?

3. Darwin analyzes his weaknesses and his strengths. What are they? Which does he discuss first? Why do you think that he arranges them in the order that he does? What other ways could they have been set out? Considering Darwin's choice and the other alternatives, which is the most effective and why?

4. Darwin discusses the "curious and lamentable loss of the higher aesthetic tastes" (5). To what does he attribute this loss, and why does he consider it "lamentable"? Taking into consideration what you have determined to be the underlying assertion of the selection, why do you think that Darwin includes this discussion in the conclusion of his autobiography?

STYLE

1. What attitude does Darwin take towards himself? Is he complacent, self-aggrandizing, modest, what? Underline the passages that convey his self-conceptions. Do you find them honest? Do you find Darwin likeable? Why or why not? What does his sense of himself lend to the piece?

2. What does Darwin say that he learns about the writing process? Do you find his conclusions true to your own experiences? Do you find the autobiography clearly and gracefully written? Underline sentences that support or refute your general estimation.

3. One difficulty in writing autobiography is the constant use of *I*, which, if the writer is not careful, can suggest egotism. One way that Darwin conveys a balanced view of himself is through his sentence structure. Reread paragraph 1. What grammatical structure does Darwin use to balance his statements that begin with *I*? Do you find the technique effective? Why or why not?

IDEAS FOR A FIRST DRAFT

Make a list of your strengths and weaknesses. You may even wish to consult your family, friends, and foes to help you compile this list.

Imagine yourself at the top of your chosen career—a famous scientist, doctor, writer, athlete, military officer, economist, business executive, lawyer, professor, artist. Write an autobiographical sketch that analyzes the personal strengths that helped you achieve success. Discuss your weaknesses as well (some may have indirectly aided your success, others may not).

Or, analyze your current strengths and weaknesses, and decide whether they will lead you to success or failure in a specific field or endeavor. Consider how you might have to change if you wish to succeed.

In either case, select an audience, such as your family and friends, strangers, descendants, or professionals in your field. Decide what personality you wish to project to your audience and whether you wish to be a model of success or an example of failure.

Look over your list, and select the characteristics most important to your purpose and to your audience. Determine which pattern of organization will be most effective by shuffling the order of the characteristics. You may wish to discuss strengths first, then weaknesses. Or the reverse. Or you may choose to alternate between the two.

And finally, decide on a tone for your sketch based upon your aims. Depending upon the sense of yourself you want to convey, your tone may be instructive, preachy, self-effacing, ambivalent, decisive—whatever you think will drive your point home.

MARK TWAIN

Remembering the Farm

Samuel Clemens (1835–1910) was born in Florida, Missouri—"an almost invisible village"—and four years later moved to Hannibal, which he made famous through its association with Tom Sawyer. Journeyman printer, journalist, riverboat pilot, traveler, speechmaker, and novelist, Clemens led a life as varied as his writing. He adopted the name Mark Twain early in his career, and his psuedonym has now almost obscured his real identity.

Samuel Clemens wrote much of his autobiography in 1906 although he began it in the early 1870s and worked on it intermittently until his death. A mixture of styles and voices, the autobiography is still distinctively his—full of anecdotes, imagery, and humor. His uncle's farm, the subject of the excerpt that follows, was four miles from his birthplace. The excerpt is notable for its freshness, all the more remarkable because Clemens is recalling a place where he had spent part of each year some fifty years earlier. He summons up the sights, smells, and sounds of his boyhood, in part by using similar sentence patterns. Try reading the selection aloud to hear the incantatory effect.

As I have said, I spent some part of every year at the farm until I was twelve or thirteen years old. The life which I led there with my cousins was full of charm, and so is the memory of it yet. I can call back the solemn twilight and mystery of the deep 1 woods, the earthy smells, the faint odors of the wild flowers, the sheen of rain-washed foliage, the rattling clatter of drops when the wind shook the trees, the far-off hammering of woodpeckers and the muffled drumming of wood pheasants in the remoteness of the forest, the snapshot glimpses of disturbed wild creatures scurrying through the grass—I can call it all back and make it as real as it ever was, and as blessed. I can call back the prairie, and its loneliness and peace, and a vast hawk hanging motionless in the sky, with his wings spread wide and the blue of the vault showing through the fringe of their end feathers. I can see the woods in their autumn dress, the oaks purple, the hickories washed with gold, the maples and the sumachs luminous with crimson fires, and I can hear the rustle made by the fallen leaves as we plowed through them. I can see the blue clusters of wild grapes hanging among the foliage of the saplings, and I remember the taste of them and the smell. I know how the wild blackberries looked, and how they tasted, and the same with the pawpaws, the hazelnuts, and the persimmons; and I can feel the thumping rain, upon my head, of hickory nuts and walnuts when we were out in the frosty dawn to scramble for them with the pigs, and the gusts of wind loosed them and sent them down. I know the stain of blackberries, and how pretty it is, and I know the stain of walnut hulls, and how little it minds soap and water, also what grudged experience it had of either of them. I know the taste of maple sap, and when to gather it, and how to arrange the troughs and the delivery tubes, and how to boil down the juice, and how to hook the sugar after it is made, also how much better hooked sugar tastes than any that is honestly come by, let bigots say what they will. I know how a prize watermelon looks when it is sunning its fat rotundity among pumpkin vines and "simblins"; I know how to tell when it is ripe without "plugging" it; I know how inviting it looks when it is cooling itself in a tub of water under the bed, waiting; I know how it looks when it lies on the table in the sheltered great floor space between house and kitchen, and the children gathered for the sacrifice and their mouths watering; I know the crackling sound it makes when the carving knife enters its end, and I can see the split fly along in front of the blade as the knife cleaves its way to the other end; I can see its halves fall apart and display the rich red meat and the black seeds, and the heart standing up, a luxury fit for the elect; I know how a boy looks behind a yard-long slide of that melon, and I know how he feels; for I have been there. I know the taste of the watermelon which has been honestly come by, and I know the taste of the watermelon which has been acquired by art. Both taste good, but the experienced know which tastes best. I know the look of green apples and peaches and pears on the trees, and I know how entertaining they are when they are inside of a person. I know how ripe ones look when they are piled in pyramids under the trees, and how pretty they are and how vivid their colors. I know how a frozen apple looks, in a barrel down cellar in the wintertime, and how hard it is to bite, and how the frost makes the teeth ache, and yet how good it is, notwithstanding. I know the disposition of elderly people to select the specked apples for the children, and I once knew ways to beat the game. I know the look of an apple that is roasting and sizzling on a hearth on a winter's evening, and I know the comfort that comes of eating it hot, along with some sugar and a drench of cream. I know the delicate art and mystery of so cracking hickory nuts and walnuts on a flatiron with a hammer that the kernels will be delivered whole, and I know how the nuts, taken in conjunction with winter apples, cider, and doughnuts, make old people's old tales and old jokes sound fresh and crisp and enchanting, and juggle an evening away before you know what went with the time. I know the look of Uncle Dan'l's kitchen as it was on the privileged nights, when I was a child, and I can see the white and black children grouped on the hearth, with the firelight playing on their faces and the shadows flickering upon the walls, clear back toward the cavernous gloom of the rear, and I can hear Uncle Dan'l telling the immortal tales which Uncle Remus Harris was to gather into his book and charm the world with, by and by; and I can feel again the creepy joy which quivered through me when the time for the ghost story was reached—and the sense of regret, too, which came over me, for it was always the last story of the evening and there was nothing between it and the unwelcome bed.

I can remember the bare wooden stairway in my uncle's 2
house, and the turn to the left above the landing, and the rafters and the slanting roof over my bed, and the squares of moonlight on the floor, and the white cold world of snow outside, seen through the curtainless window. I can remember the howling of the wind and the quaking of the house on stormy nights, and how snug and cozy one felt, under the blankets, listening; and

how the powdery snow used to sift in, around the sashes, and lie in little ridges on the floor and make the place look chilly in the morning and curb the wild desire to get up—in case there was any. I can remember how very dark that room was, in the dark of the moon, and how packed it was with ghostly stillness when one woke up by accident away in the night, and forgotten sins came flocking out of the secret chambers of the memory and wanted a hearing; and how ill chosen the time seemed for this kind of business; and how dismal was the hoo-hooing of the owl and the wailing of the wolf, sent mourning by on the night wind.

I remember the raging of the rain of that roof, summer 3
nights, and how pleasant it was to lie and listen to it, and enjoy the white splendor of the lightning and the majestic booming and crashing of the thunder. It was a very satisfactory room, and there was a lightning rod which was reachable from the window, an adorable and skittish thing to climb up and down, summer nights, when there were duties on hand of a sort to make privacy desirable.

I remember the 'coon and 'possum hunts, nights, with the 4
negroes, and the long marches through the black gloom of the woods, and the excitement which fired everybody when the distant bay of an experienced dog announced that the game was treed; then the wild scramblings and stumblings through briers and bushes and over roots to get to the spot; then the lighting of a fire and the felling of the tree, the joyful frenzy of the dogs and the negroes, and the weird picture it all made in the red glare—I remember it all well, and the delight that everyone got out of it, except the 'coon.

I remember the pigeon seasons, when the birds would come 5
in millions and cover the trees and by their weight break down the branches. They were clubbed to death with sticks; guns were not necessary and were not used. I remember the squirrel hunts, and prairie-chicken hunts, and wild-turkey hunts, and all that; and how we turned out, mornings, while it was still dark, to go on these expeditions, and how chilly and dismal it was, and how often I regretted that I was well enough to go. A toot on a tin horn brought twice as many dogs as were needed, and in their happiness they raced and scampered about, and knocked small people down, and made no end of unnecessary noise. At the word, they vanished away toward the woods, and we drifted

silently after them in the melancholy gloom. But presently the gray dawn stole over the world, the birds piped up, then the sun rose and poured light and comfort all around, everything was fresh and dewy and fragrant, and life was a boon again. After three hours of tramping we arrived back wholesomely tired, overladen with game, very hungry, and just in time for breakfast.

THE THINKING PROCESS

STRUCTURE

1. The first paragraph is unusually long but is sustained by the repetitive phrasing at the beginning of the sentences. Trace Mark Twain's introductory phrases. Which does he repeat? What pattern do you find to the repetitions? Does he sustain the repetitions through the rest of the selection? What reasons can you think of for his use of repetition? For his continuation or dropping of it?

2. Mark Twain states that his life then was "full of charm, and so is the memory of it yet" (1). Using an unabridged dictionary, look up the definition and etymology of *charm*. In what way does the descriptive language "charm" the reader?

3. Most paragraphs have an implicit or explicit topic sentence. Explicit topic sentences are useful in guiding readers through a closely reasoned piece; implicit ones draw in the readers who must then come to their own conclusions about the paragraph's main point. Reread paragraphs 2–5. Does each paragraph support Mark Twain's major assertion about charm in (1)? How so? What does each add to that assertion? Which paragraphs have implicit topic sentences? Which explicit?

STYLE

1. To evoke the atmosphere of a scene, writers often appeal to the senses, a technique common in the journal entries in chapter 1. Visual imagery is usually the most common, olfactory and tactile the least. Reread Twain's first paragraph, underlining the images that appeal to one of the less noted senses—smell, sound, touch, or taste. Be prepared to discuss in class what the variety contributes to the overall effect of the excerpt.

2. To make their writing vivid, good descriptive writers usually rely on active verbs, not on forms of *to be.* For instance, Mark Twain describes the cutting of a watermelon with the verbs *fly, cleave, fall,* and *display.* Find another sentence in the selection that illustrates Mark Twain's colorful use of verbs. Write it out on a sheet of paper, and try your own words in place of the verbs he uses. Test your choices on a few readers. Which version do they prefer and why?

3. The major difficulty in writing about the past is making it come alive in the present. Mark Twain uses a number of devices to bring the past to life: for example, present tense creates immediacy, coordinate sentences can suggest a continuum, and participles convey motion. Examine Mark Twain's use of tense in paragraph 1, his use of participles in paragraph 2, and his use of *and* in paragraph 4. Rewrite several lines, changing the element in question: alter the tense, recast the sentence to eliminate the participle, or avoid the *and.* What is gained? Lost?

4. A reader's attention is easily lost, something a writer can anticipate and prevent. Mark Twain uses varied techniques to keep the reader engaged, but perhaps the most striking is surprise. For instance, in paragraph 1 the reader does not expect a watermelon to be an active participant in its own demise, yet that is how Mark Twain describes it through personification. The melon practically invites theft by "sunning its fat rotundity." Find several other examples of the unexpected. For each, note what the reader anticipates and what Mark Twain delivers.

IDEAS FOR A FIRST DRAFT

Almost everyone has a memory of a place that holds special meaning. Perhaps, as for Mark Twain's farm, the associations are rich and pleasant, but a place can also be memorable because of painful or frightening experiences. To develop an autobiographical essay that both explores the meaning a particular place holds for you and conveys that meaning to your reader, you must first jot down the places that mean most to you, positive or negative. Select the one that you feel most strongly about, and cast your thoughts back to that place. Run through the five senses—touch, taste, sight, smell, sound—noting as many specific images as you can. Later, you may want to use sensory appeal as a principle of organization, devoting, say, one paragraph to each sense. Or you may want to tie the images to certain actions the way Mark Twain does.

When you start writing your draft, try to describe the place and your emotional response as fully as you can, and don't strain for a thesis.

Once you have a draft, determine what kind of organization came naturally to you. Perhaps the sequence in which the paragraphs presented themselves is the most natural. Or you may find, as writers often do, that you need to restructure the organization to make it seem natural. To enliven your prose, use some of Mark Twain's techniques, such as parallel phrasing, coordination with *and*, or frequent participles.

An explicit thesis may help or hinder. Your purpose in this paper is to relate what a particular place means to you so that you create in your readers a similar affinity or aversion. Give your draft to some readers. Ask them to describe the significance of the place you evoke. If their views and yours are the same, an explicit thesis would probably be redundant.

ALICE WALKER

When the Other Dancer Is the Self

Author of the recent Pulitzer-Prize winning novel *The Color Purple* (1982), Alice Walker was born in Georgia in 1944. She started teaching writing and black literature at Jackson State University, Tougaloo College, and Wellesley College and, more recently, she has taught at the University of Massachusetts and at Yale. A former editor of *Ms.*, she has received numerous grants, fellowships, and awards, including a Guggenheim grant in fiction and the Rosenthal Award from the National Institute of Arts and Letters. Walker has written a number of volumes of poetry and fiction as well as a biography of Langston Hughes. Her most recent collection of short stories, *You Can't Keep a Good Woman Down*, was published in 1981.

Walker's "When the Other Dancer Is the Self" appeared first in the May 1983 issue of *Ms.* magazine and was later published with other prose pieces in her collection *In Search of Our Mothers' Gardens* (1983). The interviewer she mentions in this autobiographical essay is Gloria Steinem, and the interview itself appeared in the June 1982 issue of *Ms.* under the title "Do You Know This Woman? She Knows You—A Profile of Alice Walker." As you read "When the Dancer Is the Self," see if you can identify the personality traits that might make Alice Walker a person of interest to the editors of *Ms.*

It is a bright summer day in 1947. My father, a fat, funny man with beautiful eyes and a subversive wit, is trying to decide which of his eight children he will take with him to the county fair. My mother, of course, will not go. She is knocked out from 1 getting us ready: I hold my neck stiff against the pressure of her knuckles as she hastily completes the braiding and then beribboning of my hair.

My father is the driver for the rich old white lady up the 2
road. Her name is Miss May. She owns all the land for miles around, as well as the house in which we live. All I remember about her is that she once offered to pay my mother 75 cents for cleaning her house, raking up piles of her magnolia leaves, and washing her family's clothes, and that my mother—she of no money, eight children, and a chronic earache—refused it. But I do not think of this in 1947. I am two-and-a-half years old. I want to go everywhere my daddy goes. I am excited at the prospect of riding in a car. Someone has told me fairs are fun. That there is room in the car for only three of us doesn't faze me at all. Whirling happily in my starchy frock, showing off my biscuit polished patent leather shoes and lavender socks, tossing my head in a way that makes my ribbons bounce, I stand, hands on hips, before my father. "Take me, Daddy," I say with assurance, "I'm the prettiest!"

Later, it does not surprise me to find myself in Miss May's 3
shiny black car, sharing the backseat with the other lucky ones. Does not surprise me that I thoroughly enjoy the fair. At home that night I tell all the unlucky ones about the merry-go-round, the man who eats live chickens, and the abundance of Teddy bears, until they say: that's enough, baby Alice. Shut up now, and go to sleep.

It is Easter Sunday, 1950. I am dressed in a green, flocked, 4
scalloped-hem dress (handmade by my adoring sister Ruth) that has its own smooth satin petticoat and tiny hot-pink roses tucked into each scallop. My shoes, new T-strap patent leather, again highly biscuit polished. I am six years old and have learned one of the longest Easter speeches to be heard in church that day, totally unlike the speech I said when I was two: "Easter lilies / pure and white / blossom in / the morning light." When I rise to give my speech I do so on a great wave of love and pride and expectation. People in the church stop rustling their new crinolines. They seem to hold their breath. I can tell they admire my dress, but it is my spirit, bordering on sassiness (womanishness), they secretly applaud.

"*That girl's a little mess,*" they whisper to each other, 5
pleased.

Naturally I say my speech without stammer or pause, unlike those who stutter, stammer, or, worst of all, forget. This is before the word "beautiful" exists in people's vocabulary, but "Oh, isn't she the *cutest* thing!" frequently floats my way. "*And got so much sense!*" they gratefully add . . . for which thoughtful addition I thank them to this day. 6

It was great fun being cute. But then, one day, it ended. 7

I am eight years old and a tomboy. I have a cowboy hat, cowboy boots, checkered shirt and pants, all red. My playmates are my brothers, two and four years older than me. Their colors are black and green, the only difference in the way we are dressed. On Saturday nights we all go to the picture show, even my mother; Westerns are her favorite movies. Back home, "on the ranch," we pretend we are Tom Mix, Hopalong Cassidy, Lash LaRue (we've even named one of our dogs Lash LaRue); we chase each other for hours rustling cattle, being outlaws, delivering damsels from distress. Then my parents decide to buy my brothers guns. These are not "real" guns. They shoot "BBs," copper pellets my brothers say will kill birds. Because I am a girl, I do not get a gun. Instantly I am relegated to the position of Indian. Now there appears a great distance between us. They shoot and shoot at everything with their new guns. I try to keep up with my bow and arrows. 8

One day while I am standing on top of our makeshift "garage"—pieces of tin nailed across some poles—holding my bow and arrow and looking out toward the fields, I feel an incredible blow in my right eye. I look down just in time to see my brother lower his gun. 9

Both brothers rush to my side. My eye stings, and I cover it with my hand. "If you tell," they say, "we will get a whipping. You don't want that to happen, do you?" I do not. "Here is a piece of wire," says the older brother, picking it up from the roof, "say you stepped on one end of it and the other flew up and hit you." The pain is beginning to start. "Yes," I say. "Yes, I will say that is what happened." If I do not say this is what happened, I know my brothers will find ways to make me wish I had. But now I will say anything that gets me to my mother. 10

Confronted by our parents we stick to the lie agreed upon. They place me on a bench on the porch and I close my left eye while they examine the right. There is a tree growing from underneath the porch, that climbs past the railing to the roof. It 11 is the last thing my right eye sees. I watch as its trunk, its branches, and then its leaves are blotted out by the rising blood.

I am in shock. First there is intense fever, which my father tries to break using lily leaves bound around my head. Then there are chills: my mother tries to get me to eat soup. Eventually, I do not know how, my parents learn what has happened. A week after the "accident" they take me to see a doctor. "Why did you wait so long to come?" he asks, looking into my eye and shaking his head. "Eyes are sympathetic," he says. "If one is blind, the other will likely become blind too." 12

This comment of the doctor's terrifies me. But it is really how I look that bothers me most. Where the BB pellet struck there is a glob of whitish scar tissue, a hideous cataract, on my eye. Now when I stare at people—a favorite pastime, up to now—they will stare back. Not at the "cute" little girl, but at her scar. For six years I do not stare at anyone because I do not raise my head. 13

Years later, in the throes of a mid-life crisis, I ask my mother and sister whether I changed after the "accident." "No," they say, puzzled. "What do you mean?" 14

What do I mean? 15

I am eight, and for the first time, doing poorly in school, where I have been something of a whiz since I was four. We have just moved to the place where the "accident" occurred. We do not know any of the people around us because this is a different county. The only time I see the friends I knew is when we go back to our old church. My new school is the former state penitentiary. It is a large stone building, cold and drafty, crammed to overflowing with boisterous, ill-disciplined children. On the third floor there is a huge circular imprint of some partition that has been torn out. 16

"What used to be here?" I ask a sullen girl next to me on our way past it to lunch. 17

"The electric chair," says she. 18

At night I have nightmares about the electric chair, and about all the people reputedly "fried" in it. I am afraid of the school, where all the students seem to be budding criminals. 19

"What's the matter with your eye?" they ask, critically. 20

When I don't answer (I cannot decide whether it was an "accident" or not), they shove me, insist on a fight. 21

My brother, the one who created the story about the wire, 22 comes to my rescue. But then brags so much about "protecting" me, I become sick.

23 After weeks of torture at the school, my parents decide to send me back to our old community to my old school. I live with my grandparents and the teacher they board. But there is no room for Phoebe, my cat. By the time my grandparents decide there *is* room, and I ask for my cat, she cannot be found. Miss Yarborough, the boarding teacher, takes me under her wing, and begins to teach me to play the piano. But soon she marries an African—a "prince," she says—and is whisked away to his continent.

24 At my old school there is at least one teacher who loves me. She is the teacher who "knew me before I was born" and bought my first baby clothes. It is she who makes life bearable. It is her presence that finally helps me turn on the one child at the school who continually calls me "one-eyed bitch." One day I simply grab him by his coat and beat him until I am satisfied. It is my teacher who tells me my mother is ill.

25 My mother is lying in bed in the middle of the day, something I have never seen. She is in too much pain to speak. She has an abscess in her ear. I stand looking down on her, knowing that if she dies, I cannot live. She is being treated with warm oils and hot bricks held against her cheek. Finally a doctor comes. But I must go back to my grandparents' house. The weeks pass, but I am hardly aware of it. All I know is that my mother might die, my father is not so jolly, my brothers still have their guns, and I am the one sent away from home.

26 "You did not change," they say.

27 *Did I imagine the anguish of never looking up?*

28 I am 12. When relatives come to visit I hide in my room. My cousin Brenda, just my age, whose father works in the post office and whose mother is a nurse, comes to find me. "Hello," she says. And then she asks, looking at my recent school picture which I did not want taken, and on which the "glob" as I think of it is clearly visible, "You still can't see out of that eye?"

29 "No," I say, and flop back on the bed over my book.

30 That night, as I do almost every night, I abuse my eye. I rant and rave at it, in front of the mirror. I plead with it to clear up before morning. I tell it I hate and despise it. I do not pray for sight. I pray for beauty.

31 "You did not change," they say.

I am 14 and baby-sitting for my brother Bill who lives in 32
Boston. He is my favorite brother and there is a strong bond between us. Understanding my feelings of shame and ugliness, he and his wife take me a local hospital where the "glob" is removed by a doctor named O. Henry. There is still a small bluish crater where the scar tissue was, but the ugly white stuff is gone. Almost immediately I become a different person from the girl who does not raise her head. Or so I think. Now that I've raised my head, I win the boyfriend of my dreams. Now that I've raised my head, I have plenty of friends. Now that I've raised my head, classwork comes from my lips as faultlessly as Easter speeches did, and I leave high school as valedictorian, most popular student and *queen,* hardly believing my luck. Ironically, the girl who was voted most beautiful in our class (and was) was later shot twice through the chest by a male companion, using a "real" gun, while she was pregnant. But that's another story in itself. Or, is it?

"You did not change," they say. 33

It is now 30 years since the "accident." A gorgeous woman 34
and famous journalist comes to visit and to interview me. She is going to write a cover story for her magazine that focuses on my last book. "Decide how you want to look on the cover," she says. "Glamorous, or whatever."

Never mind "glamorous," it is the "whatever" that I hear. 35
Suddenly all I can think of is whether I will get enough sleep the night before the photography session: if I don't, my eye will be tired and wander, as blind eyes will.

At night in bed with my lover I think up reasons why I 36
should not appear on the cover of a magazine. "My meanest critics will say I've sold out," I say. "My family will now realize I write scandalous books." "But what's the real reason you don't want to do this?" he asks.

"Because in all probability," I say in a rush, "My eye won't 37
be straight."

"It will be straight enough," he says. Then, "Besides, I 38
thought you'd made your peace with that."

And I suddenly realize that I have. 39

I remember: 40

I am talking to my brother Jimmy, asking if he remembers 41
anything unusual about the day I was shot. He does not know I

consider that day the last time my father, with his sweet home remedy of cool lily leaves, "chose" me, and that I suffered rage inside because of this. "Well," he says, "all I remember is standing by the side of the highway with Daddy, trying to flag down a car. A white man stopped, but when Daddy said he needed somebody to take his little girl to the doctor, he drove off."

I remember: 42

I am 33 years old. And in the desert for the first time. I fall 43
totally in love with it. I am so overwhelmed by its beauty, I confront for the first time, consciously, the meaning of the doctor's words years ago: "Eyes are sympathetic. If one is blind, the other will likely become blind too." I realize I have dashed about the world madly, looking at this, looking at that, storing up images against the fading of the light. *But I might have missed seeing the desert!* The shock of that possibility—and gratitude for more than 25 years of sight—sends me literally to my knees. Poem after poem comes—which is perhaps how poets pray.

On Sight

I am so thankful I have seen
The Desert
And the creatures in The Desert
And the desert Itself.

The desert has its own moon
Which I have seen
With my own eye

There is no flag on it.

Trees of the desert have arms
All of which are always up
That is because the moon is up
The sun is up
The stars
Clouds
None with flags.

If there *were* flags, I doubt
the trees would point.
Would you?

But mostly, I remember this: 44

I am 27, and my baby daughter is almost three. Since her 45
birth I have worried over her discovery that her mother's eyes

are different from other people's. Will she be embarrassed? I wonder. What will she say? Every day she watches a television program called "Big Blue Marble." It begins with a picture of the earth as it appears from the moon. It is bluish, a little battered-looking but full of light, with whitish clouds swirling around it. Every time I see it I weep with love, as if it is a picture of Grandma's house. One day when I am putting Rebecca down for her nap, she suddenly focuses on my eye. Something inside me cringes, gets ready to try to protect myself. All children are cruel about physical differences, I know from experience, and that they don't always mean to be is another matter. I assume Rebecca will be the same.

But no-o-o-o. She studies my face intently as we stand, her inside and me outside her crib. She even holds my face maternally between her dimpled little hands. Then, looking every bit as serious and lawyerlike as her father, she says, as if it may just possibly have slipped my attention: "Mommy, there's a *world* in your eye." (As in, "Don't be alarmed, or do anything crazy.") And then, gently, but with great interest: "Mommy, where did you *get* that world in your eye?" 46

For the most part, the pain left then. (So what if my brothers grew up to buy even more powerful pellet guns for their sons. And to carry real guns themselves. So what if a young "Morehouse man" once nearly fell off the steps of Trevor Arnett Library because he thought my eyes were blue.) Crying and laughing I ran to the bathroom, while Rebecca mumbled and sang herself off to sleep. Yes indeed, I realized, looking into the mirror. There *was* a world in my eye. And I saw that it was possible to love it; that in fact, for all it had taught me, of shame and anger and inner vision, I *did* love it. Even to see it drifting out of orbit in boredom, or rolling up out of fatigue, not to mention floating back at attention in excitement (bearing witness, a friend has called it), deeply suitable to my personality, and even characteristic of me. 47

That night I dream I am dancing to Stevie Wonder's song "Always." As I dance, whirling and joyous, happier than I've ever been in my life, another bright-faced dancer joins me. We dance and kiss each other and hold each other through the night. The other dancer has obviously come through all right, as I have done. She is beautiful, whole and free. And she is also me. 48

THE THINKING PROCESS

STRUCTURE

1. Readers learn about a person in an autobiography not only from the person herself but also from others' responses to her. What do you learn about Alice Walker from her interaction with her brothers (10)? Her mother and sister (14)? Her classmates (17–21)? Her daughter (45–46)? What do you learn about Alice Walker from her own perceptions in paragraphs 4, 10, and 47?

2. Autobiographical essays occasionally tell a story exploring the meaning of the writer's life rather than make an explicit point. Sometimes the thesis is implied; sometimes it is withheld until near the end of the essay. What is Alice Walker saying about her blind eye? State her thesis in your own words. Where in the essay does she come closest to stating the thesis?

3. Often a writer working on an autobiographical piece will juxtapose the past with the present. In what paragraphs does Alice Walker use both past and present? What effects does she achieve with the contrast?

4. One way to make a long essay readily comprehensible is to break it up into groups of paragraphs, with each group unified by a common thread. Work through Alice Walker's essay. How many paragraph blocks do you find? Note that each deals with a specific time in her life. What are those times? Work out the essay's chronology. How are the paragraph blocks organized: chronologically, dramatically, or a mixture of the two?

STYLE

1. Understatement can be a very effective device. Consider, for instance, the flat manner in which Alice Walker relates what she remembers about Miss May (2). The author states only bald facts; the reader then infers the exploitive relationship. Paragraphs 8, 23, and 41 use the same technique. Select one of those examples or any other: first note the facts, then your inference.

2. Understatement usually has an ironic twist to it, and irony is another of Alice Walker's techniques. Consider, for example, the essay's central image. Alice Walker is blind in one eye, lived for years under the fear of losing her sight in the other, and yet finally learns to accept, even to love, the blind eye that is the source of her anger and pain. In her dream, her dance partner is herself; the song is "Always"; the singer is Stevie Wonder, who is blind. Where else in the essay do you find examples of irony? Select one, and analyze it so that you are prepared to discuss what irony contributes to that particular passage.

3. Italics have a number of functions: among them, emphasis, repetition, and echo. Examine their use in paragraphs 5, 6, 7, 15, 27, 40, 42, 43, and 46. What conclusions can you draw about the way Alice Walker uses italics?

IDEAS FOR A FIRST DRAFT

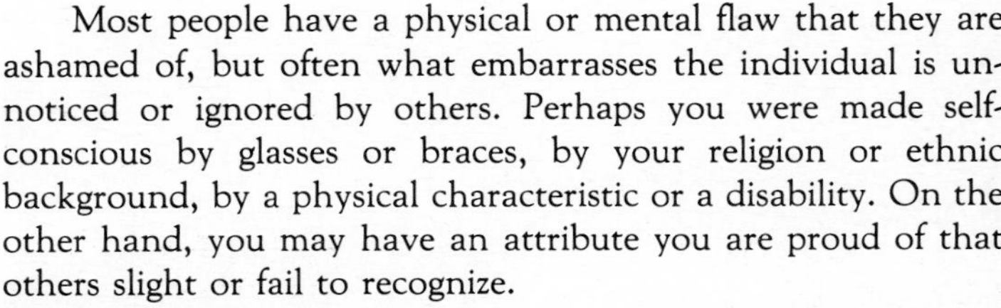

Most people have a physical or mental flaw that they are ashamed of, but often what embarrasses the individual is unnoticed or ignored by others. Perhaps you were made self-conscious by glasses or braces, by your religion or ethnic background, by a physical characteristic or a disability. On the other hand, you may have an attribute you are proud of that others slight or fail to recognize.

Consider any of your attributes or characteristics that have made you feel either ashamed or proud. Jot down examples, and then select one to write about. Choose an audience that you wish to affect by your essay—maybe one particular individual, your family, your classmates, your peers, society in general. To gather material to use in your autobiographical essay, consider your answers to the following questions: When did you first become aware of your feelings? When did you reconcile yourself to your imperfection? What events characterized those times? Who or what made you most self-conscious? What emotions do you want to create in your readers? What thoughts? How do you want your audience to be changed by reading your essay?

Review your notes to determine what to include in your

draft, and sketch out your plan for the essay. Does your paper lend itself to being built around one incident or several? What sequence best guides your organization—chronological, dramatic, a mixture of the two? Would dialogue be appropriate in your essay? Italics? Should your thesis be implicit or explicit?

THE WRITING PROCESS

INVENTION

If you are working on a previous assignment in this chapter, you already have a rough draft and can skip to Organizing and Developing. If not, review the important influences on your life by listing them under several headings: people you have known, places you have lived, dramatic incidents that have happened, themes you found reoccurring. Jot down a few examples for each category and then reread your notes to see what would work well for an autobiographical paragraph or essay. Ideally you are looking for a topic you can explore to discover something about yourself that you want to communicate to your readers. You are looking for a person, place, incident, or idea that means a great deal to you. You want to analyze just what that meaning is and then convey it effectively to your audience—the average citizen or a specific group of your choice. Think of the experiences your readers have probably had, and then look for connections between your subject and your readers' lives. Your paper will focus on you, but you want to convey your experience in such a way that you recreate it for your readers. Once you have chosen a topic, you will need to reconstruct your thoughts and feelings for readers who know nothing about them.

Whether you are writing a paragraph or an essay, you should generate more material than you think you need, so that you will be able to select the most effective examples. Explore your topic by brainstorming—that is making a list as quickly as you can without stopping to analyze your notes—on each of the following aspects of autobiography:

1. Chronology: What happened when? In what sequence?

2. Characterization: What did you think, feel? How did others respond to you? Would dialogue be effective? What descriptions of people or places are necessary?

3. Ideas: What does your subject reveal about you? How can you state that insight in a working thesis? What sub-assertions are related to your working thesis?

Keeping in mind your major assertion, review your notes, and put a check mark by the items most relevant to your point. These checks are your working outline. Begin writing a draft, incorporating the material you have marked and anything else that comes to mind as you write. Don't feel bound to your notes; they are only reminders.

ORGANIZING AND DEVELOPING

Writers may place the most dramatic material near the end of the essay to leave the reader with a final impact. Writers also may contrast the past with the present. Outline the chronology you have established to decide whether or not you want your sequencing of the dramatic time to correspond to the actual time, and then readjust your draft so that the chronology is appropriate to your point and presents it effectively.

To review your draft for coherence and effectiveness, mark any paragraph that deals with your internal world, making sure that the material can be readily understood by readers who do not know you. Then go back and note what emotion or assertion each paragraph is illustrating. Check to see that all details in the paragraph relate to your assertion. Try making that assertion implicit if it is explicit, explicit if it is implicit, and then see which you prefer. Remember that you need not use the same method in all your paragraphs.

Similarly, double-check your major assertion. Is the paper more effective with an implicit or explicit thesis? If the thesis is explicit, where is it stated? Might it be more effective placed elsewhere? Try it in different positions to determine which works best. If the thesis is implicit, check to see that it is clear by asking a few people to read the paper. What do they perceive as the thesis? If their inferences do not correspond to your thesis, you should consider changing it or reshaping your material. Given the choice, adjusting your thesis is probably the better alternative; odds are that what you have written is what you really had to say.

FINDING A VOICE

Try to determine the most effective relationship between your autobiographical material and your reader. Do you want to establish distance? Choose past tense. Do you want to make the material immediate? Choose present tense. Figure out what side of yourself you wish to portray—for example, tragic, humorous, naive, wise, vulnerable. Determine what other effects you want your essay to have on your audience. What emotions do you want your readers to feel? What ideas do you want them to be left with? What impressions of you do you want them to have?

If you can, try out your draft on a reader or two to see if the paper is having the effects you are striving for. If it isn't, discuss the paper with your readers to pinpoint the trouble spots. Usually if you ask specific questions, such as "What details led you to think I was angry (sad, happy)?," you will be able to spot the problem. More general questions, such as "Why doesn't it work?," are apt to lead to equally general answers: "Well, it just doesn't." Once you have revised the paper to achieve the responses you want, you have established your tone.

POLISHING

Review your paper to check for rambling and disunity. Autobiography tempts a reader to include too much: you need not account for every moment from the past to the present. Delete any events, details, and descriptions that do not support or heighten your main dramatic focus. Remember, the narrative mode sometimes invites excessively long paragraphs and long, strung-together sentences. Revise accordingly.

Reconsider the personality you create in your essay. When writing about ourselves, we can easily become self-indulgent and project self-pity, conceit, or any number of undesirable traits. List the characteristics you want associated with your *I*, and double-check your details to see that they support these characteristics.

Finally, remember to proofread once for each of your current problems with mechanics and usage: for example, once for comma splices and once for pronoun-antecedent agreement.

THINKING AHEAD

Your notes from your brainstorming will come in handy, particularly if you are keeping a journal. Save them for a day when you can think of little to write about, and they will provide some ready ideas.

From brainstorming to proofreading, you have been working with the narrative—with chronology and with how to view the real as drama. List the techniques you have used, such as sequence, tense change, description, dialogue, and implied thesis. You will find that the brief narrative can be used in many other kinds of writing, from the personal essay to the historic and scientific paper and that your list of techniques will serve you well in the future.

CHAPTER 3

THE PERSONAL ESSAYIST

Though the personal essay had its origins over four hundred years ago with Montaigne, today it is ubiquitous. Even with national news magazines like *Newsweek* and *Time*, specialized publications like *Field and Stream*, magazine supplements in local Sunday newspapers like *Parade*, all of us can settle down to read the private ideas of strangers. But while writers of these essays make public their private thoughts, they have edited these thoughts for an audience. Essayists usually transcend both the audience of the self, so central to the journal, and the subject of the self, so central to the autobiography. Although they write about personal experience, they must be aware that they are writing, in a sense, for an audience of eavesdroppers—for a disparate group of individuals who are listening in on them—and thus they must sound natural, even casual.

The artifice of the personal essay is similar to that of the soliloquy. The convention of the soliloquy allows the actors, still in character, to step out of the scene and reveal their past reactions and future actions. Similarly the personal essay reveals writers thinking out loud, expressing their concerns to an unseen audience. Both actors and writers attempt to make their audiences, strangers all, part of their particular worlds.

Yet paradoxically essayists must be acutely aware of their audiences—their likes and dislikes, their preconceived ideas, their frames of reference. And though the essays are monologues, they are monologues carefully tuned for the ears of a particular audience.

Edward Hoagland, an editorialist for the *New York Times*, has written a personal essay about the personal essay, "What I Think, What I Am." There he likens the essay to "the human voice talking, its order the mind's natural flow, instead of a systematized outline of ideas." The word *essay*, taking its origin from *assay*—an "examination, trial, test," originally implied "an irregular undigested piece"; now it refers to a composition "elaborate in style though limited in range."

Some contemporary essays, however, hide their elaboration and seem almost simple in design. Their ostensible "tumbling progression" is essential to the essay's informal, individual style; yet beneath the seemingly casual organization lies a fixed structure supporting the meditation. The personal essay, says Hoagland, emphasizes "mind speaking to mind" and addresses an audience typified by the "educated, perhaps a middle-class, reader, with certain presuppositions, a frame of reference, even a commitment to civility that is shared."

In personal essays, writers explore a variety of subjects, but they usually place their experiences within larger contexts so that they focus on basic human concerns. Thus Laurence Shames writes about love in "The Eyes of Fear" and Willie Morris about love and death in "A Love That Transcends Sadness." But personal essays need not solely address grand subjects; indeed they may focus on essential concerns that readers may at first think insignificant. Gary Esolen, for instance, in "Grace in Motion" pays tribute to expertise and garbage men while E. B. White in "Bedfellows" studies dogs and democracy. Whatever the subject, it must be one that the writer knows well although as Hoagland reveals,

> An essayist soon discovers that he doesn't have to tell the whole truth and nothing but the truth; he can shape or shave his memories, as long as the purpose is served of elucidating a truthful point.

As E. B. White asserts,

> There are as many kinds of essays as there are human attitudes or poses, as many essay flavors as Howard Johnson ice creams. The essayist arises in the morning and, if he has work to do, selects his garb from an unusually extensive wardrobe: he can pull on any sort of shirt, be any sort of person, according to his mood or his subject matter—philosopher, scold, jester, raconteur, confidant, pundit, devil's advocate, enthusiast.

The personal essay is one of the most versatile forms of composition. Its informal and often colloquial tone, its fluid organization, its demand for clear articulation of specialized experience, its insights into the predicaments of being human, its conscious lack of self-consciousness, make the personal essay a challenging art form. As Hoagland concludes, "the fascination of the mind is the fascination of the essay."

GARY ESOLEN

Grace in Motion

Gary Esolen, a contemporary American writer, traveled throughout the country and held a variety of jobs before moving to New Orleans, where he is the editor of *Gambit*, a weekly newspaper of politics and the arts. In addition to news stories, *Gambit* has regular features and contributors. "Standpoint" is the slot for the personal essay, and it is there that in September, 1982, Esolen's "Grace in Motion" appeared. You will find that Esolen selects the unlikely subject of garbage men, describing them in the larger context of physical laborers. And he enlarges the scope of the essay by appealing to readers in states other than Louisiana, referring to scenes in California, Florida, Michigan, and New York. Thus he connects the scene he witnessed in New Orleans with similar ones that occurred in different places and at different times.

There's a special joy in physical work when it's done well, with skill and enthusiasm; and the joy communicates itself to the watcher. I saw the Nureyev and Baryshnikov of the garbage trucks last week, working in the French Quarter, and it was pure poetry in motion. 1

They were both young men, and throwing garbage is a job that is hard on older men. One was white, one black. Both were in superb physical condition. They ran alongside the truck, ran ahead of the truck, and ran with cans and bags of garbage. 2

When they collected bags from the curbside, they would throw them, sometimes 15 or 20 feet, into the truck. I saw hook shots, bank shots, and in some cases double bank shots. They 3 never missed. With ease and grace, they performed physical feats that were astonishing. It reminded me of first-rate acrobatic clowns, who run frantically around doing things that would make Olympic acrobats flush with envy. One of these guys came running from curbside with a garbage can in each hand, held out in front of him by the near edge. He lifted both cans at once over the truck, and then upended them with a flip of his wrists. He shook both of them out and flipped them back right side up and ran back to the curb with them, whistling as he ran to alert the truck driver to move on. Try it sometime. It's like lifting a kitchen chair from the bottom of a leg with one hand.

I have a good friend who works as a consultant to city gov- 4
ernment in the San Francisco area, helping to improve city-employee relations. As part of his job, he once joined a garbage crew in Berkeley, in one of the rich neighborhoods. There the houses sit on the street but the garbage is kept behind the house, down a steep hill. The garbage men would run behind the houses, get the garbage, run to the trucks, then run back with the empties. My friend says they laughed and sang as they worked.

C. Wright Mills, the great American sociologist, once saw 5
a man digging a ditch. He noticed that the ditchdigger was the most efficient shoveler he had ever seen, lifting one shovelful of dirt after another, throwing the dirt neatly into the pile of spoil, swinging his shovel in a perfect rhythm. Mills stopped his car, got out, and took lessons from the man for an hour until he could match the movement.

I remember watching an aristocrat of labor at work in Ann 6
Arbor, Michigan once. This guy was black, a lead mason on a crew out of Detroit. He handled only the elite jobs: fireplaces and fancy work. He wore a yellow nylon shirt with an embroidered pocket and a pair of brown doubleknit pants. His shoes were polished to a mirror shine, and he wore a silver ring.

He walked up to a prospective fireplace like a surgeon going 7
into the operating room. He called for bricks, and bricks were brought to him. He called for mud, and in came a hod full of mortar, held by a dutiful attendant. He called for his trowel, and someone brought it. He removed his ring and began to work. He laid up the entire fireplace in scarcely an hour, working quickly and cleanly, laying the arch, the standard common-bond joints, the rows of upright bricks called, in the trade, English Soldiers.

When he laid the last brick he struck the last joints, handed his trowel to his assistant, wiped his hands on a towel, replaced his ring, and walked to the next fireplace.

On that same job was a roofer, a French-Canadian, who turned everybody's head when he worked. Nailing down an asphalt shingle roof is miserable work by any standard. You work in the noonday heat, fully exposed to the sun. You stand up high on a slanted surface. You lift and throw around considerable weight. You must work with exact precision, or the roof will look ridiculous. And you are under pressure to work fast. Worst of all, there is no possible comfortable working position: you must work in a perpetual crouch. 8

This man was a master. A really good roofer can set a square of roof, 100 square feet, in an hour. This guy set two square an hour, eight or 10 hours a day. He ran from place to place, ran up and down ladders, hopped across the roof, and drove each nail in one blow. I worked alongside someone almost as good once, and it is incredible to watch. He set two rows to my one, and never seemed to want to rest. The French-Canadian was so good that men on the job brought their sons to watch him: look, that's the best roofer you'll ever see in your life. 9

Driving a nail with one blow, incidentally, is called speed nailing, and with roofing nails, going into plywood, it's not really hard. The hard part is not to hit your fingers. It takes perfect timing. But speed nailing is the basis of one of the great myths among framing carpenters. 10

Let me explain what framing carpenters do. They build the two-by-four frames of houses. On big crews, that's all they do. They nail up the skeletons, perhaps throw a plywood roof on, and then they move on to the next job. Somebody else does everything else. 11

Framing carpenters are generally paid by the square foot, so they are under pressure to move fast. They make their money on speed. They use 27-ounce hammers (the normal big hammers around the house are 16-ounce) with extra long handles and a striking face that is checkered to drive nails better. It is a specialized tool: it drives three-inch long nails into pine or fir two-by-fours. Most framing is done flat on a deck and then the completed wall is lifted into place. Swinging a 27-ounce hammer at full arm's length develops some serious momentum. But I have never seen anyone who could drive a 16 penny nail in one blow. I have done it myself in two blows, and I've seen men who 12 could do that all day long: set the nail to about a third of its depth in one blow, finish it off with the second.

But every framing crew talks, over lunch and over coffee, about the great speed nailer, who can drive a 16 penny nail in one blow. If you are in New York, he's on a job in California. If you are in California, he's in Michigan. If you are in Michigan, he's in Florida. If you're in Florida, he's in New York. But there's always one guy on the crew who saw him work, and can swear to it. The speed nailer is the John Henry of the framing crew. 13

I come from a family in which the ability to do physical work well is highly valued. My great-grandfather Stephen was famous for his ability to carry a barrel of flour on his head. I learned at my father's knee how to use balance and the strength of my legs to carry large loads. I have an appreciation of such things comparable to the insight a good Sunday golfer would have into the grace of Arnold Palmer or Jack Nicklaus. 14

It is one of the special pleasures in life to be aware of the beauty of work well done. There is an aesthetic in physical work, and we all recognize it. I remember a short-order cook, a counter-man in Syracuse, New York, called The Sergeant. The Sergeant could pick up four eggs at once, two in each hand, and break all of them simultaneously. He could cook six hamburgers, two omelets, four orders of hash browns, and three orders of eggs, each with the right kind of toast and the right side orders, without missing a gesture. Every motion was fluid and effective. People would come from all over the city to eat at the little diner where he worked just so they could watch him. The urge to excellence, to perfection, can find expression in the most remarkable ways, and each of them is a tribute to our humanity. 15

THE THINKING PROCESS

STRUCTURE

1. Many personal essays present a central assertion that is often set out in the first paragraph. Compare Esolen's opening assertion to the ones he makes in the last paragraph. What similarities and differences do you find? Consider those assertions, and then state the essay's thesis in your own words.

2. The author builds his essay on examples of physical work triggered by the sight of "the Nureyev and Baryshnikov of the garbage trucks." What are the other examples of physical work? In what paragraphs do they occur? Why might he have presented them in the order he does?

3. Paragraphs are the writer's building blocks, and Esolen uses them singly and in groups in order to develop his assertions. Find the examples of physical laborers. Is each example handled in a separate paragraph, in several paragraphs, a combination? How does Esolen link one example to another? List the characteristics Esolen associates with each example. What are the general characteristics Esolen ascribes to physical laborers?

STYLE

1. Because the personal essay is based on the convention that the author is more or less thinking out loud, most writers try to achieve a natural, informal tone through diction and sentence structure. Examine Esolen's word choice. What examples can you find of informal words? Formal words? What type of sentences predominate—simple, compound, complex, compound-complex? On the whole, how formal or informal is Esolen's tone?

2. Esolen assumes that most readers think little of physical labor if they think of it at all. He not only wants to make us see it, however, but to value it as well. For instance, paragraph 1 elevates the act of collecting garbage by comparing the workers to ballet dancers and their actions to "poetry." What metaphors or similes does Esolen use elsewhere? In what way do they enhance physical labor?

3. For a reader to accept an essay's thesis, the author must have credibility. Esolen, for example, must appear knowledgeable about his subject, sincere, believable—a person whose views are worth listening to. What sort of person does Esolen appear to be in this essay? What words or phrases give rise to your impressions? In what way does his describing a variety of laborers and locales help create his credibility?

4. A writer can set up a relationship with the reader by using the second person *you* or the first person plural *we*. Trace the author's use of pronouns in the essay. Where does he use *I? You? We?* What effects does he achieve by the changes in pronouns?

IDEAS FOR A FIRST DRAFT

Make a short list of subjects that interest you and that you know about. Choose one of the subjects on your list that people often undervalue or take for granted. Perhaps you raise tropical fish, collect matchbooks, follow batting averages, read trash, collect trivia, eat junk food. Form an idea of the audience you are writing to. Perhaps they are subscribers to a magazine called *Unusual Hobbies* or perhaps you are writing to a friend you have not seen in a long time. You will want to explain the reasons behind your interest and communicate your enthusiasm for it. Because readers are likely to be intrigued by an offbeat subject they know little about, choose the subject on your list that has the most surprise value, the one your readers may be least familiar with, and jot down the attitudes they are likely to hold. Think through your own attitude and develop a working thesis. Try starting your introductory paragraph with that thesis followed by an example that you can use as a jumping-off place. What other examples can you include? Select the examples so that they represent a broad range. Have any well-known people shared your interest? Are there any legendary or mythic figures in your field? Try organizing your draft along the lines of Esolen's essay, linking examples together to form the body of your paper. Reevaluate your working thesis to see if you want to change it, and then consider your last paragraph. How can you link your initial assertion to a larger point?

WILLIE MORRIS

A Love That Transcends Sadness

Born in Jackson, Mississippi, in 1931, Willie Morris graduated from the University of Texas at Austin and as a Rhodes scholar went on to further study in England at Oxford University. He then started his journalistic career back in Texas where his success in editing the *Texas Observer* was followed by an equally impressive tenure at *Harper's.* There, he served first as editor, then executive editor, and finally as editor in chief, a position he held until 1971. Now a freelance writer of fiction and nonfiction, Morris lives not far from New York City though his ties with the South remain strong.

The essay that follows appeared in the September 13, 1981, issue of *Parade,* the Sunday magazine supplement carried by many newspapers. Thinking of the general Sunday readership, the publisher apparently felt that "A Love That Transcends Sadness" might well offend, for the essay appeared with a mildly apologetic headnote:

> This is an unusual article, dealing as it does with a subject many magazines prefer to avoid. Yet we feel that the highly personal and supremely sensitive approach taken by writer Willie Morris provides an important and touching perspective. We commend it to our readers, and suggest that some may wish to save it for a time in their lives when its meaning may seem all the more significant.

Read Morris' essay and then take another look at *Parade's* introduction. Was it necessary?

Not too long ago, in a small Southern town where I live, I was invited by friends to go with them and their children to the cemetery to help choose their burial plot. My friends are in the heartiest prime of life and do not anticipate departing the Lord's earth immediately, and hence, far from being funereal, our search had an adventurous mood to it, like picking out a Christmas tree. It was that hour before twilight, and the marvelous old graveyard with its cedars and magnolias and flowering glades sang with the Mississippi springtime. The honeysuckled air was an affirmation of the tugs and tremors of living. My companions had spent all their lives in the town, and the names on even the oldest stones were as familiar to them as the people they saw everyday. "Location," the man of the family said, laughing. "As the real-estate magnates say, we want *location.*" 1

At last they found a plot in the most venerable section which was to their liking, having spurned a shady spot which I had recommended under a giant oak. I know the caretaker would soon have to come to this place of their choice with a long, thin steel rod, shoving it into the ground every few inches to see if it struck forgotten coffins. If not, this plot was theirs. Our quest had been a tentative success, and we retired elsewhere to celebrate. 2

Their humor coincided with mine, for I am no stranger to graveyards. With rare exceptions, ever since my childhood, they have suffused me not with foreboding but with a sense of belonging and, as I grow older, with a curious, ineffable tenderness. My dog Pete and I go out into the cemeteries, not only to escape the telephone, and those living beings who place more demands on us than the dead ever would, but to feel a continuity with the flow of the generations. "Living," William Faulkner wrote, "is a process of getting ready to be dead for a long time." 3

I have never been lonely in a cemetery. They are perfect places to observe the slow changing of the seasons, and to absorb human history—the tragedies and anguishes, the violences and treacheries, and always the guilts and sorrows of vanished people. In a preternatural quiet, one can almost hear the palpable, long-ago voices. 4

I like especially the small-town cemeteries of America where the children come for picnics and games, as we did when I was growing up—wandering among the stones on our own, with no 5 adults about, to regard the mystery and inevitability of death, on its terms and ours. I remember we would watch the funerals from afar in a hushed awe, and I believe that was when I became obsessed not with death itself but with the singular community of death and life together—and life's secrets, life's fears, life's surprises. Later, in high school, as I waited on a hill to play the echo to taps on my trumpet for the Korean War dead, the tableau below with its shining black hearse and the coffin enshrouded with the flag and the gathering mourners was like a folk drama, with the earth as its stage.

The great urban cemeteries of New York City always filled me with horror, the mile after mile of crowded tombstones which no one ever seemed to visit, as if one could *find* anyone in there even if he wished to. Likewise, the suburban cemeteries of this generation with their carefully manicured lawns and bronze plaques embedded in the ground, all imbued with affluence and artifice, are much too remote for me. My favorites have always been in the old, established places where people honor the long dead and the new graves are in proximity with the most ancient. The churchyard cemeteries of England haunted me with the eternal rhythms of time. In one of these, years ago as a student at Oxford, I found this inscription: 6

Here lies Johnny Kongapod,
Have mercy on him, gracious God,
As he would on You if he was God,
And You were Johnny Kongapod

Equally magnetic were the graveyards of eastern Long Island, with their patina of the past touched ever so mellowly with the present. The cemetery of Wainscott, Long Island, only a few hundred yards from the Atlantic Ocean, surrounded the schoolhouse. I would watch the children playing at recess among the graves. Later I discovered a man and his wife juxtaposed under identical stones. On the wife's tomb was "Rest in Peace." On the man's at the same level, was "No Comment." I admired the audacity of that. 7

But it is the graveyards of Mississippi which are the most moving for me, having to do, I believe, with my belonging here. They spring from the earth itself, and beckon me time and again. The crumbling stones of my people evoke in me the terrible enigmas of living. In a small Civil War cemetery which I came across recently, the markers stretching away in a misty 8 haze, it occurred to me that most of these boys had never even had a girl friend. I have found a remote graveyard in the hills with photographs on many of the stones, some nearly one hundred years old, the women in bonnets and Sunday dresses, the men in overalls—" the short and simple annals of the poor." I am drawn here to the tiny grave of a little girl. Her name was Fairy Jumper, and she lived from April 14, 1914 to Jan. 16, 1919. There is a miniature lamb at the top of the stone, and the words: "A fairer bud of promise never bloomed." There are no other Jumpers around her, and there she is, my Fairy, in a far corner of that country burial ground, so forlorn and alone that it is difficult to bear. It was in this cemetery on a bleak February noon that I caught sight of four men digging a grave in the hard, unyielding soil. After a time they gave up. After they left, a man drove toward me in a battered truck. He wanted to know if some fellows had been working on the grave. Yes, I said, but they went away. "Well, I can't finish all by myself." Wordlessly, I helped him dig.

One lonesome, windswept afternoon my dog and I were sitting at the crest of a hill in the town cemetery. Down below us, the acres of empty land were covered with wildflowers. A new road was going in down there, the caretaker had told me; the area was large enough to accommodate the next three generations. "With the economy so bad," I had asked him, "how can you be *expanding?*" He had replied: "It comes in spurts. Not a one last week. Five put down the week before. It's a pretty steady business." 9

Sitting there now in the dappled sunshine, a middle-aged man and his middle-aged dog, gazing across at the untenanted terrain awaiting its dead, I thought of how each generation lives with its own exclusive solicitudes—the passions, the defeats, the victories, the sacrifices, the names and dates and the faces belong to each generation in its own passing, for much of everything except the most unforgettable is soon forgotten. And yet: though much is taken, much abides. I thought then of human beings, on this cinder of a planet out at the edge of the universe, not knowing where we came from, why we are here, or where we might go after death—and yet we still laugh, and cry, and feel, and love. 10

"All that we can know about those we have loved and lost," Thornton Wilder wrote, "is that they would wish us to remember them with a more intensified realization of their reality. 11

What is essential does not die but clarifies. The highest tribute to the dead is not grief but gratitude."

THE THINKING PROCESS

STRUCTURE

1. The structure of an essay can be charted. Some essays move in a straight line, others progress like building blocks from one idea to another, and still others turn in a circle and end more or less where they began. What image best describes the structure of Morris' essay? What examples can you cite to back up your decision?

2. Personal essays are based on the author's own experience, but a good writer has the ability to second-guess the readers' generalized experience. What do you think most readers associate with cemeteries? Reread the essay, noting what Morris associates with them. Does he confront his audience's notions directly or indirectly? Where and how?

3. It is not enough for a writer to make an assertion as Morris does in paragraph 3: graveyards "have suffused me not with foreboding but with a sense of belonging and, as I grow older, with a curious, ineffable tenderness." Unless the assertion has primarily a dramatic or rhetorical function, good writers explain their assertions, answering the readers' "Why so?" Paragraphs 3–11 contain bits and pieces of Morris' answer to that question. What evidence can you find that explains Morris' fondness for cemeteries? Considering both the evidence and the assertion, how would you state the thesis of the essay?

STYLE

1. Morris' subject has an intrinsic danger, for many readers would think someone with his interests was at best morose and at worst a ghoul. Yet he is neither. What sort of person does

Morris show himself to be? What details does he include that reveal his character?

2. Paragraph 8 is the first in a group of three paragraphs that all support Morris' assertion that "it is the graveyards of Mississippi which are the most moving for me." Review paragraphs 8, 9, and 10 and note the details in each. What is the predominant emotion in each paragraph? Which details support it?

3. Although the essay is a personal one, Morris places his thoughts and reactions in a wider, more universal context, seeing himself as part of "human history" (4). Where in the essay does he connect his experiences with those of earlier generations? What words or phrases emphasize "continuity with the flow of generations" (3)? How do those words and phrases relate to the subject of love and death? What assertion do you find that Morris is making about the interrelationship of love and death?

IDEAS FOR A FIRST DRAFT

Writing in your journal or on scratch paper, explore your own ideas about love and death. Write down one or two key words that represent the direct or indirect experiences you have had that dealt with death and its relationship to love. Find a place or an object that you can use as a focal point for an essay on the topic. What does that place or object look like? What emotions do you associate with it? What might your reader associate with it that you need to take into account? What emotions do you want your reader to feel? Is there any spot where humor might be appropriate?

Once you have a sense of direction, you might consult Bartlett's *Familiar Quotations* to see if you can find a particularly suitable quotation that lends itself to your concluding paragraph. Like Morris, you might want to use your introduction to set a particular scene and tone, saving the thesis for later. More than likely, you may write your way into your thesis, discovering it perhaps in the last paragraph of your first draft, in which case you may want to leave it there or try it elsewhere. If you want to start with a clearer sense of direction, however, begin by describing a central image or try stating the basic idea you wish to communicate.

LAURENCE SHAMES

The Eyes of Fear

A contemporary free-lance writer, Laurence Shames has contributed nonfiction to a variety of magazines that range from the specialized audience who reads *World Tennis* to the general one who follows *Saturday Review.* Most frequently his articles appear in *Esquire,* where he is a contributing editor and a regular writer of the "Ethics" column in which the September, 1982, selection that follows was first published.

As its name suggests, *Esquire* is written primarily for affluent, middle-class, upwardly mobile men. Appropriately the central character of Shames' narrative is a member of that group. Yet the subject of the essay, fear of intimacy, is not one traditionally found in men's magazines. As you read the piece, look for ways the author presents the potentially threatening topic of vulnerability to his audience. How might the essay be rewritten for *Ms.* or *Cosmopolitan?*

Remember how they did it in *1984?* 1

They studied you until they'd learned your deepest fear—rats, bats, darkness, whatever—and then they used that fear to turn you. The premise was that while human beings might be expected to behave with some degree of dignity and moral sense under normal circumstances, they'd crumble when confronted with their personal demons; courage and resolve would slip 2 away, and people would become abject, malleable, capable of any sort of betrayal.

A sobering proposition—but one that, in Orwell's nightmare world, proved only too accurate. How about in our world? 3

We, too, occasionally have our worst fears thrown in our face, are confronted with situations in which the choice is between staring down our private bogeymen and skulking away in safe but ignoble retreat. True, most of us will never have to deal with the primordial horror of having rodents nibble at us, but we will face other fears: the fear of intimacy, which, for many of us, is truly scarring and which can lead us to be dishonest, unfair, and self-defeating in our relationships; the fear of taking an uncharted course in a career—a fear that can turn us into morally hollow yes-men or cause us to be untrue to our real ambitions; and, in every aspect of our lives, the basic fear of change—a timidness about growth and risk that, in the long haul, can make us bitter, disappointed, and mean. 4

Consider, for example, the fear of intimacy. Intimacy offers itself as one of life's great comforts, but for all its tender appeal, many of us find it terrifying. And not without reason: intimacy means reckless self-exposure, a bold baring of the soft white underbelly, an offering of the jugular. It demands more trust than many of us grow up believing the world deserves. Yet few of us choose to be hermits or celibates; the difficulty, then, is in reconciling our need for closeness with our fear of it. And, ethically, the danger is that we may go halfway, then balk, inevitably hurting people in the process, deceiving them without intending to, being helplessly dishonest to others because we're being untrue to ourselves. 5

In college I hung around with a group of guys for whom meeting women was a major preoccupation. Some of us liked having one girlfriend at a time, in a sort of puppy-love version of what has come to be known as serial monogamy. Others preferred to juggle several entanglements at once, with results that ranged from the comical to the cruel. Then there was this fellow I'll call Arty. Arty had a style all his own. Forward, eccentric, and dapper, he insinuated himself into the favor of more young ladies than any of us could win. Yet he never seemed the slightest bit entangled. He was the consummate hit-and-run man, as adept at ending things as at starting them. 6

For a while, of course, this capacity of his impressed the 7 rest of us no end. Compared with the blistering pace of Arty's escapades, our humble efforts seemed sluggish and mundane. Gradually, however, even to us die-hard adolescents, it became clear that the fellow had a problem. His fear of getting close to women was so pronounced that it led him to all sorts of caddish behavior. Whatever his intentions may have been, he ended up misleading every woman he met, and he left behind, if not exactly a string of broken hearts, then certainly a number of ladies who had good reason to feel baffled, angry, and used. Arty was a classic case of a guy letting himself be bullied into shabbiness by his fears, not even truly enjoying his encounters because they were laced with so much anxiety. After a while, the rest of us didn't know whom to feel sorrier for—the women who crossed Arty's path, or Arty himself. *They* were victimized by Arty's fear only once; *he* was doomed to repeat the pattern again and again.

After college, some of us old friends stayed in touch, staging 8
informal reunions at various taverns in the cities where we'd ended up. True to form, we'd still discuss, among other things, our dealings with women, but the emphasis was different now. In spite of ourselves, we were getting serious. We were at the age when the question of marriage was beginning to bear down on us with the slow portentousness of a distant but oncoming train. We'd flirt with the subject and sometimes make goading conjectures about who would be the first to take the plunge. There was no consensus on this point; as to who would be the *last*, however, there was general and confident agreement.

We were wrong, of course. Arty was the first of us to wed. 9
To me, this was more than a surprise; it represented a moral victory of a high order.

I still remember when he told me of his plans. The revela- 10
tion literally took my breath away. This was *Arty*—the guy so scared of closeness that he'd hardly leave an imprint on a paramour's pillow. But people change—or *can* change. "Look," Arty said to me, "don't you think I know what I've been doing all these years? I've just been jerking around, wasting everybody's time, acting like the kind of person I really hope I'm not. I've got to take the chance and try to be different. I think I've found someone who understands how tough it's gonna be for me and who'll be able to handle it, and I've got to take a shot."

That was around three years ago, and Arty and his wife are 11
still fighting the good fight against Arty's fear of intimacy. It

hasn't been easy. It's not the sort of fear you stand up to once and conquer; it requires a more durable sort of courage, the sort that renews itself every day.

Arty—so he admits—is still clutched at times by the old terrors; he clams up, broods, gets moody and aloof. His wife, when frustrated, throws tantrums. The two of them have been known to make scenes and to indulge in extended sulks. Yet, beneath the turbulent surface of their marriage, there is a true adventure going on. 12

It's an adventure whose basis is a moral contract, a mutual pledge not to retreat into halfheartedness. And while the contract's demands are unyielding, its rewards are rich and irreplaceable. "I no longer try to get away with the sort of evasions that I never *wanted* to get away with in the first place," Arty says. "Marriage is like boxing: you can run but you can't hide. Sooner or later, you're going to end up in a clinch—and it's in the clinches where you learn the most about yourself, where your strength is really tested." 13

But the challenge of marriage is one that Arty still wonders if he's equal to. "You know," he said to me a while back, during a particularly bumpy phase, "I didn't exactly pave the way for this. I mean, I'd always been too scared even to really have a girlfriend, and all of a sudden this little voice starts telling me that maybe I should take this giant leap all the way to marriage, and I *listen.* Maybe it was just a crazy thing for me to do." 14

I disagreed with him, and told him so. To me, it was his finest hour. Because if duking it out with our personal demons is full of potential pitfalls, it also offers opportunities for real self-transcendence, for genuine heroics. Where's the virtue, after all, in taking a stand when we're *not* afraid? What's the value of a moral contract that doesn't cost us anything? 15

Big Brother, in his perverse wisdom, was correct in his assumption that every person has his private fear, his exposed nerve. But it doesn't take an all-seeing autocrat to discover that vulnerable point and to probe it—the circumstances of ordinary life will do that just as well. The way we hold our ground when that sensitive place is tweaked, when that anxiety-drenched subject is foisted on us, is the surest test of what we're made of. 16

THE THINKING PROCESS

STRUCTURE

1. An introduction may consist of a paragraph or a group of paragraphs leading into the essay's subject. In what paragraph does Shames set out his subject—the fear of intimacy? What effects does he achieve by delaying it until that point?

2. The body of the essay is taken up by a narrative, the story of Shames' friend Arty. Trace the chronological development of the narrative. Why does Shames break the paragraphs where he does?

3. Allusions to Orwell's novel *1984* frame the essay. What differences do you discern between the opening and closing references? What are the advantages and disadvantages of a frame? What principles can you derive for the function of a concluding paragraph? Does Shames' last paragraph merely close the frame? Restate the thesis? Reach a new conclusion? What functions does the last paragraph serve?

STYLE

1. One of the difficulties a writer encounters when addressing values such as courage or love is the danger of sounding pious, righteous, or overly sentimental. Does Shames avoid this difficulty? How or how not?

2. Most frequently writers use paragraphs to develop assertions; however, paragraphs may also signal a change in direction or emphasize an idea. They can be used singly or in blocks. What purpose is served by paragraphs 1 and 9? By paragraph 3? By paragraphs 6–15?

3. What does Shames' use of quotations (10, 13, 14) add to the narrative in paragraphs 6–15? Try paraphrasing the quoted material. What is gained? Lost?

IDEAS FOR A FIRST DRAFT

Fear comes in all sizes, from mouse to mountain lion, from a bump in the night to a scream in the street. Some people are afraid of heights, others of open spaces, but no matter what the cause, the fear is real. Write an essay in which you try to recreate a time when you felt fear, describing your emotions so that your audience shares your feelings. Try to make connections between what you felt and similar occasions your readers may have experienced. Think about the times you have felt afraid, jotting down a note or two for the more memorable incidents. Choose one that lends itself to a narrative and then block out the plot line. Who was involved? Where? How? Why? What occurred when? How can you break down the time line into paragraphs? What was your response to the situation? What did you learn from it?

Consider possible frameworks for your narrative. Might an allusion to a well-known book or recent movie work well? Perhaps the lyrics from a popular song would provide an ironic juxtaposition. On the other hand, maybe a more direct approach would be in order, for example, some general speculations on fear or on some important part of your narrative. Most people, for instance, find amusement parks just that, but being trapped at the top of a roller coaster can be terrifying, and the ironic contrast could provide a tidy introduction. Reread your draft aloud to see if your tone sounds natural: remember that it's easy to slip into an overly dramatic tone, which quickly becomes melodramatic. Given a choice between under- or overstatement, understatement usually has greater effect because it takes the reader by surprise.

E. B. WHITE

Bedfellows

Renowned for his wit and superb styble, Elwyn Brooks White, born in 1899, is an American writer and master of the personal essay. Since 1927, he has contributed to the *New Yorker*, the magazine in which the following essay first appeared. White also revised and enlarged William Strunk's *The Elements of Style* in 1959, coedited *A Subtreasury of American Humor* (1941) with his wife Katharine (who is quoted in paragraph 22), and wrote *Is Sex Necessary?* (1929) with American humorist James Thurber. He is the sole author of numerous volumes, including his collected letters (1976) and essays (1977) and the children's books *Stuart Little* (1945) and *Charlotte's Web* (1952). White's awards include the Gold Medal for Essays and Criticism of the American Academy of Arts and the Presidential Medal of Freedom.

When White wrote "Bedfellows" in February, 1956, President Dwight D. Eisenhower (1890–1960), known for his conservative administration, was just beginning his second term, the Korean Armistice was three years old, the Communist witch hunts of Senator Joseph McCarthy had been condemned by the Senate the year before, and Eisenhower had recently emerged optimistic from the Geneva Summit Conference. Adlai E. Stevenson (1900–1965) (1), an eloquent spokesman for liberal reform and internationalism, was the Democratic challenger whom Eisenhower had just defeated for the second time. Dean Acheson (1891–1971) (1) helped design NATO and other security pacts and early in his career served as private secretary to Louis Brandeis (1856–1941), associate justice of the Supreme Court (8). Harry S. Truman (1844–1972) (1) under whom Acheson served as secretary of state, succeeded to the presidency upon the death of Franklin D. Roosevelt in 1945. Though the polls predicted an overwhelming defeat when Truman ran for the presidency in 1948, he won a resounding victory.

I am lying here in my private sick bay on the east side of town between Second and Third avenues, watching starlings from the vantage point of bed. Three Democrats are in bed with me: Harry Truman (in a stale copy of the *Times*), Adlai Stevenson (in *Harper's*), and Dean Acheson (in a book called *A Democrat Looks at His Party*). I take Democrats to bed with me for lack of a dachshund, although as a matter of fact on occasions like this I am almost certain to be visited by the ghost of Fred, my dash-hound everlasting, dead these many years. In life, Fred always attended the sick, climbing right into bed with the patient like some lecherous old physician, and making a bad situation worse. All this dark morning I have reluctantly entertained him upon the rumpled blanket, felt his oppressive weight, and heard his fraudulent report. He was an uncomfortable bedmate when alive; death has worked little improvement—I still feel crowded, still wonder why I put up with his natural rudeness and his pretensions. 1

The only thing I used to find agreeable about him in bed was his smell, which for some reason was nonirritating to my nose and evocative to my mind, somewhat in the way that a sudden whiff of the cow barn or of bone meal on a lawn in springtime carries sensations of the richness of earth and of experience. Fred's aroma has not deserted him; it wafts over me now, as though I had just removed the stopper from a vial of cheap perfume. His aroma has not deserted the last collar he wore, either. I ran across this great, studded strap not long ago when I was rummaging in a cabinet. I raised it cautiously toward my nose, fearing a quill stab from his last porcupine. The collar was extremely high—had lost hardly 10 percent of its potency. 2

Fred was sold to me for a dachshund, but I was in a buying mood and would have bought the puppy if the storekeeper had 3 said he was an Irish Wolfschmidt. He was only a few weeks old when I closed the deal, and he was in real trouble. In no time at all, his troubles cleared up and mine began. Thirteen years later he died, and by rights *my* troubles should have cleared up. But I can't say they have. Here I am, seven years after his death, still sharing a fever bed with him and, what is infinitely more burdensome, still feeling the compulsion to write about him. I sometimes suspect that subconsciously I'm trying to revenge myself by turning him to account, and thus recompensing myself for the time and money he cost me.

He was red and low-posted and long-bodied like a dachs- 4
hund, and when you glanced casually at him he certainly gave the quick impression of being a dachshund. But if you went at him with a tape measure, and forced him onto scales, the dachshund theory collapsed. The papers that came with him were produced hurriedly and in an illicit atmosphere in a back room of the pet shop, and are most unconvincing. However, I have no reason to unsettle the Kennel Club; the fraud, if indeed it was a fraud, was ended in 1948, at the time of his death. So much of his life was given to shady practices, it is only fitting that his pedigree should have been (as I believe it was) a forgery.

I have been languishing here, looking out at the lovely 5
branches of the plane tree in the sky above our city back yard. Only starlings and house sparrows are in view at this season, but soon other birds will show up. (Why, by the way, doesn't the *Times* publish an "Arrival of Birds" column, similar to its famous "Arrival of Buyers"?) Fred was a window gazer and bird watcher, particularly during his later years, when hardened arteries slowed him up and made it necessary for him to substitute sedentary pleasures for active sport. I think of him as he used to look on our bed in Maine—an old four-poster, too high from the floor for him to reach unassisted. Whenever the bed was occupied during the daylight hours, whether because one of us was sick or was napping, Fred would appear in the doorway and enter without knocking. On his big gray face would be a look of quiet amusement (at having caught somebody in bed during the daytime) coupled with his usual look of fake respectability. Whoever occupied the bed would reach down, seize him by the loose folds of his thick neck, and haul him painfully up. He dreaded this maneuver, and so did the occupant of the bed. There was far too much dead weight involved for anybody's comfort. But Fred was

always willing to put up with being hoisted in order to gain the happy heights, as, indeed, he was willing to put up with far greater discomforts—such as a mouthful of porcupine quills—when there was some prize at the end.

Once up, he settled into his pose of bird watching, propped 6
luxuriously against a pillow, as close as he could get to the window, his great soft brown eyes alight with expectation and scientific knowledge. He seemed never to tire of his work. He watched steadily and managed to give the impression that he was a secret agent of the Department of Justice. Spotting a flicker or a starling on the wing, he would turn and make a quick report.

"I just saw an eagle go by," he would say. "It was carrying a 7
baby."

This was not precisely a lie. Fred was like a child in many 8
ways, and sought always to blow things up to proportions that satisfied his imagination and his love of adventure. He was the Cecil B. deMille of dogs. He was a zealot, and I have just been reminded of him by a quote from one of the Democrats sharing my bed—Acheson quoting Brandeis. "The greatest dangers to liberty," said Mr. Brandeis, "lurk in insidious encroachment by men of zeal, well-meaning but without understanding." Fred saw in every bird, every squirrel, every housefly, every rat, every skunk, every porcupine, a security risk and a present danger to his republic. He had a dossier on almost every living creature, as well as on several inanimate objects, including my son's football.

Although birds fascinated him, his real hope as he watched 9
the big shade trees outside the window was that a red squirrel would show up. When he sighted a squirrel, Fred would straighten up from his pillow, tense his frame, and then, in a moment or two, begin to tremble. The knuckles of his big forelegs, unstable from old age, would seem to go into spasm, and he would sit there with his eyes glued on the squirrel and his front legs alternately collapsing under him and bearing his weight again.

I find it difficult to convey the peculiar character of this ig- 10
noble old vigilante, my late and sometimes lamented companion. What was there about him so different from the many other dogs I've owned that he keeps recurring and does not, in fact, seem really dead at all? My wife used to claim that Fred was deeply devoted to me, and in a certain sense he was, but his was the devotion of an opportunist. He knew that on the farm I took the overall view and traveled pluckily from one trouble spot to the

next. He dearly loved this type of work. It was not his habit to tag along faithfully behind me, as a collie might, giving moral support and sometimes real support. He ran a troubleshooting business of his own and was usually at the scene ahead of me, compounding the trouble and shooting in the air. The word "faithful" is an adjective I simply never thought of in connection with Fred. He differed from most dogs in that he tended to knock down, rather than build up, the master's ego. Once he had outgrown the capers of puppyhood, he never again caressed me or anybody else during his life. The only time he was ever discovered in an attitude that suggested affection was when I was in the driver's seat of our car and he would lay his heavy head on my right knee. This, I soon perceived, was not affection, it was nausea. Drooling always followed, and the whole thing was extremely inconvenient, because the weight of his head made me press too hard on the accelerator.

Fred devoted his life to deflating me and succeeded admir- 11
ably. His attachment to our establishment, though untinged with affection, was strong nevertheless, and vibrant. It was simply that he found in our persons, in our activities, the sort of complex, disorderly society that fired his imagination and satisfied his need for tumult and his quest for truth. After he had subdued six or seven porcupines, we realized that his private war against porcupines was an expensive bore, so we took to tying him, making him fast to any tree or wheel or post or log that was at hand, to keep him from sneaking off into the woods. I think of him as always at the end of some outsize piece of rope. Fred's disgust as these confinements was great, but he improved his time, nonetheless, in a thousand small diversions. He never just lay and rested. Within the range of his tether, he continued to explore, dissect, botanize, conduct post-mortems, excavate, experiment, expropriate, savor, masticate, regurgitate. He had no contemplative life, but he held as a steady gleam the belief that under the commonplace stone and behind the unlikely piece of driftwood lay the stuff of high adventure and the opportunity to save the nation.

But to return to my other bedfellows, these quick Demo- 12
crats. They are big, solid men, every one of them, and they have been busy writing and speaking, and sniffing out the truth. I did not deliberately pack my counterpane with members of a single

political faith; they converged on me by the slick device of getting into print. All three turn up saying things that interest me, so I make bed space for them.

Mr. Truman, reminiscing in a recent issue of the *Times*, says the press sold out in 1948 to "the special interests," was 90 percent hostile to his candidacy, distorted facts, caused his low popularity rating at that period, and tried to prevent him from reaching the people with his message in the campaign. This bold, implausible statement engages my fancy because it is a half-truth, and all half-truths excite me. An attractive half-truth in bed with a man can disturb him as deeply as a cracker crumb. Being a second-string member of the press myself, and working, as I do, for the special interests, I tend to think there is a large dollop of pure irascibility in Mr. Truman's gloomy report. In 1948, Mr. Truman made a spirited whistle-stop trip and worked five times as hard as his rival. The "Republican-controlled press and radio" reported practically everything he said, and also gave vent to frequent horselaughs in their editorials and commentaries. Millions of studious, worried Americans heard and read what he said; then they checked it against the editorials; then they walked silently into the voting booths and returned him to office. Then they listened to Kaltenborn. Then they listened to Truman doing Kaltenborn. The criticism of the opposition in 1948 was neither a bad thing nor a destructive thing. It was healthy and (in our sort of society) necessary. Without the press, radio, and TV, President Truman couldn't have got through to the people in anything like the volume he achieved. Some of the published news was distorted, but distortion is inherent in partisan journalism, the same as it is in political rallies. I have yet to see a piece of writing, political or nonpolitical, that doesn't have a slant. All writing slants the way a writer leans, and no man is born perpendicular, although many men are born upright. The beauty of the American free press is that the slants and the twists and the distortions come from so many directions, and the special interests are so numerous, the reader must sift and sort and check and countercheck in order to find out what the score is. This he does. It is only when a press gets its twist from a single source, as in the case of government-controlled press systems, that the reader is licked. 13

Democrats do a lot of bellyaching about the press's being 14 preponderantly Republican, which it is. But they don't do the one thing that could correct the situation: they don't go into the publishing business. Democrats say they haven't got that kind of money, but I'm afraid they haven't got that kind of temperament or, perhaps, nerve.

Adlai Stevenson takes a view of criticism almost opposite to 15
Harry Truman's. Writing in *Harper's,* Stevenson says, ". . . I very well know that in many minds 'criticism' has today become an ugly word. It has become almost *lèse majesté.* It conjures up pictures of insidious radicals hacking away at the very foundations of the American way of life. It suggests nonconformity and nonconformity suggests disloyalty and disloyalty suggests treason, and before we know where we are, this process has all but identified the critic with the saboteur and turned political criticism into an un-American activity instead of democracy's greatest safeguard."

The above interests me because I agree with it and everyone 16
is fascinated by what he agrees with. Especially when he is sick in bed.

Mr. Acheson, in his passionately partisan yet temperate 17
book, writes at some length about the loyalty-security procedures that were started under the Democrats in 1947 and have modified our lives ever since. This theme interests me because I believe, with the author, that security declines as security machinery expands. The machinery calls for a secret police. At first, this device is used solely to protect us from unsuitable servants in sensitive positions. Then it broadens rapidly and permeates nonsensitive areas, and, finally, business and industry. It is in the portfolios of the secret police that nonconformity makes the subtle change into disloyalty. A secret-police system first unsettles, then desiccates, then calcifies a free society. I think the recent loyalty investigation of the press by the Eastland subcommittee was a disquieting event. It seemed to assume for Congress the right to poke about in newspaper offices and instruct the management as to which employees were okay and which were not. That sort of procedure opens wonderfully attractive vistas to legislators. If it becomes an accepted practice, it will lead to great abuses. Under extreme conditions, it could destroy the free press.

The loyalty theme also relates to Fred, who presses ever 18
more heavily against me this morning. Fred was intensely loyal to himself, as every strong individualist must be. He held un-

shakable convictions, like Harry Truman. He was absolutely sure that he was in possession of the truth. Because he was loyal to himself, I found his eccentricities supportable. Actually, he contributed greatly to the general health and security of the household. Nothing has been quite the same since he departed. His views were largely of a dissenting nature. Yet in tearing us apart he somehow held us together. In obstructing, he strengthened us. In criticizing, he informed. In his rich, aromatic heresy, he nourished our faith. He was also a plain damned nuisance, I must not forget that.

The matter of "faith" has been in the papers again lately. 19
President Eisenhower (I will now move over and welcome a Republican into bed, along with my other visitors) has come out for prayer and has emphasized that most Americans are motivated (as they surely are) by religious faith. The *Herald Tribune* headed the story, PRESIDENT SAYS PRAYER IS PART OF DEMOCRACY. The implication in such a pronouncement, emanating from the seat of government, is that religious faith is a *condition*, or even a *precondition*, of the democratic life. This is just wrong. A President should pray whenever and wherever he feels like it (most Presidents have prayed hard and long, and some of them in desperation and in agony), but I don't think a President should advertise prayer. That is a different thing. Democracy, if I understand it at all, is a society in which the unbeliever feels undisturbed and at home. If there were only half a dozen unbelievers in America, their well-being would be a test of our democracy, their tranquillity would be its proof. The repeated suggestion by the present administration that religious faith is a precondition of the American way of life is disturbing to me and, I am willing to bet, to a good many other citizens. President Eisenhower spoke of the tremendous favorable mail he received in response to his inaugural prayer in 1953. What he perhaps did not realize is that the persons who felt fidgety or disquieted about the matter were not likely to write in about it, lest they appear irreverent, irreligious, unfaithful, or even un-American. I remember the prayer very well. I didn't mind it, although I have never been able to pray electronically and doubt that I ever will be. Still, I was able to perceive that the President was sincere and was doing what came naturally, and anybody who is acting in a natural way is all right by me. I believe that our political leaders should live by faith and should, by deeds, and sometimes by prayer, demonstrate faith, but I doubt that they

should *advocate* faith, if only because such advocacy renders a few people uncomfortable. The concern of a democracy is that no honest man shall feel uncomfortable, I don't care who he is, or how nutty he is.

I hope that belief never is made to appear mandatory. One 20
of our founders, in 1787, said, "Even the diseases of the people should be represented." Those were strange, noble words, and they have endured. They were on television yesterday. I distrust the slightest hint of a standard for political rectitude, knowing that it will open the way for persons in authority to set arbitrary standards of human behavior.

Fred was an unbeliever. He worshiped no personal God, no 21
Supreme Being. He certainly did not worship *me*. If he had suddenly taken to worshiping me, I think I would have felt as queer as God must have felt the other day when a minister in California, pronouncing the invocation for a meeting of Democrats, said, "We believe Adlai Stevenson to be Thy choice for President of the United States. Amen."

I respected this quirk in Fred, this inability to conform to 22
conventional canine standards of religious feeling. And in the miniature democracy that was, and is, our household he lived undisturbed and at peace with his conscience. I hope my country will never become an uncomfortable place for the unbeliever, as it could easily become if prayer was made one of the requirements of the accredited citizen. My wife, a spiritual but not a prayerful woman, read Mr. Eisenhower's call to prayer in the *Tribune* and said something I shall never forget. "Maybe it's all right," she said. "But for the first time in my life I'm beginning to feel like an outsider in my own land."

Democracy is itself a religious faith. For some it comes close 23
to being the only formal religion they have. And so when I see the first faint shadow of orthodoxy sweep across the sky, feel the first cold whiff of its blinding fog steal in from sea, I tremble all over, as though I had just seen an eagle go by, carrying a baby.

Anyway, it's pleasant here in bed with all these friendly 24
Democrats and Republicans, every one of them a dedicated man, with all these magazine and newspaper clippings, with Fred, watching the starlings against the wintry sky, and the prospect of another presidential year, with all its passions and its distortions and its dissents and its excesses and special interests. Fred died from a life of excesses, and I don't mind if I do, too. I love to read all these words—most of them sober, thoughtful

words—from the steadily growing book of democracy: Acheson on security, Truman on the press, Eisenhower on faith, Stevenson on criticism, all writing away like sixty, all working to improve and save and maintain in good repair what was so marvelously constructed to begin with. This is the real thing. This is bedlam in bed. As Mr. Stevenson puts it: ". . . no civilization has ever had so haunting a sense of an ultimate order of goodness and rationality which can be known and achieved." It makes me eager to rise and meet the new day, as Fred used to rise to his, with the complete conviction that through vigilance and good works all porcupines, all cats, all skunks, all squirrels, all houseflies, all footballs, all evil birds in the sky could be successfully brought to account and the scene made safe and pleasant for the sensible individual—namely, him. However distorted was his crazy vision of the beautiful world, however perverse his scheme for establishing an order of goodness by murdering every creature that seemed to him bad, I had to hand him this: he really worked at it.

THE THINKING PROCESS

STRUCTURE

1. Often a personal essayist chooses a looser structure than that of an argumentative essay or a report in order to adopt an informal tone. Thus White, whose illness ostensibly allows him to ramble, can discuss such diverse matters as his dachshund Fred, security, and the press. What is the common thread that weaves together these diverse subjects? Does White have an explicit thesis? If so, underline it. If not, write his thesis in your own words. What does the title add to the essay's structure?

2. Reread White's opening and closing paragraphs. What devices does he use to introduce his subject to his readers? How does he maintain their interest? What device does he use to conclude his essay? What ideas does he leave his readers thinking about?

3. White spends the first 12 paragraphs discussing his dog Fred and then takes up Truman, Stevenson, Acheson, and

Eisenhower. He mentions Fred briefly in paragraphs 18 and again in 21 and 22. Why does White devote so much space to Fred in the opening and so little in the closing? Was it necessary for White to return to Fred at all? Why or why not? Why might White have taken up the political figures in the order that he does?

STYLE

1. Why do you think that White brings in his dachshund Fred? Does he feel compelled to write about Fred out of revenge, "by turning him to account, and thus recompensing myself for the time and money he cost me"? (3) If not, why not? What does the discussion of Fred add to the essay? How may it detract?

2. White gives Fred human qualities through the technique of personification. Find several examples of this technique. What is the function of personification in paragraph 1? In 4? In 6? In 7? In 8? In 11?

3. White enlivens his essay by describing Fred in unconventional terms. Consider how most pet owners describe their dogs, both physically and spiritually. How does White's descriptions contrast with the usual stereotypes? Is he using the contrasts to make a point beyond humor? If so, what?

4. Though the predominant tone of White's essay is serious, he includes humorous passages as well. Why? Point out some and explain what makes them funny. Do they disrupt the tone of the essay? Why or why not?

5. White plays with language throughout his essay, a technique especially entertaining to the sophisticated audience of the *New Yorker.* Consider in their contexts the following images and turns of phrases, and analyze their effectiveness: Democrats "sniffing out the truth" (12); "An attractive half-truth in bed with a man can disturb him as deeply as a cracker crumb" (13); "All writing slants the way a writer leans, and no man is born perpendicular, although many men are born upright" (13); "This is bedlam in bed" (24); and the implied pun of the title, "politics makes strange bedfellows."

IDEAS FOR A FIRST DRAFT

Imagine that you have taken to your bed sick and have your choice of any book, magazine, or TV show to keep you company. You may select any companion you wish—a classic or a best seller, *Moby Dick, Geology and World Affairs, Konan the Barbarian; The Christian Science Monitor, Superman Comics, Cosmopolitan; Days of Our Lives, The Price Is Right, Three's Company,* or a *PBS* special. Whatever you select, make sure you know it well.

Use your book, magazine, or show as a springboard for a discussion about an aspect of American culture, whether political, cultural, or social. Before you begin writing, select an audience you would like to address, perhaps blue collar or white collar, young or old, male or female. Or maybe what you have read or seen says something to you about the country, your state, or community so that you want to make a special appeal to your readers as Americans, as citizens of your community.

On separate sheets of paper or on large notecards, list from three to five main points that you wish to convince your readers of. Under those headings, note a variety of specific examples from your book, magazine, or show that supports your assertions. Now rearrange the cards until you find an order that is effective—perhaps least important to most, humorous to serious, or an inherent logical progression.

You may wish to begin by writing an introduction that sets the scene and introduces your source. Then write supporting paragraphs, using your notecards as guides. Think of an appropriate conclusion that unites your assertions and leaves the reader with some ideas to consider. Your thesis may be implied or explicit. If explicit, you may wish to include it in the introduction or save it until the conclusion.

THE WRITING PROCESS

INVENTION

If you are working on a previous assignment in this chapter, you already have a rough draft and can skip to Organizing and Developing. If you are starting anew, focus on a specific audience—perhaps the average citizen, your classmates, a group of students who are majoring in your discipline, or possibly the readers of a particular feature in a periodical (*Newsweek*'s "My Turn" or *The New Yorker*'s "Talk of the Town"). Think about the particular traits of human beings. To select a trait that you know well and have something to say about to your readers, brainstorm for ideas, jotting down as many associations as cross your mind. Don't stop to evaluate or expand them. Depending on your general attitude and on your current mood, your list will probably be largely negative or positive. You may find you've listed characteristics such as pettiness and prejudice; in a better mood, you may have listed generosity and humor.

Select one of the words on your list and give yourself five to ten minutes to write as much as possible about it, forcing words onto the paper if they don't spring into your mind spontaneously, free-associating with no particular plan in mind. If you get stuck, keep your pen moving even if it means writing the same word over and over. When you have finished, reread your passage to deduce an assertion or a primary idea. Write out that statement, and then focus on it for another timed writing. After two or three of these "wet-ink" writings, you probably will have evolved a working thesis for your essay.

To develop one of your passages into a full-length essay, you need to generate additional statements that qualify or expand your main assertion. Each of these statements with supporting illustrations can then become a topic sentence for a separate paragraph. For your conclusion, review all of your major points and see if you can tie them into a new and larger idea, one that subsumes all your others and leaves the reader something to think about.

ORGANIZING AND DEVELOPING

If you have worked on an earlier assignment in this chapter or on the one above, you now have the beginnings of a personal essay. Check what you have so far by underlining your primary assertion and numbering your supporting examples. Does your assertion still adequately express your feelings and ideas, or do you need to modify it? Make sure you have included a number of examples that support your assertions, examples that are well-developed and provide details and description.

What assertion have you used to end your rough draft? Might it serve better in the beginning of your essay? Reread the whole paper to make sure your assertion still fits, and don't hesitate to alter or discard it if it is no longer suitable.

Now reexamine your examples. How many of them come from your own experience? From the experience of others? Try to balance the two sources so that you are writing from a broad perspective. Are your examples ordered logically? You may want to use a striking example first and then build from least important to most. Or you might organize your illustrations chronologically, or from particular to general or general to particular, or from most familiar to least.

Your illustrations need to be clear to an audience unfamiliar with you and your subject. Check to see if you have used any terms or have made any references that your audience may not understand. Have you provided enough background information for an audience of strangers?

FINDING A VOICE

Creating a tone for the personal essay is challenging. Try thinking of the *I* in the essay as a character who expresses your ideas. Of course that character is closely tied to yourself, but it is yourself created to have a specific effect on your readers. Writing a personal essay is like thinking out loud and performing for an unseen but very real audience. Review your sense of your audience, keeping in mind what tone is appropriate for your readers; then reread your draft, noting the characteristics associated wtih the *I* in your essay. What details suggest these characteristics? Does your personality in the draft fit the image you want to convey? Do you sound credible?

To evaluate the essay's tone, read your draft aloud. Does your diction suit the educated but informal note you want to strike? Be on the lookout for slang or inflated diction. If you've used either extreme, try reading your essay to a listener to make sure that the diction is appropriate and not jarring.

POLISHING

Read your paper aloud again, listening to the cadences of the language. If you hesitate, stumble, or run out of breath as you read, mark the spot where the trouble occurs. These are the places that will need to be revised. Before you try to revise them, check your sentence length, paragraph by paragraph. If the majority of your sentences are short and choppy or long and complex, that may be a cause of the difficulty. Try combining or breaking some of the sentences so that your prose has variety; too many similar sentences can put a reader to sleep.

Review your paragraphs. Does their sequence support the pattern of organization that you designed earlier? Does each paragraph have an implicit or explicit controlling idea or topic sentence? Do you have a good reason for ending each paragraph where you do? Make sure that you have included transitions that lead the reader from one paragraph to another.

Finally, keep in mind your past problems with usage and mechanics, and then proofread your paper separately for each problem. If you are a poor speller and have problems with fragments, for instance, proofread once for spelling only and then for fragments. Consult a dictionary or a handbook if any doubts or questions arise.

THINKING AHEAD

Make a list of the general and particular problems that you have encountered while composing your personal essay. Next to each item, note how you resolved the dilemma. Though sometimes difficulties are tied to a particular type of writing, most are not, and the solution you found this time may work for you again later. If you did not reach a satisfactory solution for this paper, by being aware of the problem you are closer to solving it.

P A R T 2

THE WRITER AS EXPOSITOR

Exposition is probably the oldest and most frequently used form of writing. From the primitive agricultural reports of ancient civilizations, to the military dispatches of the ancient Greeks and Romans, to the wire services and technical articles of today, people have used exposition to record, convey, and explain facts. But facts themselves have a dull, prosaic connotation. Their best remembered advocate is Dickens' Mr. Gradgrind in *Hard Times* (1854) whose school was guaranteed to stifle imagination and strangle any thought that teetered on the creative. No theory, philosophy, poetry, or speculation for Mr. Gradgrind: "Now, what I want is, Facts. Teach these boys and girls nothing but Facts. Facts alone are wanted in life. Plant nothing else, and root out everything else." Yet anyone familiar with courtroom drama knows that "the facts and nothing but the facts" need not be dull.

To interpret facts, to give them shape and sense and purpose, takes all the qualities Gradgrind despises. And it takes hard work. In his essay "Writing, Typing, and Economics," the contemporary economist John Kenneth Galbraith states,

> Nothing is so hard to come by as a new and interesting fact. Nothing is so easy on the feet as a generalization. . . . My advice to all young writers is to stick to research and reporting with only a minimum of interpretation. And especially this is my advice to all older writers, particularly to columnists. As the feet give out, they seek to have the mind take their place.

Putting the feet to work is the first task of the expository writer.

Where a writer goes looking for facts depends in large part on the subject, but books, articles, newspapers, historical records, experiments, and people are the writer's primary resources. Whether collecting facts in a large, research-oriented university library, in a general public branch library, in a newspaper's "morgue," in a laboratory, or in an interviewee's office, writers need to record with accuracy what they read, see, or hear so that they know, without a doubt, the exact source of their data. Not knowing who said or did what, to whom it was said or done, or on what occasion, makes information dubious at best, dishonest at worst.

Gathering information and knowing where it comes from are only the initial steps in writing an expository essay. Tailoring that raw material to a particular audience comes next. The *Wall Street Journal*, for instance, deals with all the intricacies of business and economics, yet its editorial policy dictates that every aticle be addressed to a general, educated reader. Simple writing is not necessarily simplistic. Thomas Jefferson, Ralph Waldo Emerson, and Albert Einstein all wrote clear prose, and all wrote profoundly.

Whether the writer's stance is that of the historian or the scientist, the focus remains the same—on the *subject;* the writer's personal responses and evaluative judgments and the audience's reaction are secondary to the subject itself. Once the writer has identified and researched a topic of potential interest to the reader, he or she must then present the topic so that it both engages the audience and conveys information. The more complex the subject, the more difficult and necessary the task of presenting it clearly and effectively. Only love or money could induce someone to read expository prose that is boring or fails to inform.

A leaden writer can blunt the most interesting topic; so too an exciting writer can sharpen a seemingly dull one. Often a writer will explore a question people might speculate about, as John Stevens does in "The Black Reaction to *Gone With the Wind.*" But frequently the question will be a familiar, problematic one, like Tim Hackler's "What can you do to ease the pain of a hangover?" in his essay "The Morning After." Sometimes the writer will take an intriguing look at a topic we take for granted as James McKinley does in "If You've Got an Ounce of Feeling, Hallmark Has a Ton of Sentiment," or will make concrete what is abstract, as does Jonathan Schell in "What If the Bomb Hits Home?"

Expository writers inform us, and clear exposition undergirds the roles of observer, evaluator, persuader, and speaker. But some expository writing is more specialized, and the readings that follow are divided into two categories because each presents the writer with different situations. The historian examines the records of the past to explain its people and its events; the scientist focuses on the physical world to explain its cause-and-effect relationships and its patterns of behavior. Both inform us, but in different ways. Both have researched their subjects and then interpreted and presented their findings with intelligence and imagination. That facts alone are not enough is a lesson, at the end, even Mr. Gradgrind learns.

CHAPTER 4

THE HISTORIAN

In the first century before Christ, Marcus Tullius Cicero, writing in his *Of the Orator*, defined history as "the witness that testifies to the passing of time; it illumines reality, vitalizes memory, provides guidance in daily life, and brings us tidings of antiquity." His definition still holds true today, but it is the historian's task to apply it. The writer of historical essays must research his or her subject thoroughly in order to compose a complete picture that "illumines reality." Then to paint that picture for the reader so that it "vitalizes memory, provides guidance in daily life, and brings us tidings of antiquity," the historian must recreate the subject vividly but accurately.

Chronology is the primary tool of the historical report writer, but the time frame can vary widely. The most obvious one is an individual life span, and that is the scope of the biographer. Whether a full-length work, such as Robert Massie's recent study of *Alexander the Great*, or a thumbnail sketch, such as the Eli Whitney entry reprinted here from the *Concise Dictionary of American Biography*, or a dramatic scene such as Garrett Mattingly's "Curtain Raiser," biography is one of the basic historical genres. "The history of the world," wrote Thomas Carlyle, "is but the biography of great men." And women.

Some historical writers examine smaller, less discrete

chunks of time. John D. Stevens, for instance, scrutinizes a three-month period to ascertain "The Black Reaction to *Gone With the Wind.*" The film opened just before Christmas in 1939, and ripples of protest ran through the black newspaper community well into March of 1940. Stevens' framework for his essay, however, places his topic within a broader perspective, from the premiere of W. D. Griffith's *Birth of a Nation* in 1915 to the frequent rerunning of *Gone With the Wind* which continues into the present.

A far broader chronological framework is involved in James McKinley's essay on Hallmark cards, "If You've Got an Ounce of Feeling, Hallmark Has a Ton of Sentiment." Starting with the ancient Egyptians and the Roman Empire, McKinley takes us quickly to 1415, the date of the "earliest formal valentine." Moving on to the seventeenth century and then to 1840, the advent of the penny postage rate, McKinley next introduces Joyce Clyde Hall, the founder of Hallmark. After providing a brief biography, McKinley offers us an entertaining history of the company whose products we resort to when we "care enough to send the very best," a slogan said to be "the world's greatest guilt producer."

Whether writing a brief biography, examining a critical response to a film, recounting the history of a well-known company's product, or recreating a dramatic event, the historian needs to stay behind the scenes so that the reader's attention remains fixed on the action. Nevertheless, the writer has to project the qualities that make the account believable: *balance, reason, authority, thoroughness,* and *honesty.* Writers achieve these qualities by a judicious use of sources and fair presentation. Primary sources, such as the sixteenth-century records and narratives Mattingly consulted or the greeting cards amassed in Hallmark's archives or the newspaper accounts at the time of *Gone With the Wind*'s premiere, are the most desirable, but secondary sources, such as various full-length biographies of Eli Whitney or modern analyses of the Spanish Armada's campaign, can provide valuable information and insight. In addition, information from sources other than print can be equally valuable, as McKinley demonstrates through his interviews and research into the general history of the greeting card.

Whatever the source—old or new, book or periodical, informal interview or expert opinion—the historian's job is to weigh the data and then report honestly. Evaluating evidence is difficult. Historians must examine the credibility of their sources and the biases and the credentials of the authors they consult. When faced with conflicting views, they must conduct additional research to determine the most accurate and reliable sources. "The first law for the historian," says Cicero, "is that he shall never dare utter an untruth. The second is that he shall suppress nothing that is true. Moreover, there shall be no suspicion of partiality in his writing, or of malice."

To carry out these two laws, the writer must research the subject thoroughly and account for that research correctly. Various disciplines have evolved different systems of documentation to insure that sources are accurately noted, but most historical writing for a general audience uses a simplified method that incorporates the source into the paper itself as in the Whitney biography and the Hallmark article. Stevens uses a more formal and academic system in the report on *Gone With the Wind*, as suits its more specialized audience. Garrett Mattingly, the most academic writer represented here, has seamlessly woven his sources into his description. He relegates his notes to the end of the book where chapter by chapter, he discusses his sources in detail and points to the discrepancies he encountered.

People, places, events—all are the heart of history. From the time of the Greek historian Herodotus to the present, we have explored the past to learn about it and from it. The British philosopher and mathematician Bertrand Russell remarks:

> The past alone is truly real: the present is but a painful, struggling birth into the immutable being of what is no longer. Only the dead exist fully. The lives of the living are fragmentary, doubtful, and subject to change; but the lives of the dead are complete, free from the sway of Time, the all-but omnipotent lord of the world. Their failures and successes, their hopes and fears, their joys and pains, have become eternal—our efforts cannot now abate one jot of them. Sorrows long buried in the grave, tragedies of which only a fading memory remains, loves immortalized by Death's hallowing touch—these have a power, a magic, an untroubled calm, to which no present can attain.

That is the power invoked by serious historians, whether they be the ancient Greeks Herodotus or Thucydides, the British

Thomas B. Macaulay or Arnold Toynbee, the Americans Francis Parkman or Samuel Eliot Morison, or numerous others whose names, like the events they commemorate, pass on into history.

ELI WHITNEY

From *The Concise Dictionary of American Biography*

The *Dictionary of American Biography* is a standard source for biographies of celebrated Americans. The selection below is from the *Concise Dictionary of American Biography* (1964) and is a 500-word biography of the American inventor Eli Whitney. Because the *CDAB* is the result of many writers' work and contains many entries, the biographies are not identified by author. Note how this biography takes the form of a historical summary rather than an evaluative assessment.

Whitney, Eli *(b. Westboro, Mass., 1765; d. New Haven, Conn., 1825)*, inventor. Disinclined to study as a boy, he showed a marked proficiency for mechanical work; he made and repaired violins, worked in iron, and at the age of 15 began the manufacture of nails in his father's shop. On making up his mind to acquire a college education (at the age of 18), he taught school to obtain the necessary money and entered Yale in May 1789. Graduating in 1792, he set out for Savannah, Ga., to serve as a tutor while he studied law. Disappointed of the position he had expected, he took up residence on the plantation of Gen. Nathanael Greene's widow in Georgia, began law studies, and showed his appreciation for Mrs. Greene's hospitality by making and repairing all manner of things about the house and the plantation. 1

During the following winter he learned that many unprofit- 2 able areas of land in the South could be made profitable if the green seed cotton which could be raised on them could be cleansed of seeds by some mechanical device. Encouraged by Mrs. Greene, Whitney turned his mind to the problem and within ten days designed a cotton gin and completed an imperfect model. After further experiment, he built by April 1793 a larger, improved machine with which one man could produce fifty pounds of clean cotton a day. Entering into partnership with Phineas Miller, the plantation foreman, to patent and manufacture the new device and also to maintain a monopoly of its use, Whitney obtained his patent Mar. 14, 1794, but soon found that a monopoly was impossible because of almost universal infringement of his patent by rival machines. Whitney obtained a court decision in his favor in 1807 after a long series of infringement suits; meanwhile Miller had died. On Whitney's application to Congress for a renewal of his patent in 1812, his request was refused. All in all he received practically no return for an invention which let loose tremendous industrial forces in the nation and the world.

Prior to this, on Jan. 14, 1798, he had obtained from the 3
U.S. government a contract to manufacture and deliver 10,000 stand of arms. He proposed to make the guns by a new method, his aim being to make the same parts of different guns (for example, the locks) as much like each other as the successive impressions of a copper-plate engraving. This was perhaps the first suggestion of the system of interchangeable parts which has played so great a part in industrial development and mass production. Raising the necessary capital in New Haven, Conn., he built a factory in present Whitneyville and began design and construction of the machine tools required to carry out his schemes. He worked against great difficulties, having no experienced workmen to aid him and having to make by himself practically every tool required. Completing the contract in some eight years instead of two, he nevertheless accomplished all which he had set out to do. Workmen with little or no experience could operate his machinery and turn out the various parts of a musket with so much precision that they were readily interchangeable. In 1812 he received a second contract from the U.S. government for the manufacture of firearms and also a similar contract from the state of New York. Thereafter, his unique manufactory yielded him a just reward.

THE THINKING PROCESS

STRUCTURE

1. A biography can have chronological or dramatic structure, or a combination of the two. A dramatic structure can be organized by events in the subject's life or by the individual's contributions to society. What pattern does the author use to structure the biography of Whitney?

2. The biographical entry is divided into only three paragraphs. What are the topic sentences of each paragraph? Do you find these three organizing ideas the most central to the biography? Why or why not? What others, if any, would you write?

3. Although a full biography includes the major events in an individual's life, a short biography must eliminate a great many of those events. Reread the introductory and concluding paragraphs. What events, major in most of our lives, are missing here? Is there any other information you would like to know about Whitney that is not included?

STYLE

1. In the selection, we are given little sense of Whitney's character. The focus is on what Whitney did, not on his personality, and the effect is that the reader is distanced from the subject. What stylistic techniques does the author use to create this distance?

2. Compare the *CDAB* entry with the first paragraph of the entry in *The New Encyclopaedia Britannica* (15th ed.):

> **Whitney, Eli** Inventor, pioneer, mechanical engineer, and manufacturer, Eli Whitney is best remembered as the inventor of the cotton gin. He also affected the industrial development of the United States when, in mass-producing muskets for the government, he translated the concept of interchangeable parts into a manufacturing system. His genius as expressed in

> tools, machines, and technological ideas made the Southern United States dominant in cotton production and the Northern states a bastion of industry. The American Civil War may thus be seen as a fratricidal conflict between two economies, agricultural and industrial, on the beginnings of which Whitney's inventions were decisive.

Which selection is more factual? Find places where you think the author of the *Britannica* entry is interpreting rather than reporting. Does the writer evaluate and analyze Whitney's contributions, or does he or she simply report facts? A combination?

3. Examine the sentence structure in the first two paragraphs of the *CDAB* entry. What similarities do you note? Do these characteristics make the paragraphs more effective or less so? How?

IDEAS FOR A FIRST DRAFT

For a general biographical essay, think of someone you know whose life would lend itself well to biography: perhaps one of your parents or grandparents, an aunt or uncle, a cousin or friend of the family. Your sources will be your memory, your conversations with your subject, and any information you can obtain from others who know the person. As you accumulate information, take extensive notes and make sure that you know who said what. Your audience should be educated general readers, strangers to your family, who wish to be informed and entertained. If you elect this assignment, you can skip to paragraph 5.

For a research paper, select a historical figure who is not a household word, someone you'd like to know more about. Perhaps an individual connected with your hobby or your major: George Berkeley in philosophy, Henry George in economics, Margaret Mead in anthropology, Humphry Davy in chemistry, Norbert Wiener in mathematics, Jean Paul Getty in business, Gertrude Stein in literature, Hector Berlioz in music, Stanford White in architecture, Mary Cassatt in art history.

Start your research by finding a summary of the person's life, one that you will probably find in an encyclopedia. If you fail to turn up any information, check an appropriate volume of

Who's Who, which you will find in the reference section of your library. In addition to general notes, write down any biographical resources mentioned in the entry; encyclopedias frequently list major autobiographical and biographical works. Once you have completed your preliminary research, consult the card catalogue for further information. Think also of general headings that would be listed in the subject catalogue. You might not turn up much under the name of a relatively obscure figure, but you may still find information under a larger heading.

As you review your sources, you will accumulate a great deal of material. Then you can sift through your research to determine what you want to include. Remember, the selection process cannot take place until you have thoroughly examined a wide variety of sources. You will probably survey primary and secondary material, and if your subject is controversial, you will have to be familiar with all sides of the controversy.

Your notes will probably be an expanded version of the ones you made during your preliminary research. The major facts you noted then can now serve as categories for the information you are collecting. Review your notes to see if a pattern emerges, one you can use as an organizing principle. Perhaps chance played a significant role in the individual's life, or education, or ambition. Think of that motif as a magnet, and review your notes again, marking any of them that are drawn to the overall theme. Now your information is limited to the most relevant. (Remember, you don't need to include all the circumstances of birth, death, marriage, etc., if they do not bear on your motif.)

Start writing the body of your draft, incorporating your notes according to the chronology of the person's life or according to dramatic events, whatever best suits your focus. You may also want to devote one paragraph to each of the points you emphasize or to group several points together. Keep in mind that your audience probably knows far less than you do about the person. You can capitalize on that realization by beginning the paper with a quick comparison to a more familiar figure or by revealing an intriguing fact or anecdote.

Ending the paper presents a different problem, for by this time your reader is relatively well informed. You could close with a brief narrative, a comment from a contemporary of the individual, or a reassessment from the perspective of the present.

Remember, however, that your purpose is not necessarily to argue about the person's importance but to sift through the relevant information and present the individual's contribution to history effectively and informatively.

JOHN D. STEVENS

The Black Reaction to Gone With the Wind

At the time John D. Stevens wrote the essay that follows, he was teaching journalism at the University of Michigan and was head of the History Division of the Association for Journalism. The author of two books, *Mass Media and the National Experience* (1971) and *The Rest of the Elephant: Perspectives on Mass Media* (1973), Stevens was a regular contributor to various journals. "The Black Reaction to *Gone With the Wind*" was published in the Fall 1973 issue of the *Journal of Popular Film,* a periodical that concentrates on commercial cinema, its "stars, directors, individual films, and genres," and one that includes articles on the theory and criticism of film, as well as interviews, bibliographies, and book reviews.

Although less strident and far less familiar than the reaction to *The Birth of a Nation* (1915), there was an outcry by blacks against *Gone With the Wind* when it was released in 1939. Both films presented a pro-Southern view of the Civil War period, and black leaders felt both degraded members of their race, the Griffith film by painting them as evil and the Selznik movie by showing them as massa-loving simpletons.[1] 1

In the Griffith epic, the "black" characters (actually whites 2
in makeup) were central to the action, but in *GWTW* they were peripheral, in spite of the praise hurled by many reviewers on Butterfly McQueen and especially on Hattie McDaniel. Although Miss McDaniel became the first of her race to win an Academy Award, the focus was clearly on the romance between Clark Gable as Rhett Butler and Vivien Leigh as Scarlett O'Hara. It is doubtful that many whites even knew that the film was controversial in the black community, although blacks did picket the film briefly in several cities, including Chicago and Washington, D.C.

Much of this furor boiled to the surface in the three black 3
weekly newspapers which had national distributions. The Chicago *Defender,* the Pittsburgh *Courier,* and the Baltimore *Afro-American* published many editions and were as available in all major black population centers as in their cities of origination. Each had a circulation of more than 150,000 in 1940.

The faint outcries about the racism of Margaret Mitchell's 4
novel which sold one million copies within a year and captured the 1937 Pulitzer Prize were drowned out in the din of critical approval and ballyhoo by Hollywood publicists. In truth the racism of the book was toned down in the film, partly because of quiet pressures by the National Association for the Advancement of Colored People. The most notable change was in having a white, rather than a black, attack Scarlett.[2]

Black publications and leaders held their breath as the 5
world premiere in Atlanta in December, 1939, approached. Hoping for the best, they were prepared for the worst.

The immediate reaction was calm, even supportive. A col- 6
umnist on the Chicago *Defender*'s entertainment page on December 23 called the film inoffensive and said it exhibited "Negro artistry." The next week appeared the first small cloud, a brief notice that in Los Angeles, "Negro and progressive organizations are reported organizing a boycott against the film."

On December 30, the Pittsburgh *Courier* and Baltimore 7
Afro-American both praised Miss McDaniel for "stealing the show," and the *Courier* carried a front-page story about the firing, by the Communist *Daily Worker,* of its movie critic for refusing to pan the film at the time the party was trying to boycott it.

The attack really began January 6, 1940, when the Chicago 8
Defender published a scathing review, calling *GWTW* more

vicious than *Birth* and a "weapon of terror against black America." The reviewer, William L. Patterson, said the film "distorted and twisted the history of an era. . . . It has deliberately thrown down the gage of battle to those who are seeking to advance democracy today." That same week, the *Courier* published a four-column editorial cartoon of a wind labeled "Propaganda Films" blowing papers marked "facts" and similar things off the table of Hollywood. It was, not surprisingly, titled "Gone With the Wind." The accompanying editorial denounced the film for presenting all blacks as "happy house servants and unthinking, hapless clods." The *Afro-American* remained silent that week as it did the next when the *Defender* editorial called Selznik's epic "crude propaganda" and "subversive."

By contrast, the *Afro-American* was quiet, carrying only a short dispatch on January 13 quoting resolutions of the AFL and CIO which called the Selznik film "reactionary" and racist. On January 20, the paper's first review praised the film and Hattie McDaniel. Harry B. Webber said the movie showed the essential bankruptcy of the slave regime. Except for brief mentions or pictures of Miss McDaniel, that was all the Baltimore paper had to say until Academy Award time. 9

Not so at the other two papers. The *Defender* worked a gibe into a caption of a picture of Butterfly McQueen on January 13 and reprinted an abusive review of *GWTW* from a labor paper on January 20. A February 3 story told of the picketing of the film in Chicago by 100 persons. The leader of the protest was none other than William L. Patterson, author of the January 6 review. There was no mention of the picketing in either the Chicago *Tribune* or the New York *Times* and no followup stories in the *Defender*. 10

The same February 3 issue included a story about the refusal of the Canton (Ohio) city council to ban the film in that city and a three-column editorial cartoon showing a cowboy labeled "Gone With the Wind" using a lynch rope to prevent a black and white from shaking hands. 11

Billy Rose, New York editor of the *Courier*, reviewed the film January 13 for his paper and found "if as some say, it glorifies the South, it at the same time glorifies many great qualities of the race." He could see no reason blacks should not want to see the picture. 12

The January 27 edition of the *Courier* announced a film 13
which was supposed to right the political record of the Civil War. A headline promised, " 'Son of Thunder' Will Be Race's Answer to 'Gone With the Wind.' " In this article, the Pittsburgh paper sounded more like the Chicago *Defender:*

> The film chattel has glorified slavery. It has attempted to show that Negroes reveled in slavery. That the Negro's place was in the cotton fields, stables and kitchen. It has depicted a world that Negroes are ignorant, incapable and superstitious. Black America is indignant over the distorting of facts during that period.[3]

The January issue of *The Crisis*, official NAACP journal, 14
was anything but militant about the new film, saying it contained "little material, directly affecting Negroes as a race, to which objection can be made." This was a far cry from the comments in the same journal a quarter century earlier concerning *Birth*, which it charged showed the black as an "ignorant fool, a vicious rapist, a venal and unscrupulous politician, or a faithful but doddering idiot."[4]

All three newspapers published long, laudatory articles on 15
March 9 about Miss McDaniel's Academy Award, and both *The Crisis* and *Opportunity*, organ of the Urban League, featured pictures of her on their covers in March.

The publications obviously were faced with a dilemma. Miss 16
McDaniel was the first of her race to win an Oscar, but she had won it for the role of "Mammy," a stereotype if ever there was one. The other major black character in *GWTW* was Butterfly McQueen, who played the lying pickanniny who is too frightened to aid Scarlett with the delivery of Melanie's baby during the siege of Atlanta. Thus, in the two women, the movie personified both "modern" stereotypes: the faithful darky and the superstitious child. Hollywood created neither. In 1933, a scholar classified seven stereotypes of blacks in novels: the contented slave, the wretched freeman, the comic Negro, the brute, the tragic mulatto, the local-color Negro and the exotic primitive. Griffith used the first five, but subsequent pressures forced Hollywood to rely almost entirely on the comic and the contented.[5]

On March 9, 1940, the *Afro-American* carried four photo- 17 graphs of picketers at the Washington, D.C. premiere, but offset them with two columnists. Ralph Matthews said blacks in the District of Columbia always were too ready to feel sorry for themselves and defended the integrity of any author to present his or her own view of reality, while Lillian Johnson said the pickets were either uninformed about the film's content or were trying to mislead customers. She said *GWTW* was a "true representation of the period," even if members of her race did not like that representation. She continued to defend the film for the next two weeks. Both the *Defender* and the *Courier* limited their remarks to the historic victory by Miss McDaniel in the Oscar Derby.

The protest was all but over, although the *Defender* tried to 18
fuel it with a March 16 article about how Harlem was still divided on the merits of the film. Both the *Afro-American* and the *Courier* expressed alarm on March 23 about hints of a remake, in color, of *Birth of a Nation,* and on March 30 the Baltimore paper took its only real position when Ralph Matthews urged readers to bury the Hayes Office with protests to prevent the remake of the Griffith classic. For whatever reason, the film was not redone, of course, and on the rare occasions when *Birth of a Nation* is shown anywhere except on a college campus it still draws protests and pickets.

By contrast, *Gone With the Wind* returns and returns, with 19
nary a whisper. It is now a Broadway musical. Probably no one in the audience is aware of the short-lived ruckus the film version produced in 1939–40.

NOTES

[1]For the reaction to *Birth* see Thomas R. Cripps, "The Reaction of the Negro to the Motion Picture *Birth of a Nation.*" *The Historian* XXV (May 1963) 344–362: Everett Carter, "Cultural History Written with Lightening," *American Quarterly* XII (Fall 1969) 347–357; Stephen R. Fox, *The Guardian of Boston* (New York: Atheneum, 1970) 191–198; Charles F. Kellogg, *NAACP* (Baltimore: Johns Hopkins University Press, 1967) 142–145.

[2]Peter Noble, *The Negro in Films* (London: S. Robinson, 1948) 79.

[3]Pittsburgh *Courier,* January 27, 1940.

[4]*The Crisis* X (May 1915) 33; XLVII (January 1940) 17.

[5]Sterling A. Brown, "Negro Characters as Seen by White Authors," *Journal of Negro Education* XXII (April 1933) 179–203.

THE THINKING PROCESS

STRUCTURE

1. Time is as crucial to historical reports as cause and effect is to scientific reports. Trace the chronology involved in Stevens' essay. What times or dates are mentioned in which paragraphs? Does the time frame Stevens supplies for the black response to the film justify his use of the phrase "short-lived" (19)? How or how not?

2. Throughout his essay Stevens interweaves a comparison of *Gone With the Wind* to *Birth of a Nation.* What paragraphs mention *Birth of a Nation?* What are the similarities and differences between the films? In what way is the comparison an effective or ineffective framework for the essay?

3. What "dilemma" did *Gone With the Wind* present to the black press? How did each of the three black weeklies respond to that "dilemma"? How did each express its response? Why might Stevens have delayed mention of this dilemma (16)? What is gained or lost by his doing so? To what extent does Stevens identify the bias of his sources? Is his essay weaker or stronger for it?

STYLE

1. Stevens uses a combination of incorporated documentation and end notes. Why might he have used both methods? What do the sources he incorporates into his text have in common?

2. The historian's task is to evoke the past—to remove its vague, abstract quality and substitute fact and concrete detail. Stevens presents many facts, but what else does he include that gives us a better picture of the time?

3. To what extent does Stevens make himself credible to his readers? How does he achieve the degree of credibility that you discern? Consider not only what sources he uses and why he selects them but also the more subtle qualities implied by diction and sentence structure.

IDEAS FOR A FIRST DRAFT

Examine a historical controversy. You might consider examining the reaction to the Yalta Conference (1945), the dropping of the atomic bomb on Hiroshima and Nagasaki (1945), the partitioning of India (1947), the creation of the State of Israel (1948), or the pardoning of President Nixon (1974). Or investigate the critical reception of an idea or a book of historical interest. You might select a work in your field: in psychology, the early writings of Freud; in economics, the initial response to Thomas Robert Malthus' theories; in political science or government, the reaction to Marx' *Das Kapital*; in physics, the reception to Copernicus' findings; in history, the impact of Edward Gibbon's magnum opus; in literature, the banning of D. H. Lawrence's *Lady Chatterley's Lover*; in dance, the reviews of Isadora Duncan; and so on.

Before engaging in specialized research you would do well to consult an encyclopedia for an overview of your subject. From there you can explore the card catalogue and the books, journals, and newspapers contemporary with your topic. As you read, categorize the opinions into positive, negative, and neutral. Notecards will facilitate arranging and rearranging your material.

Whether you organize your paper chronologically or by type of response (negative, positive, neutral), your sources and their dates are crucial. When you use a source in your paper, give your reader an idea of how it should be weighed; an opinion expressed in a weekly journal with a national circulation of 30,000 is apt to have far less impact than one in the London *Times.*

Your introduction should provide whatever background is necessary. For an essay on the reaction to the Yalta conference or a historical look at the reception of *Lady Chatterley's Lover*, for example, you might want to provide a brief survey of the climate of those times. Or perhaps a current event is related to your subject and can be used to frame your essay. Your introduction, of course, is an appropriate place for your thesis if it is explicit. Your conclusion can summarize, comment, raise questions still unanswered, place the event into a larger context.

As you review your draft, keep in mind that your role is primarily to weigh responses, to assess sources, and then to explain, not necessarily to take sides or to argue for a particular position. Remember your readers are generally familiar with your subject; your job is to present new information and breathe life into your topic.

JAMES McKINLEY

If You've Got an Ounce of Feeling, Hallmark Has a Ton of Sentiment

James McKinley's essay on the history of Hallmark cards was published in the December, 1982, issue of *American Heritage*, a journal sponsored by the Society of American Historians. If you want to find out about Hallmark's marketing techniques, production systems, and management practices, you should read the original article, which is almost twice as long as the excerpt that follows and remarkable for presenting a history of both the greeting card industry and the company that has become a household name. Underpinning McKinley's account of Hallmark's evolution into "the king of American sentiment" is an explanation of "how the colossus of the 'social expression industry' always manages to say it better than you do." As you read the excerpt, see if you can count the ways.

From a distance, it looks like any other factory scene. Women, seated at small tables, hunch over piecework, their hands moving in quick, accustomed ways. 1

But up close you see this is not a common factory, not the usual piecework. A woman, her adhesive machine hissing like a gosling, is pasting lacy red pages into a folded card. Next to her a worker deftly glues three tiny Styrofoam blocks to the back of a big-eyed paper moppet and sticks it to a blue-flocked card emblazoned in gold: "Be my valentine." This is a greeting-card factory. Hallmark, to be precise. 2

What most of the fourteen thousand employees of Hallmark 3
Cards, Inc., are doing is mass-producing American sentiment. Their task is to make a product that will stand in for the bewildered, inarticulate, well-intentioned rest of us. Like the other workers in the four hundred-odd companies that make up the "social expression industry," they are fabricating dazzling John Aldens for us dull Myles Standishes. Hallmark happens to be the biggest John Alden company in the world—the king of American sentiment, with a trademarked crown on every card.

When a young entrepreneur named Joyce Clyde Hall came 4
out from the fastnesses of Norfolk, Nebraska, in 1910 to set up shop in Kansas City, he could scarcely have envisioned his effect on the sentiment industry. He was simply in the business of mailing packets of unsolicited picture postcards to druggists, hoping they'd keep them. Yet, seventy-two years and untold millions of cards later, Hallmark has estimated annual sales of a billion dollars. The exact figure is known to only a few. J. C. Hall's son, Donald, who became president of Hallmark in 1966 (his father was chairman of the board until his death last October), rightly calls it a closely held corporation. But unquestionably Hallmark sells hundreds of millions of dollars' worth of cards, gift wrap, plaques, posters, puzzles, calendars, gummed initials, party supplies, and assorted oddments. Even J. C. Hall himself may occasionally have wondered, "Whence came all this? Out of what deep need or impulse do the people buy my bunnies, flowers, Muppets, Santas, hearts—any of the thirteen thousand or so different cards produced each year in such seemingly endless categories as religious, cute, traditional, formal, juvenile, humorous, and 'suitable for serious illness'?"

Hallmark historians like to point out that precursors of the 5
greeting card, or at least of ritualized social expressions, date back as far as the ancient Egyptian and Roman custom of exchanging small gifts to celebrate the New Year. Valentines are said to have originated in the Roman Feast of Lupercalia, February 15, when young lovers slipped notes to each other in a sort of erotic lottery, the maidens putting their wishes into a large urn and the swains drawing out their courting assignments. Another version of the origin of valentines relates that the persecuted St. Valentine supposedly fell in love with his jailer's blind daughter, restored her sight through his faith, and before his martyrdom sent her a farewell note signed "from your Valentine." The

earliest formal valentine dates from 1415, when another imprisoned lover, Charles, Duke of Orleans, crafted a love message and dispatched it from the Tower of London to his wife.

But these social expressions were personal, unique, and 6
made by extraordinary people in extraordinary circumstances. Hardly mass-produced, they certainly were not the product of an official governmentally designated "day." History provided the inspiration for most of these commemorative days, the Hallmark archivists maintain. One finds, for instance, the modern Mother's Day card anticipated in the seventeenth-century letters of greeting and affection that young tradesmen sent once a year to their mothers. However, these, too, were personal, handmade messages. The verse primers of that and the next century, called valentine writers, may have pointed the way to ready-made sentiment. They offered glib poems of love, admiration, and friendship for the hurried or speechless to copy out.

But it was not until 1840, when the English approved a pen- 7
ny postage rate, that the time of Everyman's social expression had come. Valentines, embellished with elegant, machine-made paper lace and glittering with tinsel, feathers, and powdered colored glass, became a rage. The Christmas card followed the cheap postage rate by three years, when a Londoner named Henry Cole commissioned a Royal Academy Artist to design a Yule greeting. The result, a three-by-five-inch triptych, pictured a family raising a holiday toast and flanked by portrayals of Christmas charity: feeding and clothing the needy. The words—known in the business as the "sentiment" (the artwork is called the "design")—read "A Merry Christmas and a Happy New Year to You." At Hallmark this particular sentiment is called the "classic in the field" and will adorn some of the five billion or so Christmas cards posted in the United States this year. Of his original "Christmas in an envelope"—Hallmark's generic phrase for Yule cards—Mr. Cole printed only one thousand copies.

Commercial greetings flourished in the second half of the 8
nineteenth century. By the 1860s American greeting-card makers, following the English, were producing dozens of different designs, many beautifully printed and ornamented. The publisher Louis Prang took such pains that some of his cards required twenty lithograph plates, and Esther Howland's handmade, silk-fringed, jeweled, laced, and beribboned messages could set an earnest Lothario back as much as thirty-five dollars. . . . Such quality products, though, could not compete

with the flood of inexpensive cards coming off the presses by the end of the century. Customers could choose from landscapes, babies, comic Irishmen, fairies, kittens and puppies, birds, Madonnas, family scenes, just about anything imaginable. For the naughty there were "penny dreadfuls" or "rudes and crudes," forerunners of the mildly humorous and mocking "slam cards" in the current Hallmark lines. Postal officials here and in a few other countries judged some of the "dreadfuls" so bad that they banned them. But there could be no banning those phalanxes of cheap German-made picture postcards. They ran the Prangs out of business—and they provided Joyce Hall with his stock.

Joyce Clyde Hall had been born in David City, Nebraska, 9
in 1891. His birthright was what he later called the "gift of poverty." His frail mother cared for her four children as best she could, often going without food or clothing so they could be nourished and warm. His father, a feckless preacher and inventor, deserted the family when Joyce was seven. Joyce got his first job at eight, doing farm chores. At nine he started selling sandwiches, then horseradish, then cosmetics in David City. At eleven he was working for his brothers, Rollie and Bill, in the Norfolk bookshop they'd bought. There, a few years later, came the fateful introduction to the German greeting cards. Before long Joyce Hall realized there could be something more to this business than riding the local freight, the "Oconee Turnaround," drumming for card business at every whistle-stop. And so, in January of 1910, he left for Kansas City. He traveled without a high school diploma but with a suitcase full of cards and his heart full of ambition. He would do something with these cards, something profitable and not shabby. On arriving in Kansas City, Hall first lived at the YMCA, where his stockroom was the space under his bed and his distribution facility the post office. By 1915 Joyce and his brother Rollie had Hall Brothers Company firmly enough established to survive a fire that wiped out their stock of valentines. That year they acquired their own engraving plant and printed their first wholly original cards. J. C. Hall had also by then made the first of several crucial marketing discoveries: cards could be more than an easy, inexpensive form of communication. Sending them was, he decided, a deeply rooted social custom, and the carriage trade would pay for good ones. He could succeed faster by forsaking his cheaper offerings and even the popular leather postcards (one had his favorite slogan burned into it: "When you get to the end of your

rope, tie a knot in it and hang on"). What was needed were tasteful cards with envelopes for private social communication of two sorts: what his company came to call the "everyday"—birthday, sympathy, get-well—and the "seasonal"—Christmas, Valentine's Day, Mother's Day.

Hall set out to provide them; and he brought to the project 10
some other important concepts. One he learned on his very first day at Spalding's Commercial College in Kansas City, where, to please his family, he had enrolled to learn typing, commercial law, penmanship, and spelling. George E. Spalding's initial act was to have each of his students tack up a tin sign reading, "Time is money—save time." J. C. Hall was impressed but made a significant alteration when it came to his own business: "Time is everything—save time" became an enduring motto at Hall Brothers. Their business, after all, was saving time—buying a card saved the time-consuming trouble of dreaming up a sentiment.

Steadily increasing sales proved Hall's precepts right. The 11
company grew through the twenties, expanded while the national economy shrank in the 1930s, and flourished after World War II when prosperity and mobility created a tremendous market.

The cards in the Hallmark files mirror the concerns of seven 12
crowded decades. A 1928 card, playing off Lindbergh, shows lovers in a cut-out monoplane, with the sentiment, "It's PLANE to see I'm all taken up with you." Many Depression cards keep a stiff upper lip—"in this year of readjustment." Others flash breezy tough-guy lines: "Hi, Toots, Happy Birthday." Or topical word play: "There ain't no Hooey Long with this/It's just a great big wish for Happy Birthday." World War II cards, most of them pacific, send good wishes "to you in the Service." A few clearly violate J. C. Hall's belief that "good taste is good business": a 1946 number, for instance, shows a cartoon anarchist's round black bomb labeled ATOMIC, its sentiment reading, "The little atoms in this bomb can show you what to do/Just have yourself a BANG-UP TIME each minute all day through." Hallmark's efficient archivist, Sally Hopkins, smiles at the card's naiveté. And winces at the early blackface cards in her care. "We don't show those to people," she says. "It was a different time."

Changing times are evident throughout the collection. You 13
can see Mickey Mouse and the gang—Walt Disney was a friend

of J. C. Hall's—come aboard in the 1930s. Charles Schultz's Peanuts and Jim Henson's Muppets are their present-day descendants. Artists, too, change with the years from Norman Rockwell to Saul Steinberg to Alexander Girard. "Mr. J. C.," as the founder is called by longtime Hallmarkers, counted as a special coup getting Winston Churchill's paintings for a line of 1960s cards. But it's the "contemporary" cards, above all, that show how closely Hallmark has monitored the society.

Born in the late 1950s as a response to a growing irreverence 14
toward things previously held sacred, the contemporary line has, over the years, featured humorous H-bomb cards, hippie greetings, peace messages, lunar-landing missives. The archives disgorge C.B. radio cards, jogging cards, silicone-injection cards, fuel-shortage cards, streaking cards, Astro-turf cards, computer-dating cards, feminist cards, even goose-down cards. Last year there were Princess Di cards and video-game greetings. All of these, of course, merely augment the tried-and-true everyday and seasonal products. . . .

"Trust," like "taste" and "very best," is a touchstone at Hall- 15
mark. In the headquarters there is an atmosphere that all is well and will continue so. A public relations man confides: "I worked in government and had to quit because there were so many klutzes. Here everybody knows their job and does it well." Thus, management trusts that each product line will emerge attractive enough and various enough to snare most sentiment seekers. If a card fails, the computer ensures the concept will be discarded and a new one created. The new card, in good taste and carefully focused, will come down a folding chute somewhere in a Hallmark factory, if necessary at a one-million-per-shift rate. At the plant in Lawrence the supervisor of production stood and mused as the machines clanked, hissed, stamped, cut, silk-screened, folded. "You know," he said, "we automate as much as we can, but you still can't take the personal touch out of a greeting card."

The cards whiz past, on their way to plastic bags and then 16
to distribution centers and then to the Hallmark counters. One of them fits virtually every occasion a customer might encounter. Perhaps the time is right for Hallmark Lights, a new line of cards to allow young people to communicate lightheartedly and at a distance. Perhaps one of the new ready-made occasional cards strikes home: congratulations on a nurse capping,

new job, new apartment, new pet. Or maybe what's wanted is something for an old holiday like Halloween that's receiving fresh emphasis ("You know," says Daniel Drake, " we sell them in England, and they don't even celebrate Halloween in England"). Whichever, Hallmark trusts that one or another concept will strike you, that something will articulate your particular sentiment. Something made for you, something quick, convenient, and the very best money can buy.

THE THINKING PROCESS

STRUCTURE

1. A relatively long essay, 1500 words or more, usually requires more than one paragraph to introduce its subject. What paragraphs provide the introduction to "If You've Got an Ounce of Feeling, Hallmark Has a Ton of Sentiment"? Explain your reasons for identifying the introduction as you do. Does one paragraph or several function as a conclusion? Does the conclusion restate, sum up, predict, raise a new point?

2. Which paragraph focuses on the history of the greeting card? On the history of Hallmark? What principle mode—cause and effect, comparison and contrast, description, narration, and so forth—lies behind McKinley's arrangement of paragraphs in the body of the essay? Show how the principle unites the paragraphs.

3. Trace McKinley's interweaving of the present and past. Which paragraphs bring in the present? Given that the essay is historical, what reasons can you find for McKinley's frequent mention of the present?

STYLE

1. While McKinley sets out historical facts, he also projects a distinct sense of his own personality. Humor, for instance, is one of the characteristics that lend the essay its tone. What examples can you find of McKinley's wit? How would you characterize it—mild or biting, good-natured or sardonic, what?

2. Paragraph 9 provides a brief biography of Joyce Clyde Hall, starting with his birth and ending with his vision for the company. Such a narrative lends itself to a trite, Horatio Alger rags-to-riches tale. Does McKinley fall into this trap? If so, what are the qualities within the paragraph that lead to your conclusion? If not, what saves the paragraph?

3. Throughout most of the essay, McKinley begins his paragraphs with a topic sentence. Identify the paragraphs that are organized by topic sentence. Does McKinley keep this pattern from becoming formulaic? What evidence supports your opinion?

4. Allusions are intended to add meaning to a point, but if they are obscure or inappropriate, they disrupt the reader's understanding. Evaluate McKinley's use of allusion in paragraphs 3 and 13. Do the allusions add or detract? How so?

IDEAS FOR A FIRST DRAFT

If you are planning a career in business, you would probably enjoy exploring the history of a particular product associated with a large corporation: the typewriter and IBM; Coke and Coca-Cola; the hamburger and MacDonald's; Band-Aids and Johnson & Johnson; Kleenex or Kotex and Kimberly-Clark. If your interests are more general, think of some of the rituals that we engage in: for example—fireworks, handshakes, Halloween, or burial.

For a paper on the history of a product, you should research both the product and the company associated with it, tracing the product back to its precursors. Business publications such as *Business Week, Forbes,* and the *Wall Street Journal* will aid you in your research, as may discussions with members of your school of business and interviews with local management. Products like Coca-Cola have been the subject of numerous books, so don't overlook what your library can offer you.

If your instructor agrees, you might conduct the assignment

as a group project, with one person responsible for either a specific type of source or question. You will need to know when the product was first marketed, who developed it, what its precursors were, and how it is produced. More specialized information will come to light as you conduct your research, and you will want to include it. Watch for any advertising campaign, slogan, song, or character associated with the product; look for any indication of its future and for any successful (or unsuccessful) spin-offs.

Organizing the body of the paper is difficult only because you have so many choices. All historical reports use chronology, but what is stressed may vary. Instead of emphasizing dates, for instance, you can emphasize change, organizing the paper according to the major technological developments that led to the present product. If you've found that individuals brought about those changes, then individuals might provide you with a valid organizing principle. Or perhaps you want to present first the historical context of the product and then the history of the company.

A paper on a ritual lends itself to similar patterns of organization and to a group approach. You can assign tasks by type of source (books, periodicals, interviews) or by question (origin, evolution, current variants). Your sources will be found in the library's social science holdings: sociology, anthropology, psychology, and history. Like the paper on a product, yours can be organized by stressing various elements within the overall chronology: dates, significant changes, notable individuals, cultural practices, historical contexts, and twentieth-century varieties.

No matter how you organize the body of the paper, you will want to save some material for the introduction. Using a descriptive framework can be effective, for example, opening with a particular present-day scene and returning to it in your conclusion. An introduction that asks a question or reveals a surprising but relatively unimportant fact would also catch the reader's attention. If your reader is familiar with your topic, so much so that it may seem mundane, you will have to devise a snappy or unusual opener that indicates you have interesting information to impart. An effective conclusion might be to place your subject in a wider, more far-reaching context.

GARRETT MATTINGLY

Curtain Raiser

Garrett Mattingly (1900–1964) earned his B.A., M.A., and Ph.D. degrees in history at Harvard University. After joining the faculty of Columbia in 1960, he was appointed to the university's first chair in European history.

Mattingly served in the Army in World War I and in the Navy in World War II, experiences that lent a practical background to his research on military and diplomatic history. His books include *Catharine of Aragon* (1941), *Renaissance Diplomacy* (1954), and *The Armada* (1959). The *New York Times* called this last "a work of art as well as of scholarship," an evaluation echoed by the Pulitzer Prize committee from whom the book received a special citation.

The selection that follows is the first chapter of *The Armada* and contains a number of historical allusions. Rizzio, Darnley, Huntly, Norfolk, and Babington (4), all figured in the Scottish and English intrigues that surrounded the Catholic Mary Stuart, and all paid for their association with her with their lives. Outraged by Mary's failure to punish the earl of Bothwell, believed to be her husband's murderer, and angered further by her marrying Bothwell, the Scots had forced Mary to abdicate in favor of her son, James I. She fled to England and spent the next sixteen years under the protection of Elizabeth I, against whom Mary continuously schemed. Finally implicated beyond all doubt in a plot to murder Elizabeth, Mary was arrested and taken to Fotheringay Castle, where she was tried and found guilty. It is her death warrant that Mr. Beale, Elizabeth's messenger, delivers (1).

The dean of Peterborough (7), the official representative of the Church of England, was, of course, a Protestant; "the heretic" (8) is Elizabeth.

Fotheringhay, February 18, 1587

Mr. Beale had not brought the warrant until Sunday evening but by Wednesday morning, before dawn outlined its high windows, the great hall at Fotheringhay was ready. Though the earl of Shrewsbury had returned only the day before, nobody wanted any more delay. Nobody knew what messenger might be riding on the London road. Nobody knew which of the others might not weaken if they waited another day. 1

The hall had been cleared of all its ordinary furniture. Halfway along its length a huge fire of logs blazing in the chimney battled against the creeping chill. Towards the upper end of the hall they had set up a small platform, like a miniature stage for traveling actors, jutting twelve feet into the hall, eight or nine feet wide, and less than three feet high. At one side a pair of stairs led up to it, and the fresh wood of the scaffolding had been everywhere decently covered in black velvet. On the platform, in line with the stairs, stood a single high-backed chair, also draped in black, and three or four feet in front of it a black cushion. Next to the cushion and rising above it something like a little low bench showed where the velvet imperfectly concealed an ordinary wooden chopping block. By seven in the morning the stage managers were satisfied, the sheriff's men trying to look soldierly in morion and breastplate and to hold their halberds stiffly had taken their places, and the chosen audience, two hundred or more knights and gentlemen of the neighborhood peremptorily summoned for that early hour, had filed into the lower end of the hall. 2

The star kept them waiting more than three hours. In the almost thirty years since she had wedded a future king of France in the glittering, devious court beside the Loire she had failed repeatedly to learn some of the more important lessons of politics, but she had learned how to dominate a scene. She entered through a little door at the side, and before they saw her was already in the great hall, walking towards the dais, six of her own people, two by two, behind her, oblivious of the stir and 3 rustle as her audience craned forward, oblivious, apparently, of the officer on whose sleeve her hand rested, walking as quietly, thought one pious soul, as if she were going to her prayers. Only for a moment, as she mounted the steps and before she sank back into the black-draped chair, did she seem to need the supporting arm, and if her hands trembled before she locked them in her lap, no one saw. Then, as if acknowledging the plaudits of a multitude (though the hall was very still), she turned for the first time to face her audience and, some thought, she smiled.

Against the black velvet of the chair and dais her figure, 4
clad in black velvet, was almost lost. The gray winter daylight dulled the gleam of white hands, the glint of yellow gold in her kerchief and of red gold in the piled masses of auburn hair beneath. But the audience could see clearly enough the delicate frill of white lace at her throat and above it, a white, heart-shaped petal against the blackness, the face with its great dark eyes and tiny, wistful mouth. This was she for whom Rizzio had died, and Darnley, the young fool, and Huntly, and Norfolk, and Babington and a thousand nameless men on the moors and gallows of the north. This was she whose legend had hung over England like a sword ever since she had galloped across its borders with her subjects in pursuit. This was the last captive princess of romance, the dowager queen of France, the exiled queen of Scotland, the heir to the English throne and (there must have been some among the silent witnesses who thought so), at this very moment, if she had her rights, England's lawful queen. This was Mary Stuart, Queen of Scots. For a moment she held all their eyes, then she sank back into the darkness of her chair and turned her grave inattention to her judges. She was satisfied that her audience would look at no one else.

The earls of Kent and Shrewsbury who had entered with 5
her, almost unobserved, had seated themselves opposite, and Mr. Beale was standing, clearing his throat and crackling the parchment of the warrant he had to read. He need not have been nervous. One doubts whether anyone was listening. "Stubborn disobedience . . . incitement to insurrection . . . against the life and person of her sacred Majesty . . . high treason . . . death." Nothing in the phrases could have mattered to Mary Stuart or to any person in the hall. Everyone knew that this was not the sentence for a crime. This was another stroke in a political duel which had been going on as long as most of them

could remember, which had begun, indeed, before either of the enemy queens was born. Sixty years ago the parties had begun to form, the party of the old religion, the party of the new, and always, by some trick of fate, one party or the other, and usually both, had been rallied and led by a woman. Catherine of Aragon against Anne Boleyn, Mary Tudor against Elizabeth Tudor, Elizabeth Tudor against Mary of Lorraine, and now, for nearly thirty years, Elizabeth Tudor against Mary Stuart, the prisoner on the scaffold. The shrewdest politicians might wonder how for almost two decades England had managed to contain both these predestinate enemies and keep them both alive.

Whatever Elizabeth had done, Mary Stuart had, of course, 6
sought by every means in her power to destroy her cousin and bring her low. In a duel to the death like theirs there were no foul strokes. When the arms of strength had fallen from her hands she had used whatever weapons weakness could grasp: lies, tears, evasions, threats and pleadings, and the hands and lives of whatever men her crowns, her beauty or her faith could win to her cause. They had proved two-edged weapons at last; but if they cut her now, she had dealt wounds with them, and kept her cousin's realm in greater turmoil from her English prison than ever she had been able to do from her Scottish throne. And she meant to strike one blow more. She turned a bored chin on Mr. Beale's concluding phrases.

The dean of Peterborough was even more nervous than Mr. 7
Beale. She let him repeat his stumbling exordium three times before she cut him contemptuously short. "Mr. Dean," she told him, "I shall die as I have lived, in the true and holy Catholic faith. All you can say to me on that score is but vain, and all your prayers, I think, can avail me but little."

This, she was sure, was the one weapon which would not 8
turn in her hand. She had been closely watched at Fotheringhay, but not so closely that she could have no word from the daring, subtle men who slipped in and out of the Channel ports in disguise. The north was Catholic, they said, and the west, and even here in the heretic's own strongholds, even in the midlands, even in London, more and more turned daily to the ancient faith. While the heir to the throne was a Catholic, likely to succeed without a struggle on her heretic cousin's death, those thousands had been quiet, but now, should the heretic slay her orthodox successor, surely they would rise in their wrath to sweep away all this iniquity. And there were Catholic kings

beyond the seas who would be more eager to avenge the Queen of Scots dead than ever they had been to keep her alive.

That Mary herself was a devout Catholic is one of the few 9
things about her not open to dispute, but it was not enough for her simply to die in her faith. The duel would go on. All men must know that she had died not only in her faith, but for it. Perhaps she had not always been its steadiest pillar. Perhaps her dubious intrigues had sometimes harmed her cause more than her devotion had helped it. Now the glittering sweep of the axe would cut off forever the burden of old mistakes, silence the whispered slanders, and her blood would cry out for vengeance on her enemies more unmistakably than her living voice could ever have done again. For years she had favored an ambiguous motto, "My end is my beginning." Martyrdom might make good both the promise and the threat. She had only to play this last scene well.

So she held the crucifix high, visible all down the long hall 10
as she flung defiance at her judges, and her voice rose with a kind of triumph above the voice of the dean of Peterborough, always higher and clearer than his rising tones, arching over the vehement English prayers the mysterious, dominating invocations of the ancient faith. The queen's voice held on for a minute after the clergyman had finished. Her words were in English now; she was praying for the people of England and for the soul of her royal cousin Elizabeth; she was forgiving all her enemies. Then for a moment her ladies were busy about her. The black velvet gown fell below her knees revealing underbodice and petticoat of crimson silk and she stepped forward, suddenly, shockingly, in the color of martyrdom, blood red from top to toe against the somber background. Quietly she knelt and bowed herself low over the little chopping block. "In manus tuas, domine . . ." and they heard twice the dull chunk of the axe.

There was one more ceremony to accomplish. The execu- 11
tioner must exhibit the head and speak the customary words. The masked black figure stooped and rose, crying in a loud voice, "Long live the queen!" But all he held in his hand that had belonged to the rival queen of hearts was a kerchief, and pinned to it an elaborate auburn wig. Rolled nearer the edge of the platform, shrunken and withered and gray, with a sparse silver stubble on the small, shiny skull was the head of the martyr. Mary Stuart had always known how to embarrass her enemies.

NOTES

There are a large number of "relations" of the execution of Mary Queen of Scots which have some claim to credibility, but except for the official report signed by Shrewsbury and his associates (Bod. Ashmole 830 fol. 18) and Bourgoing's *Journal* printed in R. Chantelauze, *Marie Stuart* (1876), their provenance and authenticity and their relationship to one another and to the two earliest printed accounts, *Mariae Stuartae . . . supplicium et mors* (Cologne, 1587) and *La Mort de la Royne d'Ecosse,* n.p., n.d. [Paris? 1587?] (see Jebb, *De Vita . . . Mariae,* Vol. II, London, 1925), pose many problems. Besides the official report and Bourgoing one seems to discern at least four eyewitnesses who concur in most details but differ in some. Some extant accounts depend on only one source, others are mixed. E.g. Bod. Ashmole 830 fol. 13, Tanner 78; B. M. Landsdowne 51 fol. 46, Yelverton 31 fol. 545; *Aff. Et. Corresp. pol. Angleterre,* XXII fol. 471 (Châteauneuf), XX fol. 454 (Bellièvre) (both printed in Teulet, *Relations,* IV); *Bib. Nat. MSS Fds. Fr.* 15890 fol. 27; Vat. *Francia* 21. Cf. Ellis, *Orig. Letters,* 2nd ser. III, 113, and M. M. Maxwell-Scott, *The Tragedy of Fotheringhay,* Appendices. One would say that two of the witnesses were Protestant in sympathy, two Catholic, but the small visual details in which they differ do not seem to be related to their sympathies. For instance, the color of Mary's undergarments is variously described as "crimson" or "cramoisie," "pourpre" and "a black bodice and brown petticoat," sometimes with, sometimes without "scarlet ribbons." Doubtless the light in the great hall was bad, but the last witness must have been color-blind. I have opted for crimson, not so much because it is in more early MSS than any other, but because if Mary had crimson undergarments (and we know she had) I think she would have worn them.

THE THINKING PROCESS

STRUCTURE

1. Mattingly structures his scene dramatically, chronologically, and thematically, relying on the motif implied in the chapter's title, "Curtain Raiser." Of the three structural elements, which predominates? How?

2. The journalist's *who, what, where, how, when,* and *why* point out the essentials of a story. In what paragraphs does Mattingly identify each of these components? What reasons can you find for his sequence of presentation?

3. Although Mattingly recounts the details of the morning of the execution, he places the event itself in a wider context. What paragraphs focus on the meaning of the event, not just on the fact of it? To what extent is that focus necessary to understanding this moment in history?

4. Narration, description, cause and effect, comparison and contrast, definition, example, and process analysis are the most frequently used modes of organization. Reread Mattingly's chapter, noting where he draws upon these modes. Which does he use most often? Least? What reasons can you find for his choices?

STYLE

1. Paragraph 2 describes the place of execution in great detail, depicting it so that the reader can see it clearly. What words or phrases does Mattingly use to indicate spacial relationships? Size? What specific details make the scene come to life?

2. Contrast, paradox, irony, juxtaposition—all are related techniques that achieve their effect by similar means, dramatic comparison. What sentences can you find that contain contrasts? What elements within the sentences are contrasted? In which passages does Mattingly use descriptions that depend primarily on contrast? What overall thematic contrasts unify the piece?

3. Sometimes the structure of a sentence will parallel the action it describes. The first sentence of paragraph 10, for instance, tell us how Mary's voice overpowered that of the dean of Peterborough, filling the great hall. So, too, the sentence's structure builds and rises, and its participles (*arching* and *dominating*) sustain the action. Where else do you find Mattingly using this technique of sentence structure paralleling action? Analyze the interrelationship you find in your example.

4. As a serious historian, Mattingly has researched his

topic thoroughly and weighed his evidence before drawing his own conclusions. In the last sentence of paragraph 3, for instance, he reveals his judicious use of sources: ". . . and, *some thought,* she smiled." Where else do you find evidence of Mattingly's dependence on his sources? Does his use of them seem responsible? How or how not?

IDEAS FOR A FIRST DRAFT

The you-are-there approach to history can be glib and sensational or it can be serious and dramatic. If you are assigned a term paper or a research project, consider taking a historian's approach to a particular event. You might want to focus on the signing of the *Declaration of Independence* or the *Emancipation Proclamation,* or perhaps on the assassination of a political leader or on the turning point in a battle—the Napoleonic Wars' Waterloo, the Civil War's Antietam, World War I's Battle of the Bulge, World War II's Dunkirk, and the like.

To make your topic manageable, find some obvious chronological limits to your scene. Like Mattingly, you will want to give your scene a context, so you will be incorporating background material and perhaps looking to the future. But even so, your scene should have distinct boundaries.

First, you may want to get an overview of the event by consulting an encyclopedia; however, books, articles, and newspapers are far more complete sources and will probably turn up some firsthand accounts. Pictures, too, can tell a story, as Matthew Brady's photographs of the Civil War attest. Your library's card catalogue and newspaper indices will reveal useful sources, and the bibliography following the encyclopedia entry will guide you to the more authoritative ones.

As you conduct your research, make sure you note down where the information comes from and any indication of how it might be weighed. A French account of Waterloo will differ from an English one. Be thinking, too, of your role as narrator and interpreter, for you will have to make choices among conflicting information and account for any substantial discrepancy.

When you start your draft, you may wish to set out *who, what, where,* and so on immediately, or you may want to build up suspense by withholding a crucial element until you have created the atmosphere you find appropriate to your subject. Chronology will probably structure your essay, but drama and a unifying theme can be used to underscore your time line. Once you have set your scene, look for appropriate ways to place it in a larger context. Mattingly, for instance, uses the reading of the warrant to point out, "Everyone knew that this was not the sentence for a crime" (5). From there, Mattingly discusses the political duel that lead up to the execution.

You may conclude by describing the last event in the chronology of your scene, or you may turn up an apt quotation. Looking ahead to the future is another possibility, and you may choose to close by drawing a parallel to the present. Throughout your paper, however, you want to focus on the past event, bringing it to life and giving it meaning.

THE WRITING PROCESS

INVENTION

If you have been working on one of the writing assignments that follow the essays in this chapter, you already have a rough draft and may move on to Organizing and Developing. If you are starting from scratch on an historical report, however, you might consider researching what was going on in the world on the day you were born, or tracing the history of one particular word or phrase, or looking into the circumstances surrounding the emergence of a new nation.

1. To find out about the events that occurred on the day you were born, start with several copies of different newspapers: your local one of course, but also perhaps the *New York Times* or the *Los Angeles Times*, the *Washington Post*, the *Atlanta Constitution*, the *Chicago Tribune*, or the *Wall Street Journal*. Most if not all of these sources will be available only on microfilm, but don't let that deter you: if you have not used microfilm before, a librarian will assist you.

Read through a paper quickly before you start to make notes so that you can get an overall view of the day's news; then go back and reread more slowly, jotting down what interests you. You will probably devise your own categories, but if you have trouble, the following may help: international news, national news, local news, special stories or features, entertainment (television and radio shows, concerts, plays, movies), noteworthy ads, obituaries, classified ads.

Look over your categories and select one topic that particularly appeals to you; to broaden the base of your research by providing additional background, consult several weekly publications, for example, *Newsweek* or *Time*, the *National Review* or the *New Republic, Sports Illustrated, Rolling Stone.* Armed with this preliminary research, you should then refer to the card catalogue to discover additional material.

2. To write a historical essay on a word or phrase, you might consider words such as *flirt*, *robber*, or *fussbudget* and phrases such as *good-bye*, *beat it*, or *get one's goat*, though almost any will do. You might try leafing through an unusual dictionary such as *Brewer's Dictionary of Phrase and Fable*, a dictionary of slang, or books on word origins that you find listed in the card catalogue of your library. Once you have identified some likely subjects, look them up in an etymological dictionary, such as the *Oxford English Dictionary*, a primary source that will also give you the history of the word's usage. Also check your word or phrase in concordances and books of quotations like Bartlett's *Familiar Quotations* as well as in a thesaurus, the card catalogue, and foreign dictionaries.

After a preliminary search, narrow your subject to one word or phrase and then research it thoroughly, taking careful note of the information and its source as you go. Look for the etymology, origins, changing meanings, and different uses. You may end up with quotations, translations, books that use the key term in their titles, and several entertaining stories.

3. To report on the emergence of a recent nation, first compare a map of, say, Africa in the early 1900s to one that was published within the last five years. Maps of Asia and the Far East also lend themselves to this assignment. Make a list of the new countries that appear on the recent map, and then narrow down the list to those you want to know more about. You may find, for instance, that you know little about Bangladesh or Benin or Botswana or Burundi or Sri Lanka. Or you might want to explore a country recently prominent in the news, such as Zimbabwe, Nigeria, or Uganda. Once you have chosen a country, start researching it in encyclopedias and their supplements to gain a broad view of the people, culture, geography, government, economy, and standard of living.

The next step is to trace the events leading to the country's emergence. Noting the year the country came into being, look under its old and new name in the appropriate volumes of the

Reader's Guide and *New York Times Index.* These sources will list what articles were written about the country. Then check the card catalogue for more detailed histories or other information. Your preliminary reading will have given you general categories to pursue: major events prior to change or independence, pressures immediately preceding the formation of the new government, effects of change or independence, and subsequent major events.

ORGANIZING AND DEVELOPING

If you are working on assignment 1 and have thoroughly conducted your research on the events that occurred on your birthday, you already have discovered a broad context with which you can frame your specific topic. That context may make a good introductory paragraph.

Using a broad context may also make an effective introduction for assignment 3. A thumbnail sketch of the country until the time just preceding its new form of government would give your reader some necessary information while at the same time setting the stage for the events that follow.

For assignments 1 and 3, the body of the paper will probably be organized chronologically, but within that broad category you can emphasize whatever seems most dramatic: dates, places, people, events, or a combination. In a report on a new country, for instance, you may find that dates and events are important but that equally crucial are the political beliefs of a person or political party. Your pattern of organization should capitalize on whatever drama is inherent in your topic by building up to that key event or figure. The present, too, can provide an effective conclusion. You might report briefly on how the country has fared or on how the event you selected looks from the perspective of the 80s.

If you are working on assignment 2, you may find that rather than making an assertion, a simple indication of purpose better suits your project. Or you may end your first paragraph with a series of questions that indicate what the rest of his essay will address. Try stating your purpose or thesis in your first paragraph together with a brief working definition if your term is unusual. You might then organize what follows by origins, meanings, and current usage, weaving in whatever narratives and examples are appropriate. Remember as you write that you should focus on the term itself; if your word is *love*, for example, don't get sidetracked into preaching. For your conclusion, you might point out some of the spin-offs of the word or phrase or end with an entertaining anecdote you unearthed in your research.

FINDING A VOICE

No matter what your topic, you are faced with the same question: what personality do you wish to project in your paper? Because you are writing a historical paper, you want to make sure that your focus stays squarely on your topic and that the reader is not distracted by your presence as the narrator. Thus you will probably want to avoid first person and the informal *you*, unless you are using a you-are-there approach. Your sources, manner of presenting them, overall organization, paragraph and sentence structure, word choice, and allusions will create your tone.

You will want to impress your reader as an objective, knowledgeable observer, someone who can be believed. Careful attention to transitions, for instance, can create the impression that you have not only assimilated your source material, but that you cared enough to rework it so the reader can follow your report easily. Your word choice can have a similar effect: too simple a vocabulary suggests you are condescending; one too complex suggests you want to impress not inform.

POLISHING

The more details you can add to your report, the more your reader is going to be able to see, feel, and hear, and the more your reader will acquire a distinct impression of the history you are recreating. Review your draft looking for any small imprecision. If you use dates, make them exact; if you include people, give them names. Try going one step further: describe the times and days; describe what the people looked like and thought.

If your organization has any gaps, you should be able to

spot them by outlining your latest draft. You might try the system described on page 196; it should also reveal any flaws in the paper's logic as well as in its organization.

Finally, find someone who represents the audience you are addressing, perhaps one of your classmates. Read the paper aloud to your audience to hear how it sounds and to discover how clearly you have communicated. Ask your listener to tell you in a sentence or two the major point you are making. The response should correspond roughly to your thesis. If it doesn't, perhaps you should revise your thesis to suit your paper. Ask what particular points or details the person recalls from hearing the paper. Those points should be the ones you want to stand out. If they don't, compare the sentences that your listener noted to the ones you wanted to emphasize. Does the sentence structure explain the discrepancy? The diction? Or what? Revise accordingly.

THINKING AHEAD

Review your paper to see how you have handled chronology. Make a list of all the terms and techniques you have used to indicate time: words such as "now," "next," "when," and techniques such as repeating phrases and listing dates. Note the paragraph in which you used the term or technique. Is there any unnecessary repetition? Write a paragraph or two about the problems you encountered dealing with chronology and the solutions you found for them. Your solutions will help you in organizing and tightening up your future papers. Chronological organization is one of the basic organizational patterns that can undergird almost any kind of paper: autobiography, personal essay, report, evaluation, argument.

CHAPTER 5

THE SCIENTIST

Lewis Thomas, a biologist and head of the Sloan-Kettering Cancer Center, recently summarized the public's attitude toward science when he wrote, "Science is thought to be a process of pure reductionism, taking the meaning out of mystery, explaining everything away, concentrating all our attention on measuring things and counting them up." Yet, he points out, "The greatest single achievement of science in this most scientifically productive of centuries is the discovery that we are profoundly ignorant; we know very little about nature and we understand even less." The writer of scientific reports who addresses a general audience is thus faced with a double task: to counter the popular notion of science as reductionist while at the same time explaining what it is that science does and does not know.

The writer of scientific essays focuses on the subject and the intended audience; what the writer may feel about the subject and what argumentative stand the writer may want to take is usually secondary. Thus Jonathan Schell in "What If the Bomb Hits Home?" concentrates on explaining and describing the effects of a nuclear explosion. He explains those effects using the example of New York City, and he describes them graphically, making real the abstract statistics involved in such an event; so too, he uses his facts and figures to imply an argumentative stand. Tim Hackler, in his essay on hangovers, also explains and describes though he takes no stand for or against drinking. Nuclear holocaust and hangovers are problems of dramatically different magnitudes, though both subjects share the characteristic of built-in audience interest. In contrast, Mark Mikolas must not only explain what many readers regard as so commonplace as to be self-explanatory—the egg, but he must first engage his reader's curiosity, which he attempts to do from the start—his title. J. B. S. Haldane's dilemma is somewhat similar; he too explains the obvious—that animals are different sizes. Far less obvious, however, are the reasons behind an animal's optimum size.

All four writers share the difficult task of shaping scientific research for the general reader and doing justice to both audience and subject. To overestimate the reader's knowledge is to bewilder, to underestimate is to condescend; to overcomplicate the subject is confusing, to oversimplify is dishonest. Seeking a balance, the writer of scientific reports draws upon many techniques; *summary*, *quotation*, *paraphrase*, *definition*, *example*, *simile*, *comparison*, and *analogy* are just a few.

Some of these techniques can be carried to extremes as Alex Heard illustrates in his recent parody of folksy scientific writing. Imagining a question-and-answer column in a magazine called *Science 'n' You*, Heard explains the concept of the "black hole":

> To conceive of the density of this black hole, defrost and toast a grocery-store-bought bagel. Bite into it. Pretty dense, right? Now imagine the same bagel that has packed into it all the hot dog buns ever sold at any major league ball game ever played, even rainouts, every pizza crust ever flipped, every cake from every birthday on this 4.3 billion-year-old planet, all the pfeffernusses, pigs-in-blankets, French bread, day-old bargain loaves, scones, black bread, Earl's Famous Chocolate Chip Cookies, tortillas, kaiser rolls, Wonder Bread, Swedish rosettes, gingerbread men, dumplings, Whatta Wheatz, snickerdoodles, Ho Hos, Yuk Yuks, marmalade upside-down cakes, crunchy-crumb brownies, grain silos—in fact, everything that has ever contained any kind of grain, all packed into one super-nutritious bagel. A bagel like that could curb your appetite for eternity, *but you couldn't eat it*. If you put it in the toaster oven it would go through the floor, *through the very Earth itself*. And that's nothing compared to your typical black hole.

Overwritten, yes; funny, yes. But you also understand the density of a black hole.

In a more serious essay, the nineteenth-century English biologist T. H. Huxley uses a similar technique, explaining the unfamiliar in terms of the familiar:

> The method of scientific investigation is nothing but the expression of the necessary mode of working of the human mind. It is simply the mode at which all phenomena are reasoned about, rendered precise and exact. There is no more difference, but there is just the same kind of difference, between the mental operations of a man of science and those of an ordinary person, as there is between the operations and methods of a baker or of a butcher weighing out his goods in common scales, and the operations of a chemist in performing a difficult and complex analysis by means of his balance and finely-graduated weights. It is not that the action of the scales in the one case, and the balance in the other, differ in the principles of their construction or manner of working; but the beam of one is set on an infinitely finer axis than the other, and of course turns by the addition of a much smaller weight.

From this point, Huxley turns his essay toward scientific methods: induction, deduction, and the posing and testing of hypotheses—methods that, as he aptly shows, we use in daily life.

Lewis Thomas finds the motivating forces behind science in "curiosity . . . and the open acknowledgement of ignorance." And indeed most scientific essays start with questions: Mikolas' essay is a good answer to "what's so special about an egg?" Hackler responds to "what can be done about a hangover?" Schell tackles "what if the bomb hits home?" and Haldane explores "why are animals the size they are?" You will note, however, that while all the essays supply information, none of them purports to be definitive. Science is not a body of knowledge, but, as its etymology reveals, is a way of knowing.

MARK MIKOLAS

Useful and Surprising Facts About Eggs

Mathematicians have called the egg the most perfect form in nature, but most consumers are content to see it poached, hard-boiled, or sunny-side up. Yet like many of the everyday objects that surround us, the egg is a complex entity, and Mark Mikolas' "Useful and Surprising Facts About Eggs" shows us just how complex it is. Mikolas' essay appeared in 1983 in *The (Old) Farmer's Almanack.* As the title page declares, the Almanack, which was established in 1792, contains "besides the large number of Astronomical Calculations and the Farmer's Calendar for every month in the year, a variety of NEW, USEFUL, AND ENTERTAINING MATTER." As you read Mikolas' essay, see if you agree.

You may or may not keep them all in one basket, they are difficult to walk on, and you can't make an omelet without breaking them. Although we often think of eggs as symbols of fragility, it is nearly impossible for an adult to break an egg by squeezing it with one hand. Put it endwise between your palms with your fingers interlaced, and it can defy the pressure of both hands. You can even throw it out your second-story window onto the lawn; chances are it will survive. 1

Egg dropping actually became big news in England in 1970. 2

After a headmaster of a school dropped an egg out of a window
to demonstrate its strength, a local fireman climbed to the top of
a 70-foot ladder and dropped ten eggs. Seven survived. Then an
officer of the Royal Air Force took 18 eggs in a helicopter to a
height of 150 feet and dropped them. Only three broke.

The eggshell has a number of other interesting features. In 3
1863 John Davy of Edinburgh placed one under water and filled
it with air under pressure. Bubbles poured out of the shell over
its entire surface. He was the first to demonstrate that an eggshell has 6,000 to 8,000 microscopic pores. These pores allow oxygen to pass in and carbon dioxide to pass out as the embryo
develops.

When a pullet reaches sexual maturity, some of its roughly 4
3,600 ova begin to develop into mature yolks one by one. The
entire yolk is actually only one cell, one of nature's largest. In
fact, an ostrich egg—which according to *The Joy of Cooking* can
serve 24 for brunch—is probably the largest cell nature is currently manufacturing.

The hen's oviduct is a sort of egg assembly line about 20 to 5
30 inches long. Along the assembly line the yolk spends its first
three hours in the magnum, where the thick white albumen (egg
white) is deposited around it. The hen also performs a tricky
maneuver of rotating the yolk while secreting dense cordlike
fibers of mucin that are twisted into chalazae at opposite ends of
the yolk. These help to anchor the yolk in the middle of the
milky albumen. Eggs are always packed blunt side up because
that chalaza is the stronger of the two.

The yolk then continues down the oviduct to the uterus as 6
alternating layers of thick and thin white are added. The egg remains in the uterus about 20 to 21 hours, during which time the
inner and outer shell membranes are added and then calcium
carbonate creates the shell around the egg.

Within about 30 minutes of an egg's being laid, the next 7
yolk starts its trip down the oviduct until it too comes off the
end of the assembly line about 25½ hours later.

All assembly lines require a source of raw materials. Yellow 8
pigment to color the yolk is obtained from the pullets' feed and
then stored in their beaks, shanks, toes, vents, eye rings, and in
the white of their ear lobes (in white-earlobed breeds).

This pigment is then diverted as needed to the hen's single 9
ovary to color the yolks yellow. The beak, shanks, toes, and so

on of a hen that continues to lay become slowly bleached as its store of yellow pigment is used up.

Another raw material required to make an egg is calcium. A 10
good hen will lay about 300 eggs a year. How does a five-pound bird produce 21 pounds of calcium? It is measured out in its feed, generally in the form of ground oyster shells. If she does not get enough calcium in her diet, the hardworking hen will begin to draw it out of her own skeleton.

Egg coloring is not only an Easter pastime. Some hens color 11
their eggs while they are still in the uterus—these are brown eggs. The color of the shell is strictly a function of the breed of the bird. English birds, such as Rhode Island Reds, lay brown-shelled eggs. Mediterranean birds, like White Rocks and Leghorns, lay white eggs.

Whether producing white or brown eggs, modern-day agri- 12
cultural Henry Fords are working to make a more streamlined, efficient producer out of the hen. In the early 1800s the average barnyard hen laid about 15 eggs a year. Selective breeding was introduced, and by the turn of the century an average hen was laying about 150 eggs a year.

Today a well-run operation achieves an 85 percent produc- 13
tion rate, meaning that each day 85 percent of the hens have produced an egg. That works out to over 300 eggs per year per hen. Genetic researchers at the University of Missouri College of Agriculture managed to coax hen #2988 to lay 371 eggs between August 30, 1979, and August 29, 1980—a world's record of 1.02 eggs a day for an entire year.

Whether they are brown or white, Peewee or Jumbo, have 14
pale or bright yellow yolks, Americans consume an average of 281 eggs per year. That's down from 313 per capita in 1969, but it still keeps about 285 million hens busy day and night.

You can recognize a fresh wholesome egg by first shaking it. 15
If you feel a rattle, it is not fresh. A top-grade egg, when broken, will stand up firm with very little spreading of the white. Government grades are based on the size of the air cell in the egg, the egg's quality, and its freshness. A Grade AA egg must be less than ten days old from packing, a Grade A, 30 days.

An old-fashioned but valid test for egg freshness is accom- 16
plished by gently dropping a whole uncooked egg into a salt solution (two tablespoons of salt in two cups of water). If very

fresh, the egg will be full and heavy and it will sink and tip to one side. If moderately fresh it will remain suspended in the middle of the water in an upright position, and if it bobs up to the top it is stale.

Unwashed eggs, available from some health food stores or local farms, will stay fresh up to six times longer than commercially processed eggs. In fact, if eggs are to be stored or shipped long distance, packers often oil them with a colorless, tasteless mineral oil to seal the egg after the "bloom"—the egg's natural protection—has been washed off. 17

When you next open a carton of eggs and contemplate their perfection, take a minute to ponder which side of the philosophical fence you prefer. Some of us may stand with Cervantes, who was the first to advise, "'Tis the part of a wise man to keep himself today for tomorrow, and not venture all his eggs in one basket." The more daring may hail Mark Twain and his admonition, "Put all your eggs in one basket and—WATCH THAT BASKET!" 18

THE THINKING PROCESS

STRUCTURE

1. Writers often use the title of an article to engage the reader's interest and highlight the subject. Mikolas' title does both: "surprising" piques the reader's curiosity while the title as a whole tells exactly what the report will cover. The report itself brims with facts. Which did you already know? Which surprised you? Which do you find useful?

2. What is the overall pattern of the essay's organization? Does Mikolas present useful facts first, then the surprising ones, or does he vary them, moving from one to another? Why might he have structured the essay as he does?

3. Reread the last paragraph. Is Mikolas asking us to make a decision between Cervantes or Mark Twain, or do the quotations serve another purpose? If so, what?

STYLE

1. Though *The (Old) Farmer's Almanack* is read by many people who have never been on a farm, most are so familiar with the egg that they take it for granted. Mikolas' task is an interesting one: how to engage people in scrutinizing a familiar object. Examine the first two paragraphs, and identify the techniques Mikolas uses to engage his reader's interests.

2. What analogy does Mikolas use in paragraphs 5 through 7 to explain the unfamiliar? Where else in the essay does he bring in the same analogy? To what extent is it effective or ineffective? How so?

3. Paragraph 5 is the most technical one in the report, containing terms such as *oviduct, albumen, mucin,* and *chalazae.* Why might Mikolas have chosen to include a parenthetical definition of *albumen* but not of the others?

IDEAS FOR A FIRST DRAFT

As an exercise in general expository writing that requires the detailed observation essential to scientific studies but does not require research, select a familiar object that most people do not usually distinguish from others in its category: an orange, a pair of blue jeans, a used pencil, a pair of jogging shoes, your thumb or hand. Note down all the relevant features of your subject, including size, shape, textures, colors, distinguishing features—any detail that makes your subject different. Write up your observations, and test them out on the class or on a small group. Faced with several similar objects, a basket of oranges, for example, would your description identify the subject of your paper?

To find a topic that calls for research, you can probably come up with a fair-sized list of commonplace objects by just looking around you. Consider the seemingly ordinary baseball or the dollar bill, the nectarine or the aspirin tablet. Make a short list of everyday objects that invite closer scientific scrutiny.

Select the object from your list that most piques your curiosity, and set up notecards (or separate sheets) for each of the following headings: *facts*, *terms*, *history*, *production* or *chemical process*, and *use*. Before beginning your research, jot down any assumptions the average reader is apt to hold about the object. (Confronting and contradicting your reader's assumptions can make an interesting introductory paragraph.) Next, write down as many questions and curious facts as you can. The life span of a dollar bill, for instance, is probably surprisingly short. Then list any technical words associated with the object. Your list of words and facts will grow as you conduct your research.

Only research will reveal the history of your object, so write down questions you need to answer: When did the object first appear? Who invented or discovered it? What did it originally look like and consist of? What uses did it have? How did the public respond to it? Depending upon your subject, these questions will vary. Current uses of your object may lead to some entertaining stories, and one might make a good concluding paragraph. Don't hesitate to ask your instructor or a librarian for leads to sources that will provide you with the necessary information.

You can organize the body of your draft by using one of a number of patterns. You might consider the chronological process involved in your object's manufacture or development. Or you might begin with a brief history and a description of its evolution as a way of leading into a discussion of its uses. If you stress the technical side of your subject, you will be writing from the perspective of a scientist; if you emphasize its origins and development, you will be adopting the role of a historian. No matter what your approach, remember not to belabor the obvious; most likely your thesis will be readily apparent, so you need not make it explicit.

TIM HACKLER

The Morning After

In "The Morning After," Tim Hackler explores a common ailment, the hangover—an occasional headache for social drinkers and a chronic one for alcoholics. Hackler interprets complex scientific data, transforming them for the general reader into the common sense of prevention and remedies. *Mainliner,* the monthly where the article first appeared in July, 1981, is found in the seat pockets of United Airlines jets. The magazine identifies Tim Hackler as "a science and medical writer whose reports on executive health matters appear [in the *Mainliner*] regularly." As you read the essay, ask yourself if Hackler, writing for a general audience, does justice to the complexity of his subject.

"A dark brown taste, a burning thirst/A head that's ready to split and burst/No time for mirth, no time for laughter/The cold gray dawn of the morning after," wrote George Ade in a 1903 poem about what doctors today call the alcoholic headache. Its victims call it a hangover. Either way, it's a pain in the head, frequently accompanied by nausea or heartburn, that follows consumption of alcohol. 1

It's a problem that can plague even moderate, "socially constructive" drinkers (such as Jackie Gleason, who supposedly once said, "I drink to remove warts and pimples from the people I'm looking at"). It is curious that so much mythology has grown up around the treatment of the hangover, in light of the fact 2 that there are simple, effective steps to take before, during and after drinking alcohol in order to minimize the problem.

A hangover headache is one type of vascular headache, a 3
category characterized by a throbbing sort of pain on one side of the head. The pain is caused by blood vessels in the skull swelling and becoming distended; the throbbing is the result of blood pulsing through the swollen arteries in time with the pulsing of blood from the heart. At first, the arteries are soft and rather flexible, but if the headache goes on for hours, the blood vessels tend to become rigid and less susceptible to the pulsation of the blood. This is why a throbbing pain is replaced by a constant, unwavering pain.

There are two home remedies that help relieve the throb- 4
bing quality of the hangover. The first is to get out of bed and drink a cup of coffee. Blood flows through the blood vessels in the head with greater force when the body is horizontal rather than vertical. Coffee not only serves as a stimulant, it causes the blood vessels to constrict. This effect can also be achieved by taking ergotamine, a drug commonly prescribed for migraine (Gynergen and Ergomar are two trademarked brands) or by using another popular home remedy and reliable vasoconstrictor, the ice pack.

Complete rest, isolation and a dark room can also alleviate 5
the symptoms. One doctor puts it this way: "Alcohol increases our ability to sustain light and sound and noise during a party, but on the morning after the brain may be exhausted and fatigued, and the world seems larger than life at a time when peace and anonymity are desired by the drinker."

One of the most effective ways to prevent—or once unpre- 6
vented, to cure—a hangover is to consume large amounts of fructose, which helps speed up the body's metabolism of alcohol. Only a very small amount of the alcohol consumed in a drink is excreted unchanged—about 5 percent. The rest is metabolized in the body, chiefly in the liver. However, it is possible to modify the rate at which alcohol is metabolized. Thirty grams of fructose will increase the rate of metabolism of alcohol by 15 to 30 percent. No other sugars, including glucose (white table sugar), have this effect on alcohol metabolism. The best sources of fructose are honey, ripe fruits and tomatoes. A thoughtful host or hostess would provide some fructose-rich foods as part of the hors d'oeuvres scheme.

According to Dr. Donald J. Dalessio (writing in the journal *Headache*): "A slice of toast well spread with honey, taken prior to bedtime after an evening of drinking, is a simple and effective remedy for hangover. The ingestion of vegetable juices during the hangover hours may be helpful in hastening the metabolism of whatever alcohol remains in the body to be metabolized. Thus, the standard morning-after cocktail of tomato juice with some added spices may be more therapeutically sound than suspected previously." Party veterans often wonder if "hair-of-the-dog" treatment is a good idea. The answer from doctors is an emphatic no. Although the alcohol in a Bloody Mary, for example, may temporarily deaden the senses, it will only create anew the syndrome that led to the hangover in the first place. The best morning-after drinks would appear to be a cup of coffee and a virgin mary. 7

As anyone with any experience has recognized for himself, the morning after arrives more peacefully if the alcohol of the evening before was consumed along with a generous portion of food. But the type of food is important, too. Fatty foods, especially meats and such dairy products as milk and cheese, absorb the alcohol. These foods not only help reduce the amount of alcohol entering the bloodstream, they help prevent stomach irritation and the consequent nausea and heartburn that some hangover victims suffer. It's not a bad idea to drink a glass of milk along with your toast and honey before going to bed. 8

The first thing many victims of the morning-after syndrome want is a glass of water—and sometimes several glasses of water. This is because alcohol acts as a diuretic, stimulating the flow of urine. Water taken before drinking may help somewhat to reduce the subsequent dehydration, but it is also a good idea because it helps prevent rapid absorption. Water makes sense as a mixer in drinks—better than fizzy carbonated beverages that hasten the absorption of alcohol. (That's why you get such a kick out of champagne.) 9

It is still being investigated, but it is now widely believed that substances known as congeners have a lot to do with causing hangovers. Congeners are small molecules that are produced during the processes of fermentation, distillation and aging of liquors and wines. These "by-products" come primarily from the barrels in which alcohol is aged. In the book *Body, Mind and Behavior* (Dell) by Maggie Scarf, Dr. Morris E. Chafetz, director of the National Institute of Alcohol Abuse and Alcoholism Pre- 10 vention, says, "You tend to find congeners in your better whiskeys—good bourbon, for example—because aging is one of the marks of fine whiskey. And the longer that whiskey is in the wood, the more of the congeners it is going to take on. They give alcohol flavor; they give it that smoothness of taste that we associate with good liquor. But the suggestion remains, nevertheless, that there are miniscule aftereffects from these congeners. They are toxic substances; if you had them in large doses, they would be absolutely deadly."

Whiskeys that are stored, such as bourbon and Scotch, con- 11
tain more of these substances than, say, vodka, which is simply a mixture of pure grain alcohol and distilled water. However, any liquor produced by the distilling process will contain fewer congeners than will those beverages produced by fermentation—which includes all wines.

To complicate the picture somewhat, about 30 percent of 12
those persons who suffer from migraine headaches react to substances called tyramines. These are chemicals found in many foods and alcoholic beverages. Beverages that contain large amounts of tyramines are beer, red wine, bourbon, gin and vodka: in general, anything that's fermented. Rosé wines, white wine (except Sauterne), brandy, cordials, Scotch and rum will not cause a tyramine reaction in migraine patients.

It is possible that some people consider their "morning 13
after" headaches to be common hangovers, when in fact they are migraines caused by the tyramine-laden drinks of the night before. (The migraine, like the hangover, is a vascular headache.) The only way to find out the true culprit is to abstain from these two different groups of alcoholic beverages one at a time to see if either is responsible for causing or exacerbating the "morning after" headache.

People are sometimes surprised to wake up with a hangover 14
after a night of relatively light drinking. The explanation may be that the individual was psychologically on edge or simply physically tired while doing his or her drinking. Alcohol anesthetizes the nervous system and therefore masks the physical or mental tension you may be feeling. This often leads to unrealistic demands on the body, which can cause the morning-after syndrome to become evident after the anesthetic mask of the alcohol has worn off.

Science writer Maggie Scarf asked Dr. Chafetz why she 15
would occasionally find herself feeling bad after only light social

drinking. "I think that when you are bored, when you are at a place where you really can't stand being," Dr. Chafetz explains, "you tend to hold yourself with a certain degree of tenseness. And, however much alcohol you happen to drink, it suppresses your own sense of that tension—for the time being. You do experience it later on, however, in the form of a hangover." According to Dr. Chafetz, "A lot of body tension can result from the way you are forced to hold your body—I mean simply to *stand*—because you happen to be doing your drinking in a very crowded room."

Drinking while under emotional strain may also lead to a hangover. In fact, another type of headache—the tension headache—may compound the miseries of the normal alcoholic headache. "That kind of headache is often related to anxiety a person might be feeling about something he or she had done the night before—especially if it was in circumstances where misbehavior might be threatening," says Dr. Henry Murphree of Rutgers Medical School (quoted by, again, Scarf). 16

For all of these reasons, Dr. Chafetz recommends that you take a nap before attending a party, in order to be mentally and physically more relaxed. He concludes: "Don't take that drink if you happen to be feeling physically exhausted or perhaps distressed for some reason." 17

Anyone wishing further information on the medical effects of alcohol or alcoholism may write the National Clearinghouse for Alcohol Information, NIAAA, PO Box 2345, Rockville, MD 20852. 18

THE THINKING PROCESS

STRUCTURE

1. Cause and effect is a pattern of organization basic to the form of a scientific report, and Hackler's paragraphs 4 through 9 use cause and effect to explain how various remedies work. Paragraphs 10 through 17 focus on the causes of hangovers: trace these cause and effect relationships.

2. Scientific exposition also relies on chronology as a method of organization. Hackler states about hangovers: "there are simple, effective steps to take before, during, and after drinking in order to minimize the problem" (2). Of the paragraphs that follow, which focus on the steps "before"? "After"? "During"? Is chronology or cause and effect the primary pattern? What evidence do you have to support your opinion?

3. How does Hackler conclude his essay? Do you find this type of ending satisfactory? Try adding a sentence or two to Hackler's conclusion or write a paragraph to serve in its stead. Which is more effective and why?

STYLE

1. Reread the essay, listing the sources Hackler uses. Which does he quote from directly? Paraphrase? Are the number and type of sources sufficient to his purpose? How or how not?

2. Anyone who writes an article that incorporates scientific information must temper the highly specialized sources for the general reader. Examine paragraphs 10 through 13. How does Hackler shape complex technical information to interest the reader? What different techniques does Hackler use to "translate" technical terms and causal relationships?

3. Hackler uses qualifiers in his essay; in paragraph 14, for instance, he chooses *sometimes, relatively, may be, often, can cause.* Find several other examples of qualification. What do the qualifiers add to the essay's tone? What characteristics of Hackler's personality do they suggest?

IDEAS FOR A FIRST DRAFT

Consider some common physical complaints that have both scientific and folk remedies: bad breath, warts, burns, sprains, acid indigestion, hiccoughs, insect bites, dandruff, muscle cramps, ingrown toenails, and the like. Select a subject, and set up the following headings: *definition, folk remedy, medical remedy, physiological causes.*

To research your subject, look it up in various indices (*Reader's Guide, New York Times,* etc.) and the *Index Medicus,* which surveys a large number of medical journals. Your college librarians may also know of other useful sources, and the card catalogue listing for "folk remedies" might also prove fruitful. As you conduct your research, use a separate sheet for technical terms, recording the definitions as you discover them.

After you have collected sufficient information to write knowledgeably about your subject, rough out the body of the paper. You may want to structure the paper by moving from the unscientific to the scientific, using the medical remedies to introduce a discussion of the physiology of the problem in question. Or you may want to construct the body of the paper entirely by cause and effect. You may first discuss the physiological causes and their effects—the symptoms—or you may first discuss the symptoms, then their causes. Examine how the possible remedies may affect those symptoms.

For an introduction, perhaps write a brief, entertaining narrative, history, or description of the symptoms. A short definition may be in order. If you want your thesis to be explicit, try including it here. Your concluding paragraph may sum up, predict the ailment's future, narrate an amusing or horrifying story—whatever best suits your tone and purpose.

JONATHAN SCHELL

What If the Bomb Hits Home?

In *The Fate of the Earth,* the 1982 book from which this excerpt is taken, Jonathan Schell argues for nuclear disarmament. "What If the Bomb Hits Home?" however, explains and describes in lay terms the effects of a one-megaton bomb on the city of New York. Manhattan, the most populated of New York City's five boroughs, is an island that runs from Battery Park (1) at the southern end to the Harlem River, near the George Washington Bridge (1), at its northern tip. The Empire State Building (1), over which Schell's hypothetical bomb bursts, stands at 34th Street; Greenwich Village is just below 14th Street; and Central Park (6) begins at 58th Street. Staten Island (1), another of New York City's boroughs, lies off lower Manhattan between New York and New Jersey.

As you read the piece, note that the description is not neutral, and see if you can discover how Schell combines description and narration to give an expository piece a persuasive edge.

One way to begin to grasp the destructive power of present-day nuclear weapons is to describe the consequences of the detonation of a one-megaton bomb, which possesses 80 times the explosive power of the Hiroshima bomb, on a large city, such as New York. Burst some 8,500 feet above the Empire State Building, a one-megaton bomb would gut or flatten almost every 1 building between Battery Park and 125th Street, or within a radius of four and four-tenths miles, or in an area of 61 square miles, and would heavily damage buildings between the northern tip of Staten Island and the George Washington Bridge, or within a radius of about eight miles, or in an area of about 200 square miles.

A conventional explosive delivers a swift shock, like a slap, 2
to whatever it hits, but the blast wave of a sizable nuclear weapon endures for several seconds and can surround and destroy whole buildings. People, of course, would be picked up and hurled away from the blast along with the rest of the debris. Within the 61 square miles, the walls, roofs and floors of any buildings that had not been flattened would be collapsed, and the people and furniture inside would be swept down onto the street. (Technically, this zone would be hit by various overpressures of at least five pounds per square inch. Overpressure is defined as the pressure in excess of normal atmospheric pressure.)

As far away as 10 miles from ground zero, pieces of glass and 3
other sharp objects would be hurled about by the blast wave at lethal velocities. In Hiroshima, where buildings were low and, outside the center of the city, were often constructed of light materials, injuries from falling buildings were often minor. But in New York, where the buildings are tall and are constructed of heavy materials, the physical collapse of the city would certainly kill millions of people.

The streets of New York are narrow ravines running be- 4
tween the high walls of the city's buildings. In a nuclear attack, the walls would fall and the ravines would fill up. The people in the buildings would fall to the street with the debris of the buildings, and the people in the street would be crushed by this avalanche of people and buildings.

At a distance of two miles or so from ground zero, winds 5
would reach 400 miles an hour, and another two miles away they would reach 180 miles an hour. Meanwhile, the fireball would be growing, until it was more than a mile wide, and rocketing upward, to a height of over six miles. For ten seconds, it would broil the city below. Anyone caught in the open within nine miles of ground zero would receive third-degree burns and would probably be killed; closer to the explosion, people would be charred and killed instantly.

From Greenwich Village up to Central Park, the heat would 6
be great enough to melt metal and glass. Readily inflammable materials, such as newspapers and dry leaves, would ignite in all five boroughs (though in only a small part of Staten Island) and west to the Passaic River, in New Jersey, within a radius of about nine and a half miles from ground zero, thereby creating an area of more than 280 square miles in which mass fires were likely to break out.

If it were possible (as it would not be) for someone to stand 7
at Fifth Avenue and Seventy-second Street (about two miles from ground zero) without being killed instantly, he would see the following sequence of events. A dazzling white light from the fireball would illumine the scene, continuing for perhaps 30 seconds. Simultaneously, searing heat would ignite everything flammable and start to melt windows, cars, buses, lampposts, and everything else made of metal or glass. People in the street would immediately catch fire, and would shortly be reduced to heavily charred corpses.

About five seconds after the light appeared, the blast wave 8
would strike, laden with the debris of a now nonexistent midtown. Some buildings might be crushed, as though a giant fist had squeezed them on all sides, and others might be picked up off their foundations and whirled uptown with the other debris. On the far side of Central Park, the West Side skyline would fall from south to north. The 400-mile-an-hour wind would blow from south to north, die down after a few seconds, and then blow in the reverse direction with diminished intensity. While these things were happening, the fireball would be burning in the sky for the 10 seconds of the thermal pulse. Soon huge, thick clouds of dust and smoke would envelop the scene, and as the mushroom cloud rushed overhead (it would have a diameter of about 12 miles), the light from the sun would be blotted out, and day would turn to night.

Within minutes, fires, ignited both by the thermal pulse and 9
by broken gas mains, tanks of gas and oil, and the like, would begin to spread in the darkness, and a strong, steady wind would begin to blow in the direction of the blast. As at Hiroshima, a whirlwind might be produced, which would sweep through the ruins, and radioactive rain, generated under the meteorological conditions created by the blast, might fall.

Before long, the individual fires would coalesce into a mass 10 fire, which, depending largely on the winds, would become either a conflagration or a firestorm. In a conflagration, prevailing winds spread a wall of fire as far as there is any combustible material to sustain it; in a firestorm, a vertical updraft caused by the fire itself sucks the surrounding air in toward a central point, and the fires therefore converge in a single fire of extreme heat. A mass fire of either kind renders shelters useless by burning up all the oxygen in the air and creating toxic gases, so that anyone inside the shelters is asphyxiated, and also by heating the ground to such high temperatures that the shelters turn, in effect, into ovens, cremating the people inside them.

In Dresden, several days after the firestorm raised there by Allied conventional bombing, the interiors of some bomb shelters were still so hot that when they were opened the inrushing air caused the contents to burst into flame. Only those who had fled their shelters when the bombing started had any chance of surviving. (It is difficult to predict in a particular situation which form the fires will take. In actual experience, Hiroshima suffered a firestorm and Nagasaki suffered a conflagration.) 11

In this vast theatre of physical effects, all the scenes of agony and death that took place at Hiroshima would again take place, but now involving millions of people rather than hundreds of thousands. 12

THE THINKING PROCESS

STRUCTURE

1. Schell's perspective in the essay is like a camera's; he begins with a long shot and then zooms in on particulars. Distance is one of the elements by which he organizes paragraphs 1 through 6. Which distances does Schell introduce in what paragraphs? What is the direction of movement, from smaller to greater distance, or what?

2. Paragraphs 7 through 10 are organized chronologically. Which times are presented in what paragraphs? What is Schell implying by using the rapid time frame in paragraphs 7 through 10?

3. A writer will use comparison and contrast as a basic pattern of organization or as a motif that gives the essay unity. Trace the comparisons Schell employs, marking each example and its paragraph. Does Schell use comparison and contrast as a motif to provide unity or as a fundamental organizational principle? What else is gained by the comparisons?

STYLE

1. Good writers make action more vivid by using concrete verbs. Schell, for instance, uses *strike, laden, crushed, squeezed, picked up, whirled, fall, blow, die down, envelop, rushed, blotted out,* and *turn* (8). Find a sentence with several active verbs and try substituting forms of *to be.* Which kind of verbs make the event more immediate? Now substitute different concrete verbs, comparing them to Schell's original choices. Which do you prefer and why?

2. A writer can make the unfamiliar concrete and clear by comparing it to the familiar. Schell uses this technique in paragraphs 2 through 8; a nonnuclear blast is "like a slap," and buildings "might be crushed, as though a giant fist had squeezed them on all sides." Create different similes for these sentences. What differences do you discern? Which do you prefer and why?

3. One of the techniques a writer uses to make the abstract concrete is precise detail. The city in the essay is not Main Street, U.S.A., but New York City, and Schell uses street names and recognizable landmarks to pinpoint the effect of the explosion. To what extent is that technique effective? What other kinds of specific details does Schell use?

IDEAS FOR A FIRST DRAFT

Start by thinking of natural phenomena that lend themselves to a cause-and-effect explanation: tornados, earthquakes, hurricanes, tidal waves, thunderstorms. Or perhaps you would rather explain how an instrument or machine or component works—an electron microscope, a CAT scan, a turbocharger, a transit, a microchip, or the like. If those subjects don't appeal, you may want to explore how scientists make predictions—of the weather, of earthquakes, of the greenhouse effect. Whatever your subject, you will be writing for a general audience, your classmates or perhaps the readers of *Science 1984* or *Science Digest*.

If you want to write a less scientific paper, perhaps one with an argumentative edge, think of the disasters that could happen to an area you know well: natural catastrophes such as a flood, hurricane, earthquake, tornado, or those man-made disasters such as a nuclear power meltdown, dam rupture, or power outage. Ask yourself "What would happen if . . . ," and then finish the question with one of the examples above or with one of your own choosing. Establish a time, day, and specific location for the event and then set up two lists, one for the time sequence, another for place.

Your research will progress more quickly if you are looking for answers to specific questions. If you are writing about the causes or effects of an earthquake hitting San Francisco, for instance, under *time sequence* you would need to know its various stages or the duration of your hypothetical quake and the duration and number of the aftershocks. Under *location*, you would need to know where earthquakes are likely to occur or the various degrees of devastation at significant distances from the epicenter and what landmarks are associated with those lines of demarcation.

Whether your essay is a scientific or a more general exposition, your introduction should include any information essential to what will follow—a definition of central terms or an explanation of central data, like the force of a quake on the Richter scale, for example. You may also want to summarize the force of a natural phenomenon or the function of the machine you are examining or your event's effects, citing the abstract numbers before presenting concrete details.

Using the facts you have garnered from your research, sketch out your introductory paragraph and the body of the paper. You may want to organize the body by chronology or process or degree of devastation, working from least affected to most or the other way round. As you write your draft, use active verbs, and try to particularize the subject you are describing by using names, simile, and history. If discussing tornados, for instance, you might mention some particularly devastating twisters; your machine may be descended from a far earlier and more primitive one; or your hypothetical earthquake may be a step above the one that destroyed much of San Francisco in 1906, in which case the effects can be contrasted to dramatic advantage.

Your conclusion might predict future technological developments or the possibility of a natural disaster or refer to a different catastrophe; or you might make a comment about the rate of technological progress or your area's state of preparedness for a natural disaster. Your object is to make statistics and the unfamiliar come to life, so that you can both engage your reader and explain a complicated process.

J. B. S. HALDANE

On Being the Right Size

The noted English scientist John Burdon Sanderson Haldane (1892–1964) was educated at Oxford University and later taught at Cambridge University, the Royal Institution in London, University College in London, and the University of California. Haldane held professorships in biochemistry, physiology, genetics, and biometry (the statistical study of biological data).

The author of some fifty volumes, Haldane wrote political works, autobiography, and essays as well as scientific treatises such as *Animal Biology* (1927), *New Paths in Genetics* (1941), *The Biochemistry of Genetics* (1954), and *Physiological Variation and Evolution* (1960).

Haldane, a world authority on heredity and inherited diseases, is known for formulating the mathematical theory of natural selection. The first scientist to map a human chromosome, Haldane was a master of scientific method, even experimenting on himself to study poisonous gases and the effectiveness of inoculation.

The essay that follows reflects Haldane's interest in biometry. Published in 1928 in his collection of essays *Possible Worlds*, "On Being the Right Size" retains a surprising freshness of information and style. The characters Christian, Pope, Pagan, and Despair, to whom Haldane refers, all appear in John Bunyan's seventeenth-century, Protestant allegory *Pilgrim's Progress* (1678), in which Christian journeys from the City of Destruction to the Celestial City, encountering all manner of impediments on the way.

The most obvious differences between different animals are differences of size, but for some reason the zoologists have paid singularly little attention to them. In a large textbook of zoology before me I find no indication that the eagle is larger than the sparrow, or the hippopotamus bigger than the hare, though some grudging admissions are made in the case of the mouse and the whale. But yet it is easy to show that a hare could not be as large as a hippopotamus, or a whale as small as a herring. For every type of animal there is a most convenient size, and a large change in size inevitably carries with it a change of form. 1

Let us take the most obvious of possible cases, and consider a giant man sixty feet high—about the height of Giant Pope and Giant Pagan in the illustrated *Pilgrim's Progress* of my childhood. These monsters were not only ten times as high as Christian, but ten times as wide and ten times as thick, so that their total weight was a thousand times his, or about eighty to ninety tons. Unfortunately the cross sections of their bones were only a hundred times those of Christian, so that every square inch of giant bone had to support ten times the weight borne by a square inch of human bone. As the human thigh-bone breaks under about ten times the human weight, Pope and Pagan would have broken their thighs every time they took a step. This was doubtless why they were sitting down in the picture I remember. But it lessens one's respect for Christian and Jack the Giant Killer. 2

To turn to zoology, suppose that a gazelle, a graceful little creature with long thin legs, is to become large, it will break its bones unless it does one of two things. It may make its legs short and thick, like the rhinoceros, so that every pound of weight has still about the same area of bone to support it. Or it can compress its body and stretch out its legs obliquely to gain stability, like the giraffe. I mention these two beasts because they happen to belong to the same order as the gazelle, and both are quite successful mechanically, being remarkably fast runners. 3

Gravity, a mere nuisance to Christian, was a terror to Pope, Pagan, and Despair. To the mouse and any smaller animal it presents practically no dangers. You can drop a mouse down a thousand-yard mine shaft; and, on arriving at the bottom, it gets a slight shock and walks away, provided that the ground is fairly soft. A rat is killed, a man is broken, a horse splashes. For the resistance presented to movement by the air is proportional to 4 the surface of the moving object. Divide an animal's length, breadth, and height each by ten; its weight is reduced to a thousandth, but its surface only to a hundredth. So the resistance to falling in the case of the small animal is relatively ten times greater than the driving force.

An insect, therefore, is not afraid of gravity; it can fall with- 5
out danger, and can cling to the ceiling with remarkably little trouble. It can go in for elegant and fantastic forms of support like that of the daddy-longlegs. But there is a force which is as formidable to an insect as gravitation to a mammal. This is surface tension. A man coming out of a bath carries with him a film of water of about one-fiftieth of an inch in thickness. This weighs roughly a pound. A wet mouse has to carry about its own weight of water. A wet fly has to lift many times its own weight and, as everyone knows, a fly once wetted by water or any other liquid is in a very serious position indeed. An insect going for a drink is in as great danger as a man leaning out over a precipice in search of food. If it once falls into the grip of the surface tension of the water—that is to say, gets wet—it is likely to remain so until it drowns. A few insects, such as water-beetles, contrive to be unwettable; the majority keep well away from their drink by means of a long proboscis.

Of course tall land animals have other difficulties. They 6
have to pump their blood to greater heights than a man, and therefore, require a larger blood pressure and tougher blood-vessels. A great many men die from burst arteries, especially in the brain, and this danger is presumably still greater for an elephant or a giraffe. But animals of all kinds find difficulties in size for the following reason. A typical small animal, say a microscopic worm or rotifer, has a smooth skin through which all the oxygen it requires can soak in, a straight gut with sufficient surface to absorb its food, and a single kidney. Increase its dimensions tenfold in every direction, and its weight is increased a thousand times, so that if it is to use its muscles as efficiently as its miniature counterpart, it will need a thousand times as much food and oxygen per day and will excrete a thousand times as much of waste products.

Now if its shape is unaltered its surface will be increased 7
only a hundredfold, and ten times as much oxygen must enter per minute through each square millimetre of skin, ten times as

much food through each square millimetre of intestine. When a limit is reached to their absorptive powers their surface has to be increased by some special device. For example, a part of the skin may be drawn out into tufts to make gills or pushed in to make lungs, thus increasing the oxygen-absorbing surface in proportion to the animal's bulk. A man, for example, has a hundred square yards of lung. Similarly, the gut, instead of being smooth and straight, becomes coiled and develops a velvety surface, and other organs increase in complication. The higher animals are not larger than the lower because they are more complicated. They are more complicated because they are larger. Just the same is true of plants. The simplest plants, such as the green algae growing in stagnant water or on the bark of trees, are mere round cells. The higher plants increase their surface by putting out leaves and roots. Comparative anatomy is largely the story of the struggle to increase surface in proportion to volume.

Some of the methods of increasing the surface are useful up 8
to a point, but not capable of a very wide adaptation. For example, while vertebrates carry the oxygen from the gills or lungs all over the body in the blood, insects take air directly to every part of their body by tiny blind tubes called tracheae which open to the surface at many different points. Now, although by their breathing movements they can renew the air in the outer part of the tracheal system, the oxygen has to penetrate the finer branches by means of diffusion. Gases can diffuse easily through very small distances, not many times larger than the average length travelled by a gas molecule between collisions with other molecules. But when such vast journeys—from the point of view of a molecule—as a quarter of an inch have to be made, the process becomes slow. So the portions of an insect's body more than a quarter of an inch from the air would always be short of oxygen. In consequence hardly any insects are much more than half an inch thick. Land crabs are built on the same general plan as insects, but are much clumsier. Yet like ourselves they carry oxygen around in their blood, and are therefore able to grow far larger than any insects. If the insects had hit on a plan for driving air through their tissues instead of letting it soak in, they might well have become as large as lobsters, though other considerations would have prevented them from becoming as large as man.

Exactly the same difficulties attach to flying. It is an elemen- 9
tary principle of aeronautics that the minimum speed needed to keep an aeroplane of a given shape in the air varies as the square root of its length. If its linear dimensions are increased four times, it must fly twice as fast. Now the power needed for the minimum speed increases more rapidly than the weight of the machine. So the larger aeroplane, which weighs sixty-four times as much as the smaller, needs one hundred and twenty-eight times its horsepower to keep up. Applying the same principle to the birds, we find that the limit to their size is soon reached. An angel whose muscles developed no more power weight for weight than those of an eagle or a pigeon would require a breast projecting for about four feet to house the muscles engaged in working its wings, while to economize in weight, its legs would have to be reduced to mere stilts. Actually a large bird such as an eagle or kite does not keep in the air mainly by moving its wings. It is generally to be seen soaring, that is to say balanced on a rising column of air. And even soaring becomes more and more difficult with increasing size. Were this not the case eagles might be as large as tigers and as formidable to man as hostile aeroplanes.

But it is time that we pass to some of the advantages of size. 10
One of the most obvious is that it enables one to keep warm. All warm-blooded animals at rest lose the same amount of heat from a unit area of skin, for which purpose they need a food-supply proportional to their surface and not to their weight. Five thousand mice weigh as much as a man. Their combined surface and food or oxygen consumption are about seventeen times a man's. In fact a mouse eats about one quarter its own weight of food every day, which is mainly used in keeping it warm. For the same reason small animals cannot live in cold countries. In the arctic regions there are no reptiles or amphibians, and no small mammals. The smallest mammal in Spitzbergen is the fox. The small birds fly away in winter, while the insects die, though their eggs can survive six months or more of frost. The most successful mammals are bears, seals, and walruses.

Similarly, the eye is a rather inefficient organ until it reaches 11
a large size. The back of the human eye on which an image of the outside world is thrown, and which corresponds to the film of a camera, is composed of a mosaic of "rods and cones" whose diameter is little more than a length of an average light wave.

Each eye has about a half a million, and for two objects to be distinguishable their images must fall on separate rods or cones. It is obvious that with fewer but larger rods and cones we should see less distinctly. If they were twice as broad two points would have to be twice as far apart before we could distinguish them at a given distance. But if their size were diminished and their number increased we should see no better. For it is impossible to form a definite image smaller than a wave-length of light. Hence a mouse's eye is not a small-scale model of a human eye. Its rods and cones are not much smaller than ours, and therefore there are far fewer of them. A mouse could not distinguish one human face from another six feet away. In order that they should be of any use at all the eyes of small animals have to be much larger in proportion to their bodies than our own. Large animals on the other hand only require relatively small eyes, and those of the whale and elephant are little larger than our own.

For rather more recondite reasons the same general princi- 12
ple holds true of the brain. If we compare the brain-weights of a set of very similar animals such as the cat, cheetah, leopard, and tiger, we find that as we quadruple the body-weight the brain-weight is only doubled. The larger animal with proportionately larger bones can economize on brain, eyes, and certain other organs.

Such are a very few of the considerations which show that 13
for every type of animal there is an optimum size. Yet although Galileo demonstrated the contrary more than three hundred years ago, people still believe that if a flea were as large as a man it could jump a thousand feet into the air. As a matter of fact the height to which an animal can jump is more nearly independent of its size than proportional to it. A flea can jump about two feet, a man about five. To jump a given height, if we neglect the resistance of the air, requires an expenditure of energy proportional to the jumper's weight. But if the jumping muscles form a constant fraction of the animal's body, the energy developed per ounce of muscle is independent of the size, provided it can be developed quickly enough in the small animal. As a matter of fact an insect's muscles, although they can contract more quickly than our own, appear to be less efficient; as otherwise a flea or grasshopper could rise six feet into the air.

THE THINKING PROCESS

STRUCTURE

1. Examine the last sentence of paragraph 1 and the first sentence of paragraph 13. Which is the essay's thesis? What is the function of the sentence that is not the thesis?

2. Cause and effect is a mode of thought and organization basic to scientific study. Note in the margins where Haldane uses this mode. Mark where he uses examples and definitions. How do these other techniques of exposition support Haldane's overall pattern of cause and effect?

3. Haldane begins the body of "On Being the Right Size" by explaining essential proportion, in this case the proportion of bone to weight. To what extent is the concept of proportion tied to the mode of cause and effect?

4. Consider the progression of Haldane's essay. The body of the article starts with giants and the necessary relationship of bone to weight; it ends with cats and the relationship between weight and brain. Why might Haldane present his explanations in the order he does?

STYLE

1. Humor, surprise, understatement, exaggeration are all techniques a writer can draw upon to enliven a subject. What examples can you find of these techniques in Haldane's essay? What audience can you infer for the essay? Given Haldane's audience and subject, how effectively does he engage the reader?

2. How would you characterize Haldane's tone? Is it formal or informal? If formal, is it pompous, academic, intellectual, what? If informal, is it casual, colloquial, intimate, conversational? What words or phrases can you cite that help establish the tone you deduce?

3. Most handbooks will warn you about beginning consecutive sentences with the same syntax, yet in paragraph 5, Haldane introduces four sentences with the same phrasing. What effects does Haldane achieve with this technique? To what extent does the parallelism contribute to or detract from the paragraph's impact on the reader? Where else in the essay do you find examples of parallel phrasing?

4. Where in the essay does Haldane use scientific words and phrases? How does he explain them—by context, example, synonym, formal definition? Do any need further definition?

IDEAS FOR A FIRST DRAFT

Our understanding of the physical world rests upon certain scientific laws and theories. Haldane, for instance, refers to the law of universal gravitation to explain the relative effects of a fall from a considerable height. Depending upon your interests and scientific knowledge, choose one of the major laws or theories basic to one of the sciences: the theory of relativity, of chemical bonds, of evolution, Planck's quantum theory; or Boyle's law, the first or second law of thermodynamics, Mendel's laws. Your aim is to write a paper explaining your subject to an adult audience more familiar with the phrase than the principle (for instance, your classmates).

Or perhaps you would rather work on a paper that explains a technical term crucial to a scientific, technical, or social science discipline. In that case, think of a word or phrase that has a complex, specialized meaning, such as the concept of the black hole, probability, solid state physics, systems analysis.

Your college textbooks will provide a clear explanation of your subject, but you will probably need to know more about your topic. Many texts include a bibliography for each chapter, and specialized encyclopedias usually list a brief bibliography for each important entry. Using the sources at your disposal, work out the cause-and-effect relationships central to your subject. To make relationships comprehensible, you might note in the margins of your draft the examples, analogies, and comparisons that would help your audience follow your explanation. Also look for places where you will need to stop and define terms, as does Haldane. Like Haldane, you might want to begin with the idea that we take certain things for granted and then follow with your thesis. And you may wish to conclude with a short restatement and a dispelling of a myth.

THE WRITING PROCESS

INVENTION

If you are working on a previous assignment in this chapter, you already have a rough draft and can skip to Organizing and Developing. If not, start with a general area of interest to you or with the specific career you have in mind. If you intend to specialize in medicine, you might want to recreate the role of a medical detective and report on how a recent outbreak of botulism, lead poisoning, or Legionnaire's disease was tracked down. Rather you may want to report on one of the diseases that have recently received popular attention: AIDS, Alzheimer's disease, herpes, heart disease, cancer. Or you may choose to investigate new developments in the treatment of disease, such as organ transplants and prosthetics.

If you are majoring in engineering, you know that engineers face a similar explosion in new techniques and designs. Recent discoveries that stabilize soil, for instance, have made it possible to build skyscrapers in areas with a high water table, and new developments in automobile technology have lead to safer, more fuel-efficient cars with fewer toxic emissions. Not all modern engineering feats have been successful, however, and you might want to explore the design or construction faults that led to a specific bridge or dam collapse, airplane crash, or major hotel fire.

If your interests are more general, you can still find a subject that appeals to you—ecology or space exploration, for example. Think of questions you would like answered, and don't be deterred if the answers are not definitive. No one may know if life exists in space, but current scientific discoveries combined with mathematical probabilities can point us toward answers. Recent information from space probes, for instance, have changed the traditional scientific views of Mars and Saturn and even of our moon. Any of these subjects or their spin-offs would make good topics for a paper. Perhaps you are concerned with the ecological issues that face us: Just how real is the threat of acid rain or the destruction of the earth's ozone layer? How can toxic wastes be disposed of safely? What are some of the successful non-chemical ways of combatting insect pests?

After you have selected a topic that intrigues you, work out your reader's preconceptions, the questions you have, and the sources you might use. Your readers probably know as much about your subject as the readers of *Time* or *Newsweek.* At this initial stage, your sources will probably be general ones that will lead you to more specific books and articles. You should consult, for example, the *Reader's Guide*, the card catalogue, the *New York Times Index*, the *Index Medicus*, the *Applied Science and Technology Index*, or the *General Science Index.* An encyclopedia entry may provide background information. After you've consulted general sources, talk with a professor in the area of your topic and with the science librarian. Your lists of questions and sources will continue to grow as you conduct your research.

ORGANIZING AND DEVELOPING

Two obvious ways to organize your notes are by questions and answers or by causes and effects. Whatever your subject, you can focus your paper on one overriding question and on a number of smaller ones. If you want to adopt this pattern of organization, rearrange your notes under the headings of the various questions. When you write your first draft, you can use the major question in the title and the smaller ones as subheads, one for each section of the body of the paper. Papers under 2000 words usually are too short to be divided into sections, so when you review your draft, try turning the questions into declarative topic sentences. To provide paragraph variety, try experimenting with the placement of the topic sentence by putting it in the beginning, middle, and end positions. Then take your major question and decide if you want to keep it as the title or incorporate it into an introductory paragraph. See too if you want to leave it as a question or rework it into a statement.

If you decide to use cause and effect to organize your paper, sort out your notes accordingly, but be careful: a cause can have an effect that in turn becomes a cause, and so on. If you set out a specific time line, odds are your cause-and-effect relationships will fall into place. Someone tracking down the source of an outbreak of food poisoning, for instance, would start with the effect, that is the symptoms, and then try to discover the cause. Writing about a known disease, however, presents a slightly different situation. You would start with the symptoms and then discuss the probable causes and possible cures, which may take you from the past to the present and into the future.

Writing the introduction is where your notes on the readers' preconceptions come into play. If the attitude toward the topic is apt to be negative, then try to catch your readers' interest from the first. Use a narrative or a startling statistic; try suspense or irony. Even if you don't have to worry about a negative reaction, you will still have to sustain your readers' interest beyond the initial attraction of the topic. One of the techniques mentioned above might work, or you might aim the paper at a specific audience and address them directly. An article on bypass surgery, for instance, is apt to be of particular interest to those affected by heart trouble.

The concluding paragraph might summarize what science does and does not know about the subject, indicate the unanswered questions, set the topic within a larger context, or predict what developments may occur and when.

FINDING A VOICE

Reread your draft, paying particular attention to your word choice. Have you used any technical terms? If so, double-check to make sure they are explained in context, or that you've included a brief definition. Is your diction more formal or informal? Which best suits your audience? Also consider the role you play in your paper. Are you an invisible narrator, or do you use first person? If you do use first person, make sure you don't shift the reader's focus from the subject to you.

You want to keep a low profile yet at the same time impress upon your reader that you are intelligent, knowledgeable, and credible; that you have known what questions to pose; have chosen sources wisely; and thus are worth listening to. Pay particular attention to your use of sources, checking to see that you have made their information your own while still acknowledging them. If you string together quotations, the reader may question your ability to assimilate material; if you mention too few sources, the reader may wonder if you've done your homework.

POLISHING

Check with your instructor to see if your sources should be incorporated into the paper or placed as footnotes or end notes. Ask if you can use the method of documentation called for in your major, or find out what system you should use. Then check to see that you have documented all your secondary material.

Outline your paper, using the traditional method of Roman and Arabic numbers, capital and lower case letters. Expand the outline into at least three levels (I., A., 1.), noting the content of each level. See if the outline reveals any holes, an A. not followed by a B., for example. Fill in any gaps you discover. Then reread your outline labeling each level's rhetorical function: *example, definition, comparison, analogy,* and so on. (Your first paragraph may appear as I., its subject as "Brief History," and its function as "introductory narrative.") Next review the outline to see where the thesis appears. If it is implied instead of explicitly stated, check the elements of the outline to make sure that they all contribute to the paper's implication.

To evaluate your style, read the paper aloud and mark any spot that seems awkward, trails off, or causes you to misread. These are the sentences you need to revise.

THINKING AHEAD

If your topic is related directly to your major, make a list of the basic sources that you found useful—bibliographies, encyclopedias, crucial journals, indices—together with a descriptive sentence or two for each one. When you next need to research a topic in that area, your time will be spent more efficiently. Also write down the system of documentation required in your field and the source in which it is fully explained.

To assist in future writing assignments, you might note any trick or gimmick you used that you found successful. Poor spellers, for instance, find that they catch more errors if they proofread from end to beginning; reading the last sentence first and so on makes each word stand out because the sentence is separated from its context.

PART 3

THE WRITER AS EVALUATOR

We depend on evaluations by auto mechanics, electricians, industrial designers, engineers, and pathologists. We also rely on the expert judgments of jewelers, realtors, art collectors, and rare stamp dealers. And we trust the opinions of psychologists, sociologists, economists, lawyers, and criminologists.

The writer's repertoire offers many roles for the evaluator—critic, reviewer, analyst, commentator—and all require similar skills. Good evaluators must be able to mediate among their personal observations and responses, their research and factual data, and the external standards established for reasoned judging. They should be able to put aside their personal biases and prejudices, gather their information with impartiality, and shape their material for their audience—the final judges.

In this section, we have divided the role of the evaluator into the reviewer and the analyst—two frequently used rhetorical stands. The reviewer usually evaluates current cultural events—books, films, plays, movies, concerts, and the like—while the analyst considers and reconsiders nearly everything else from stock market trends to presidential addresses. The analyst discerns, weighs, inspects, digests, speculates, synthesizes, and then renders judgment. While most evaluations are more complex, averaging from 2000 to 6000 words, most reviews are short essays of 500 to 2000 words.

In order to be a credible evaluator, you must not only know yourself, your subject, and your audience, but also the established standards and criteria essential to the subject at hand—whether aesthetic, cultural, or technical. Obtaining this knowledge is only half the trial; writing it down is the other half. To have your audience consider your evaluation seriously, you must convince your readers that your powers of observation are acute and accurate, that you have conducted your research thoroughly and fairly, that you have performed your evaluations objectively and impartially, and that you have considered your readers' needs and best interests. The voice of the evaluator is one of authority, of expert opinion, of careful consideration and deliberation.

Though analysts are not necessarily argumentative, they reach judgments and support them. Thus the writers of the article on cake mixes that follows clearly make judgments, but they do not try to persuade us to scrap mixes altogether; nor do they dissuade us from buying the lower-rated brands. So too, the author of "The Confrontation of the Two Americas" does not recommend one candidate over another, and Donald Hall, in his literary analysis, simply lays bare the process of explication to reveal the delicate machinery of a poem.

In reviews as well as in analyses, writers may express personal opinions, but these opinions do not become the driving force of the piece as they do in argumentative essays. Though the line between review and argument is thin, we can see that Peter Rainer and Tom O'Brien encourage their readers to see the movie *E.T.* by focusing on the qualities of the film rather than on their partiality. John Bull tantalizes us with a dinner at Le Train Bleu through vivid gustatory and visual imagery. And not only by his opinion, but by the force of his detailed analysis, John Pluenneke takes us on a short Continental tour as he reviews *The Europeans.*

Evaluations are integral to our lives. As citizens, as

employer or employee, as teacher or student, we are evaluated—by officers of the law, by customers, by supervisors, by professors. Written evaluations are also often essential to hiring and to promotions. They demand judicious, balanced appraisal, and because they are composed by human beings about human beings, to be read by still other human beings, written evaluations are difficult to compose. A well-written evaluation can make a crucial difference in an individual's career.

In the first section, The Writer As Observer, we explained the differences between a personal observation of a wolf and a report from an encyclopedia. An evaluation of the wolf's distant relative, a dog named Djinn, appears in Evelyn Waugh's dark comedy *A Handful of Dust:*

> Djinn . . . was a very unrepaying dog who never looked about him and had to be dragged along by his harness; . . . when loosed he stood perfectly still, gazing moodily at the asphalt . . . ; only once did he show any sign of emotion, when he snapped at a small child who attempted to stroke him; later he got lost and was found a few yards away, sitting under a chair and staring at a shred of waste paper. He was quite colourless with pink nose and lips and pink circles of bald flesh round his eyes. "I don't believe he has a spark of human feeling," said Marjorie.

The writer observes, the writer reports, and through the character of Marjorie, the writer evaluates. Whether comic or crucial, evaluations are central to our lives and to our writing.

CHAPTER 6

THE REVIEWER

All of us rely on informal evaluations—an assessment of a car mechanic, a new computer, a just-discovered restaurant, an old friend, a new acquaintance, our health, the day at work or school. Yet word-of-mouth "reviews" are often incomplete and rarely impartial.

Formal, written reviews, however, are based on standards and values established most often by experts in the field. They range in length from short paragraphs to a dozen pages, and they vary in subject from books and films, to plays and concerts, to restaurants and speeches, to television shows and live performances. Yet their purpose is always the same: to inform the readers about the subject and to appraise its quality.

Reviewers, then, report on their subjects, but they go beyond reporting to make judgments. Thus in his review, John Pluenneke not only provides factual information about *The Europeans* but also likens reading it to "the rich pleasures of conversation with an urbane, widely traveled, elderly acquaintance who has spent his entire adult life seeking out interesting people and important trends."

The word *review*, of course, originally meant "to look again," and a good reviewer considers and reconsiders the subject after the immediacy of the experience. The reviewer, or critic, is a writer who expresses judgments of recent cultural events according to certain standards or values that vary from expert to expert and from culture to culture. Reviewers who write for specialized audiences know their audience's values and use them to shape their reviews. The review for *Mademoiselle*, for instance, emphasizes *E.T.* as entertainment while the review for the Catholic periodical *Commonweal* assesses the film's religious significance.

Thus reviewers can provide their own opinions after attempting to formulate exact judgments according to aesthetic standards and cultural values. A film critic may not like horror films, for instance, and may make that bias known in the review; yet he or she is still expected to judge a new film of that genre by using standards established by horror classics like *Frankenstein*, *Dracula*, *Phantom of the Opera*, and *Invasion of the Body Snatchers*.

As you read the reviews in this section, you will notice that though the critics may incorporate their own experiences into their evaluations, not one reviewer here expresses judgments in the first person. Peter Rainer comes closest in his review of *E.T.* when he writes: "It can make you feel indescribably happy or indescribably sad; I can't recall a fantasy film that was so simple, yet so moving." Here Rainer tempers his opinion with second person and qualifies his praise. He does not say that *E.T.* is the best film he's ever seen (though it may be); rather he states that *he*, personally (implying other film experts might disagree) cannot remember a "fantasy film" (not any film, but one in a particular genre) that was "so simple, yet so moving" (not "best," "greatest," or other similarly vague terms).

In the course of your reading, you'll find reviewers creating a variety of styles, from casual to very formal, from humorous to sophisticated. But even the most casual review incorporates the technical vocabulary required by established standards. Examine, for instance, the specialized diction in a simple restaurant review by John Bull in his weekly column "Dining Out." And even the most formal reviews often relieve their formality to include second person, placing the reader at the scene in the heart of the experience.

Reviewers do not try to persuade their audience to skip a film, avoid a restaurant, or ignore a book; rather they present the information in the light of past evaluations and trust the readers to make their own decisions. Some moviegoers might enjoy overly sentimental love stories. Some restaurant-goers might prefer elegant decor and atmosphere to the quality of the food.

Readers soon learn to recognize a columnist's particular biases and know how much weight to give the evaluation. Sometimes columnists become popular, not because they are impartial critics, but because they write entertaining reviews. Gene Shalit's fans, for example, may appreciate his humorous style more than his evaluations. As a form of writing, the review may appear insignificant, yet clear and entertaining prose will always attract an audience. ❧

JOHN PLUENNEKE

An Informal Tour of Europe As A State of Mind

John E. Pluenneke, a Senior Editor for *Business Week,* was based in London for five years and supervised the magazine's foreign news coverage. Thus he is an appropriate reviewer for Luigi Barzini's book, *The Europeans.* The review appeared in the June 20, 1983, issue of *Business Week.* One of the most prestigious business publications, *Business Week* "reports and interprets the week's news about all phases of business—production, labor, finance, marketing, research, economics, exports, transportation, labor relations, and new products." Published weekly since 1929, *Business Week* now has a subscription list of 763,000, as well as Industrial and International editions of 10,000 and 71,000, respectively.

As you read the review, see if you can discover how Pleunneke tailors his writing for his audience.

The "improbable funny burlesque character" received a group of foreign journalists. "His mustache surprised me. It had a third dimension that was not apparent in photographs. It was thick and bristled horizontally forward, somewhat like the quills of a porcupine, almost as far as the tip of his nose. . . . I was fascinated above all by his tearful eyes. . . . I told a friend that he had the eyes of a bird dog or a hound. My friend corrected me: 'No. He has the eyes of an orphan.' " 1

2 It was 1934, and the mustache and tearful eyes were those of Adolf Hitler, Germany's new chancellor, as seen by a young Italian journalist, Luigi Barzini. In his new book, *The Europeans*, Barzini recalls the meeting: "When my turn came, Hitler shook my hand, held it for a while between his two, looked steadily at me, and delivered a short statement for my benefit. Sometimes I like to think he delivered to me personally a pregnant political proposal which, if relayed to the right persons, followed through, and made the basis for negotiations, could have prevented World War II. Whatever his short speech meant, it was wasted on me. I did not understand a word."

3 Barzini, who later spent the war under arrest for his antifascist views, never saw Hitler again. But his job as a newspaper correspondent took him all over Europe in a long and varied series of assignments that has now enabled him, at 75, to sum up impressions gathered during a journalistic career that spans 45 years.

4 The result is the kind of book that accurately reproduces the rich pleasures of conversation with an urbane, widely traveled, elderly acquaintance who has spent his entire adult life seeking out interesting people and important trends. Conversational in style, anecdotal in construction, *The Europeans* is an informal tour of Europe as a state of mind, plus discussions of the British, Germans, French, Italians, Dutch, and Americans as seen through European eyes.

5 One of Barzini's recurrent themes is that the Europeans, like the young Italian journalist listening to the German madman, simply do not understand one another. An important source for many of these misunderstandings—apart from national pride—has been, Barzini writes, the self-destructive aping of the British by the establishments of other European countries.

6 It was not auspicious for European unity, therefore, to encounter residual traces of haughty British disdain for continentals after the end of World War II. "Didn't the ordinary inferior human beings still begin at Calais?" writes Barzini, describing the attitude. "Most of them were bizarre, slippery, and often incomprehensible. They ate incredible things such as octopuses, frogs, and snails."

7 At times the emulation of things British could reach startling extremes or, in the case of men's attire, funereal ones. "The continental aristocracy and elite abandoned the glossy silks or

the vivaciously colored worsteds of previous generations for opaque fuliginous wools, generally imported from across the Channel," Barzini notes. "In the end, everybody—statesmen and bankers, kings and emperors in mufti, scientists, rentiers, revolutionaries . . . all dressed like clergymen, undertakers, seconds at a duel, or as if in mourning."

The look of fine English tailoring did not reach the masses 8
in the streets, however. Barzini tells of "an Italian count, who prided himself on the meticulousness of his English elegance." Visiting London with his manservant, the count sent the servant out into the streets the first morning to see how the natives were attired. "Signor conte," the man reported, "there is nobody in London dressed like an Englishman except you and me."

According to Barzini, European ideas of America are equal- 9
ly superannuated. There is, he says, "an antique, family-album view of America that should not be dismissed [because] it is still very much alive." This is an America believed to be "a virile, proud, unafraid country led by a conservative, moneyed, Protestant oligarchy of gentlemen who lovingly followed British examples of the previous century, handled the economy with skill, were addicted to monopolies, and adored the almighty dollar."

Superimposed on this "like layers of successive snowfalls" 10
are other Americas: World War I, World War II, Truman's America, and the doubts and controversies of the contemporary U.S. The upshot is a country seen as healthy and hardy, if somewhat turbulent, "which in the end always finds its way." To be sure, this is not a consistently held view. Even America's closest friends in Europe are sometimes thrown for a loss by what they regard as bizarre or erratic action. Barzini quotes Helmut Schmidt's celebrated sigh: "They are what they are, but they are the only Americans we have."

Barzini, like any good journalist, has a deft way of sketching 11
physical appearance. Konrad Adenauer's "old and wrinkled face reminded you of an ancient turtle or a Japanese mask." Valéry Giscard d'Estaing, "a bloodless upper-class economist," looked "vaguely like a Protestant bishop." The author also has a flair for arrestingly sweeping aphorism: "De Gaulle gave the French the monarchy many of them longed for under every republic, and at the same time the republic many of them longed for under every monarchy."

Organizationally, however, Barzini's book is a hopeless 12

hodgepodge, rambling on interestingly but with scarcely any evidence of a framework. What organization there is comes naturally from the treatment of the various nationalities in separate chapters. There is no index—it could have been useful—and the book shows some evidence of haste, particularly in proofreading. For a book leaning so heavily on the dropping of names, for instance, it is shocking that the surname of French President François Mitterrand is consistently misspelled.

THE THINKING PROCESS

STRUCTURE

1. Why does Pluenneke begin with a quotation? What is the effect of withholding the name of the person he introduces in the first paragraph?

2. A reviewer needs to speak to a variety of issues when analyzing the book at hand: the author, a general description of the contents, organization, style, theme, strengths, flaws, and any special features—for example, photographs. Does Pluenneke discuss each element? Which paragraph(s) does he devote to which topic? What principles lie behind the sequencing of the paragraphs?

3. A writer's thesis can be overt—neatly stated in one sentence—or more subtle, forcing the reader to deduce it from various sentences in the work. What is Pluenneke's thesis? If it is obvious, which sentence is it? If it is subtle, which sentences are crucial to it?

STYLE

1. A good reviewer should provide enough information about a book's contents and style so that the audience can decide whether or not they want to read it. What elements in Pluenneke's review would encourage his *Business Week* audience to read *The Europeans?* What elements might dissuade them? What in the review attracts you to the book? What puts you off?

2. Quotations provide necessary details about a book's style and content. Nevertheless, reviewers must balance the quotations they select with their own analysis or they will end up with a mass of undigested quotations. Mark the quotations that Pluenneke uses. Approximately what percentage of his review do they make up? Are they appropriate? How or how not? Does Pluenneke achieve a balance between text and quotations? Would you eliminate some or add others?

3. Even though reviewers should try to present their material objectively, they necessarily form opinions about their subjects. Does Pluenneke project his own personality in his review? How would you characterize his personality? What details lead you to draw the conclusions you do? What are Pluenneke's feelings about *The Europeans?* What details point to these feelings?

4. Reading between the lines, judging from what Pluenneke praises and criticizes and from the quotations he selects, what standards do you find he uses to judge the book? Do you find these standards similar to other reviews you have read? How or how not? Does Pluenneke present these standards directly or indirectly?

IDEAS FOR A FIRST DRAFT

Select a book that you have read recently, and make notes under the following headings: *author, style, organization, plot, theme, special features, sample quotations, audience.* Using a separate page for each element, write a paragraph describing that element, and write a paragraph or two considering accuracy, completeness, thoughtfulness, and complexity. Under special features, for instance, you may have noted photographs and a thorough index. If the book is a biography, photographs add another dimension to the printed portrait, and the index would be invaluable to a researcher; both of these facts and assessments would be incorporated into your paragraph, which would probably be introduced with a summarizing topic sentence.

After you have sketched out a paragraph for each aspect, decide on your overall reaction to the book: is it positive or negative? Go back over your notes and paragraphs to find the elements that caused your reactions. Try using these elements to pinpoint the book's strengths and weaknesses.

Determine what standards of evaluation you wish to use. You may rely on past discussions of books in class or on other reviews that you have read. This determination is difficult, so you will probably need to consult your instructor. Also, you need to consider an audience for your review. Your audience may be based in part on the book itself. Some books are written explicitly for specialists and would have little or no interest for the general audience. Are you writing to the general public, to an intellectual audience, to an audience that prefers humor, to college-aged readers, to some other readers? Determining an audience might be easier if you imagine a specific place of publication—your school newspaper, a local publication, a national magazine.

Consider what overall organization might best suit your purpose. You can arrange your material by elements, weaving the pros and cons throughout the review, or you might begin with the favorable and end with the unfavorable (or the other way around), sorting out the elements into those two categories. Having written each paragraph on separate pages, you can juggle them to see which order is most effective.

After you have determined an appropriate order, work on making the transitions between paragraphs smooth and effective. You now have the body of the paper and lack only introductory and concluding paragraphs. Try opening with a brief attention-getting narrative or quotation from the book and then closing with a summary of its salient features.

PETER RAINER

E.T. The Extra-Terrestrial

Peter Rainer, the author of the first review of *E.T.* reprinted in this chapter, is a movie reviewer for *Mademoiselle*, a "fashion and beauty magazine for young women" that includes articles on travel, entertainment and decorating, college and career, fiction and poetry, features, book and movie reviews, and recipes. *Mademoiselle* is a monthly magazine with a circulation of 1,065,659. With that description in mind, see if you can determine the average age group and the sophistication of *Mademoiselle*'s readership.

Steven Spielberg's *E.T. The Extra-Terrestrial* is the funniest, most magical fantasy-adventure film since *The Wizard of Oz*. It can make you feel indescribably happy or indescribably sad; I can't recall a fantasy film that was so simple, yet so moving. Spielberg and his screenwriter, Melissa Mathison *(The Black Stallion)*, have accomplished the near impossible: With the help of E.T. designer Carlo Rambaldi, they've created a spindly, dwarf-sized, lizard-necked, flat-topped munchkin of an extra-terrestrial—and they make us care about it as we would a human. Only artists with a direct pipeline to childhood imaginings could accomplish that. 1

The story is about an orphaned extra-terrestrial adopted by a trio of children: Elliott (Henry Thomas), who is perhaps eight or nine; his older brother Michael (Robert MacNaughton); and their baby-doll little sister (Drew Barrymore, John's granddaughter). This new addition to the family is like a wonderful toy. It can levitate tennis balls, rejuvenate flowers and mimic human speech; in one breathtakingly lyrical scene, E.T. and Elliott fly across the moon on a bicycle. 2

The bond between E.T. and Elliott is the heart of the film. Even though we never find out how old E.T. is, or even if it has a gender—Elliott insists it's a boy—the two are soul mates. (Elliott, in some ways, feels orphaned himself—his parents are divorced.) We see E.T. as Elliott sees it, as a lopsided but beautiful creature whose human-looking eyes are so expressive and intelligent we always seem to know what it's thinking. E.T. isn't treated as a pet by the children; it's more like an honored guest. The underlying sadness, however, is that E.T. wants to return home. 3

Children, Spielberg seems to be saying, are the predestined welcoming committee for the extra-terrestrials; their innocence and sense of wonder make them spiritually closer to E.T. than to the adults of their world. The one adult sympathetic to the outer space visitor is a NASA scientist (Peter Coyote) who looks strikingly like a grown-up Elliott; he tells the boy, "Ever since I was ten I've been dreaming of this." In this film, as was true in *Close Encounters*, adults who have retained their childlike awe are the true believers. And, ultimately, just as in the fairy tale, their beliefs are vindicated. 4

Within the context of the sci-fi fantasy genre, Spielberg has spun a simple little fable that encompasses more about love and friendship and separation than do most serious films. And he incorporates references to some of the great children's classics of the past: *Peter Pan, Bambi, Alice in Wonderland, The Wizard of Oz* and, of course, the *Star War* movies—*E.T.*'s lineage. Like those films and books, *E.T.* is the sort of experience parents will want to share with their children. There's something restorative about a movie that convinces you childhood is an enraptured time when anything is possible and everything is magical. 5

THE THINKING PROCESS

STRUCTURE

1. Rainer obviously likes *E.T.* Does he have a thesis that supports his overall view? If so, is it implicit or explicit? Which sentence is the thesis, or which comes closest to expressing the thesis? What are Rainer's criteria for evaluating a film? To what extent are those standards reflected in his thesis?

2. What elements are common to all films? Which of them does Rainer consider here and which does he omit? What reasons can you think of for his choices? What principle(s) can you discern behind Rainer's sequencing of his paragraphs?

3. Examine each paragraph in the review, and see if you can identify its topic sentence. What paragraphs have clear topic sentences? Where in the paragraphs are those sentences placed? What pattern can you find in that placement? Does each paragraph have a topic sentence?

STYLE

1. In his introductory paragraph, Rainer uses a variety of modifiers. Underline them. In paragraph 1, what is the difference between the group of modifiers in the first two sentences and the group in the last two? Do you find Rainer's use of modifiers effective? Why or why not?

2. Parentheses either pack information into a sentence or add an incidental thought. Good writers, nonetheless, use parentheses sparingly. To what use(s) does Rainer put parentheses in paragraphs 1–4? Do you find his use effective?

3. Writers rely on punctuation to clarify their ideas and to build in pauses that aid in reading. Rainer uses semicolons, colons, dashes, and commas with some frequency. Select a sentence that relies heavily on punctuation, and rewrite it so that you change the punctuation. (The second sentence of paragraph 3, the first and last of 4, and the second sentence of 5 are good examples.) Read your version and the original sentence aloud. What is gained? Lost?

IDEAS FOR A FIRST DRAFT

List all the elements that you consider essential to a film. Then turn to Ideas for a First Draft following the next reading.

TOM O'BRIEN

Very High Sci-Fi

The author of the second review is Tom O'Brien, an English teacher at the Manhattan School of Music and an occasional film reviewer for the biweekly Catholic magazine *Commonweal.* A magazine that covers public affairs, religion, literature, and the arts, *Commonweal* is at the opposite end of the spectrum from *Mademoiselle.* Although both reviews are appropriate to their audiences, the differences are more striking than the similarities. The reader of *Mademoiselle,* for instance, is not apt to know that the "*l'homme moyen sensuel* who lives in one of Spielberg's Ville Nouvelles Condeaux" is the modern man of average sensibilities. The reader of *Commonweal,* however, is expected to recognize the French phrase.

After you have read both reviews, determine which you think is the better of the two by comparing both information and style. Which review do you think more fully explores the meaning of the film? Which gives more attention to the techniques associated with film? If you haven't seen the movie, which review better captures your interest and why?

1 The summer's crop of science fiction movies proves two things. First the price of special effects may have risen from a dime a dozen but a good story is still hard to find. Second, despite all the novel gizmos, something old remains at the center of the best films, a strong if heterodox religious sensibility which

uses special effects to evoke the marvelous and uncanny. In a famous essay, "The UFO Is a Religious Symbol," C. G. Jung suggested that modern man appropriates machine images to his own magical purpose, and turns the stuff of science to myth and religion. No filmmaker does this better than Steven Spielberg, a suburban animist with a tinge of Manicheanism.

Watch Spielberg's pizzas, watch his toys, dolls, and train sets. In *E.T.*, watch his use of Coors beer and Pez candies. On one level, this mass of details explains part of the appeal of his films—the lovingly nostalgic recreation of American life, particularly suburban life, that engages viewer sympathy, tickles humor, and establishes credibility for the weird events about to happen. On another level, however, these physical, almost palpable recreations of the material world are not the antithesis of Spielberg's interest in the uncanny; rather, their intensity explains it. 2

Consider only the opening scenes of *E.T.*: we are saturated in an atmosphere of Fresca and Coke, game boards and softball mitts, video games and ringing telephones, pets and unwashed dishes. Spielberg's televisions are always on and always full of—what else?—commercials; the stage business of his films reads like a combined Sears catalogue and grocery list. But only someone so overwhelmed by this proliferation of things could so need religion that he has to invent one—or at least something supernatural—to believe in. Spielberg's roving camera shots of sunlit but emotionally vacuous California settings underline in panoramic terms what his details imply: amid all these things, something is missing, something (as in *Poltergeist*), is unaccounted for. 3

Science fiction as a genre developed historically in concurrence with science, the industrial revolution, and modern material civilization; America in the 1960s, when Spielberg grew up, was simply the apex of these developments. His "materialism" is thus an inversion of the so-called "post-materialism" of those in his generation who dropped out or pursued unlucrative careers. Instead of revolting against things, however, Spielberg presents a private vision: he sees through them. In his films, kitchen chairs suddenly become possessed *(Poltergeist)*, a woodshed becomes alive *(E.T.)*, or mashed potatoes—in a classic scene from *Close Encounters*—become a key to finding extraterrestrial life. To the spiritually enlightened—the kids in the recent 4 films, or Richard Dreyfuss in the older one—ordinary things open up to reveal unearthly wonders. E.T.'s plaintive cry, "Home!" is thus not just the center of his story, but an expression of Spielberg's own religious longing for a transfiguration of earth.

Spielberg's animism is complicated by the religious extremism which he shares, to some degree, with other directors of science fiction. According to their plots, whatever comes out of a spaceship must either save us or destroy us; no E.T. can be the kind of *l'homme moyen sensuel* who lives in one of Spielberg's Villes Nouvelles Condeaux. His own E.T., despite all the fuss over his creation and engineering, belongs to hallowed moral tradition—from films like *2001, Superman,* or the earlier *Red Planet Mars* and *The Day the Earth Stood Still*—where something or someone Godlike or Christlike saves, or at least renews, humanity—or reaffirms its best impulses. If in doubt, check out the print ad for *E.T.*, borrowed from the Sistine Chapel. 5

Curiously, Spielberg almost made a science-fiction film in the other tradition—alive in films like *Blade Runner* or *The Thing* (an awful remake of a 1951 classic)—where humanity must confront demonic and sadistic threats and where Apocalypse hovers in every special effect. According to Kathleen Kennedy, who co-produced *E.T.*, its original plot was "about an extraterrestrial siege, an attack," in which we would see "ten or twelve creatures in a rather unsympathetic light—scared, frightened, and at the same time, very aggressive." According to Kennedy, however, "Steven became so uncomfortable with the idea of horrific aliens descending to earth and hurting people, which was completely an opposite point of view from what he had done with *Close Encounters*, that the story had to change." As much as Spielberg's change of heart, "completely the opposite" is the key here; in sci-fi, there are only two options, angels or devils. 6

In effect, Spielberg gives us something like the rejected E.T. in *Poltergeist*, although that film is not exactly sci-fi but the closely related ghost genre. Produced, co-written, but not directed by Spielberg, the film suffers from several divisions of responsibility, and the plot involving the demonic is weak. One notes, moreover, that the operative demon gains leverage because of human evil—developers careless about some old cemeteries when bestowing progress on one of Spielberg's archetypal condo wastelands. The poltergeists belonging to the corpses aroused by 7 this mistreatment are enlisted by a satanic force, terrorize a family, and are finally, if fitfully, exorcised. Despite this hocus-pocus, however, the haunting is chilling and well prepared: beware the dead pet bird at the film's opening and the initial excavation for the swimming pool. Beneath affluence and rational exteriors, the film implies, lie unrepented sins ready to explode and destroy the (slightly funky) sanctity of a Spielberg home.

In *E.T.*, the sanctity of home is threatened too, but not by 8
the alien, who is cloaked in extensive religious symbolism. A child befriends him with offerings of M & M's, Coke, and Pez (an evocative anachronism from Spielberg's childhood); the whole scene looks curiously like a sacramental ritual. With the child at school, E.T. has a "field day" at home, learning the letter "B" from TV's *Sesame Street*, mastering computers, raiding the refrigerator, and finally guzzling Coors, another communion symbol. By telepathy, when E.T. drinks, his friend at school belches and grows woozy. In addition, the crucial events of the plot occur on Halloween, All Saints Day, and All Souls; when E.T. dies, he has the power to rise again. He can make bikes leap into the sky at a single bound. His UFO has a spire. When he leaves, his message to the child parallels some words of Christ at the Ascension.

The real aliens in *E.T.* (like the developers in *Poltergeist)* are 9
the "establishment": scientists, police, teachers. They first patrol the house after their suspicions are aroused by geiger counter readings; they hover around like a stalking pervert from "Quincy" or, with a radio car to listen in, like the Gestapo in resistance films. We never see their whole bodies; the camera views them at waist level, like the biology teacher whose frog dissection class the child disrupts when inspired by a new respect for life. In effect, the camera thus mimics a child's physical point of view; it also turns the adults into disembodied, dissected, humanoid forms of power without heart or head. When they finally invade the house, the child's mother protests, "This is my home," echoing some of E.T.'s homesickness. But even she can't see him; when her little girl tries to introduce them, she knocks him down with a refrigerator door, missing him amid all the things in her kitchen. In the film's best scene, she misses him in a closet because he looks exactly like the dolls stored there. In Spielberg's universe, only as a child can you enter the kingdom.

Spielberg's defects are glaring: escapism, romanticism about 10 children, a counter-cultural depiction of alienation, both literal and figurative. Nevertheless, he has great power to lift the soul and move the heart by combining great effects with small, and in the past such gifts have usually been called art. As a mythmaker, however, he shares the defect of other creators of science fiction, not excess but defect of imagination. Their substitute religion is based on an unspiritual premise: something physical is going to save or destroy us, depending on whether the E.T.'s involved are angelic or satanic. If extra-terrestrial intelligence exists, however, it might just be morally mediocre, however bright at engineering (like the Swiss, for example). It never occurs to any sci-fi director or writer, except Swift—who was, naturally, thought mad—that alternate physical worlds, whatever the differences of their creatures in size and shape, must in the nature of things be as gray as ours, as haunted by defect and excellence. Such imaginings would demythologize the skies, and bring us back to square one, where real belief in the spiritual was required. Spielberg's limit is that things inhabit the other side of his things. But other worlds aren't *other*, and salvation is more uncanny than special effects.

THE THINKING PROCESS

STRUCTURE

1. What implicit standards does O'Brien use to judge *E.T.*? Given those standards, state the reviewer's thesis. What sentence or sentences of O'Brien's come closest to your version of the thesis? Why might the author have positioned his thesis where he does?

2. Often a writer uses a theme to unify an essay or review. O'Brien, for instance, relies on the idea of religion. Where in the review does he introduce this theme? Where else does he incorporate it? How does religion influence his standards of evaluation? His thesis?

3. The last paragraph begins with two sentences that state some of the film's faults and successes. What sentences in the previous paragraphs prepare the reader for these statements? What other connections can you find between the conclusion and the earlier paragraphs?

STYLE

1. Usually a writer's diction is relatively consistent, whether formal or conversational. O'Brien, however, alternates between formal and informal diction. What examples can you find of informal or colloquial words? Be prepared to discuss in class the effect of his changes in diction levels.

2. Credibility is essential for all writers, but particularly for argumentative essayists and reviewers. O'Brien's diction and sentence structure as well as the information he chooses to include can contribute to or detract from his credibility. What personal and professional characteristics does O'Brien appear to possess? What image do these characteristics project? What information and techniques contribute to that impression?

3. Like Rainer, O'Brien uses the semicolon, colon, and dash frequently. Select one of these marks of punctuation and compare both authors' use of it. What differences do you note? What similarities? Which of the two writers uses which type of punctuation more effectively? How so?

IDEAS FOR A FIRST DRAFT

Jot down the titles of several movies you've seen recently. List the following categories, filling in the appropriate information: *credits* (actors, director, producer, screenwriter, etc.), *story line, characterization and acting, dialogue, photography, editing, themes, location,* and *costumes* and *special effects.* If any other features strike you as significant (music, for example) list them as well. Determine your basic response to each film on your list, and then select the film that you have the most to write about. What genre does it belong to? What are the "classics" within the genre? Determine your audience and what tone you want to adopt in your review. You may want to shape your review for an audience of your peers, for your instructor, or for a particular periodical.

On separate pages, write a paragraph for each element that you consider noteworthy, so that you can juggle the pages to determine an overall order. Which element is essential? Least significant? Number the elements in order of importance. Are there any you want to omit? To stress at the expense of others? Figure out what paragraphs you want to include, and number them according to their order of presentation. What principle have you used to arrange the paragraphs?

Is there an overall context in which you can place the film that would serve as a framework for your review? You might think of starting with some mention of similar films familiar to your readers and ending with an evaluation of how your film rates within its genre. If it's a fear- and suspense-film, for instance, is it closer to the psychological terror of *Psycho* or to the physical horror of *Friday the Thirteenth?* Is it destined to be a classic or just another spinoff?

JOHN V. R. BULL

Food Matches Elegant Decor

A staff writer for the *Philadelphia Inquirer,* John V. R. Bull writes weekly reviews of area restaurants in his column "Dining Out." The restaurant he evaluates in the June 19, 1983, article that follows is located in King of Prussia, a suburb of Philadelphia. Bloomingdale's, Bloomies' for short, is a long-standing, sophisticated New York department store that only in the last twelve years opened branches in the Philadelphia area. The *Inquirer,* servicing the area since 1829, has a circulation of 416,605, and since the demise of the *Evening Bulletin* in 1982 is the only substantial local paper.

Bloomingdale's knows a lot about merchandising. But restaurants? 1

Well, if you visit Le Train Bleu, the classy restaurant at the Court at King of Prussia, you'll find that Bloomingdale's does indeed know a lot about food service. 2

The restaurant on Bloomies' third floor is copied after the Blue Train, the famed 19th-century French luxury dining car: Masses of mirrors, brass fixtures, and walls and ceiling covered with rich green, quilted fabric create a stunning decor. 3

Beveled mirrors in place of windows reflect brass candlestick lamps with gorgeous turn-of-the-century, peach-colored silk 4 shades, their scalloped edges bordered in black. The mirrored reflection of these beautiful lamps is breathtaking as you look down the length of the extra-wide train.

5 Tables are set with white linen tablecloths and napkins, and comfortable chairs upholstered in green. Overhead are brass luggage racks and Victorian light fixtures with crimped glass shades. Elaborate silk flower bouquets grace recessed nooks paneled with mirrors; classical music plays softly in the background.

6 The imaginative, beautifully prepared food is just as delightful as the decor.

7 Creamy, silk-smooth chicken liver paté ($3), rich in cognac and spicy from little green peppercorn bursts, was garnished picture-pretty with cornichons, tiny Niçoise olives, a cherry tomato half with serrated edges, and a sprig of parsley. Shrimp appetizer ($5) offered three firm shrimp in a crisp, beer batter, with a delicate, slightly sweet dipping sauce of orange marmalade touched with ginger and horseradish.

8 The main courses were delightful. Small, tender cubes of lamb curry ($10) came in a slightly spicy brown sauce sprinkled with grated coconut. Along with sultana-flecked saffron rice, the lamb had a lid of crisp, deep-fried Indian bread. Spicy mango chutney was filled with crisp apples and onions.

9 Pillow-soft Florida bay scallops ($9.50) in *crème fraîche* sauce that was grainy with tiny crunches of chopped hazlenuts, was prettily sprinkled with julienned carrots. Vegetables of the day were red-skinned potatoes with chopped parsley and a medley of sauteed mushrooms, wild rice, and julienned carrots and zucchini.

10 The chef does not slight desserts. Linzer torte ($3.50), an uncommonly rich cookie batter with raspberry jam, was accompanied by real whipped cream sprinkled with orange zest. White chocolate mousse (also $3.50), light in texture but rich in flavor, was colorfully topped with grated chocolate, pistachio nuts and a candied violet. The egg-rich custard of *crème brulée* ($3.75) quivered beneath a thin layer of carmelized brown sugar. Complimentary Bloomingdale's chocolate coins accompanied the check.

11 Service, while not overly friendly, was almost *too* efficient: It was nearly impossible to get the waitress to stand still long enough for me to ask for water or a fork replacement.

Le Train Bleu
Bloomingdale's, the Court at King of Prussia.
Telephone: 337-6290
Open: Lunch 11 a.m.–3 p.m. and dinner 5:30–9:30 p.m. Mon.–Sat. Closed Sun.
Price range: Dinner for two about $35
Credit cards: American Express, Bloomingdale's
Atmosphere: Stunning

THE THINKING PROCESS

STRUCTURE

1. Does Bull's review have a thesis? Is it explicit or implicit? If explicit, which sentence is it? If implicit, which sentences suggest it?

2. A writer can organize a restaurant review in several ways: by aspect—from positive to negative or from negative to positive; by chronology—from entering to leaving, from soup to nuts; by dramatic order—leading up to the best or to the worst aspect; or by combining methods. What pattern(s) of organization does Bull use in his review of "Le Train Bleu"? To what extent do you find the organization effective?

3. Because restaurant reviewers deal with such diverse elements as decor, food, and service, they need to construct transitions that lead the reader naturally from one element to another. Examine Bull's transitions. What are they? Are they functional and unobtrusive?

4. The bordered block of information is standard in the column "Dining Out." What does it add to the review? Why is the information presented in that format rather than integrated into the text of the review?

STYLE

1. Titles of reviews should encapsulate what the writer considers essential about the subject under evaluation. Bull's title, originally a headline, is appropriately brief and informative, but try devising other appropriate titles for his review. Which improve on Bull's? Which fall short and why?

2. One of the challenges in reviewing a restaurant is appealing to the reader's gustatory, tactile, and visual senses. If the review is largely positive, as is Bull's, then the reader should be tantalized. If negative, the reader should feel queasy (but not repulsed). Examine the sentences in paragraphs 7 through 10. What is the secret of Bull's vivid description? Try changing three of these sentences from positive to negative by substituting your own adjectives, verbs, and adverbs in place of Bull's. Some negative examples from another review of Bull's read that the shrimp was "slightly over-cooked," the meat "was over-cooked, tough and stringy"; "a restuffed potato with soggy skin was eminently forgettable"; the service was "molasses-slow." Can you make your descriptions equally effective? Notice also that Bull incorporates the second person in paragraphs 2 and 4. What is the effect of this usage? Is it effective or ineffective? How so?

3. Restaurant reviewers rely on sophisticated vocabulary, not only to evoke sensual responses but to describe the food and decor precisely. Make a list of the furnishings Bull describes in paragraphs 3 through 5. How many details does he pack into each paragraph?

4. One problem the writer encounters when describing food and decor is that both are static, and repeating the verb *to be* dulls mind and palate quickly. Underline the verbs Bull uses in his review. What active verbs does he use to make Le Train Bleu and its offerings come to life? Because he focuses on the food and not on the preparer, Bull is forced to use the passive voice more than a writer normally would. What are the passive verbs he uses? Are they varied? Try changing several sentences to active voice. Which is more effective? Why?

IDEAS FOR A FIRST DRAFT

When evaluating a restaurant, the reviewer must consider the food, the service, the decor, the atmosphere, the clientele, and the cost. The challenge is to appeal to the gustatory and tactile senses of your readers as well as to the visual. As a reviewer, you first need to sharpen your powers of description.

You might want to warm up for your review by writing a paragraph that focuses on a single course. The best place for this study is at home, at the school cafeteria, or at a casual restaurant where your note-taking can be surreptitious. Concentrate on one course and make notes about its visual appearance, texture, and taste. If you are keeping a journal, record your observations there.

For a longer paper, jot down the names of some restaurants you know well or perhaps some you'd like an excuse to visit. The restaurants can vary from the school cafeteria and pizza parlors to French or Thai. But remember to restrict yourself to reviewing the kinds of food you are familiar with, so that you have some basis for relevant standards. Most restaurant reviewers dine out with friends so that they can taste several dishes, have help identifying ingredients, and can survey others' opinions. When reviewing a pizza parlor, for instance, you must know whether the mushrooms are fresh or canned, whether the dough and seasonings are consistent, and which toppings are best. So unless you're prepared to eat several pizzas by yourself, go with some friends or make a couple of visits.

After you've selected and visited your restaurant and made your observations, jot down notes as soon as possible after the meal. You are now prepared to begin drafting your review. Consider your audience. Are they college students? Local residents? Tourists? A combination? How familiar are they with the cuisine you will be describing? What terms will you need to define? What expectations might they have?

Decide on the best way to organize your review—by aspect, from positive to negative or from negative to positive; by chronology, from entering to leaving or soup to nuts; by dramatic order, leading up to the best or worst aspect; or by combining methods. Number your notes in the order you wish to use them, and write separate paragraphs to flesh out the different aspects that you're evaluating. After an initial sketch, if you want to rearrange your paragraphs, number them according to the new sequence, or cut them out and rearrange them, taping them to new sheets of paper.

Finally you are ready to write an introduction and a conclusion. Your introduction might identify the type of restaurant under review, the location, the owner, the chef, or it might present a general statement of your reaction. The conclusion may be a restatement of your reaction, a summary of minor aspects not complex enough for separate paragraphs, or a comparison of your restaurant with others of similar cuisine in the area. And you might want to add a block of information like Bull's.

THE WRITING PROCESS

INVENTION

If you are completing an assignment in this chapter, you already have a rough draft of a review and can skip to Organizing and Developing below. If not, select a TV show that you know well, or a play, a talk, or a concert that you've recently attended. Consider the elements that you can evaluate: a TV show, for example, can be evaluated by examining plot, characterization and acting, dialogue, theme, pacing, emotional and intellectual responses. Jot down notes under each category and any other you consider appropriate. On separate pages sketch out a paragraph for each aspect. Remember to be specific: include, for example, dialogue, lyrics, names of performers, a description of the set, bits of the story line.

Shuffle your paragraphs until you are satisfied with the sequence. Check to see that a principle of organization undergirds your sequencing, and then work on an introduction and a conclusion. You might want to begin with an engaging plot summary, quotation, or narrative and end with a summing up of your opinion. You might start by declaring your opinion and end by restating it, or you might set your review within the context of a particular genre.

ORGANIZING AND DEVELOPING

Reread your paper. Does it have a thesis? If not, would adding one make your paper clearer? Often the reviewer's thesis is simply his or her basic judgment of the subject under consideration.

Have you added a rich variety of support for your thesis and its sub-assertions? Have you discussed all the essential elements? If you have omitted some, have you been fair to your reader by doing so? You may want to include more quotations, a further discussion of plot, an extended context, or a comparison of other works in the same genre. Be cautious. Bringing in too many other plays, films, books, concerts, or restaurants can blur your focus. You may also want to eliminate some of the quotations if they detract from the flow of your paper. And if plot is crucial to your subject, you don't want to disclose too much; you want only to evaluate your subject, not spoil it for your readers.

FINDING A VOICE

Determine your attitude toward what you are reviewing—positive, negative, mixed—and select an audience to write for, perhaps single women, sports enthusiasts, college students. It might help to have a specific magazine in mind, perhaps *Cosmopolitan*, *Working Woman*, *Sports Illustrated*, *Playboy*, or your campus newspaper. Decide what special coverage you want to provide for your particular audience: What elements are apt to concern them most? What elements will you emphasize? Determine the personality you wish to project—enthusiastic, humorous, sophisticated, bored? Try reading your drafts to people who fit your audience, and ask them to describe the character of the speaker your review suggests. If they hear silliness where you meant humor, superciliousness where you meant sophistication, revise accordingly.

POLISHING

Read your paper aloud. Is the tone you established what you really want it to be? Is it consistent? Remember, when writing reviews it is easy to be overly enthusiastic or highly critical. Though you want to project a personality your readers will rely on, your primary aim is to inform your audience about your subject and interest them in the validity of your opinion not in yourself.

Have you opened with a zinger to get your audience's attention? Have you used varied and rich adjectives and adverbs? Have you included vivid details?

THINKING AHEAD

Jot down the trouble spots you encountered. What about the nature of the writer's role caused those problems? Reviews offer ideal opportunities to practice stating a simple thesis and developing it through examples. Reviews also offer suitable occasions to experiment with voice. You might want to write several reviews of the same piece, each in a different voice. You can be savage like John Simon *(New York)*, sophisticated like Pauline Kael (the *New Yorker)*, or humorous like Gene Shalit ("Today").

CHAPTER 7

THE ANALYST

Analysis, whether chemical, mathematical, linguistic, psychological, historical, literary, political, consumer, or product, separates the whole into its parts to discover their nature, properties, function, and interrelationship. While the reviewer considers a recent cultural event—a film, a book, an album, a concert—the analyst examines more complex subjects in greater detail. Like the report writer, the analyst deals with facts and research, but the analyst goes beyond the reporter to interpret the data and to judge it by standards established by experts in the field.

The analyses presented in this chapter represent a variety of subjects: products, literary texts, and political events. Product analysts are closest to scientists in that they strive for impartiality by establishing objective standards and, when possible, by conducting laboratory tests. They present their findings without trying to persuade the reader to take a specific stand or action. "Cake Mixes," to the reader's surprise, is an entertaining and informative study of the boxed mixes on the market today. Though many readers may not care about baking cakes, most care about eating them, and it is this principle that the writers use to attract their audience.

Literary critics set out to explain works of fiction—poetry, drama, short stories, and novels—by using the language of nonfiction. They conduct their evaluations by applying aesthetic standards, and they address their analyses to a specialized audience. The literary analysis included here, Donald Hall's explication of Robert Frost's "Stopping by Woods on a Snowy Evening," is written in large part to introduce the college student to poetry.

Most literary analysis, when not written for specialized journals, is incorporated within other types of writing. Practicing literary analysis has advantages beyond its integration into other forms of writing. It sharpens our sensitivity to the minute shadings of words, individually and in combination, and words are the blood of all writing.

Political analysts examine political events—campaigns, elections, protests, national and international issues—and place them within a historical context. "The Confrontations of the Two Americas" examines the Presidential campaign of 1972 between Richard Nixon and George McGovern. The author examines the particular events of the campaign itself—the reaction of the eligible voters, and the ideals and values projected by the candidates—expanding the analysis to show the two political leaders symbolizing the roots and rituals of our American culture and heritage.

All analysis demands a thorough understanding of the subject at hand—in its broad perspective and in its narrow focus, in its established standards and in its prescribed criteria. Analysis calls for the writer to see the forest for the trees and each tree for the forest.

from CONSUMER REPORTS

Cake Mixes

Consumer Reports is a monthly magazine published by Consumers Union, first issued in 1936, and now boasting a circulation of three million. As the copyright pages explain, Consumers Union is a nonprofit organization accepting no advertising and "not beholden in any way to any commercial interests." Its aim is "to provide consumers with information and counsel on consumer goods and services," and its "ratings are based on laboratory tests, controlled-use tests, and/or expert judgments of the purchased samples."

The magazine is largely a collection of evaluative reports (reports with judgments and recommendations), compiled by a variety of staff and directors, a technical department divided into units such as appliances, autos, chemistry, food, standards, and statistics—each with its own staff and project leader.

The selection below on cake mixes is nearly complete. The only materials excised are recipes for making cakes from scratch and most of the individual ratings of the different brands. Though fifty-eight brands were tested and summarized under "Recommendations," space permits including only a small but representative selection of the actual ratings, to illustrate the writing style employed.

They've taken a lot of the mystery out of cake-baking, but what have they added in return? Only a few of the chocolate, yellow, and white cakes we tested were really good.

Cake has always been more a symbol than a food. In the days when refined white flour was costly and sugar was scarce, cake was a food of the rich, an emblem of status coveted by the poor. Now that most Americans eat princely fare as a matter of course, the status conferred by cake has diminished. 2

But cake remains a ritual food. It accompanies the organized rites of birthdays and weddings. It appears at the conclusion of special feasts. It is eaten in personal rites of indulgence. 3

The ritual aspects of cake extend to the home kitchen, where, tradition has it, the best cakes are made. Central to cake iconography is a tintype vision of Grandmama surrounded by fresh creamery butter, eggs, and flour in a cloth sack. The cakes she made, the layer cakes "made from scratch," have been elevated into legend since the coming of packaged cake mixes in the late 1940's. 4

The packaged cake mix took a lot of the mystery out of baking. Anyone who could break open an egg and wield a spoon or mixer, and who had a fairly constant oven, could produce a decent home-baked layer cake. 5

Ritual is still important, however. The principal ceremony is the breaking open of the eggs. An early version of layer-cake mixes didn't need any added eggs. Home bakers resisted. They wanted to put more of themselves into the baking. So Betty Crocker let them add eggs. 6

During the 1950's, the opening of the Convenience Food Era, cake mixes were basically a handy assemblage of the sort of dry ingredients you would use to make a cake from scratch. 7

By the 1960's, the mixes had been changed. Using a lower-gluten flour and some products of food technology, the mixes produced a higher-volume batter and a fluffier cake. The best home baker would have been hard-pressed to duplicate the results without a mix. 8

The fluffy phase is now drawing to a close. "Moistness" is the new byword, and the "pudding added" cake its manifestation. 9

Pillsbury, one of the three companies that dominate the cake-mix market, was the first to notice that creative home bakers were adding, among other things, instant pudding mix to cake mix to get a moister, richer cake. In 1977, Pillsbury came out with its *Pillsbury Plus* line, with "pudding in the mix." Betty Crocker (a division of General Mills) and Duncan Hines (a divi- 10 sion of Procter & Gamble) followed shortly with their *Super Moist* and *Pudding Recipe* lines. So great was the demand for moistness that General Mills and Pillsbury have dropped their lines of puddingless cake mixes. Supermarket brands now offer mixes "with pudding," too.

But a cake mix plus pudding is a bit of a put-on. Instant pudding is mainly sugar and "modified food starch," both of which can be found in puddingless cake mixes. You, the baker, add to the moistness of pudding-added mixes by adding an extra egg and some oil or butter. 11

Comparing the Cake Mixes. The mixes we tested fall into three broad categories—chocolate, yellow, and white. Some have pudding, some don't. Included in our samples were the products of the three major cake-mix companies, as well as three supermarket brands—*A&P*, Safeway's *Mrs. Wright's*, and *Kroger*. 12

Chocolate is the most popular overall cake flavor, with subflavors ranging from devil's food to milk chocolate. One of those tested is a *Pillsbury Bundt* cake, part of that company's line of ring-shaped *Bundt* cakes begun in 1972. 13

Yellow cakes are the most popular single flavor. Among our yellow mixes are a few pound cakes, usually baked as loaves, and a *Pillsbury Bundt* pound cake. 14

White cakes are far less popular. Included in the white mixes are some angel-food cakes, the only tested mixes to which you add just water. 15

Our sensory consultants tasted the cakes plain, without frosting, so any flaws in flavor and texture would not be disguised. The results of their tests showed that no one company's mixes consistently outdid another's. The results also showed that mixes with pudding didn't taste consistently better—or moister—than mixes without. But our expert tasters did find similarities by flavor: The chocolate and yellow cakes, overall, had fewer flaws than the white cakes. 16

A few cakes earned a Rating of very good. Most of the rest were undistinguished, and some were worse than that. . . . 17

Cake Chemistry. A cake's lightness and evenness of texture depend on complex interactions among its ingredients. In any cake, those ingredients perform certain roles. 18

Flour adds substance. Eggs provide a framework and help 19

emulsify fats or oils in the batter. Leavening raises a cake and makes it light. Sugar is a tenderizer and helps a cake rise higher. The fat or oil found in most cakes is a tenderizer, too, producing a fine, velvety crumb.

Commercial mixes may also contain several ingredients not 20
found in the usual kitchen repertory to enhance a cake's texture. Chemical emulsifiers such as mono- and diglycerides and polysorbate help produce the extremely fine, spongy texture common in cakes made from mixes. So do such ingredients as propylene glycol monoesters, isolated soy protein, and guar or cellulose gum.

When the chemistry of a cake works correctly, the result is a 21
cake with an excellent texture. A few of the mixes produced cakes with just such a texture. The cakes were moderately firm and not crumbly. Their crumb texture was even, and there was enough air in them to make them moderately light. They were quite moist, but not gummy. They didn't stick to the mouth and teeth.

About half the sensory defects found in the mixes were 22
defects of texture. The chocolate cakes tended to be a bit gummy. Most of the white cakes left a residue of fine grit in the mouth—our sensory consultants termed them "chalky." Some of the white cakes were also dry and crumbly. The yellow cakes were often slightly gummy, chalky, or both. Frosting can disguise dryness and, to some extent, chalkiness. But it can't hide such texture problems as gumminess or crumbling.

Artificial flavors. Aside from the textural problems, the 23
other main flaw we found in the cake mixes was the nearly ubiquitous presence of artificial flavors.

As a group, the chocolate cakes had the fewest problems. A 24
chocolate cake is supposed to taste and smell like cocoa or chocolate. Many of those tested did; most just didn't have *enough* cocoa flavor. All had at least some real flavoring in them. But half the mixes made cakes with the tell-tale artificial fruity overtones of a poor imitation-chocolate flavoring. Many of the chocolate cakes also had some vanilla flavor. That's not in itself a defect, but the use of artificial vanilla may have contributed to the fake taste found in some of those cakes.

A yellow cake is supposed to taste and smell like egg and 25
vanilla. Most of ours did. In all but the *Jiffy Golden* mix,

however, the vanilla tasted artificial. Compared to the rich, resounding taste of real vanilla, artificial vanilla has a weak, one-dimensional taste.

The "butter recipe" cakes or cakes with "sour cream" in the title usually tasted even more artificial. Most of them added a fake butter taste (like that of movie-theater popcorn) or a fake sour-cream taste to the artificial vanilla taste. 26

White cakes are supposed to smell and taste of vanilla. In more than half of the ones we tested, that taste was artificial, too. Nearly all the rest tasted instead of some other artificial flavor, generally almond or coconut. Two of the three angel-food cakes also tasted or smelled of dehydrated egg whites. 27

Obviously, cakes are supposed to be sweet. But a few cakes were *too* sweet. A few were also too salty. 28

All but the most egregious of the artificial tastes, our sensory consultants decided, could be successfully covered up with frosting. 29

Recommendations. The three top-rated chocolate mixes produced cakes that were very dark and flavorful, with a good texture. The three were rated very good and had only minor flaws. *Betty Crocker Super Moist Chocolate Fudge* left a faint fruity aftertaste. *Jiffy Dark Fudge* was a bit too dense. And *Duncan Hines Deluxe II Deep Chocolate* left a very slight coating in the mouth. 30

The best of the yellow cakes was not a layer cake but the *Betty Crocker Golden Pound Cake*, rated very good. It was moist and dense, with a mostly vanilla taste. Unfortunately, its vanilla taste was artificial, and its texture was very slightly chalky. The best yellow layer cake was *Jiffy Golden*, rated good. 31

The white cakes were led by the *Pillsbury* and *Betty Crocker* angel-food cakes, rated very good. One was a bit too dry with a slightly uneven crumb texture, the other had a very slight aroma and flavor of dehydrated egg whites. The best white layer-cake was a *Pillsbury Plus* mix, rated good. 32

The majority of the mixes tasted just ordinary. But since a strongly flavored frosting can cover a multitude of flavor and texture sins, you could make a satisfactory cake with nearly any of them. So you might choose a mix by how much it costs. 33

The cheapest mixes were usually *Jiffy* or the store brands, at about 75 cents for two layers' worth. *Betty Crocker*, *Pillsbury*, and 34

Duncan Hines layer-cake mixes generally cost about $1, with *Duncan Hines* typically the most expensive by a few cents. The specialty cakes—the pound cakes, the angel-food cakes, the *Bundt* cakes—were more expensive still, costing from $1 to more than $2 per box. But some of them make larger cakes than the layer-cake mixes.

RATINGS

Cake Mixes

Listed by types. Within types, listed in order of overall sen- 35
sory quality as judged by CU's consultants. Differences between closely ranked products were slight. Unless otherwise noted, each mix makes 2 layers, 9×5-in. loaf, or 10-in. ring. Prices are average paid by CU shoppers.

CHOCOLATE

Very good

Betty Crocker Super Moist Chocolate Fudge. 91¢. Very dark 36
brown cake with mostly cocoa and a little vanilla flavor; less sweet than most. *Defects:* Very slight fruity aftertaste. . . .

Good

Pillsbury Triple Fudge Bundt. $2.05. Very dark brown cake 37
with mostly cocoa and some vanilla flavor and very good, slightly dense texture. *Defects:* Bland; poorly blended flavor; a bit too firm. . . .

YELLOW

Very good

Betty Crocker Golden Pound. $1.03. Moist, dense cake with 38
mostly vanilla and some egg and a little butter flavor; less sweet than most. *Defects:* Vanilla artificial; very slightly chalky. . . .

Good

Kroger Pudding Cake. 81¢. Moist cake with mostly vanilla 39
and a little egg flavor. *Defects:* Vanilla artificial; too salty; not quite firm enough; slightly gummy and sticky. . . .

Fair

Nabisco Dromedary Pound. $1.12. Mostly vanilla and some 40
egg flavor. *Defects:* Vanilla artificial; very slight medicinal

aroma, very slight metallic feeling left in mouth; very slightly chalky and sticky. . . .

WHITE

Very good

Pillsbury White Angel Food. $1.56. Light-textured cake with mostly almond and baked egg-white flavor. *Defects:* A bit too dry; crumb texture slightly uneven. . . . 41

Good

Duncan Hines Deluxe Angel Food. $1.37. Light-textured cake with mostly almond and some egg-white flavor, less sweet than most. *Defects:* Almond flavor artificial; some aroma of dried egg whites and cardboard; too dry; grainy and spongy. . . . 42

Fair

Mrs. Wright's Pudding Delight. 83¢. Moist cake with a little vanilla flavor. *Defects:* Vanilla artificial; too sweet and salty; chalky; dissolved too slowly and became gummy mass in mouth. . . . 43

THE THINKING PROCESS

STRUCTURE

1. What is the function of the title? Of the introductory blurb? Does "Cake Mixes" have a thesis? If so is it explicit or implicit? If explicit, where is it presented? If implicit, state it in your own words.

2. Product analysts divide their evaluations into various sections: background information or history of the product; type and range of products tested; definition of standards and criteria; testing conditions; general results, recommendations, and specific ratings. The list, of course, varies with the nature of the product. What standards do they use to rate cakes? Are they appropriate? What other standards might be used? How is the evaluation of cake mixes organized? Do you find the organization satisfactory or confusing? Why or why not?

3. Examine the specific recommendations of cake mix brands at the report's conclusion (36–43). Do you find the summaries helpful? What four elements are included in each of these paragraphs? Would you include others? Why or why not?

STYLE

1. "Cake Mixes" is an interesting mix of casual and formal language. Find examples of both types. What are their functions? Why do you think the analysis is not purely formal or purely informal?

2. The report includes an elaborate discussion of the importance of cake in our lives and a history of cake mixes. Are these discussions important to the evaluation? If so, why? If not, why do you suppose the writers included them?

3. How does the style describing the individual brands (36–43) differ from that of the main analysis? Is it appropriate? Why or why not?

4. "Cake Mixes" is an unsigned article and is most likely a group effort. The use of *we* and *our(s)* in paragraphs 12, 16, 23, and 25 may indicate multiple authorship, or it may simply be a device used by one writer to establish a tone. Study the prose styles in each section (Comparing the cake mixes, Cake chemistry, Artificial flavors, and Recommendations). Are there variations in style that suggest different authors? If so describe the differences. If not, what tone is established by an individual author using *we?* Compare the voice of the essay here to that of O'Brien in "Very High Sci-Fi." What differences can you deduce between the voice of the reviewer and that of the analyst?

IDEAS FOR A FIRST DRAFT

Cast yourself in the role of a product analyst, and select a product of interest to you, one that is simple to evaluate—perhaps ice creams, colas, tissues, ball-point pens, household cleaners. Avoid complicated appliances and machines like stereo components, computers, and automobiles. Once you have selected your topic, make sure that you can secure a reasonable number of different brands of your product to evaluate—say no fewer than five, no more than twelve.

Next, define the type and range of your product. Make sure the brands you select are comparable. If you choose ice cream, for example, you may decide to limit your tests to either store-bought brands or to specialty shops; it is unfair to compare prepackaged ice cream with ice cream made fresh daily. You will also need to limit your tests to one or two flavors, depending on the number of brands available.

If you are testing products that depend on expert judgment rather than on controlled-use or laboratory tests, you should collect a minimum of three other testers. You must then define the standards and criteria. Keep in mind your audience, the general consumer (which includes family-conscious parents). You can devise the standards using your own judgment and by consulting others. When testing ball-point pens, for instance, you need to consider the consumer, and thus you might decide that clear writing without spotting, skipping, or smearing is essential. Perhaps also essential is the pen writing over grease splotches and when held upside down. Is it important that the pen feel comfortable in any size hand? Is aesthetic appearance a consideration? Perhaps the color of ink and selection of colors is a criterion.

If you are using several testers, make sure that your group understands the criteria—perhaps provide them with a list of what you consider essential or, better yet, draw up the list together before the tests. Make sure too that when tested the brand names remain secret (which may call for blindfolds) and that the conditions for the tests are identical for each brand and for each tester. And don't let your judges confer with one another during the tests. Remember to make sure you take thorough notes. Don't rely on memory.

Once you have obtained your results, try categorizing and summarizing them. Rate your brands. Perhaps construct a chart. (You might want to browse through issues of *Consumer Reports* and study some of the charts presented there.)

Next research the history of your product. When did it come into use? Who was responsible? What was the public reaction at the time? What is the popularity of the product now? If you have a scientific bent, you might want to research the chemical composition or production.

When you begin writing your evaluation, remember that you are an impartial experimenter. Report your findings objectively, but be accurate. It is acceptable to conclude that Brand X ice cream has a grainy texture, a plastic aftertaste, and a noticeably artificial flavor, but it is unacceptable to state that it is *gross, the worst ever, insufferable,* and so on. In other words, avoid imprecise and charged language.

Before you begin writing, consider your audience. You want to engage the interest of the average individual who will use your product, and you want to be clear and informative. If you are discussing technical information, make sure that you emphasize the effects and results, not the terminology. Explain and define only what is necessary. (See paragraph 20 in "Cake Mixes" for an example.)

Organization of your material will depend in part on the nature of your product, but a basic structure might begin with its history, the identification of the types and range of the products tested, and other background information. An explanation of testing procedures and criteria as well as particular problems encountered might follow. A general discussion of results, specific recommendations, and either a chart or a simple summary might conclude your report. You also may want to consider adding headings to divide a long report into sections.

If your instructor wishes, writing a product analysis is a good assignment for a group paper, a frequent business practice. One writer could handle history, another science, a third the testing and writing of results.

DONALD HALL

An Explication of Frost's "*Stopping by Woods on a Snowy Evening*"

Donald Hall is a poet, writer, editor, and teacher. His books of poetry include *The Dark Houses, The Alligator Bride,* and *Kicking the Leaves.* His prose works include *String Too Short to Be Saved, Henry Moore,* and *Remembering Poets.* Hall has edited various poetry anthologies, among them *The Poetry Sampler, Contemporary American Poets,* and *American Poetry,* and he has written several textbooks including *To Read Poetry,* published in 1982, from which this selection is excerpted.

This analysis opens chapter 1 of the text that Hall explains is written "to help students read poetry with intelligence, gusto, and discrimination." Only a short discussion of explication and paraphrase, some incidental comments, and a fuller discussion of ambiguity and poetry are excised.

According to Hall, an explication "tries to account for the whole poem in its sounds, in its minute suggestions of meaning, in its shapeliness." As you read, see if Hall does account for the whole poem in meaning, sounds, and shape.

Stopping by Woods on a Snowy Evening

Whose woods these are I think I know.
His house is in the village though;
He will not see me stopping here
To watch his woods fill up with snow.

My little horse must think it queer
To stop without a farmhouse near
Between the woods and frozen lake
The darkest evening of the year.

He gives his harness bells a shake
To ask if there is some mistake.
The only other sound's the sweep
Of easy wind and downy flake.

The woods are lovely, dark and deep,
But I have promises to keep,
And miles to go before I sleep,
And miles to go before I sleep.

When you've read a poem two or three times—slowly and quickly, silently and out loud, and when you have arrived at a tentative paraphrase—you are ready to go back to the poem and look at it bit by bit, as if you were taking apart a machine in order to understand how it works. 1

Start with the title; sometimes it gives us information we need to understand a poem's wholeness. This title, "Stopping by Woods on a Snowy Evening," is a description or label; it tells us what we're going to see, and then we see it. This particular title requires little work on the reader's part. 2

In his first line—"Whose woods these are I think I know"—Frost turns normal word order around. Ordinary word order would have us say something like "I think I know whose woods these are." By moving *woods* to the start of the sentence, Frost gives it more prominence or power. . . . 3

In the second line, "His house is in the village though," the last word makes no logical sense; *though* or *although* should make some sort of contradiction or qualification to the statement that *I* know who owns this woodlot. But Frost writes as we usually speak—and the *though* qualifies something left out. To understand *though*, we might paraphrase the whole statement, bracketing what is implicit: "I know who owns this land [and I would feel self-conscious if the owner saw me standing and staring into space this way] but he doesn't live out here, and therefore he won't see me pausing to gaze idly." The word *though* implies more than its one syllable would seem able to contain. 4

At the same time *though* implies something, it rhymes with the word that ends the first line. A rhyme word must feel natural 5 or the poet will seem to have chosen it for the sake of rhyming. Looking to the rest of the stanza, we see that Frost doesn't rhyme the next line with anything nearby but that the fourth line rhymes with the first and the second, tying the stanza together. Because we have the word *snowy* in the title, the idea of snow is important to this poem before we start reading it. Then the word *snow* ends a three-line sentence that makes snow the object of our attention. The last two lines of the stanza are a natural, inevitable journey to the culminating word *snow.* As soon as we get there, we realize that this is where we had to go, all the time. This inevitability is underlined by the rhyme, where *know* and *though* build up a sound-expectancy to culminate in *snow.*

Maybe the speaker's self-consciousness is the most important element in the first stanza. (I say "the speaker"—though it feels awkward—because I don't want to say "Robert Frost" and make the mistake of thinking that *I* in a poem necessarily means the poet.) To sense his embarrassment is to catch the tone of voice, the way we all learn to catch the tone of people talking, when we understand by hundreds of small signals whether the person's tone is ironic or straightforward, conniving or sincere. 6

As the stanza ends we learn something besides the speaker's embarrassment; we learn his motive for stopping: "To watch his woods fill up with snow." Frost's language here is plain, but it could be plainer or flatter still; *I* could have said . . . "to look at the snow falling on his forest." Saying *fill up* contributes to the image or picture made by the poet; *his woods* becomes a container—empty or partly empty—which *snow* can fill. 7

As mentioned before, *here* doesn't rhyme with anything around it. If we hold the sound of the word in our ears, however, we are rewarded when we read the first line of the second stanza. We experience the pleasure of completing something begun earlier, like the moment in a piece of music that a theme (or a phrase or a chord) returns. Rhyme in this poem holds parts together, linking stanzas more firmly than many poems try to do. The third line of each stanza, unrhymed to the lines near it, rhymes with three of the lines in the stanza following. The four stanzas together are like four groups of four dancers doing the same dance, with one member of each foursome holding hands with the group beyond it. 8

If it's a dance, it must move to a tune. *Rhythm* is an approxi- 9 mate recurrence or repetition in the pacing of sound; rhythm is fast or slow, staccato or flowing. *Meter,* which is a measure or count of something, puts its own mark on certain rhythms. "Stopping by Woods" is written in meter, and this meter helps define the rhythm of the poem. Counting *evening* as two syllables, in every line the even-numbered syllables (two, four, six, and eight) are louder than the odd-numbered syllables. Not all the even syllables are loud, but they are louder; in *promises, prom-* is louder than the *have* before it, and *-ses* is louder than the *-i-*—just barely louder; you cannot say *prom*-IH-*ses.* This alternation of louder and softer syllables is the meter of the poem. Other matters besides meter contribute to differing lengths of pause at lines' ends. A poet can manipulate punctuation to speed or slow rhythm. . . . Frost uses the line's pause and avoids a comma, which would slow the stanza down more than he wants it slowed. . . . The poet slows his rhythm, however, at the measured ending of the poem, and he puts a comma after *keep.* Notice that Frost manipulates commas only where commas in prose would be optional.

The second stanza, picking up the *here* rhyme, tells us that 10
the *little* horse (*little* sounds affectionate; this person seems to care about his horse's feelings) *must think it queer.* Consider the word *must* as we use it in speech. If we know that it's raining, we say "it's raining"; if we only think so—because of forecasts or the distant sound of falling water—we say "It *must* be raining." We only claim that something must be true if we don't know it for certain. When Frost writes "My little horse must think it queer," he uses the doubtful *must* because he knows a human cannot mindread his horse. The speaker in the poem attributes doubts to his horse because he himself believes it weird or eccentric to stop one's horse for no good reason out in the middle of nowhere to watch snow falling in the darkness. This man's uneasiness shows in his self-mockery: even his horse *must* think he's crazy.

As this stanza continues, ostensibly telling what the horse 11
must think queer, the poet gives us more information, and he gives us information in images that carry feeling on their backs. The road, we learn, passes between *the woods*—which are like a container filling with snow—and the *frozen lake.* Sometimes an image informs us by what it omits. While *frozen* adds cold to the poem (an image records not just pictures but *any* experience of

the senses, like cold), the line also increases the solitude of the scene: the lane runs between wood and lake only, no houses or factories here, no inns or filling stations, just these cold and natural things, on "The darkest evening of the year."

This last detail . . . is strange if we take it literally, and 12
when we read a poem we ought to try at first to take it literally. We cannot take it literally that this man has determined scientifically, using some instrument that measures light, that this clouded—moonless, starless—night contains fewer candlepower units than any other night in the preceding twelve months. . . . Poetry usually works by common sense, not on riddles that ingenuity must solve. It's just too complicated to explain this line as telling us that tonight is the winter solstice. Probably we do best to take the line as an expressive exaggeration, the way people always talk about the weather. . . .

In the third stanza, the little horse does what horses do; he 13
shudders or shakes, standing still in the cold night, and to the driver who still feels foolish pausing to gaze at snow in the woods, the horse's jingling harness bells seem like the horse's reproach. The jingling is another image—so far we've had images of sight (*to watch*), of touch (*frozen lake*), and of sound (*bells*)—and now the sound images multiply: "the sweep / Of easy wind and downy flake." Notice that images often appeal to more than one sense. If *frozen* is an image of cold in *frozen lake*, it is an image of sight also, because we know what a frozen lake looks like. And *the sweep* is a swooshing sound, but it's also (at least distantly) a visual broom moving.

The phrase *easy wind* is not an image at all. We could not 14
draw (or play on an instrument, or hear) an easy wind as opposed to a difficult wind or an uneasy one. Does it mean anything at all to call the wind easy? First let us paraphrase, using alternative words. Perhaps this wind is light and gentle—*easy* as "full of ease," like the softness of *downy* that *easy* is parallel to. If this paraphrase is accurate, someone might ask why the poet doesn't call the wind "light and gentle" or, to keep line length the same, just "gentle." Because *gentle* is not the same as *easy* and *easy* does it better; the paraphrase is only intellectual, and *easy* says it better because of its sound. It is a long and luxuriant word. That long *e* stretches itself out like a big cat on a sofa, and then the *z*-sound (spelled with an *s*) slinks sensuously and stretches again into a shorter *e*, spelled *y* this time. These two

syllables take longer to say than half a line elsewhere in the poem.

I would not argue that "sound imitates sense" in this word 15
the way the sound of *drop* or *squish* is similar to the meanings of the words. (When sound imitates sense, we call it *onomatopoeia.*) I am not sure that a light wind speaks in long *e*s and in *z*s. But I am sure that the grateful tongue delights in this word, picking up the long *e* of *sweep*, looking ahead to the long *e* that ends *downy*, and that these words, giving us in our minds qualities of the scene, at the same time give us a sound-pleasure. We have two pleasures at once, one in our minds as we assent to a description, the other in our mouths as the poet arranges vowels and consonants, much as a chef arranges flavors for our pleasure.

We have concentrated on *easy*. *Downy* gives pleasure also. 16
The *y* picks up the *e* sound earlier in the line; the *ow* picks up a vowel from *sounds* in the line before. (This repetition of vowel sounds is called *assonance*.) If you don't know the word *downy*, look it up. Always look up words you are not certain of. *Down* means a good many things; among others it means goosefeathers, soft and white, and *downy* is an adjective made from the noun *down*. Because down is soft (touch) and white (vision), it gives us two kinds of image at once, and perhaps also distantly gives us an image of the snow as a great white bird. It is also a rural image, connected with barnyard and countryside. . . . Finally, the word *down* works its power on us for at least one more reason: it reminds us of the direction in which, relentlessly, snow must fall.

By the end of the third stanza the poem has erected a dra- 17
matic conflict, like a story or a play. The conflict lives in the mind of the speaker, who attributes one side of his feeling to his horse; of course, it is the speaker who thinks it queer to pause where he pauses; at the same time it is the speaker who stops to gaze into the lovely beauty of the wood, exercising the other side of his feeling. He is "of two minds about it," in the old expression. In the final stanza, mind 1 writes the first line and mind 2 answers with the second, third, and fourth; the mind with the most lines has the last word.

In our daily lives, we are often ambivalent—of two minds, 18
sometimes of three or four—about what we do. . . . In our deepest selves we are never one-hundred percent *anything*, neither loving nor hating, and if we tell ourselves we are pure, we

fool ourselves. . . . This poem is almost *about* ambivalence and its conflicts. . . . What for Frost's speaker was a quarrel between woods and duties can translate, in our lives, into the quarrel between birdwatching or writing a letter. When one set of particulars can stand in for another set of relationships, we have a *symbol.*

Symbols raise another subject: in interpreting a poem, 19
where does the reader stop? Many people find further complexities—"levels," "meanings"—in this poem. Some readers have found this poem suicidal and claimed that it contains a wish to die. People have often tended to look for a death wish in Frost because in his lifetime Frost spoke about suicidal feelings. But should we *therefore* consider that when Frost's speaker looks into the woods he takes the woods as a symbol for death and longs for the darkness of his own death? Not *therefore,* at any rate, for then we would be leaping from life to poem as if it were always possible to make equations between the facts of the life and the facts of the poem.

What can we say, finally, about the meaning of this poem— 20
looking only at the poem itself? Meaning is not paraphrase, nor is it singling out words for their special effects, nor is it accounting for rhythm and form. It is all these things, and it is more. Meaning is what we try to explicate: the whole impression of a poem in our minds, our emtions, and our bodies. . . .

A poem makes a contract with the reader: I agree to use 21
words as thoroughly as I can; you agree to read them the same way.

Because this is a poem, we shall do well to examine even 22
the simplest words. First, we have the bald statement of attraction: "These woods are lovely, dark and deep." The word *lovely* has the word *love* in it, as *downy* included *down.* So the woods pertain somehow to love. *Dark* and *deep* go together, not just for their *alliteration* (the repetition of initial consonants). The woods are dark in this evening, filling up with snow that by definition is white; and they are deep, like a vessel with room for the filling. The woods are mysterious, perhaps a place suitable for hiding, and this sensation of mystery has an attraction like the attraction people feel for each other; so the woods are *lovely. Dark and deep* work together as a double adjective, explaining the *kind* of "lovely." How different the line would be if Frost had punctuated it differently and used a comma after *dark.* "The woods

are lovely, dark, and deep"—pronounced as punctuated—makes a different sound, and even a different *meaning*: the extra comma makes the three adjectives enumerate separate qualities of the wood; in the line as Frost wrote it, instead of enumerated qualities we have a rush of feeling. . . .

Apparently the feelings in this poem are universal, and all of us find in ourselves on occasion a desire to abandon the track of duty, the track of the everyday, and to embrace the peace of nothingness. But perhaps I go too far—in trying to name the unnameable—when in my paraphrase I say "the peace of nothingness." My naming is not so good as Frost's naming, and some readers will prefer their own different naming. "The peace of nothingness" attempts to paraphrase a feeling that for some people apparently sounds suicidal—and for others merely sleepy. My inadequate phrase attempts to bring together the two sides. 23

THE THINKING PROCESS

STRUCTURE

1. Most literary explications are organized in one of two ways: either the poem is analyzed chronologically—line by line or stanza by stanza, or the poem is analyzed element by element—imagery, meter, alliteration, rhyme, and so on. How does Donald Hall organize his analysis? How effective is the organization? Would you change it? If so, how?

2. The primary purpose of Hall's analysis is to explicate Frost's poem. A secondary function, however, is to teach students how to analyze a poem. How does Hall incorporate this latter purpose into his essay? Cite examples in several paragraphs.

3. Explication, like all analysis, deals with the whole in relationship to its parts. One way to structure a paper clearly is to announce in each paragraph what part of the whole that paragraph deals with. Underline each paragraph's opening phrase if it underscores the essay's structure.

STYLE

1. Donald Hall's analysis is a pleasant mixture of technical terms and casual language. Find examples of each. What is his purpose for using casual language in a seemingly formal process like an explication?

2. A poet himself, Donald Hall incorporates similes and metaphors in his prose as do all good writers. Reread paragraphs 1, 5, 8, 13, and 14. Identify the simile or metaphor. What is being compared to what? Is the comparison effective? Why or why not?

3. During his explication, Hall frequently changes point of view. For example, he opens with *you* (1 and 2), then changes to *we* (2), next to *he* as Frost (3), then back to *we* (4), and finally to *I* (6). Some paragraphs include several points of view (6, 7, 15, 16, 18, and 22). What distinctions is Hall making among *I*, *we*, and *you?*

4. As a teacher and a poet—an expert in the field—Hall has his own criteria for what makes a good poem. What standards can you deduce that he is using? Are they implicit or explicit?

IDEAS FOR A FIRST DRAFT

Select a short poem that you find intriguing, preferably one that you've never discussed before. The Middle English lyric "Western Wind" is a good example:

Western Wind when will thou blow?
The small rain down can rain.
Christ, that my love were in my arms.
And I in my bed again.

In order to explicate the poem, to get as close to its meaning as possible, you need to include a discussion of tone, imagery, metaphor, rhyme, rhythm, alliteration, symbols, and other poetic devices and elements of poetic form that you have discussed in class.

Read the poem silently and then aloud several times. Write a line-by-line or sentence-by-sentence paraphrase of the meaning, looking up any words you're not sure of. Then answer the following questions: Who is speaking in the poem? Who is being addressed? What is the speaker's message?

Next on separate pages write out the title and each line of the poem. Identify all the devices you can discover in each line, including rhythm and meter. See whether you can discover any repeating patterns among the lines, for example, in rhythm, alliteration, and imagery. Then consider how the lines interrelate—in meaning, in form, in poetic devices. What do you determine is the overall theme of the poem?

Now you are ready to begin writing your analysis. Open, perhaps, with a general statement of the poem's whole meaning, and then analyze the poem line by line, bringing in as Hall does the different poetic devices and the shades in meaning and implications of single words, the denotations and connotations, that intensify the overall meaning. For a conclusion, return to the whole poem; perhaps discuss symbolism. As with any analysis, your paper should progress from the whole to the parts back to the whole.

For this analysis, your audience can be a classmate much like yourself, who understands as you do the terminology, so you won't have to define any poetic terms. Remember that your purpose is to explicate—to interpret the poem as fully as possible—not to judge its value.

from TIME

The Confrontation of the Two Americas

"The Confrontation of the Two Americas," an unsigned article, appeared as the cover story of *Time* magazine on October 2, 1972, and surveys the 1972 presidential campaign between incumbent President Richard Nixon and Senator George McGovern of South Dakota. In the 1968 election, Nixon had narrowly edged out Hubert Humphrey; this time the polls showed he had a strong lead over McGovern, which the actual vote verified. Nixon's term ended abruptly, however, when he resigned from office in August, 1974, as a result of the Watergate scandal.

Because of its length, "The Confrontation of the Two Americas" appears here in excerpted form. Among the material excised is an analysis by a psychologist and most of the interviews with a cross section of voters, five supporting Nixon, five McGovern. The war referred to (1) is of course the Viet Nam War. And abortion (35) was not yet legal. Hugh Sidey (11) was then and is now *Time's* Washington correspondent.

The country seemed in an odd, suspended mood. The great quadrennial division of the national house to elect or re-elect the President did not yet seem to have seriously begun—or else had already taken place so early and quietly that in effect there would be no real contest. Certainly the campaign has thus far failed to catch the national imagination, a fact that has some- 1 thing to do with the candidates who are running. There was little buoyancy and no euphoria in the American mood, but some of the stronger political poisons seemed to have been drained. The war, taxes, inflation, unemployment, the environment—no one could claim that these issues had disappeared, but they were festering less now. Some curious instauration of the '50s seemed to be at work in the psychology of 1972, almost a conscious revolt against the extravagant, Halloween '60s.

One saw it, for example, on the nation's campuses as the 2
first fragrances of autumn suffused the air and the football season started. If the hair was often as long as before, there was also a *déjà vu* of cardigans, Bass Weejuns and button-down collars. Fraternities were pursuing pledges as if Pat Boone and Johnny Mathis had never gone away. One recent night at George Washington University in Washington, the student rathskeller and the bowling alleys were jammed. Berkeley, cradle of the free speech movement, reverberated to the thock of tennis balls.

In large and small ways, the Republican political effort re- 3
flected and enhanced this mood. By campaigning little, Nixon suggests, as he means to, an air of ordered normalcy, of the business of the country going along as usual. When he does swing out on a rare foray, as he did last week to Texas, there are overtones of other days. His major remarks there were an old-fashioned scolding of "permissive" judges whose leniency from the bench in dealing with hard-drug traffickers is a "weak link" in the attack on the heroin problem. At one point during the trip, visiting a high school in Rio Grande City, he sat down at a piano like Harry Truman and banged out *Happy Birthday* on the old 88 for a Democratic host Congressman while the students chorused the words. In fact, of course, Nixon has moved way beyond the '50s politically and philosophically, as is shown by his major diplomatic moves of conciliation toward the Communist powers and a number of his domestic proposals. But in his manner and calculated appeal, he invites the electorate to come home to an earlier, no longer quite real America.

In contrast, the McGovern campaign marches to the 4
rhythms of the long, Wagnerian '60s: the blacks' upheaval, the war and the defense machine, a generation's uprising (or dropping out), the industrial-ecological dilemma, the battle for privacy, the feminist movement, the sexual revolution. It was in

this context that McGovern's candidacy was shaped and his nomination became possible. For McGovern and his people it is not possible after such events to envision the nation relapsing quietly into some smooth semblance of the middle Eisenhower years. Too much has changed. Another awareness, another America was born in those years of the last decade.

Hurting in morale and above all for money because of his 5
bad showing in the polls, McGovern lashed out: "I think the polls are a lot of rot. I think they make these things up in the back room." Nonetheless, he released his own poll, which showed his cause not nearly so hopelessly behind as the general surveys. Touring the big cities last week, sometimes he was the angry, fundamentalist McGovern. Holding aloft a U.S. pineapple bomb in Philadelphia, he cried, "Does it increase our honor because the color of the bodies has been changed from white to yellow? Their blood is still red. They are still children under God." Before an assembly of unionists in Detroit, where antibusing sentiment runs high, he was uncompromising. With the exception of the war, McGovern said, "there is no darker chapter in the presidency of Richard Nixon than his exploitation of the difficult questions and emotions surrounding this issue of busing." . . .

McGovern is trying to fight his way clear of association 6
with past radical excess. As he told a group of New Jersey labor leaders almost apologetically: "It's nothing radical to call this nation to the principles on which it was founded." The central theme of his candidacy, he argues, is not that darker side of the '60s, but the decade's loftier impulses: civil rights, equality, more open and humane government, the older and classically Democratic concern for the little man against special interests and corporations. In those enthusiasms he has had a wider following, and probably a firmer hold on the future, than his polls would indicate. It was Nixon who first declared that the election offered the clearest choice of the century—and McGovern quickly and happily agreed. Both candidates may have been right. What seems to have intervened is McGovern's personal failure.

Professor Sidney Hook of New York University believes 7
that the country is ready for most of McGovern's domestic proposals, but that "what people fear most is his unpredictability." Or, as a Princeton student told an interviewer scornfully: "You can say that I'm 1,000% behind McGovern." In modifying his

stands on some issues, in failing to control his staff, particularly in the Eagleton affair, whose negative resonance across the country still haunts McGovern to a remarkable degree, the Democratic nominee emerged in the public view as an ineffectual leader and manager. Indeed, his seeming ineptness may well have become the issue obscuring all others, thus diluting the purity of the "clearest choice in a century" between two programs and philosophies. If McGovern is turning off the voters to the extent that the latest polls suggest, it is nearly impossible to determine to what degree they are resisting his program—or their perception of it—and to what extent they merely distrust his effectiveness as a leader.

McGovern's program as amended is actually less radical 8
than many voters seem to think; with some exceptions, it is a quantitative extension of past Democratic propositions, and in some areas it comes quite close to Richard Nixon's own plans. But the two men are nonetheless each embodiments of ideas larger than either of their somewhat unprepossessing personalities. They represent different instincts about America. In their casts of characters and processes, the Republican and Democratic conventions this year said much of it. They suggested almost two different countries, two different cultures, two different Americas.

In the face of the ruinous polls, where is the McGovern 9
America? McGovern apparently commands a majority of only the college young, the blacks and the Jews. But the McGovern constituency, actual and potential, is not a matter of race, economic class or education. Like Nixon, McGovern has support among millionaires, blue-collar workers, suburbanites—not nearly so much as the President of course. But it may be that as an idea, an instinct, the McGovern phenomenon is more widespread than the polls indicate. "In a broad sense," writes Arthur Schlesinger Jr., "the election of 1972 will be the politics of authority and the Establishment versus the politics of change. If McGovern is right on the currents of change, his appeal will reach into every part of our society."

Republicans smile at such thinking as a species of self- 10
delusion. Nixon, they argue, is just now in the process of mobilizing an extraordinary new G.O.P. coalition from blocs pirated from, or abandoned by the Democrats—the South, Catholic ethnics, blue-collar workers, the noncollege

young—along with more traditional Republican voters. Says Kevin Phillips, author of *The Emerging Republican Majority*: "McGovern represents a new radical elite that has taken control of the Democratic Party and alienated much of the traditional party structure in the process."

The ideas of the two Americas can be found deeply laminated in the characters of the candidates themselves. It may be, as *Time*'s Hugh Sidey observes, that the difference is rooted in the Sunday schools of Yorba Linda, Calif., and Mitchell, S. Dak. Richard Nixon was the Quaker, sitting in a tiny loft room with a few neighborhood children beside his father, who was the teacher. The children were taught to look inward. The emphasis was on the individual, what he felt, what he could and should do. Each person created his own world. 11

For George McGovern, there was the constant cry for self-sacrifice, to reach out beyond oneself to help and teach and preach. Personal striving was part of it, but people should be uplifters, missionaries, and should share with the poor, comfort the bereaved. 12

In youth, Nixon carved out his commercial and educational way in a California that was luminous with opportunity, even in Depression days. The Nixons worked hard and suffered, but always there was opportunity through discipline. Sheltered but driven, he was molded by the society of merchants in which he developed. 13

Out in George McGovern's prairie, the dreams faded in the '20s. Mitchell would never be Detroit. For some reason—climate, falling farm prices, no jobs—people left South Dakota. Instead of the sunny optimism that glowed through the hard years in California, there was little more than grasshoppers and blizzards in answer to the prayers of country parsons. They were people who felt overpowered not only by the elements but by other men. McGovern saw it from the front pew, saw it when he hunted rabbits over the parched countryside. Always there were the Scriptures ringing in his head—someone worse off to be helped, someone more unhappy to cheer. 14

Nixon went after personal achievement and material success. Life became a contest where the strong and persistent endured, the controlled and clever won the field. Each person looked out for himself and his, worried about his own life more than his neighbor's. Horatio Alger may have entered McGov- 15 ern's life, but not nearly so much as the apostle Peter. If there was endurance and struggle and self-improvement, it was often related to other people or grander designs. In those small towns of Depression days the churches taught history through the Bible and the music that came out of musty pump organs. There was the faint whiff of adventure from the missionary letters. So McGovern went out to serve people and to understand the world a little better.

Not much has really changed in the two men since they 16
both went off to war. They learned their arts, studied their legislative and political crafts. But Nixon sees the world as an arena of individual initiative, where each man is expected to do all he can within his abilities. His nation, he still insists, is a place of almost limitless opportunity where hard work and brains can bring a man wealth or power, which translate very easily with Nixon into happiness. George McGovern still sees the world as a place of natural cruelties, where strong men are supposed to help others before themselves.

In the world of the presidency, Nixon believes that the peo- 17
ple can pretty much run themselves if left alone. A spirit of laissez-faire—to the point of "benign neglect"—suffuses his thinking. Thus a major purpose of Washington is to guard against too much governmental encroachment. It is ironic that under Nixon, the Government has imposed economic controls and grown bigger than ever. But he believes that he has stirred more initiative in the courthouses and state capitols.

In a more missionary spirit, McGovern would use govern- 18
ment as a moral force to create equal rights, to give to the poor, to provide jobs for the jobless, food for the hungry, security for families that cannot compete, medical care for the old and the very young. He sees government as the problem solver. His view is fundamentally domestic, concentrated on the problems around him that he can see and hear and understand. The foreign scene tends to intrude only in cases like Viet Nam, which he feels is a moral outrage that has depleted the nation's resources.

Nixon, in his preoccupation with personal achievement, 19
with toughness and endurance, assumes finally that almost every American has had the same open field before him as he has had. Classic competitive liberalism too often leaves little room for compassion. His best friends are self-made millionaires.

His inner sense of America harbors no place for failure and limited room for mistakes. Work is all. "Because I believe in human dignity," Nixon has said, "I am against a guaranteed annual wage. If we were to underwrite everybody's income, we would be undermining everybody's character." Yet he himself has proposed a guaranteed annual income. He admires strength, both moral and physical, and equates negotiating strength with military power.

Nixon calls them "the old values"—parental authority, a stand against permissiveness, law-and-order before civil rights. In the process he has presided over increasing surveillance and broader arrest patterns. Despite his praise for traditional values, the question of privacy has been submerged in the fight against crime and subversion. He too often lacks compassion and equates conformity with conscience. He is apt to ignore basic changes occurring in the U.S. by simply conjuring up an image of national well-being, perhaps a sentimentalized vision emanating from the America of his young manhood. 20

McGovern's America, by contrast, is tinged with utopia—a land of peace and prosperity. The rich would still be rich, but a lot less so. The poor would be poor no more. The hungry would be fed, the unemployed would have work, crime would be curbed, schools and hospitals built and the drug pushers jailed. There would be no war, but the nation's defenses would remain strong. Aid for Israel, but none for Viet Nam. The environment would be cleansed. Inflation would end. 21

It is a glowing vision, but is it realistically attainable? And if so, how much would it cost to sustain it? Most of his life, McGovern has been an influencer, a talker, a thinker. He has the visionary sense, but his campaign thus far reflects his distaste for details, for organization—a quality that has disturbed many American voters, even among his own followers. 22

Each candidate has a resonance to his own America. Within each constituency, voters repeat their candidate's themes and even rhetoric with a precision that is sometimes eerie. A one-word common denominator prevails in the Nixonian America: the sense of "system." The free enterprise system, the law-and-order system, even the "family unit" system—they are the recurring images among Nixon supporters. Their antonym is "chaos," not utopia. They are apprehensive of the disorders that the late 23

'60s adumbrated to them, the turmoils that they suspect a McGovern accession might bring.

In two weeks spent in interviewing Nixon supporters across the nation, *Time* Correspondent Champ Clark found that "Nixonians are not against change. I have yet to meet one who wants the U.S. to stay exactly the way it is. But they have in kindred spirit a sense of orderliness, of tidiness. They are fond of saying that their political stance is 'evolutionary, not revolutionary.' It was in this meaning that Richard Frank, vice president of Schenley Distillers, Inc., rolled his eyes heavenward and summed up his political desires: 'Please don't rain on my parade.' " 24

The Nixon nation is a varied and obviously populous place. The issues of the campaign, strangely enough, strike little fire—the talk is apt to be more of principles. Where Nixon supporters do discuss issues, their opinions tend toward the predictable: "peace with honor" in a war that the President inherited and is only trying to end—just don't turn it over to the Communists overnight. (It is interesting that the word Commie has all but disappeared from the political lexicon.) No amnesty for draft resisters. Busing is bad, or else does not matter much any more. 25

Nixonians generally are against wage and price controls in principle. But in practice they are not so sure. McGovern's economics, they agree, would be disastrous, especially the Senator's proposals to tax capital gains as regular income. Welfare arouses even more emotion—against it. A retired Floridian summed up the Nixonian attitude: "Give 'em a shovel." 26

• Ewell Pope is a 44-year-old self-made Atlanta millionaire who came back from Korea with a Silver Star, a Purple Heart and a lucidly aggressive desire to "aspire and achieve in the system." Today he is a partner in Crow, Pope & Land Enterprises, one of Atlanta's largest real estate developers. Having grown up on a tiny Georgia farm, he feels entitled to declare: "This country has always been a place where anyone who was willing to work at it could rise up to some degree." He is antiracist: "If someone asked my wife to sit in the back of the bus, I'd be the meanest man alive." He explains part of the reason he is voting for Nixon: "The political values of this country are mainly middle-class. Because this group believes in human rights, people have sometimes been too anxious to right any human wrong 27 that occurs, and they have given the Federal Government powers to go in and right what seems wrong at the time. But you are never going to get those powers back from the Federal Government. I have been in almost every country in the world by now. Every time I get a little bit upset with our system, I can still come back and marvel at how great it is." . . .

• Sanford Fray, 58, a black optometrist in Harlem, disputes 28
the Democrats' complete hold on black Americans. "Our country needs a strong President if we are to survive," he says, explaining why he favors Nixon. "There is no doubt in my mind that McGovern will get a lot of votes in Harlem, it being a heavy welfare area. But America didn't become great by the inhabitants sitting down and stretching their hands out to the Federal Government. You know, I can't get an errand boy. It's more profitable to be on welfare."

If in Nixon's America the language tends to be angular 29
and mechanical, to speak of systems and order, in McGovern's nation it is a more humanistic vocabulary of "decency," "compassion" and "integrity." The idea of "a restoration of faith in government" recurs, a vaguely spiritual impulse focusing on confidence and trust. If Nixonians talk of what is "right with the country," McGovernites almost by definition are impelled by a sense of what is wrong with it and what could be better. They express a sense of the U.S. gone awry, of government wrested from the people to serve unholy ends—a war the people did not want, or corporate privilege.

In two weeks of interviews in McGovern's America, *Time*'s 30
Gregory Wierzynski found that the operative word is almost always "tone"—to change the tone of government, of the country. A young McGovern pollster, Pat Caddell, explained his feelings: "It is more a question of moral leadership than of program. It is the goal of reconciliation and salvation, of the spirit he gives the country more than the bills he proposes or programs he initiates." Yet if McGovern's America is a reflection of his personality, the man himself evokes none of the adulation that characterized, say, the John and Robert Kennedy campaigns, or even the Eugene McCarthy campaign. Even among his own faithful, he comes across as a cool and somewhat distant figure, perhaps a touch pedestrian. No waves of shrieking teen-agers engulf him; his cuff links are always in place when he emerges from a crowd. . . .

• Harold Willens, 58, calls himself "a dyed-in-the-wool capitalist." A wealthy Los Angeles realtor, he started out in utter poverty. "McGovern," says Willens, "is a man whose concerns are deeply human and deeply moral. As things are, we are putting our money where our myths are—like the myth of the domino theory—and we napalm little children and contravene the ideals for which this country was founded. We have lost our soul in Indochina, and this has created a fantastic crisis of confidence. People have lost faith in their Government, and the economy depends on confidence in our democracy." Nixon, says Willens, "is looking at the world through a rear-view mirror. Meantime these devastating problems are creeping up on us. We need leadership that's interested in the country and the world rather than its own hang-ups—clichés like not being the first President to lose a war." Nor is Willens concerned that McGovern's tax policies would ruin his own fortune. "We will get what we pay for," he says. "Not an extra mink coat for Mrs. Willens, but more stability and the survival of the system that I love and that has worked for me. We must share in order to keep." . . . 31

• Marjorie Benton, 37, is the daughter-in-law of former Connecticut Senator William Benton, the publisher of the *Encyclopaedia Britannica.* Active in politics since the first Adlai Stevenson campaign, she has been an effective McGovern fund raiser, drumming up over $1,000,000 from wealthy acquaintances and friends. "There are a lot of people being left out of the benefits of the society," she argues. "Benefits such as being able to get off welfare and get a job. To have decent cities and play areas and unpolluted lakes. It sounds utopian, but I really feel that way. I feel very privileged, and I just wish everyone had as much as I do. And I'm willing to give up something and try to have that happen. Money is a product of society, and I really feel that you owe it back to society." 32

Harvard Sociologist David Riesman sees the McGovern constituency as an expression of the anti-institutional force that has long existed in American life—a force today heavily represented in the press, the advertising community and the liberal Protestant and emancipated Catholic clergy. Says Riesman: "Their attitudes have strong roots in frontier anarchism and feelings of independence"—though it is a frontier and an independence quite different from Nixon's version. 33

Riesman argues that the McGovern constituency is basically a professional elite but "is not part of the institutional, organizational, day-by-day America. They don't think this America is really necessary, that it can all be done mechanically. They have very little sense of that other day-by-day America." It may be that McGovernites, in espousing income redistribution and higher inheritance taxes, have profoundly misjudged the American character and some of its deepest aspirations. Even some of McGovern's own supporters use the curious argument that such proposals are not to be taken entirely seriously because, after all, Congress would still be there to put the brakes on any idea it thought too radical. 34

As an example of that lack of touch with the other America, Riesman cites the abortion issue. "It was madness to confront the country with it at the convention," he says. "It's an issue of great importance to liberated women—and others of course—but think of the unliberated women. For many of them the right to get an abortion simply means that they have no way of holding on to their men when they get pregnant. A considerable part of the blue-collar and farm population only gets married when the girls get pregnant." That tactical judgment is quite aside from the moral substance of the question which matters greatly to many people who consider abortion simply wrong. Nor is abortion in any sense a significant campaign issue; McGovern's present official stand is the same as Nixon's—the matter should be left to the states to decide—and there is no doubt that in the near future the U.S., as a whole, will allow women to have abortions more or less at will. To Riesman, the whole question is simply an illustration of how McGovern comes across to the voters. . . . 35

So for the moment, the Nixonian star is ascendant—not so much because the President has captured and guided the nation's imagination but almost by default. Indeed, there are those who suspect that this election has as much to do with 1976 as 1972: an enormous Nixon victory might enhance the party's post-Nixon chances four years hence. 36

For this year, neither candidate so far has been much of a national inspiration. In fact, it may be that the American people themselves are far ahead of both Nixon and McGovern—more 37 conservative perhaps than they used to be but weary of simplicities on both sides. Within the two Americas, one common denominator is a sophistication in the people that neither candidate has been respecting very much, and beyond that, there is a desire for one America rather than two—something that neither candidate seems capable of meeting.

THE THINKING PROCESS

STRUCTURE

1. A report or an exposition presents facts; an analysis presents facts and evaluates them. To clarify that evaluation, the thesis is crucial. Is the thesis of "The Confrontation of the Two Americas" explicit or implicit? If explicit, which sentence is it? If implicit, which sentences suggest it?

2. The basic pattern of organization of the analysis is comparison and contrast though the pattern is not introduced until paragraph 3. What then is the purpose of paragraphs 1 and 2?

3. Examine paragraphs 11–32. Construct an outline by briefly labeling each paragraph according to both the candidate(s) it describes and its main assertion(s).

Comparison and contrast usually takes one of two forms. One form is block, where several paragraphs discuss one element of the comparison followed by a similar block of paragraphs discussing the other. Thus if comparing Margaret Thatcher, prime minister of England, with Golda Meir, former prime minister of Israel, the writer may devote two paragraphs to Margaret Thatcher's education and political background and then follow that block of paragraphs with a block of two devoted to Golda Meir, her education and political background. Comparison and contrast can also take the form of alternating paragraphs (or even sentences). In one paragraph a writer could discuss Margaret Thatcher's education and in the next, that of

Golda Meir. Then paragraph 3 would take up Margaret Thatcher's politics followed by paragraph 4 on Golda Meir's. Some writers use a combination of both methods.

In "The Confrontation of the Two Americas" is the predominant pattern block or alternating paragraphs? Do you find the pattern effective? Why or why not? What does comparison and contrast add to the political analysis?

4. The essay includes an overview of the era, a discussion of the candidates' likes and views, citizen-on-the-street interviews, and the expert opinion of a sociologist. In what order are these elements incorporated into the analysis? Why do you think the writer structures them in the order that he or she does?

STYLE

1. *Time,* a monthly news magazine with a current circulation of 4,273,962, is written for the general reader. Yet the vocabulary and allusions in "The Confrontation of the Two Americas" are fairly sophisticated. Noting that *Time* focuses on "national and international affairs in a framework of historical perspective" and having identified the allusions and defined any unfamiliar words, how would you characterize the particular section of the general audience the piece is directed to? Why?

2. The author of this political analysis cleverly interweaves the general and particular. Examine the first two paragraphs. Which elements are general? Which are specific?

3. The author focuses on two separate individuals and through an ever-increasing spiral has them represent the diversity and complexity of a nation that is nearly two hundred years old. Reread paragraphs 11, 14, 15, 20, 21, and 29. What levels of associations and symbols does the writer use to accomplish this task?

4. What personality does the author project in this analysis? What about the diction and subject matter leads you to your conclusions? Can you deduce the standards and criteria used in the analysis? If so, what are they? Are they direct or indirect? Which political candidate do you think the writer supports? What evidence do you find for your opinion?

IDEAS FOR A FIRST DRAFT

Writing a political analysis requires familiarity with the current news, the ability to conduct research, and, ideally, a knowledge of history and government. Select a current political event or issue that you find intriguing. You may wish to restrict yourself to campus or local politics, or you may want to examine a local or national campaign, a scandal, an international crisis, a domestic problem. Whatever your subject, it should be current.

First, explore in detail the particulars of the case you have selected for analysis. Campus and local papers for local issues and current news magazines and newspapers for wider issues make excellent starting places. For national and international concerns, check *Time, Newsweek, U.S. News and World Report, National Review, New Republic,* the *Washington Post,* and the *New York Times.*

Next you need to place your issue or event in a historical context, so further research is necessary. Has anything similar occurred before? What comparisons and contrasts can you draw? Or perhaps your event or issue is unique. Explain how.

Other possible sources of information are experts in the field. Consider interviewing professors from the disciplines your event or issue touches on. If you are focusing on a personality, talk to a psychologist. If group behavior is related to your issue, consult a sociologist. A political scientist may be able to place the event in another context, and if the issue concerns the economy, an economics professor can help you. If you don't know where to start, your instructor can direct you to the experts in your field.

If you would like to enrich your analysis further, you may wish to find out what the citizens think. Perhaps conduct citizen-on-the-street interviews, collecting responses from a representative sample of society: different age groups, sexes, economic and marital statuses, vocations, political persuasions, and so forth. (For further ideas, see chapter 10, The Interviewer.)

Once you have gathered your materials, you are ready to begin organizing your paper. You might want to open by presenting background information or by defining the current issue or event you've selected. After you introduce the issue and sketch in the background, present your research and then perhaps bring in your experts and your citizen-on-the-street interviews. You may conclude with a summary, a prediction of the outcome, or suggestions for best handling the issue or event. Or if the case is well known, you can begin with the interviews, turn to the experts, and conclude by redefining your issue and discussing its history. If you are comparing two candidates or two points of view, you may decide to use comparison and contrast as your dominant pattern of organization. Because the pattern is a difficult one, you will want to make an informal outline listing the information you plan to include in each paragraph.

Before you begin writing, consider your audience. Are you writing for a local paper or magazine? A general, national newspaper or magazine? A conservative or liberal one? Shape your material accordingly. If you intend to remain impartial, balance your experts' opinions and your other interviews as well as your own comments to show both sides of the issue.

THE WRITING PROCESS

INVENTION

If you are working on a previous assignment in this chapter, you already have a rough draft and can skip to Organizing and Developing. If not select one of the two following topics.

1. Visit your university or city art museum, or browse through your library's collection of art books. Select any work of art that you think possesses *beauty*, first forming your own definition of the term with the help of a dictionary and an encyclopedia. One typical dictionary definition is "that which gives the highest degree of pleasure to the senses or to the mind and suggests that the object of delight approximates one's conception of an ideal . . . as by line, color, form, texture, proportion, rhythmic motion, tone, etc." For a topic, you might choose the Parthenon, the *Venus de Milo*, Michelangelo's *Pietà*, Brancusi's *The Kiss*, or a painting by Monet, van Gogh, or Picasso. Scrutinize your subject thoroughly, noting down all the details of form, shape, color, texture, composition, balance, quality of execution, verisimilitude, and so on.

If you wish to turn the paper into a research assignment, you might want to investigate the aesthetic standards of the age and culture in which the artwork was produced or consult literature in the museum on the work selected.

Your essay will be an analysis of that art object. You will have to define beauty, and you will have to examine the parts in relationship to the whole. Your introduction might be a discussion of the object's historical background, the artist, the nature of beauty. Your conclusion might be a discussion of how the object influenced other artists, where it is displayed today, any innovations it might demonstrate. You can organize your essay by the elements of beauty, by spatial relationships, whatever suggests itself naturally from your observations and definition.

2. Thumb through some magazines addressed to specific audiences and look for an eye-catching full-page advertisement: *Cosmopolitan* or *Mademoiselle*, *Gentlemen's Quarterly* or *Esquire*, *Science '84* or *Science Digest*, *Audubon* or *Natural History*, and the like are good sources. The purpose of the ad is twofold: to attract your attention and then to motivate you to buy the product. Examine the advertisement carefully, breaking it down into its various components: copy, design, and layout. Next, divide the elements even further; copy, for instance, can probably be divided into headline and descriptive paragraph, or headline and declarative sentence(s). After you have identified as many elements as you can, analyze what each contributes to what you deduce as the purpose behind the ad. Consider the ad's audience. What characteristics does the ad appeal to? How does it manipulate them? An ad in *Playboy*, for instance, may make its pitch based on sex appeal, but it may include status and savoir faire as well.

You can organize the body of your draft according to the elements you have examined (moving from least to most important) or by the sequence that catches the reader's eye. If you choose the latter, re-create your impressions the moment you saw the ad. Perhaps color first arrested you, then headline, next picture, and finally copy. A brief discussion of advertising gimmicks like those used in your example or a brief description of the magazine and its audience would make a good introductory paragraph because it would place the advertisement in the wider context that you will use later in your analysis. Your conclusion can summarize your analysis of the parts, returning again to the whole and assessing it according to how well it fulfills its persuasive purpose. (For a further discussion of analyzing advertisements, see chapter 8.)

ORGANIZING AND DEVELOPING

Reread your draft. If there is a thesis, make sure you have stated it clearly. Many analysts rely on process as an organizational structure when they examine a subject part by part, step by step. Underline the first sentence of your paragraphs. Many of them should indicate what part of the whole you are discussing; if they don't, you may want to clarify your essay's structure by reworking your opening sentences.

Reread your opening and concluding paragraphs. Check to see that your paper begins with a statement about your subject as a whole and that it concludes by synthesizing the parts and returning to the complete subject. Make sure that in the body of the paper you have examined all the appropriate parts of the subject, each according to its significance, that you've stated clearly any criteria you're using, that you've defined any technical terms that might be unfamiliar to your audience. Double-check that the sequencing of paragraphs is logical and easy to follow. If it is not, number your paragraphs and consider various rearrangements.

FINDING A VOICE

Remember that although you are an authority on your particular subject and in your field, you are writing to a general audience who will use your evaluation to help them make their own decisions—perhaps to buy a particular brand of product, to vote for a specific candidate, to appreciate and value a particular literary work, to understand the pitch behind a product or the nature of beauty. Try to strike a balanced tone: excessive formality and overuse of technical language will alienate and bore your audience, while too much informality, a lack of specificity, and charged language will undermine your authority and thus your evaluation. Because you must establish your credibility, you want to project a tone of expertise and impartiality. Let the thoroughness and orderliness of your evaluation speak for itself. Remember that the readers are interested in your results, not in you.

POLISHING

Give your paper to readers who fit your audience, and ask them to answer the following questions as specifically as they can: Is the subject under evaluation clearly defined? Are the standards and criteria used for the evaluation clearly evident and reasonable? Does the projected speaker sound knowledgeable about the subject? Is the tone impartial? Is there any other information about the process of the evaluation, about the results of the research, about the subject itself that a reader would like to know? Make sure that your readers are being honest rather than kind, and revise your paper according to their responses.

THINKING AHEAD

Writing evaluations is one of the writer's most difficult roles, for evaluations demand not only observation and research but educated judgment. List the problems you had in writing your evaluation. Was impartiality one of them? Because you are now an expert on your subject, you most likely have formed definite opinions. At this point you are ready to adopt the role of the argumentative essayist and turn your balanced study into a persuasive essay that argues for a specific point of view or course of action.

PART 4

THE WRITER AS PERSUADER

Whether or not the pen is mightier than the sword or whether the word processor is mightier than the atomic bomb remains to be seen, but no matter what the current medium, persuasion still takes only two forms—physical force and language.

We use language daily to persuade. "Hi! How are you?" ("Fine, thanks.") and "Please?" ("My pleasure!") are social graces and verbal niceties that we practice from childhood through adulthood to persuade others that we are friendly and courteous, that we as well as they are worth caring about and doing favors for. The greater our control over language and its diction, syntax, and voice, the greater our chances for success. The letter of application, the business correspondence, the advertisement, the political platform, the travel brochure—the success of each depends largely on the writer's control of language, on the ability to persuade the vice-president to offer the job, the client to sign a contract, the consumer to buy a product, the voters to vote, the travelers to visit the city, state, or country.

The greater our control over language, the more effectively we can argue for essential ethical and moral concerns—whether they be justice and liberty, the rights of the individual versus society, or a particular moral action. We can persuade citizens, legislators, and leaders of the state, country, or world, not only to adopt specific viewpoints and ideas but to act on them. Aristotle, Plato, Milton, Descartes, Kant, Emerson, Hegel, Susan B. Anthony, and Bertrand Russell are only a few of the philosophers and thinkers who have transformed individuals and society by persuasive arguments. Within our own American heritage, The Declaration of Independence is an excellent example of effective persuasion that has become a statement of our society's beliefs.

The writer as persuader can adopt a variety of roles ranging from the advertiser to that of the argumentative essayist. Both use persuasive techniques, but *argument* refers specifically to the formal essay, which is analytical and reflective. Where the advertiser calls attention to products, places, and even people, the argumentative essayist calls attention to ideas. The former strives for a commercial success, the latter for a moral or ideological one. How effective the writers are depends upon several characteristics: the quality of their research, their understanding of the audience, the voices they project, the nature of their appeal—whether intellectual, emotional, or ethical—and ideally on the truth of what they say.

From carnival barkers to Madison Avenue executives, advertising promotes everything from freak shows to computers. Advertisers must attract our interest, sustain it, and sell their wares, whether bearded ladies or Apples. The same is true of publications. The cover of the June, 1983, *New York* magazine, for instance, proves irresistible. Against a background of white, a large red block sets off white print that announces

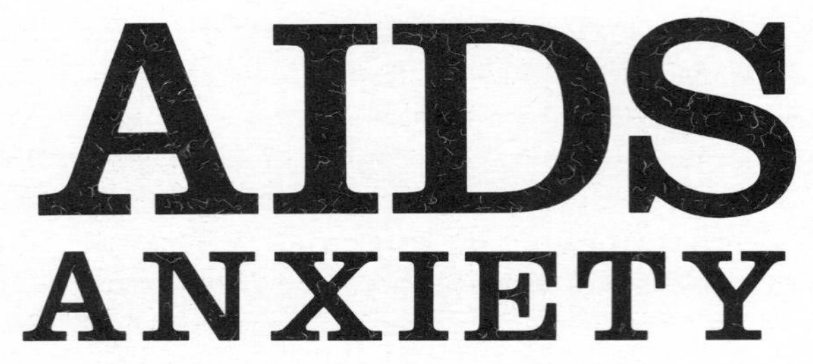

The name of the feared and much publicized disease arrests the reader. The alliteration in the article's title, the predominance of the high-pitched, long vowels, and the connotations of *anxiety* further rivet the reader's attention, as does the color of the block which screams "red alert." What follows the headline is an excerpt guaranteed to alarm even the most placid of readers:

> Not one of the hundreds of doctors who are studying AIDS has suggested that we are facing some twentieth-century version of the Black Death. Yet, as imaginations have become infected with fear, paranoia, and superstition, AIDS victims have been fired from their jobs, driven from their homes, and deserted by their loved ones. Any homosexual or Haitian has become an object of dread. And New York in 1983 has become a place where a woman telephones Montefiore Medical Center and asks if her children should wear gloves on the subway.

"Black Death," "infected," "fear," "paranoia," "superstition"; "victims" who are "fired," "driven," and "deserted"; "homosexual," "dread" are all examples of charged language, compelling us to turn the page.

Such sensationalism, however, is not the norm. For every blaring front page of the *National Enquirer* and *Star*, dozens of headlines and magazine covers appeal to the reader's intellect or values. Periodicals such as *Science Digest*, *Science '84*, and *Discover*, for instance, satisfy the general reader's need to be informed about scientific and technical matters, but these magazines also raise ethical issues for the reader to ponder, as Lewis Thomas' "On the Need for Asylums" illustrates. This kind of ethical appeal is more subtle but still evident in advertising, where some ads rely on the consumer's desire for quality and aesthetic design, not just on status and image.

And wit too can sell products, for advertisers often rely on word play, anthropomorphism, and pure literary entertainment, as in the Apple advertisement reprinted in this section.

Argumentative essayists depend largely on appeals to reason and ethical values, less so on emotion, as the argumentative pieces included here illustrate. They also demonstrate how other types of writing, cut and honed to a persuasive edge, can be transformed into argument. "Hooray for Jewish Mothers!" has some characteristics of a personal essay, but it is shaped to persuade; "On the Need for Asylums" could have been an analysis, but the call to action gives it an argumentative edge; "TV Violence: The Shocking New Evidence" could well have begun as a report, but the weight of the evidence tipped it toward persuasion; and "Active and Passive Euthanasia" is a traditional meditative essay transformed into practical argument.

Persuasion has been pervasive ever since the time of the great persuader, Satan. The honey-tongued seducer in a more modern shape is depicted in Gustave Flaubert's *Madame Bovary*, where the ruthless roué Rodolphe de Boulanger woos and wins the dreamy, romantic, unhappily married Emma Bovary. From their first meeting, Rodolphe plans simultaneously to seduce and to jettison her. In the excerpt that follows, we see Rodolphe at his desk, pen in hand, puzzling how best to tell Emma that he will not run off with her:

> He began to write:
>
> "You must be courageous, Emma: the last thing I want to do is ruin your life. . . ."
>
> "That's absolutely true, after all," he assured himself. "I'm acting in her interest; I'm only being honest."
>
> "Have you given really serious thought to your decision? Do you realize into what abyss I was about to hurl you, poor darling? You don't, I'm sure. You were going ahead blind and confident, full of faith in happiness, in the future. . . . Ah! Poor wretched, insane creatures that we are!"
>
> Here Rodolphe paused, looking for some good excuse.
>
> "I could tell her that I've lost all my money. . . . No—that wouldn't stop her anyway: I'd have to go through the whole thing again later. Is there any way of making such women come to their senses?"
>
> He thought for a while, then added. . . . "Forget me! Why was it ordained that we should meet? Why were you so beautiful? Is the fault mine? In God's name, no! No! Fate alone is to blame—nothing and no one but fate!"
>
> "That's always an effective word," he remarked to himself. . . .
>
> "That marvelous intensity of feelings you have—such a delight for those who know you, such a source of anguish for yourself!—kept you—adorable woman that you are—from realizing the falsity of the position the future held for us. . . ."
>
> "Maybe she'll think I'm giving her up out of stinginess. . . . What's it to me if she does! Let her. . . . And let's get it over with!"
>
> "The world is cruel, Emma. It would have pursued us

everywhere. You'd have been subjected to indiscreet questions—calumny—scorn—even insult, perhaps. You—insulted! Oh, my darling! And I would have been the cause of it—I, who wanted to put you on a throne—I, who shall carry away the thought of you like a talisman! Yes—away—for I am punishing myself for the harm I have done you—I am going into exile! Where? How can I tell? My poor mad brain can give no answer. Adieu, Emma! Continue to be as good as you have always been! Never forget the unfortunate man who lost you! Teach your child my name: tell her to include me in her prayers." . . .

"That's all, I guess," he said to himself. "Oh—just this little bit more, to keep her from coming after me":

"I shall be far away when you read these unhappy lines; I dare not linger—the temptation to see you again is all but irresistible! This is no moment for weakness! I shall come back; and perhaps one day we'll be able to speak of our love with detachment, as a thing of the past. Adieu!"

And he appended one more, last adieu, this time written as two words—"*A Dieu!*": it seemed to him in excellent taste.

"How shall I sign it?" he wondered. " 'Devotedly'? No . . . 'Your friend'? Yes—that's it."

"Your friend."

He read over his letter and thought it was good.

"Poor little thing!" he thought, suddenly sentimental. "She'll think me as unfeeling as a stone. There ought to be a few tears on it, but weeping's beyond me—what can I do?" He poured some water in a glass, wet a finger, and holding it high above the page shook off a large drop. It made a pale blot on the ink. . . .

Whereupon he smoked three pipes and went to bed.

We see how cleverly Flaubert has Rodolphe consider his audience, his subject, and his voice. Flaubert teaches us to read and write between the lines as well as on them. And once we understand the techniques of emotional appeal and logical fallacies, we will not only learn to read and write more effectively, but we will learn to be wary of both false philosophers and seducers—we will learn to seek the truth.

CHAPTER 8

THE ADVERTISER

"You can tell the ideals of a nation by its advertisements." So wrote British essayist Norman Douglas in 1917. If his assertion holds true today, we may be in trouble. We see relatively few ads that appeal to our community responsibilities and to our traditional values and virtues. Consider the paste-over cover on the newsstand edition of the January 1983 *Reader's Digest*, a cover that advertises the magazine as opposed to the bound cover that lists its contents: a sexy, young woman sporting a red leotard extends a shapely, long leg over an exercise bar. A large-print caption is juxtaposed with a small. The larger headline alerts the reader to an article on thin thighs; the smaller one queries the effects of herpes on American morality. Headlines announcing the body beautiful and venereal disease perhaps attract more magazine buyers than morality and social issues. The picture and sensationalism are more arresting than the less exotic and homespun titles listed on the bound cover: "All About Caffeine," "Struggle for Supremacy in Space," "A Kidney for Krista," "Do You Know Where Your Church Offerings Go?," "America's Forgotten Crops," and "How to Be Your Dog's Best Friend."

Advertising can be a tricky business. Not only must an ad stay varied and entertaining, but it must highlight the product by focusing on its name and powers. Advertisements incorporate the conventional poetic devices whose job it is to call attention to language. So billboards sport puns: "People Who Drink Old Fitzgerald Don't Know Any Better." TV jingles are metrical: "IN-di-GES-tion. . . .PEP-to-BIS-mol." Magazine slogans rhyme: "Timex . . . takes a licking and keeps on ticking." Personification flourishes: "Nothin' says lovin' like somethin' from the oven, and Pillsbury says it best." Metaphor dominates: "Put a tiger in your tank." Imagery tantalizes: "Two all beef patties, special sauce, lettuce, cheese, pickles, onions on a sesame seed bun." And sexual innuendo titillates: "Flick My Bic!"

Advertising slogans encapsulate the times. Thus in the conservative fifties, Coke was a "Sign of Good Taste." In the radical sixties, a decade that boasted philosophical reflection, Coke declared "It's the Real Thing." To the seventies, the years of economic recession, "Coke Adds Life." And now in the eighties, a time of hot competition in the soft-drink market, Coke announces, "Coke Is It!"

The eighties also are the computer age, but when IBM decided to market a personal computer it had to change its business-only image to attract a general audience. As a *Time* analysis explains, "The firm has always been seen as efficient and reliable, but it has also been regarded as somewhat cold and aloof." To humanize its image IBM adopted Charlie Chaplin's Tramp, who "with his ever present red rose, has given IBM a human face." Other techniques of selling computers are skillfully portrayed by the Apple advertisement that follows in this chapter.

In this commercial, media-centered world, persuasion can help advertise more than products. Politicians and political lobbies, charities and universities, camps and resorts, and even religions, can proclaim, promise, and persuade. Travel brochures beckon weary urban dwellers or bored country folks to "get away from it all" or "to live it up." A case in point is the essay included in this chapter that invites us to visit New Mexico, a place of "Timeless Beauty Under Gorgeous Skies."

And we don't stop with products, places, or proclamations, for we advertise ourselves as well not only in serious letters of application and letters of recommendation but with T-shirts and bumper stickers, designer jackets and jeans, initialed bracelets and briefcases, with popular music and personal classifieds. By emblazoning the slogans, logos, and emblems that we do, we are in danger of internalizing the superficial values that advertising sometimes projects. When advertising relies on excessive emotional appeal, we must be able to recognize its dishonest pitch; yet we also need to realize that advertising, like argument, can use emotional, logical, and ethical appeals to achieve a legitimate end.

Apple Advertisement

One place where the Apple advertisement that follows appeared was in the *New Yorker*, a weekly magazine that focuses on the arts and on New York's cultural events. Featuring extensive film, theatre, music, and dance reviews, it contains cartoons, poetry and short fiction, as well as articles on domestic and international news, and comments on sports and fashions. As you study the Apple advertisement, see if you can deduce what attraction it might have held for the *New Yorker* audience.

The two-page ad is primarily black and white. A blue pen and handwriting in blue ink appears on the left page. Green print and a green apple are displayed on the video monitors of the right page. A final spot of color is the multicolored Apple emblem of green, yellow, orange, red, violet, and blue. A Nehru jacket, which is a secondary concern in the ad, was made popular by the Hindu leader Jawaharlal Nehru and is a military-collared, fitted, five- or six-button, tunic-length jacket without lapels.

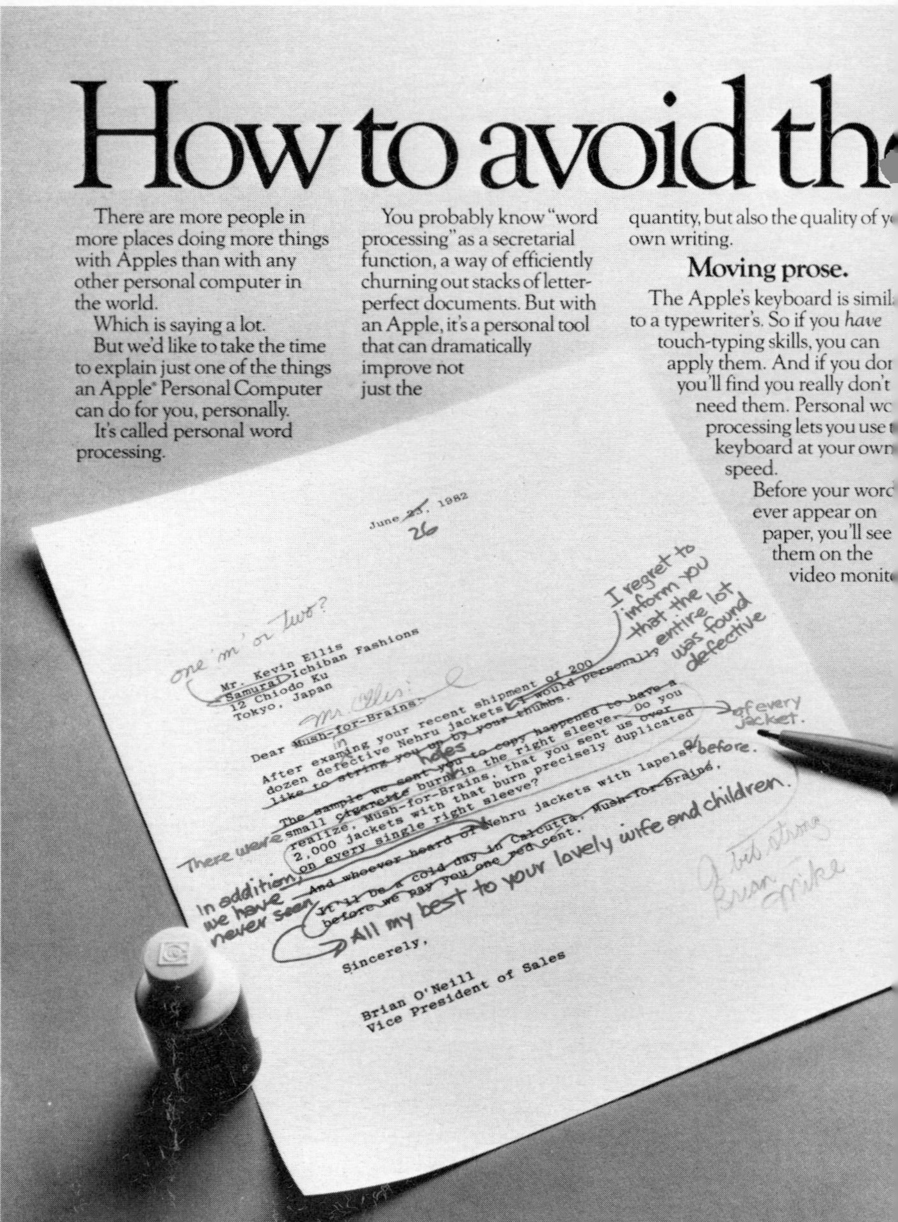

How to avoid th
There are more people in more places doing more things with Apples than with any other personal computer in the world.
Which is saying a lot.
But we'd like to take the time to explain just one of the things an Apple® Personal Computer can do for you, personally.
It's called personal word processing.
You probably know "word processing" as a secretarial function, a way of efficiently churning out stacks of letter-perfect documents. But with an Apple, it's a personal tool that can dramatically improve not just the
quantity, but also the quality of y
own writing.
Moving prose.
The Apple's keyboard is simil
to a typewriter's. So if you *have* touch-typing skills, you can apply them. And if you dor
you'll find you really don't
need them. Personal wc
processing lets you use t
keyboard at your own
speed.
Before your word
ever appear on
paper, you'll see
them on the
video monit
June 25, 1982
26
Mr. Kevin Ellis
Samurai Ichiban Fashions
12 Chiodo Ku
Tokyo, Japan
Dear Mush-for-Brains:
Sincerely,
Brian O'Neill
Vice President of Sales

Reproduced with permission of Apple Computer, Inc.

lraft.

ıd when you need to make a ange, there's no need to cross ings out. Or scribble. Or scrawl. r retype.

Instead, a few keystrokes allow u to dart instantly to any part the document, to move words, ragraphs or entire pages,

r first draft. You may decide "Mush-for-Brains" appropriate in a business letter. With one simple mand, you can change every occurrence of ush-for-Brains" to "Mr. Ellis."

asing and replacing them in a atter of seconds.

And when you feel the text is rfect, your Apple—teamed th a printer—can put it down on paper. A lot faster than any typist could.

Play tricks on our memory.

Most business ople find there are times hen it really pays to remember hat they've written.

Word for word.

The Apple can assist them in e of two ways:

By putting it on paper, which n be filed away.

Or, more conveniently, by storing your document on a "floppy disk" to be recalled later (it's smaller than a 45 rpm record and holds approximately 48 pages-worth of double-spaced typing).

Want to update a manual? Or send the same basic letter customized for several different companies? Or insert new names and information in a standard contract?

Simply load the document from the disk back into the computer, make your changes

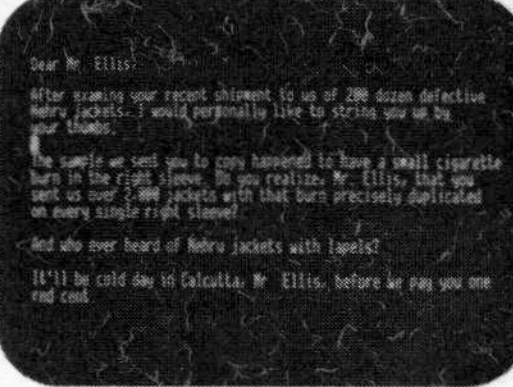

You did that in an instant. And it's just as easy to delete words and whole paragraphs. As soon as you give the command, the words realign themselves in perfect form.

and print out a letter-perfect copy every time.

There's even a feature that lets you change or delete specific words wherever they occur. So every reference to "Smith vs. Jones" can be changed to "Mugwump vs. Gretzky," with one simple command.

A better choice of words.

There are more word processing programs available for Apples than for any other personal computer.

Including our Apple Writer text-editing software, for both the Apple II and Apple III.

We even have a program that catches misspelled words. And another that will keep the names and addresses of all your customers at your fingertips.

Since revisions are so easy with no retyping or scrawled corrections, you may decide to do a still more diplomatic rewrite. There's even a program that will catch the misspelling of "examining."

Apple also offers a complete line of printers, for everything from rough drafts to finished letter-quality. Some can even print on your own letterhead or forms. And it's all backed by over 1300 authorized dealers.

Free screen test.

Word processing is just one of the thousands of things an Apple can help you do, from accounting to zoology.

Not surprising. There's more software available for Apples than for any other personal computer. So visit your nearest authorized Apple dealer. And try your hand at screenwriting.

apple

The most personal computer.

(800) 538-9696 for the location of the authorized Apple dealer nearest you, or for information regarding corporate purchases through our National Account Program. California (800) 662-9238. Or write Apple Computer Inc., Advertising and Promotion Dept., 20525 Mariani Ave., Cupertino, CA 95014. © 1983 Apple Computer Inc.

THE THINKING PROCESS

STRUCTURE

1. An advertisement is composed of copy and photo. Examine the layout of the photographs, and explain why you think they are positioned as they are.

2. Contrast and compare the structure of the ad's letter and handwritten comments on the left page with the video monitors and captions on the right. How do the differences underscore the message of the advertisement?

3. While keeping the reader's attention, the copy in the advertisement must present an orderly explanation of why the reader should own the product. In what order does the copy take up the computer's functions? Do you find the organization effective? Why or why not?

STYLE

1. As all persuasive writing, ads appeal to their audience's intellect, emotions, senses, and values. The sensual appeal of the Apple advertisement is limited but apparent, while the emotional and intellectual appeals are fully developed. Describe the sensual, the emotional, and the intellectual appeals. To what values of the prospective buyer does the ad appeal? Do you find the appeals effective, or would you change any of them? If so, how?

2. The pun, or play on words, is a popular advertising technique and is pervasive in the Apple ad, contributing to its overall humorous tone. What pun does the headline suggest? What puns do the other headings suggest?

3. The writer of this advertisement had to face the dilemma of shaping technical information for an audience concerned with the arts. How does the advertisement humanize the machine? What different methods does the writer use to incorporate the technical terms *computer, keyboard, video monitor, key-*

strokes, floppy disks, load, word processing, software, program? Are they effective? Why or why not?

4. Another technique advertisers use is revitalizing clichés. Find several embedded clichés in the ad. What are their purposes? How do they affect the reader?

5. Compare the first draft and final version of Brian O'Neill's letter to Mr. Ellis. What are the substantive changes? What do you think were the reasons behind the changes?

IDEAS FOR A FIRST DRAFT

Imagine a product you'd like to compose an advertisement for, inventing your own brand name and slogan. Select an audience for your ad, perhaps a particular magazine, and decide which primary pitch would be most effective. Intellectual—like True cigarettes? Emotional—like Virginia Slims and Marlboro? Sensual—like Eve and Satin? Do you want a slogan that sells through sex—"Ultra Brite gives your mouth sex appeal!"—use *Playboy* or *Playgirl.* Is motherhood more your style—"If it's not your mother, it must be Howard Johnson's"—try *Ladies' Home Journal* or *House and Garden.* Warm and runny—"Reach out and touch someone"—choose *The Saturday Evening Post.* Intellect—"Viceroy, the thinking man's cigarette"—select the *Nation.* Whatever you choose, consider the possibilities carefully, and study the ads in the magazine of your choice.

Sketch out or describe a photo (depending on your artistic or photographic talents), and then add copy, headline(s), and slogan. Make sure that both the photo and headline are arresting, and that the copy sustains your audience's interest as well as informs and persuades them. In the brand name, slogan, and copy, you may want to incorporate what you know about poetic devices—rhythm, alliteration, assonance, rhyme, metaphor, imagery, and so on. Consider the brand names Bonz and Lolly Pups dog snacks; Kwell for head lice; Byte Back modems, Ajax cleanser, Arrid Extra Dry deodorant, Ball Park Franks, Hercules Moving Company. Try to devise your ad to catch the reader's eye and focus it on the product. Test your ad on several friends, and check to see that it has the effects you desire.

from GUESTLIFE

Timeless Beauty Under Gorgeous Skies

Walk into almost any hotel or motel room in Aspen, Snowmass, or Vail, Colorado, or in New Mexico, or on the Monterey Peninsula, and you will find a copy of *Guestlife,* a tourist-oriented publication replete with color photographs, advertising, and guides to dining, shopping, and hotels. The entire magazine is an exotic travel brochure, and its copyright blurb declares *Guestlife,* published annually since 1979, "the prestige hotel room magazine." "New Mexico: Timeless Beauty Under Gorgeous Skies" appeared in the New Mexico edition in 1982.

New Mexicans affectionately refer to their state as the Land of Enchantment. It could just as aptly be called the Land of a Thousand Sensations. 1

Besides being intensely beautiful and a cultural gold mine, it's also one of the few places where you can catch a glimpse of what this country must have looked like to the first explorers. 2

There's an overpowering desire to protect it, put it under glass, turn it into a protected area or a park. Of all the states, New Mexico truly retains the last remnants of the wild, wild West. It is also one of the few remaining spots where the trammelings of civilization don't blot out the stars at night. 3

It's constantly said that New Mexico is a state of immense contrasts, physically and spiritually. Great antiquity juxtaposed 4 with such vanguards of the nuclear age as the laboratories of Los Alamos. You'll find the nation's oldest house, public building, church, Madonna, bell, road and state capital. You'll also find some of the nation's newest ideas.

Great, soaring mountains hover over barren flatlands and 5
deserts. Pueblo homes, still warmed by crackling pinyon fires, sit next to space laboratories where scientists plot a pathway to the stars. There are places where feathered dancers chant and importune the gods at home, then don business suits and speak of Dow Jones averages in their offices.

Here is a faithful adherence to traditions, a reverence for the 6
past—yet a thrust into the future at the same time. While potters' hands shape their clay on wheels, other New Mexicans pore over geothermal and seismologic charts. Some hands carve kachina dolls; others launch Hercules missles into the dawn sky.

Ancient New Mexico is also the site of the largest all-land 7
missile test center in the western hemisphere, and the center of a massive uranium mining industry that supplies almost half the uranium oxide produced in the United States.

It's been said that New Mexico is one state in which the 8
"melting pot concept" just didn't work. Throughout the year, the past and ancestral ways of doing things are constantly celebrated. Maybe it's because the roots from which New Mexicans spring are just so interesting.

There are New Mexicans who are descendants of the great 9
Mogollon and Anasazi civilizations; others whose forefathers were conquering Spaniards or Mexicans. Then there were the miners, railroaders, homesteaders, army men, rustlers, gunslingers. Good guys and bad guys.

More recent additions to the population have been the 10
artists who flocked to Santa Fe and Taos as these two spots became internationally known as artistic hotbeds. Among the newest New Mexicans are the escapees from New York, Los Angeles and Chicago. People looking for beauty and peace and a lifestyle where quality is more important than quantity.

The land and the climate have created what geographers 11
call an "oasis civilization" in New Mexico. Almost a third of the population lives in greater Albuquerque; more than a half occupies the narrow Rio Grande Valley that runs from Colorado to Mexico.

Throughout the state, there's pride in keeping the scene 12

from succumbing to urban sprawl and rural despoliation. In Santa Fe a city ordinance insists that the architecture remain faithful to the pueblo or Spanish traditions. And a brochure begs visitors to "take nothing but pictures, leave nothing but footprints and kill nothing but time."

New Mexico could also be named the Land of a Thousand Surprises. To begin with, New Mexico is not where many expect it to be. *The Wall Street Journal* once insisted Santa Fe was in Mexico. It's constantly being confused with Arizona, and a dean of a Midwestern college once sent a New Mexican student an application which read: "We are enclosing a form for you to fill out which will expedite your entry into the United States." 13

It's a surprise to find highly educated and cultured people of Indian heritage living in simple pueblo communities by choice. It's a surprise to find one of the nation's finest opera houses in a city of 49,000. It's a surprise to find an 18-channel recording studio in an old opera house in a tiny ghost town. 14

To put New Mexico in a nutshell: It is 121,666 square miles and the fifth largest state. Population: 1,300,000. It was admitted into the Union January 6, 1912, as the 47th state. Official nickname: Land of Enchantment. Official motto: "It grows as it goes." As of 1980, the per capita personal income was $7,841. Wheeler Peak, at 13,161 feet, is its highest mountain. There are six of the seven life zones in North America found in New Mexico. Annual rainfall ranges between 7 and 24 inches and the sun shines from 75 to 80 percent of the time. The state has one of the highest per capita ownerships of boats in the nation. 15

To be completely in the know, there's a whole raft of official state symbols the astute visitor should be familiar with. He should know, for example, that the official state slogan is "Everybody is Somebody in New Mexico." The official state flower is the yucca, a member of the lily family that grows to tree-like heights. The state bird is the roadrunner (but not the one making Wile E. Coyote's life a misery) and the state fish is the New Mexico native cut-throat trout. State mammal? *Ursa Americanus*, also known as the Black Bear (but in New Mexico, sometimes brown and often cinnamon). State gem is, of course, the turquoise and the state tree the delicious, omnipresent *Pinus edulis* or Rocky Mountain Nut Pine or Pinyon. 16

If there's one pastime that can be called truly New Mexican, it would be learning the art of cracking pinyon nuts. You might 17 have cracking sunflower and pumpkin seeds down to a fine art, but the round, slippery, pinyon shells demand a special sort of skill. Tricky as the cracking can be, the delicate, addictive taste makes it all worthwhile.

Besides producing nuts that can be eaten plain or turned 18
into candy, this wonder of a tree is used for construction, gives off a smoke of great fragrance when it's burned, supplies an unusual carving material and makes a terrific Christmas tree.

There is a long justification for naming the pinto bean and 19
the chile as New Mexico's state vegetables. Apparently, in combination, they constitute a well-balanced diet of minerals, vitamins and protein. Cliff-dwelling Indians were using pinto beans long before the Spaniards arrived and the two vegetables became the common diet of many early settlers. They were also said to account for New Mexico having a low incidence of heart disease.

And, last but not least, the state song is "O Fair New Mexi- 20
co," written by Elizabeth Garrett, daughter of Sheriff Pat Garrett, who shot Billy the Kid.

Four distinct seasons divide the New Mexico year. Summer 21
means warm days and cool, clear nights. Climbing in the mountains, fishing in mountain streams, fiestas and rodeos and tapestries of wild flowers.

Autumn is color—first the quaking aspens changing to gold, 22
then the cottonwoods, oak and maple trees enflaming the hills. Certain signs of the season are the chains of scarlet ristras, plaited red chiles hung like grape clusters from the roofs of houses, over fences, everywhere.

Winter turns New Mexico into ski country—downhill and 23
touring. It's a time when the smell of burning pinyon and juniper logs fills the air. A time for Christmas luminarias and farolitos to light the way. Of folk plays and ceremonial dances.

Spring, with its blooming yucca, the "candles of the Lord," 24
launches yet another season.

There are as many ways to see New Mexico as there are 25
reasons for coming. For lovers of the arts, Albuquerque has theater, opera and ballet. Santa Fe is a haven for painters and poets, sculptors and writers. The Santa Fe Film Festival is among the world's most successful film events. In Santa Fe there are operas in the summer and moonlight concerts. Some people come for the art galleries alone. Taos is the perfect artists' colony.

History buffs can travel the nation's oldest road, El Camino Real, the King's Highway, that runs from El Paso to Santa Fe. See ancient history in the elegant old missions and poke through ghost towns and old forts. Listen to the ghostly laughter of painted dance hall girls who once entertained raucous miners in those towns. Or is it just the wind? 26

Sportsmen will find the mountains alive with activity all year round. And everyone will love the well-preserved monuments, parks, deserts, caverns, ancient pueblo ruins. 27

Archaeologists will head for the Folsom and Clovis areas to contemplate evidence ancestors 25,000 years ago left behind. 28

New Mexico has the distinction of being the place where the earliest man living on the North American continent was discovered. Sandia Man (who left tools and the bones of near extinct animals behind in the Sandia Mountain caves) is estimated to have lived 17,000–20,000 years ago. Other early North American stone age men were also discovered in New Mexico—the Folsom Man and Clovis Man. 29

New Mexico is so bewitching, enchanting, everlasting and special, people who live outside the state keep insisting it's a different country. Just chalk it up as one of the nation's best surprises. 30

THE THINKING PROCESS

STRUCTURE

1. Does the essay have a thesis that is stated in one sentence or implied? Explain. State the thesis in your own words.

2. One element that makes a brochure successful is the large variety of examples that bring a particular place to life. Reread paragraphs 4 and 9, and count the number of examples included. Does the number support or overwhelm? How so?

3. Although examples structure the essay's organization, in paragraph 4 the writer presents New Mexico as a land of contrasts, a theme developed in paragraphs 4 through 8. What underlying pattern of organization do you find in these paragraphs? Do you find any other distinct patterns of organization in the essay? Do you find they detract from the essay's overall organization?

4. Travel brochures should attract the widest possible audience while honestly portraying the offerings of the city, state, or country. List the different groups of people that the essay is designed to attract. Why does the author organize these groups in the order presented? Can you find a more effective structure? If so, what?

STYLE

1. Powerful verbs, adjectives, and adverbs make persuasive description effective. Examine paragraphs 4 and 5, underlining all three parts of speech. Try rewriting several of the sentences, eliminating the adjectives and adverbs and making the verbs inert. What are the differences in effect? Which do you prefer and why?

2. In order to persuade their audience to visit a particular place, writers of travel brochures appeal to their readers' emotions by using charged language, words used primarily for their emotional connotations rather than for their strict denotations. For example, invoking American ideals like truth, freedom, and liberty constitute charged diction. Examine paragraphs 1 and 8, and write down the charged words. What other examples can you find throughout the essay? Are they effective in persuading you to visit New Mexico? Why or why not?

3. Writers of travel brochures, like all advertisers, sell their products by appealing to the intellect, senses, and emotions. On a separate sheet, write down the headings *Intellect* and *Senses*; reread the essay jotting down examples of each appeal. What senses are evoked? What can you conclude about the diversity of appeals in the essay?

4. Travel brochure writers often make factual information inviting for a general audience. In paragraphs 15 through 20, for instance, the writer identifies the state flower, bird, tree, and vegetables, yet makes them unique and colorful by explaining their origins and by comparing the more foreign-sounding ones to the familiar—like the cartoon roadrunner and the legendary Billy the Kid. How else does the writer enliven factual information?

5. One major theme that the writer of "New Mexico" uses is the "Get-away-from-it-all" motif, popular in vacation advertising. An example appears in paragraph 10: "Among the newest New Mexicans are the escapees from New York, Los Angeles and Chicago." Find other examples of this theme. Do you think the references to the motif subtle or obtrusive? How effective is this motif?

IDEAS FOR A FIRST DRAFT

To write a paper that uses slanted facts and charged language, consider a two-part assignment—a travel brochure and a "Sixty Minutes" exposé.

Think about a state or the cities you know well or would like to know more about. Select one. On a sheet of paper, create separate columns for the following headings: *history*, *location*, *terrain*, *climate*, *populace*, *sports*, *culture*, *general entertainment*, and *special attractions*. Under each heading, fill in as many specifics as you can—whatever comes to mind, whether positive or negative. Next mark all the positive elements with a plus and the negative with a minus. For now, only consider the positive elements. Under *entertainment*, for instance, you may have listed by name the top night spots, the best restaurants, and the finest shops.

If you need additional factual information, visit the library to consult an atlas, almanac, or city or state publication. Remember to acknowledge your sources if you are quoting directly (you needn't document common statistics like size of population, area, average temperature, etc.). Determine whether you will write a brochure to attract tourists or prospective residents.

Now you need to decide on the best way to organize your material. You may want to discuss history and location first and lead up to the variety of attractions, or the reverse. Remember it is crucial to keep your audience reading by entertaining and informing them. Be sure to use colorful verbs, adjectives, and adverbs; and appeal to the emotions with charged language, to the intellect with reason and facts, and to the senses with vivid imagery.

For the flip side of your travel brochure, consider your town, city, or state again, but this time think only about the negative aspects you have listed and any others you can think of, whether economic problems (such as finance, unemployment), legislative problems (tax base, zoning), scandals (government graft, kickbacks), social problems (vandalism, crime, prostitution). Amass your negative facts, and write a "Sixty Minutes" exposé. Because your audience is the average television viewer or newspaper reader, you may have to remind the listeners where your city or town is and what it professes to be.

You can focus on one major flaw, or you might expose a number of them, depending on your place and on your facts. You may write your exposé as a TV script, an investigative report, or a straight essay. As in the first assignment, you will exaggerate by using charged language and vivid description, but this time describe only the negative. Don't exaggerate at the expense of the truth, however; even "Sixty Minutes" gets sued for libel.

THE WRITING PROCESS

INVENTION

If you are working on a previous assignment in this chapter, skip to Organizing and Developing; if not, consider the possibilities of advertising. You may want to write a column advertising your college or university in a neighborhood paper. Your audience would be prospective students and their parents, perhaps indirectly the legislature if state or federal funding is involved, perhaps the alumni, but most certainly high-school juniors. Your tone, therefore, needs to be dignified but inviting. Start with your library to collect data about your college or university—including history, size, enrollment, campus(es), faculty, and majors.

Or perhaps rather than your school, you'd prefer advertising your major. Concentrating only on your discipline, locate a description of the department's course offerings and degree programs, find out the credentials and publications of the faculty, discover what prime jobs past majors have received after graduation or what famous men and women the department can claim as alumni.

If you'd rather advertise yourself, you have a variety of choices. You can compose a personal classified, a letter of application for a job, a fictitious letter of recommendation (for yourself or a friend), or a political statement.

Beginning with a classified is a good exercise for creating a voice. Think of a classified ad you might put in your school newspaper or local singles magazine. To get you started, here are some examples from a very different source, *New York*, a weekly magazine aimed at would-be urban sophisticates; the format calls for a heading followed by the ad, and the individual supplies both: "*Slightly Out-Of-Sync*—Female, 40, enjoys short walks, TV dinners beneath a 200 watt bulb; looking for similarly inclined male between puberty and death." Or "*Slender, Attractive, Mature*—White female, 24, seeks bright compassionate single man 26–36, 5′11″ plus who likes hiking, nature, Vivaldi and rollercoasters. No smokers. Send photo with reply." Or "*Male*—41; tall, attractive, bright and witty (isn't everybody?). Wishes to meet female for friendship, relationship, whatever. Will answer all replies (assuming I get any). Be the first on your block."

Before you begin your own classified, write down the attributes you'd like to project. After you've composed your paragraph (anywhere from 25–100 words), ask a friend or classmate to read it and jot down the attributes he or she infers from the ad. If the lists jibe, you've projected your voice properly; if not, revise.

After you've practiced advertising yourself in a classified, you're ready to write a letter of application. Imagine that you are a graduating senior looking for a job or perhaps an undergraduate seeking summer employment. You find a job you'd like and the appropriate person to write to. In your letter, you need to cover several points: the position you are applying for, your credentials, your academic record, your previous work experience, and what you can do for the company. To distinguish your letter from the rest, you should express knowledge of and interest in that particular company, which means some research on your part. You must sell yourself by appearing self-assured and competent without seeming self-aggrandizing or obsequious; emphasize *you* (the company) in your letter rather than *I*, but don't sound smarmy.

Next, assume a different identity—for instance, a former employer, a present supervisor—and write a letter of recommendation for yourself or for a friend for the same job. Here you can take a different approach and summarize what you consider your or your friend's essential qualities and potential contributions. Remember to support any generalization with specific examples or incidents. This assignment will help you develop a voice and a sense of audience for the complex professional world. Remember that both letters of application and recommendation use primarily the intellectual and ethical appeal.

Or if you'd prefer codifying your political views, find a position or office you'd like to hold—school board representative, city or state legislator, mayor or governor—and write a political platform to appear in your local newspaper, outlining your credentials, what you perceive are the current local problems, and how you would alleviate them. Most likely, you will have to conduct research to present the facts and issues. Your paper can take the form of an ad or a press release.

ORGANIZING AND DEVELOPING

Reread your draft. Make sure that your thesis is either explicit or clearly implicit; in either case it should be persuasive: Buy this product! Hire me! Come visit! Vote for me! Make sure that you have included all of the essential points that you think will persuade your readers to act and that you have explained the points clearly and logically. Where appropriate have you included appeals to the emotions, to the intellect, and to the senses?

FINDING A VOICE

In an advertisement, style makes the man, woman, place, or product, and thus how you project yourself is critical. To a certain extent, of course, your voice will depend on your audience and on your basic sales pitch. If you're hustling jockey shorts in *Sports Illustrated*, for example, it's fine to use Jim Palmer as a model, but in *Mademoiselle* you would advertise young women's undergarments with Brooke Shields.

You want to impress with facts and figures, move with emotions, and tantalize (where appropriate) with the senses. Your voice should be lively, sincere, and authoritative, but not overpowering or braggadocio. Avoid the hard sell; rather, let the qualities of your product, place, or yourself do the selling for you. Reconsider your audience, and if their main concerns are intellectual, for example, as a prospective employer's would be, make sure that reason is your primary emphasis. If you are planning to sell a product or advertise a place through emotional appeal, make sure the persuasive point is clear.

POLISHING

Reread your draft, underlining your verbs, adjectives, and adverbs. Are they vivid and descriptive? Do they create a unique picture of your product, place, or yourself? Do they emphasize or overpower? You want to distinguish what you are selling from the competition without sounding bizarre. Check through your draft once more and see if you've used charged language to your advantage as well as any appropriate poetic devices—alliteration, assonance, consonance, metaphor, imagery, and rhythm. Remember these devices can be most effective in advertising products, in travel brochures, and in political tracts, but much less so in letters.

To insure that your voice is tempered, give your draft to a friend who will evaluate your tone, making sure that it is both persuasive and sane. Your reader can also tell you if your points are clear and effective and if he or she is "sold." If your reader feels alienated or finds your pitch distasteful, ask why, and make the appropriate changes.

And finally, make sure that your grammar, mechanics, and spelling are correct and that your usage is appopriate. In the professional world, errors in writing can easily undermine your credibility.

THINKING AHEAD

Writing advertisements for products and places is good practice for focusing on the subtleties of words—on their connotations and denotations, on their sounds and rhythms. Writing letters of application is good practice for the time in the future when you will most need to sell yourself by writing an effective letter, and self-evaluation is often more difficult than evaluating others. Projecting your qualities and accomplishments convincingly without appearing on the one extreme self-centered and on the other self-effacing is a difficult role for any writer. Jot down in a journal or notebook what you've learned about language and about yourself while writing these assignments and what techniques you want to remember for the future.

CHAPTER 9

THE ARGUMENTATIVE ESSAYIST

Argument triggers the image of two people shouting at each other, gesticulating wildly, while words and tempers fly; *persuasion* doesn't fare much better, conjuring up visions of snake oil hustlers and propaganda artists. Yet both terms have a reasoned, objective meaning when used in connection with essay writing. Within the context of nonfiction, *argument* refers to the reasons marshalled for or against a particular position. An argumentative essay takes one side of an issue, and its author *argues,* in the sense of makes a case for, that side being the right one. The very word derives from the Latin *argumentum* meaning evidence or proof.

Evidence is one of the basic tools of argument. Historical precedent, causal relationships, statistics, examples, analogies, the findings of research, the statements of authorities—all constitute varieties of evidence a writer can cite to support a position, and all are ways of persuading the reader by appealing to reason. Other types of appeal, however, are also at work and often operate beneath the surface of the argument. Appeals to emotion, for instance, can be subtle, hiding perhaps in the shading of a word—the choice of "lurid" over "vivid," as in the example that follows. Or they can be overt as in the attention-getting, emotionally laden examples that open Eugene H. Methvin's essay on television violence:

> San Diego: A high-school honor student watches a lurid ABC-TV fictionalization of the 1890s Lizzie Borden ax murder case; then chops his own parents and sister to death and leaves his brother a quadriplegic.

Far more subtle, however, is the appeal evoked by the character of the writer. As readers, all of us are inclined to believe an individual of obvious good will, someone who advocates the greater good and speaks from a position of authority, whose view of the issue is balanced, who takes opposing beliefs into account and treats them honestly and with respect. In "Active and Passive Euthanasia," for instance, James Rachels urges doctors to reconsider the American Medical Association's current policy on passive euthanasia. Rachels strikes the reader as courteous, reasonable, and cool-headed even though he obviously feels strongly about convincing his audience of his thesis. He values the opinions of those who support the document, and he augments his appeal by basing his argument on moral and humanitarian grounds.

The object of all argumentative writing is to convince the reader to adopt the convictions or actions urged by the writer. Often the essay falls short of that goal, but even if the writer has only induced the reader to stop, think, and reconsider the basis for an opinion, the piece has been successful. Francine Klagsbrun's essay "Hooray for Jewish Mothers!" may not force "those closet Jewish mothers of all races and religions" to declare themselves, but it may cause us to reevaluate our concept of stereotypes. So too Lewis Thomas' essay "On the Need for Asylums" may not resolve the problem, but it will probably make us examine how society "treats its most disadvantaged, its least beloved, its mad." And Gary Pavela's essay "Cheating on the Campus" may not provide any definitive answers, but it will encourage us to reconsider "who's really to blame."

Like all writers, an argumentative essayist cannot see the reader. But here the problem is more acute, for the writer cannot spot the frown, catch the look of puzzlement, hear the words of disbelief; instead the argumentative essayist must anticipate these reactions by engaging in an imaginary debate. Acquiring this ability to predicate the existence of a reader whose views are different from one's own is what makes argumentative writing difficult, but that same ability to think through the twists and turns and logical pathways and irrational biases of another's mind is what makes argument a challenge. "Where there is much desire to learn," said seventeenth-century poet John Milton, "there of necessity will be much arguing, much writing, many opinions: for opinion . . . is but knowledge in the making."

FRANCINE KLAGSBRUN

Hooray for Jewish Mothers!

"Hooray for Jewish Mothers!" appeared in the March 28, 1983, *Newsweek*'s "My Turn" column, a regular feature in which the magazine's readers express their views. *Newsweek*'s editors note that "When she is not overprotecting her daughter, Francine Klagsbrun is a writer, currently working on a book about marriages that last." In the essay that follows, Klagsbrun faces an unusual dilemma: how to get readers to take seriously what so many consider to be a joke—the Jewish mother—and how to expand an ethnic stereotype to include a wider audience, the readers of *Newsweek*. See if you can discern the techniques Klagsbrun uses to resolve these problems.

1 Have you heard the latest light-bulb joke? *How many Jewish mothers does it take to change a light bulb? None—"Don't bother, I'll sit in the dark."*

2 I've been treated to this barb at least three times in the past month, each time prefaced by a good-natured "you'll really enjoy this one." If you're Jewish and a mother, as I am, you are subjected to every new Jewish-mother quip that makes the rounds. Worse, you're never quite certain the jokes aren't aimed directly at you. If you're not Jewish, but a mother, you still find yourself

vulnerable, for the Jewish-mother stereotype has long since cut across religious and racial boundaries. You can be Chinese, black, Puerto Rican or Italian. All you need to do to be labeled a Jewish mother is to demonstrate one or more of the maligned characteristics of the species—that is, to be overprotective, demanding, self-sacrificing or guilt-inducing.

The Jewish-mother caricature first burst upon us in the early 1960s, when Jewish writers and comedians (all of them male, few of them fathers) discovered in their immigrant mothers useful targets for both their humor and their anger. Since then, the Jewish mother has come to be viewed as the embodiment of a parent's worst impulses. As a result, all mothers have learned to be self-conscious and cautious in their child-rearing practices. Do you want to remind your daughter to wear a scarf and gloves on a cold winter day? Stop it. Don't be one of those overprotective Jewish mothers who swaddles her children in snowsuits and galoshes. Do you think your son should work harder to improve his school grades? Boy, you really are a pushy Jewish mother! 3

I believe the time has come for us to take a new look at the Jewish-mother stereotype. God knows, we don't seem to have improved much as parents since we began renouncing the Jewish-mother way. Our adolescent suicide rate has doubled in the last two decades, teen-age pregnancies rise year after year, drug abuse continues to plague many families and cults lure the innocent and insecure. Perhaps we can find some insights we overlooked within those very qualities we have ridiculed and rejected for the last 20 years. 4

Take, for example, overprotection. The proverbial Jewish mother is nothing if not overprotective, drowning her children in chicken soup at the slightest sign of a sniffle (Did you know that chicken soup has been found to be a medicinally sound remedy for a cold?). She doesn't know, as we do, that overprotection stifles independence. Or does it? I would submit, in our revisionist view, that overprotection builds a firm base of security in a child. Children who are carefully protected know that they are loved and important, and because they are important to their parents they become important to themselves. Fortified with their self-esteem, they can become strong and independent adults. Moreover, studies have shown that overprotected children are far less susceptible to peer pressure than children turned loose on their environment at a young age. 5

True, some Jewish mothers have been known to slip from overprotection to smothering, but often kids are able to carve out their own identities because of the very need to push away from their parents. In pushing hard against encircling arms, they strengthen their own muscles, shape their own space, develop their own centers.

Oh, but the demands—what of those demands and expectations Jewish-mother types have placed on their children? Sure, when parental demands exceed the abilities of a child, they can be dangerous and destructive. But we've also seen the dangers of leaning over backward not to pressure kids, not to burden them with expectations. The results are young people who feel confused, lacking in self-discipline, reluctant to put themselves on the line. Intelligent "pushiness" often pushes children to stretch as far as they can. 6

And self-sacrifice? Portnoy complained that his mother was "vying with twenty other Jewish women to be the patron saint of self-sacrifice." I don't deny that a little sigh of martyrdom may occasionally have escaped the lips of Jewish mothers. Still, if I had to choose between excessive self-sacrifice and excessive self-fulfillment as parental goals, I would stick with self-sacrifice. Jewish mothers have known how to give of themselves. In doing so, they provided not only love and support, but models for their children of what commitment and caring are all about. 7

Ah, you may say, but what about guilt, the Jewish mother's ultimate weapon? There's guilt and there's guilt. If a mother threatens to put her head in the stove at the slightest sign of disobedience, that's a bad use of guilt. But parents have to set standards. If you forbid your 15-year-old son to drink beer at a party and he drinks anyway, his feeling guilty may prevent his drinking next time or the time after that. This is guilt well used. Jewish mothers of old knew this. They stood firm on what they believed to be right and wrong, and minced no words in conveying those beliefs. Many of us today have lost either our convictions or our ability to transmit them, or both. And many "guilt free" kids are the worse for it. 8

We've all known extremist Jewish mothers—just as we've known extremist mothers of the remote, "Ordinary People" school—and extremists deserve to be laughed at. The negative 9 stereotypes, however, have gone much further, undermining the many good values of Jewish motherhood. It has been said that the stereotypes will disappear soon because the Jewish mother herself is becoming extinct, now that so many women work outside their homes. Possibly. I prefer to believe that there are still plenty of Jewish mothers in our midst, working or not. They have simply gone underground in the past two decades, practicing their art clandestinely for fear of becoming the butt of yet one more round of jokes.

To those closet Jewish mothers of all races and religions, I 10
say: come out. We need you now. We want to observe you. We want to learn from you. And we want to celebrate you with the traditional toast of our people: *l'chaim*, may you live and be well, and go on mothering for 120 years!

THE THINKING PROCESS

STRUCTURE

1. Most effective introductory paragraphs have more than one purpose. Examine Klagsbrun's introduction, paragraphs 1 through 4. What techniques does she use to engage her reader? What other functions does the introduction perform? What words or phrases can you cite to support your opinion?

2. The body of the essay is composed of paragraphs 5 through 8. What paragraphs discuss which characteristics of the Jewish mother? Where in the essay are those characteristics introduced? What are the cause-and-effect relationships involved with each of the traits?

3. Paragraphs 9 and 10 serve as the essay's conclusion. In what ways do they support Klagsbrun's line of argument? What ideas in the conclusion can you connect with other ideas in the essay? Consider the introduction together with the conclusion: in your own words, what is the thesis of the essay? What action does Klagsbrun call for?

STYLE

1. Voice is crucial to the argumentative essay, for the writer must appear reasonable and credible, present convincing evidence and persuasive details, and address and overturn the opposing views. Where does Klagsbrun incorporate the negative characteristics of the Jewish mother? Examine the paragraphs that contain both Klagsbrun's points and those of the opposition. What words or phrases does she use to change the focus from one side to the other? What is the sequence of pros and cons behind Klagsbrun's discussion?

2. Klagsbrun's tone balances the formal and the colloquial, an effect she achieves by dramatizing her argument as a dialogue. What evidence can you find that she has set up her essay as an imaginary dialogue? How does this technique affect the distances among the subject, the author, and the reader?

3. On the surface, Klagsbrun's changes in point of view and choice of pronouns are just what beginning writers are cautioned against: she uses the second person *you*; she begins with first person singular, changes to first person plural, and then uses both. What reasons can you find for Klagsbrun's choice of pronouns? Does the "we" of paragraph 10 refer to the same group as the "we" of paragraph 4? How or how not?

4. To reinforce the argument, writers depend on persuasion that appeals to our emotions. Where in the essay does Klagsbrun appeal to emotion? How would you assess the weight of her logical appeal, her marshalling of evidence? Are her sources accurate? Are her assumptions valid? Her cause and effect relationships sound? How or how not?

IDEAS FOR A FIRST DRAFT

Consider the various stereotypes associated with ethnic origins (Polish, Italian, Irish), occupations (absentminded professor, conservative banker, uneducated blue-collar worker), and the sexes (men are dominating and insensitive; women, weepy and weak). Jot down several familiar stereotypes, and for each list the negative characteristics society associates with it. Then think how each element of the negative stereotype can be turned to advantage, just as Klagsbrun turned the negative traits of the Jewish mother into positive ones. Choose a stereotype, and then list the positive and negative sides associated with each characteristic. You may find that one trait spins off another, just as Klagsbrun's "overprotective, demanding, self-sacrificing . . . guilt inducing" (2) are interrelated.

If negative stereotypes don't appeal, consider categories of people society admires: the hero or heroine, the professional athlete, the top student, the celebrity. Add your own categories, and then for each think first about the advantages of the role and then about its disadvantages. Choose the topic that you find most engaging, and write down the negative and positive aspects of the role. Where in the first assignment you would argue for the positive sides of a seemingly negative stereotype, here you will argue for the disadvantages inherent in a seemingly advantageous position.

No matter what topic you choose, your list will develop into the body of the paper, and the only questions that remain are in what order to present the items and how to incorporate opposite opinions. If you bring out the major objection to your position and dispose of it, you will have accounted for the strongest line of argument that can be used against you. Where you choose to fit in the opposition depends on how you arrange your own points. One of the most effective sequences is dramatic arrangement. Narrow your list to three or four characteristics: start with the least significant and work up to the most, or start with the least known trait and work up to the most familiar. You will probably achieve the greatest success by devoting a single paragraph to each characteristic and its counterpart.

Address your paper to a general readership or, if you prefer, to the group most apt to be concerned with your topic. Your essay may make a successful guest opinion for your school or local paper or, like Klagsbrun's essay, it may appear in *Newsweek.* Your purpose is to convert your audience to your position or to the course of action that you recommend. Like Klagsbrun, you may want to reserve overtly stating your position or recommended action for the last paragraph and perhaps finish on an amusing or ironic note. Your introduction may describe the background of the stereotype or role, review its opposite effects, and set out your essay's focus.

Both assignments lend themselves to humor, but a parody or a satiric tone is one of the most difficult to sustain, so don't attempt either unless you are confident of success. Whether your tone is serious or comic, test your ideas on a friend or two before you begin so that you can see if your approach is convincing. To be successful, argumentative essayists must not only support their own positions while influencing the undecided readers, they must also engage readers who don't share their opinions.

LEWIS THOMAS

On the Need for Asylums

Physician, researcher, and writer, Lewis Thomas was born in Flushing, New York, in 1913. His medical career spans a number of fields—neurology, pediatrics, pathology, and cancer research—and a number of medical schools—Johns Hopkins, Tulane, the University of Minnesota, New York University, and Yale. In 1973, he became president of the Memorial Sloan-Kettering Cancer Center, where he now serves as chancellor.

In 1971, Thomas began writing "Notes of a Biology Watcher," a regular column in the *New England Journal of Medicine.* His columns were collected in *The Lives of a Cell: Notes of a Biology Watcher* (1974), which won a National Book Award, and in *The Medusa and the Snail: More Notes of a Biology Watcher* (1979). Since that time, Thomas has been contributing to *Discover*, a monthly magazine published by Time Inc. that is aimed at educated general readers interested in the sciences. The essay that follows appeared first in *Discover* and has since been reprinted in Thomas' third collection of essays, *Late Night Thoughts on Listening to Mahler's Ninth Symphony* (1983). If you look up the definition of *asylum* in an unabridged dictionary, you will find that Thomas' essay takes on an added meaning.

From time to time, medical science has achieved an indisputable triumph that is pure benefit for all levels of society and deserving of such terms as "breakthrough" and "medical miracle." It is not a long list, but the items are solid bits of encouragement for the future. The conquests of tuberculosis, smallpox, and syphilis of the central nervous system should be at the top of anyone's list. Rheumatic fever, the most common cause of heart disease forty years ago, has become a rare, almost exotic disorder, thanks to the introduction of antibiotics for treating streptococcal sore throat. Some forms of cancer—notably childhood leukemias, Hodgkin's disease, and certain sarcomas affecting young people—have become curable in a high proportion of patients. Poliomyelitis is no longer with us. 1

But there is still a formidable agenda of diseases for which there are no cures, needing much more research before their underlying mechanisms can be brought to light. Among these diseases are some for which we have only halfway technologies to offer, measures that turn out to be much more costly than we had guessed and only partly, sometimes marginally, effective. The transplantation of major organs has become successful, but only for a relatively small number of patients with damaged kidneys and hearts, and at a financial cost much too high for applying the technologies on a wide scale. Very large numbers of patients with these fatal illnesses have no access to such treatments. Renal dialysis makes it possible to live for many months, even a few years, with failed kidneys, but it is a hard life. 2

The overestimation of the value of an advance in medicine can lead to more trouble than anyone can foresee, and a lot of careful thought and analysis ought to be invested before any technology is turned loose on the marketplace. It begins to look as if coronary bypass surgery, for example, is an indispensable operation for a limited number of people, but it was probably not necessary for the large number in whom the expensive procedure has already been employed. 3

There are other examples of this sort of premature, sweeping adoption of new measures in medicine. Probably none has resulted in more untoward social damage than the unpredicted, indirect but calamitous effects of the widespread introduction twenty or so years ago of Thorazine and its chemical relatives for 4 the treatment of schizophrenia. For a while, when it was first used in state hospitals for the insane, the new line of drugs seemed miraculous indeed. Patients whose hallucinations and delusions impelled them to wild, uncontrollable behavior were discovered to be so calmed by the treatment as to make possible the closing down of many of the locked wards in asylums. Patients with milder forms of schizophrenia could return, at least temporarily, to life outside the institutions. It was the first real advance in the treatment of severe mental disease, and the whole world of psychiatry seemed to have been transformed. Psychopharmacology became, overnight, a bright new discipline in medicine.

Then came the side effect. Not a medical side effect (al- 5
though there were some of these) but a political one, and a disaster. On the assumption that the new drugs made hospitalization unnecessary, two social policies were launched with the enthusiastic agreement of both the professional psychiatric community and the governmental agencies responsible for the care of the mentally ill. Brand-new institutions, ambitiously designated "community mental health centers," were deployed across the country. These centers were to be the source of the new technology for treating schizophrenia, along with all other sorts of mental illness: in theory, patients would come to the clinics and be given the needed drugs, and, when necessary, psychotherapy. And at the same time orders came down that most of the patients living in the state hospitals be discharged forthwith to their homes or, lacking homes, to other quarters in the community.

For a while it looked like the best of worlds, on paper, any- 6
way. Brochures with handsome charts were issued by state and federal agencies displaying the plummeting curves of state hospital occupancy, with the lines coinciding marvelously with the introduction of the new drugs. No one noted that the occupancy of private mental hospitals rose at the same time—though it could not rise very high, with the annual cost of such hospitalization running around $40,000 per bed. The term "breakthrough" was used over and over again, but after a little while it came to be something more like a breakout. The mentally ill were out of the hospital, but in many cases they were simply out on the streets, less agitated but lost, still disabled but now

uncared for. The community mental health centers were not designed to take on the task of custodial care. They could serve as shelters only during the hours of appointment, not at night.

All this is still going on, and it is not working. To be sure, 7
the drugs do work—but only to the extent of allaying some of the most distressing manifestations of schizophrenia. They do not turn the disease off. The evidences of the mind's unhinging are still there, coming and going in cycles of remission and exacerbation just as they have always done since schizophrenia was first described. Some patients recover spontaneously and for good, as some have always done. The chronically and permanently disabled are better off because they are in lesser degrees of mental torment when they have their medication; but they are at the same time much worse off because they can no longer find refuge when they are in need of it. They are, instead, out on the streets, or down in the subways, or wandering in the parks, or confined in shabby rooms in the shabbiest hotels, alone. Or perhaps they are living at home, but not many of them living happily; nor are many of their families happy to have them at home. One of the high risks of severe mental disease is suicide, and many of these abandoned patients choose this way out, with no one to stop them. It is an appalling situation.

It is claimed that the old state hospitals were even more ap- 8
palling. They were called warehouses for the insane, incapable of curing anything, more likely to make it worse by the process known in psychiatric circles as "institutionalization," a steady downhill course toward total dependency on the very bleakness of the institution itself. The places were badly managed, always understaffed, repellent to doctors, nurses, and all the other people needed for the care of those with sick minds. Better off without them, it was said. Cheaper too, although this wasn't said so openly.

What never seems to have been thought of, or at least never 9
discussed publicly, was changing the state hospitals from bad to good institutions, given the opportunity for vastly improved care that came along with the drugs. It was partly the history of such places that got in the way. For centuries the madhouses, as they were called, served no purpose beyond keeping deranged people out of the public view. Despite efforts at reform in the late

nineteenth and early twentieth centuries, they remained essentially lockups.

But now it is becoming plain that life in the state hospitals, bad as it was, was better than life in the subways or in the doorways of downtown streets, late on cold nights with nothing in the shopping bag to keep a body warm, and no protection at all against molestation by predators or the sudden urge for self-destruction. What now? 10

We should restore the state hospital system, improve it, expand it if necessary, and spend enough money to ensure that the patients who must live in these institutions will be able to come in off the streets and live in decency and warmth, under the care of adequately paid, competent professionals and compassionate surrogate friends. 11

If there is not enough money, there are ways to save. There was a time when many doctors were glad to volunteer their services on a part-time basis, indeed competed to do so, unpaid by state or federal funds and unreimbursed by insurance companies, in order to look after people unable to care for themselves. We should be looking around again for such doctors, not necessarily specialists in psychiatric medicine, but well-trained physicians possessing affection for people in trouble—a quality on which recruitment to the profession of medicine has always, we hope, been based. We cannot leave the situation of insane human beings where it is today. 12

A society can be judged by the way it treats its most disadvantaged, its least beloved, its mad. As things now stand, we must be judged a poor lot, and it is time to mend our ways. 13

THE THINKING PROCESS

STRUCTURE

1. Reread the first sentence of paragraph 3, and reread paragraphs 11 and 13. Which of the statements best serves as the essay's thesis? How so? Why do you think Thomas places his thesis where he does?

2. Examine Thomas' essay as an interweaving of problems and solutions. In which paragraph is this structure first introduced? How is it developed throughout the essay?

3. To what extent is Thomas' essay structured chronologically? Trace the time line through the essay and be prepared to discuss in class whether chronology or dramatic order controls the essay's structure.

4. Underline the first sentence in each of the essay's paragraphs. Which serve as topic sentences? Which do not? For the ones that do not, find the topic sentence of the paragraph. Why do you think that Thomas opens most of his paragraphs with topic sentences?

5. Considering the overall length of the essay, its introduction is relatively long and its conclusion short. What reasons can you find for this seeming imbalance?

STYLE

1. Passive voice has the effect of distancing the reader by blunting the action, and for that reason, many handbooks warn against its use. Thomas, however, uses passives with some frequency; paragraphs 5, 6, 8, and 9 contain several examples. Choose several sentences that contain passive constructions, and rewrite them in the active voice. What is gained? Lost?

2. Often writers use two or more parallel phrases to expand or emphasize a point. Thomas, for instance, writes of the mad "out on the streets, or down in the subways, or wandering in the parks, or confined in shabby rooms in the shabbiest hotels, alone" (7). Where else in the essay do you find him employing this technique? Is its effect intended to appeal to the reader's emotions? Reason? What does the technique allow the reader to deduce about the writer?

3. Thomas often varies the length and structure of his sentences, sometimes using a short rhetorical question or a sentence fragment. Analyze the different kinds of sentences in paragraph 5, 8, or 10. What does the sentence variety contribute to the essay's overall tone?

4. If you read Thomas' essay out loud, you will not only hear how his phrases lend cadence to sentences but also how certain sounds are repeated. In paragraph 7, for instance, alliteration reinforces the impact of the sentence's meaning: "Or perhaps they are living at home, but not many of them living happily; nor are many of their families happy to have them at home." Where else in the essay does Thomas use repetition or alliteration? Select an example and rewrite the sentence. What differences in effect do you note?

IDEAS FOR A FIRST DRAFT

If you have read chapters 4 and 5, you may have written a report that can provide the research for an argumentative paper on the same subject. If not, consider other topics like drug abuse, drunk driving, ecological hazards, or racial imbalance that invite solutions to ongoing social problems. As in reports, any of these subjects requires research. Jot down several topics about which you have strong opinions and are well informed. For each, briefly note the changes you want to take place.

After you've made your initial list of topics, select one or two, and write down for each the sources you have access to. *The Reader's Guide to Periodical Literature*, the *New York Times Index*, the index to your local newspaper, and your library's card catalogue are obvious starting points, but you may find other leads to books and articles that are even more helpful. Browsing at a newsstand that carries a comprehensive selection of magazines may turn up a journal or two that is pertinent though not surveyed by the *Reader's Guide*. Odds are as well that you know a number of people you could interview who are useful sources of information. If a questionnaire or poll is in order, you might ask an instructor in the social sciences how to devise one.

Like Thomas, you may wish to write your essay for the educated general reader, or you may want to address your paper to the individuals who are in positions to effect the changes you propose. You should review your notes to determine which audience is most appropriate for your solutions: perhaps a letter to your local school board member, legislator, city council member, or newspaper editor; or an essay in the newsletter of a professional group, such as business people in the Chamber of Commerce or members of the local bar or medical association. With your audience in mind, briefly state the problem as you see it, and then reduce your list of solutions to those most important and most feasible.

Figure out how you want to sequence your solutions. Perhaps you want to list the solution easiest to implement first, saving the hardest until last; or perhaps you want to start with the most fundamental and then discuss the related solutions. Once you have established the order for your points, begin writing the body of the paper. Devote at least one paragraph to each alternative, and preface it with a clear topic sentence. Later, when you review the draft as a whole and check its tone, you may want to reposition the topic sentence in the paragraph. But for the moment rely on these introductory topic sentences to structure your essay and to give your readers a clear sense of what actions they should take.

Your introduction may state the problem as you see it or provide a brief history either of the problem itself or of the solutions that were tried and failed. For a conclusion, try one or more of the following: call for immediate action, describe the consequences of not heeding your advice, briefly narrate your personal involvement, or include any other idea that will reinforce your argumentative purpose.

When you reread your draft, make sure that your diction and your presentation of evidence will not insult or alienate your audience. Whether your readers are predisposed in your favor or opposed because they have different solutions, your job is to win them over by the force of your authority and your evidence.

GARY PAVELA

Cheating on the Campus: Who's Really to Blame?

"Cheating on the Campus: Who's Really to Blame?" appeared in the February 9, 1981, issue of *The Chronicle of Higher Education*, a weekly publication addressed to college and university faculty members, administrators, and boards of trustees. Gary Pavela, the author of the essay, delineates how university policies and the people entrusted with them inadvertently contribute to cheating. An academician and a lawyer, Pavela specializes in both law and education at the College Park campus of the University of Maryland where he is director of judicial programs. As you read his essay, compare the situation he describes to the one on your own campus. Is Pavela's assessment accurate?

A faculty member generated national publicity for the University of Maryland last year by apprehending several students who had taken examinations for others. The story that was not adequately told, however, was that lethargy and confusion among many university administrators and faculty members were major contributors to problems of academic dishonesty that were being blamed exclusively on the deficient moral standards of our students. 1

Academic dishonesty is nothing new. In 1930, F. W. Parr 2

observed in the *Journal of Higher Education* that more than 40 per cent of students were "likely to be dishonest in the college classroom." Similar warnings were issued in subsequent decades, including William Bower's widely publicized report in 1964, which contained the "alarming finding" that "at least half the students in the [nationwide] sample have engaged in some form of academic dishonesty." In short, the willingness of students to engage in academic dishonesty seems to have remained relatively constant over the years, partly because, as Mr. Parr wrote, "any individual will or could be made to deviate from what is considered 'proper' conduct if confronted with a sufficiently potent incentive."

The incentives to engage in academic dishonesty on our campus included a lack of attention to even rudimentary precautions in the preparation and proctoring of examinations, vague and cumbersome policies and procedures that discouraged faculty members from reporting cases, and lenient penalties that suggested to the campus community that academic dishonesty was not regarded as a serious offense. The consequences were predictable. Students systematically stole and distributed examinations, forged dozens of "grade change" forms and related documents, infiltrated an administrative office (where over 40 grades for the members of a campus fraternity were falsified), and engaged in open and rampant cheating during examinations in several large lecture courses. 3

Moral condemnation and sociological generalizations were not sufficient responses to the serious incidents we were encountering. What was also needed was careful attention to the ways in which our own policies and procedures were compounding the problem of academic dishonesty on the campus. Some of our efforts in this direction have progressed to the point that we can share a few suggestions with others: 4

Develop a definition of "academic dishonesty." It is difficult to discourage academic dishonesty effectively if students and faculty members don't know what the term means. At Maryland, for example, we simply had prohibited all "academic irregularities," which, if taken literally, could have included chewing gum in class. As a result, we frequently wasted a considerable amount of energy in protracted and frustrating debates about whether or not academic dishonesty included negligent as well as intentional acts, or whether or not it was improper to submit portions 5 of the same academic work in more than one class. The board of regents recently resolved these and several other dilemmas by adopting a document that divides academic dishonesty into four categories: "cheating," "fabrication," "facilitating academic dishonesty," and "plagiarism," with specific definitions for each.

Reaffirm the importance of academic integrity. Academic dis- 6
honesty has had relatively strong peer support and acceptance among some students, partly because we did not make a serious effort to explain why such behavior is contemptible. It is imperative to remind ourselves and our students that the university is dedicated to learning and that academic dishonesty undermines the very foundation of that enterprise. Furthermore, academic dishonesty deceives those who may eventually depend upon our knowledge and integrity, even to the point of jeopardizing their lives or property. A recent study reported in the *Journal of Medical Education,* for example, found a "positive correlation between cheating in school and cheating in patient care" by young physicians.

Reduce temptation. We normally recognize that certain forms 7
of negligence may tempt otherwise decent people to be dishonest. Why is it, then, when we hear of students cheating in insufficiently proctored examinations, or misusing official forms left carelessly outside administrative offices, that we are so inclined to make pronouncements about the decadence of youth and the decline of Western civilization? Instead, we should review the procedures followed by administrators and faculty members and eliminate those that encourage academic dishonesty.

Eliminate proceduralism. Many administrators, paralyzed by 8
a misconception of "due process," have erroneously assumed that full adversarial hearings, technical rules of evidence, multiple appeals, and the like are required "by law" in student disciplinary cases. Not surprisingly, faculty members are reluctant to involve themselves in such proceedings. As a consequence, some of them ignore academic dishonesty altogether, thereby putting honest students at a competitive disadvantage. Others simply lower the grades of students whom they presume guilty of cheating or plagiarism. Both practices injure students without any due process at all, and prevent the university from identifying repeat offenders.

Colleges and universities across the country are now re- 9
vising disciplinary regulations. It is important to develop

equitable procedures that are compatible with the needs of the academic community. For example, the new *Code of Student Conduct* at our institution provides for streamlined "disciplinary conferences" rather than formal hearings in most cases.

Impose strict penalties. Last year's report by the Carnegie 10
Council on Policy Studies in Higher Education contained the observation that "colleges and their faculties have generally tended to be lax in punishing students for academic dishonesty." The most common example, on our campus and elsewhere, has been the practice of simply giving the offending student a failing grade. Such a policy misleads other schools to which the student might apply, and does not deter those students already in danger of failing the course. Instead, if clear definitions of academic dishonesty have been developed, and if a reasonable effort has been made to inform students that such offenses are treated seriously, the appropriate punishment for a willful offense should be some form of separation from the university, a permanent notation on the student's official transcript, or both. It is often painful to impose such sanctions in a specific case, but it is imperative to do so if we wish to eliminate a campus climate that not only is tolerant of academic dishonesty, but may also have the perverse effect of encouraging students who did not cheat at home or in secondary school to adopt such practices in college and throughout their lives.

One of the journalists who visited our campus stopped 11
taking notes when I shifted the topic of our conversation from the moral values of contemporary students to the shortcomings at the university. The article that he later wrote was not inaccurate, but his primary focus upon student attitudes did not encompass the full scope of the problem. Academic dishonesty does indeed reveal the moral deficiencies of those students who engage in it. Responsibility also lies, however, with administrators and faculty members who knowingly tolerate conditions that would allow academic dishonesty to flourish in any generation of students.

THE THINKING PROCESS

STRUCTURE

1. When an introduction is composed of a block of paragraphs, the author must be careful to interrelate the ideas so that the introduction functions as a recognizable unit. Pavela opens the essay with a description of the recent cheating scandal at the University of Maryland and then states that the newspaper accounts attributed the cheating to the "deficient moral standards of our students," ignoring the part played by many of the university's faculty and administrators. Examine the rest of the introduction (2-4). How does the information in paragraphs 2 and 3 relate to that in paragraph 1? What is the function of paragraph 4?

2. Paragraphs 5 through 10 delineate five measures that should be taken to reduce or eliminate the conditions that are conducive to cheating. What reasons can you find to explain Pavela's sequencing of those measures?

3. In his conclusion, Pavela reasserts his position that students alone are not to blame for cheating. Examine how the essay states a problem, and then sets out solutions. Putting both problem and solutions together, state in your own words Pavela's argumentative position.

STYLE

1. Argumentative writers often face the dilemma of writing to reform the very audience they criticize. Pavela's audience, for example, is composed of the same faculty members and administrators who are "to blame," which makes his argumentative task difficult: he must show them the error of their ways and point the way to reform without alienating them. For instance, Pavela chooses "reaffirm" in paragraph 6, which implies that his audience already believes in the "importance of academic integrity." What other words or phrases does Pavela use that indicate his audience is not wrong, only misguided?

2. Parallel sentence structure can add unity to an essay or become repetitious. Pavela's paragraphs 5 through 8 and 10, for instance, all begin with an italicized, imperative sentence. How does this technique affect the essay's structure? Pavela's argumentative position? Change one or two of the sentences from the imperative to the indicative or subjunctive. What is gained? Lost?

3. The level of diction in an essay depends on the writer's audience. A list of the three- and four-syllable words that Pavela uses reveals a high proportion of formal, Latinate words. Select several and rewrite the sentences they appear in using informal diction. Try making the sentence structure more conversational. What is gained? Lost? Given the essay's intended audience, what level of diction is more appropriate?

IDEAS FOR A FIRST DRAFT

Like Pavela, you will be investigating a topic to distinguish between real and illusory causes of a particular problem and then making a case for who is to blame. List some questions that you have about professions or cultural concerns. You might explore why some jobs are race- or sex-related: Why are there few black geologists? Male nurses? Female dentists? If exploring a profession doesn't appeal to you, try thinking of questions related to our culture: Why do people like fast food? Why do so many people criticize the quality of popular shows on television? Why are punk fashions popular? What is Michael Jackson's attraction?

Think too of the audience you wish to address. Like Pavela, you might address readers who are in a position to adopt what you are arguing for. If you are pinpointing discrimination within an occupation, consider aiming your argument at the appropriate professional group like the American Bar Association or the American Medical Association. If your subject is a cultural concern, direct your argument to people in a position to effect change, perhaps the local legislature, or write to a more general audience such as the readers of the *Washington Post* or a weekly magazine.

Once you have devised your list of questions, select two or

three to examine in closer detail. For each, jot down possible sources of information. Where can you find facts and figures? Whom might you interview for further information? Are your sources reliable? Now see if you can come up with some tentative answers to your questions. At this point you should be able to tell which subject will be the most fruitful to pursue, and you can sketch out your working argumentative position. Be prepared, however, to abandon any hypothesis that is not borne out by your research.

Your next step is the research itself. Refine your list of possible sources so that it is feasible yet appropriately thorough. Start with facts and figures. For instance, if you are examining a career, find out how many dentists practice in the United States. How many are women? How many students are in dentistry school? How many of them are women? You might also survey any career information distributed by the relevant professional organizations; your college placement office is a good resource.

If you are examining an aspect of popular culture, determine what definitions are necessary. One useful technique is to define your subject by comparing it to something familiar. For instance, when writing for an audience who were teenagers in the 1950s and 1960s, you could explain punk haircuts as a combination crewcut and ducktail. You will also need to place your sources in a larger context to explain who your authorities are and why you chose them. As for facts and figures, you need to know just how popular fast-food chains are. Answers to questions such as these are apt to be found in articles indexed in *The Reader's Guide to Periodical Literature*, a standard index of many popular magazines.

Sometimes it's easier to write an introduction after you've written a rough draft of the basic argument, so try working on the middle of your argument first. Perhaps see if you can summarize the answers your sources provided, and try that summary as a lead-in paragraph to your argument. The body of your essay, like that of Pavela's, can then argue for the changes you think should be made. Like Pavela, you might want to introduce each paragraph with a short, imperative statement that functions as a topic sentence. For a conclusion, you might want to use a closing narrative, an apt quotation, or a restatement of your own opinion.

EUGENE H. METHVIN

TV Violence: The Shocking New Evidence

The correlation between violence on the television screen and violence in everyday life has long been scrutinized, and in the subtitle of the essay that follows, Eugene H. Methvin gives us the latest word—"Massive research over the past decade leaves little doubt: television is seriously damaging to our children." But all is not lost, says Methvin: "We can do something about it." His article appeared as the feature story in the January 1983 *Reader's Digest*, a magazine whose thirty-one million copies a month appear in sixteen languages. Although many of its articles are reprinted from other sources, this particular one was written specifically for *Reader's Digest*; Methvin is one of the magazine's senior editors in the Washington bureau.

• San Diego: A high-school honor student watches a lurid ABC-TV fictionalization of the 1890s Lizzie Borden ax murder case; then chops his own parents and sister to death and leaves his brother a quadriplegic. 1

• Denver: *The Deer Hunter* is telecast and a 17-year-old kills himself with a revolver, acting out the movie's climactic game of Russian roulette. He is the 25th viewer in two years to kill himself that way after watching the drama on TV. 2

• Decatur, Ill.: A 12-year-old overdoses on sleeping pills after her mother forbids her to date a 16-year-old boy. "What gave you the idea of suicide?" an investigating psychiatrist asks. The answer: A little girl tried it on a TV show, was quickly revived and welcomed back by her parents with open arms. 3

Ten years ago, after studying massive research on the subject, the U.S. Surgeon General, Jesse L. Steinfeld, declared, "The causal relationship between televised violence and antisocial behavior is sufficient to warrant immediate remedial action." Called before Congress, the presidents of the three networks solemnly agreed. 4

Yet the University of Pennsylvania's Annenberg School of Communications, which for 14 years has charted mayhem in network programming, reports that violent acts continue at about six per prime-time hour and in four out of every five programs. The weekend children's programs are even worse. 5

Last May the National Institute of Mental Health (NIMH) issued a report summarizing over 2500 studies done in the last decade on television's influence on behavior. Evidence from the studies—with more than 100,000 subjects in dozens of nations—is so "overwhelming," the NIMH found, that there is a consensus in the research community "that violence on television does lead to aggressive behavior." 6

Television ranks behind only sleep and work as a consumer of our time. In fact, according to the 1982 Nielsen Report on Television, the average American family keeps its set on for 49½ hours each week. The typical youngster graduating from high school will have spent almost twice as much time in front of the tube as he has in the classroom—the staggering equivalent of ten years of 40-hour weeks. He will have witnessed some 150,000 violent episodes, including an estimated 25,000 deaths. 7

Despite the mayhem, the viewer sees little pain or suffering, a false picture that influences young and old. At a Capitol Hill hearing on TV violence, a dismayed Rep. Billy Tauzin complained to network executives that his three-year-old son had poked his fist through a glass door—in imitation of a TV cartoon character—and almost bled to death. In New Rochelle, N.Y., a killer who re-enacted a TV bludgeon murder told police of his surprise when his victim did not die with the first crunch of his baseball bat, as on the tube, but instead threw up a hand in defense and groaned and cried piteously. 8

The effect of all this? Research points toward these conclu- 9
sions:

1. TV violence produces lasting and serious harm. University of 10
Illinois psychology professor Leonard Eron and colleagues compared the television diets and level of aggressive behavior of 184 boys at age eight and again at 18. His report: "The more violent the programs watched in childhood, the more combative the young adults became. We found their behavior studded with antisocial acts, from theft and vandalism to assault with a deadly weapon. The children appeared to learn aggressive habits that persisted for at least ten years."

2. Those "action" cartoons on children's programs are decidedly 11
damaging. Stanford University psychologist Albert Bandura found cartoon violence as potent as real-life models in increasing violence among youngsters. A University of Kansas researcher reported that Saturday-morning cartoons markedly decreased imaginative play and hiked aggression among 66 preschoolers. In a year-long study of 200 preschoolers, Yale University Drs. Jerome L. and Dorothy Singer found that playground depredations like fighting and kicking were far greater among steady action-cartoon viewers.

Indeed, the Saturday-morning "kid vid" ghetto is the most 12
violent time on TV. It bathes the prime audience of youngsters from 3 to 13 years old with 25 violent acts per hour, much of it in a poisonous brew of violent programs and aggressive commercials designed to sell such products as breakfast cereals and action toys. According to one study, these commercials have a rate of violence about three times that of the programs themselves.

3. TV erodes inhibitions. With a $290,000 grant from CBS, 13
British psychologist William A. Belson studied the television diets and subsequent behavior of 1565 London boys ages 12 to 17. He found cartoon, slapstick or science-fiction violence less harmful at this age; but realistic fictional violence, violence in close personal relationships, and violence "in a good cause" were deadly poison. Heavy viewers were 47-percent more likely to commit acts such as knifing during a school fight, burning another with a cigarette, slashing car tires, burglary and attempted rape. To Belson's surprise, the TV exposure did not seem to change the boys' opinions toward violence but rather seemed to crumble whatever constraints family, church or school had built up. "It is almost as if the boys then tend to let

go whatever violent tendencies are in them. It just seems to explode in spontaneous ways."

4. The sheer quantity of TV watching by youngsters increases hurtful behavior and poor academic performance. "When the TV set is on, it freezes everybody," says Cornell University psychologist Urie Bronfenbrenner. "Everything that used to go on between people—the games, the arguments, the emotional scenes out of which personality and ability develop—is stopped. When you turn on the TV, you turn off the process of making human beings human." 14

Studies in the United States, Canada, Israel, Australia and Europe show that the amount of TV watched, regardless of program content, is a critical variable that contributes heavily to children's later aggressive attitudes and behavior. Dozens of other studies indicate that TV impairs the children's verbal skills and creativeness. 15

What parents can do. First of all, they can help by realizing that their own TV viewing affects the quality of family life. Until recently most adults worried that violent programming might be harmful to children, but assumed they could gorge themselves with impunity on whatever programs caught their fancy. Not so. 16

In one study, U.C.L.A. researchers Roderic Gorney and David Loye divided 183 husbands, ages 20 to 70, into five comparable groups. The groups were assigned 21 hours of varied TV fare at home during a single week, and each man kept a diary of his "moods." Wives, without knowing which TV diet the husbands watched, recorded "hurtful" and "helpful" behaviors. The result: husbands who watched violent programming recorded a significantly higher level of aggressive moods. Furthermore, their wives noted about 35-percent more daily incidents of hurtful behavior than did wives whose husbands watched "prosocial" programming. 17

"The important lesson of our experiment is that adults, by their own programming choices, may actually *reduce* aggressive moods and hurtful behavior," says Gorney. "In a home the climate generated by parental moods and conduct is surely as crucial as what children see on TV in determining the family's mental health." 18

Further, parents can curtail the total time children watch 19 television. Investigators find that parents are consistently unaware of how long their children are watching, and underestimate how much violence they see and how much it disturbs them. Experts agree that three hours a day should be an absolute maximum for subteen children and far less than that of action drama, cartoons and other violence-packed programming. Advises syndicated columnist Ann Landers: "Be firm. You wouldn't allow your child to eat garbage, would you? Why, then, let him put it in his head?"

Parents can avoid using TV as a baby-sitter, and they can 20
watch with their children—making certain that incidents of violence or sex never go without comment. Parents can encourage children to identify and watch programs of educational and social value. They should not hesitate to change channels or turn off the set. As an aid, Yale University's Family Television Research and Consultation Center has produced a carefully tested program for parents and teachers of children ranging from nursery to junior high: *Getting the Most Out of TV*, published at $7.95 by Scott, Foresman & Co., 1900 East Lake Ave., Glenview, Ill. 60025.

What everyone can do. In legal theory, "the airwaves 21
belong to the people," and the nation's 1067 television stations enjoy their federally awarded monopoly only in return for programming "in the public interest." In general, the government cannot deny any corporation the right to advertise on any program it chooses. But the viewer has a right to declare that he is not going to help pay for those programs by buying the advertised products.

Both the American Medical Association and the National 22
PTA have urged their members to bring public pressure against advertisers on high-violence programs. The National Coalition on Television Violence (NCTV), formed by psychiatrists, pediatricians and educators, carefully grades network prime-time and weekend children's programs. Each quarter it publishes lists of the companies and products that sponsor the most mayhem, and also companies that allot the largest portion of their television budgets to violent programming. (The NCTV's address: P.O. Box 2157, Champaign, Ill. 61820.) It promotes legislative

action and urges school, church and parent groups to publish its lists and to complain to advertisers.

Some companies need little prompting. Kodak has always shunned violent programming and consistently ranks low in NCTV monitoring lists. Kraft, Inc., also has a long-standing policy against programming that depicts excessive violence. Other companies that rate well with NCTV include Hallmark Cards, Schering-Plough and Campbell Soup. 23

Too much TV watching—and violent programming in general—can indeed be harmful to viewers' health. Says NCTV's chairman, Dr. Thomas Radecki, a psychiatry professor at Southern Illinois University, "Each of us bears a responsibility in stopping this ubiquitous teacher of rage and hate. Each of us must live in the world it is destroying." 24

THE THINKING PROCESS

STRUCTURE

1. Most essays have a relatively short introduction, but Methvin's introduction is fairly lengthy—eight paragraphs, one third of the essay. What is the purpose of paragraphs 1 through 3? Paragraphs 4 through 6? Paragraph 7? Paragraph 8? Could the introduction be reduced without adversely affecting the essay? How or how not?

2. Within the body of the essay (10-23), which paragraphs focus on television's harmful effects? Why might Methvin have presented them in the order he does? The first and third of Methvin's conclusions each receive one paragraph's worth of attention, but the second and fourth conclusions each receive two paragraphs. What reasons can you find for these differences? Why might Methvin have followed his enumeration of research findings with the actions parents, as opposed to general viewers, can take?

3. Examine the evidence. What variety is there among the sources Methvin cites? What information does he provide to reinforce his readers' belief in the studies he cites? How would you rate Methvin's use of evidence: convincing, adequate, inadequate? Why?

4. The author ends his essay with a paragraph that summarizes the effects of "too much TV watching" and then cites a medical authority. Combine Methvin's summary and his quotation from Radecki to form a statement of the essay's thesis. At what point in the essay does Methvin's thesis become clear to you? What evidence supports your opinion?

STYLE

1. When Methvin discusses boycotting products as an effective action, he mentions companies selectively. What examples does he cite? What examples does he omit and why? To what extent, if any, does Methvin's selective use of examples compromise his argument?

2. As well as appealing to reason, Methvin intensifies his persuasive tone by appealing to the readers' emotions. The essay's title, for instance, smacks of sensationalism. Where else in the essay does Methvin play on the readers' emotions? How does he do so? Do you find the technique effective or off-putting? Explain.

3. In an essay such as this one, the author must walk a fine line. Here parents and other adults, not just sponsors and programmers, are to blame for the quality and quantity of television watching and for the degree of violence in the programs. Yet if Methvin were to lecture his readers on their bad habits, they would probably be affronted and stop reading. What techniques does Methvin use to avoid pointing the finger at his readers?

4. The essay's typographical layout, its numbered and italicized sentences and subheadings, emphasize its major points and make it easy to follow. To what extent, if any, does the layout contribute to the essay's effectiveness? Considering the article's format, vocabulary, sentence structure, and information, what characteristics of its audience can you deduce?

IDEAS FOR A FIRST DRAFT

Think about laws that you believe unjust or about antisocial acts that could be mitigated if society took firmer measures. Perhaps you think that drunk drivers deserve harsher sentences than most states now allow or that victims of crimes should be compensated for their losses or that states should outlaw smoking in public places. Or maybe you want to consider some of the antisocial acts that plague us, such as vandalism, violence in the schools, and lack of common courtesy. Your research need not be as extensive as Methvin's, but you will need to collect enough evidence to show that the problem is of sufficient magnitude to warrant your reader's attention and action.

Check the *Reader's Guide*, the FBI annual crime statistics, and the *New York Times Index* as well as the index to your local paper to gather your evidence. Collect your notes under various appropriate headings such as history or background, present status, and recommended actions. If, in the course of your research, you discover someone has one of the same ideas you have, jot down the source and the person's qualifications as an authority so that you can support your opinion. Also watch for changes or proposed solutions that have failed; citing them can strengthen yours. Pay particular attention to statistics and to dramatic incidents. A news story with the headline "Drunk Driver Kills Family of Five" is a guaranteed attention-getter. Less dramatic but also impressive is the amount of money a city or a school system spends to repair the work of vandals.

To explore one way of tentatively organizing your paper, see if you can divide your notes into sections: *introduction, problem, solution, conclusion.* For the introduction, try opening with a set of short dramatic incidents similar to Methvin's first three paragraphs, and then state the problem and the fact that your readers can rectify it.

In the body of your paper, you might first discuss the ramifications of the problem, its history, and its current state. Maybe then consider moving on to the actions your readers can take. In the case of a law that needs changing, perhaps suggest whom to write to and what to say; in the case of behavior that the readers can affect directly, possibly spell out what the parent and average citizen can do, for instance, to promote discipline in the schools. If you have chosen a more abstract topic like common courtesy, you might try drawing up a checklist of ways to encourage polite behavior.

If you get stumped for a conclusion, review your notes to see if you have a quotation that lends itself to a concluding paragraph. If you have, see if you can introduce it with a brief summary of the problem. If you have no suitable quotation, perhaps update statistics or predict what the future holds if the problem continues at its present pace. Or instead you may want to wind up and make one final, strong-arm pitch to your readers.

JAMES RACHELS

Active and Passive Euthanasia

As medical technology has improved, it has brought with it a paradox: though doctors can now save lives that before would have been lost, they can also sustain life when death may be preferable. The American Medical Association's code of ethics allows withholding treatment when death is irreversible and dying is torture, but both the law and the AMA oppose active mercy killing. In the essay that follows, James Rachels argues that passive and active euthanasia are morally the same. A philosopher whose field is moral problems, Rachels is eminently qualified to argue his point; his audience is equally appropriate, doctors who subscribe to or actively support the AMA's position. The article first appeared in the January 9, 1975, *New England Journal of Medicine*, one of the more widely circulated and prestigious medical journals.

The distinction between active and passive euthanasia is thought to be crucial for medical ethics. The idea is that it is permissible, at least in some cases, to withhold treatment and allow a patient to die, but it is never permissible to take any direct action designed to kill the patient. This doctrine seems to be accepted by most doctors, and it is endorsed in a statement adopted by the House of Delegates of the American Medical Association on December 4, 1973: 1

> The intentional termination of the life of one human being by another—mercy killing—is contrary to that for which the medical profession stands and is contrary to the policy of the American Medical Association.
>
> The cessation of the employment of extraordinary means to prolong the life of the body when there is irrefutable evidence that biological death is imminent is the decision of the patient and/or his immediate family. The advice and judgment of the physician should be freely available to the patient and/or his immediate family.

However, a strong case can be made against this doctrine. In what follows I will set out some of the relevant arguments, and urge doctors to reconsider their views on this matter.

To begin with a familiar type of situation, a patient who is 2
dying of incurable cancer of the throat is in terrible pain, which can no longer be satisfactorily alleviated. He is certain to die within a few days, even if present treatment is continued, but he does not want to go on living for those days since the pain is unbearable. So he asks the doctor for an end to it, and his family joins in the request.

Suppose the doctor agrees to withhold treatment, as the 3
conventional doctrine says he may. The justification for his doing so is that the patient is in terrible agony, and since he is going to die anyway, it would be wrong to prolong his suffering needlessly. But now notice this. If one simply withholds treatment, it may take the patient longer to die, and so he may suffer more than he would if more direct action were taken and a lethal injection given. This fact provides strong reason for thinking that, once the initial decision not to prolong his agony has been made, active euthanasia is actually preferable to passive euthanasia, rather than the reverse. To say otherwise is to endorse the option that leads to more suffering rather than less, and is contrary to the humanitarian impulse that prompts the decision not to prolong his life in the first place.

Part of my point is that the process of being "allowed to die" 4
can be relatively slow and painful, whereas being given a lethal injection is relatively quick and painless. Let me give a different sort of example. In the United States about one in 600 babies is born with Down's syndrome. Most of these babies are otherwise healthy—that is, with only the usual pediatric care, they will proceed to an otherwise normal infancy. Some, however, are

born with congenital defects such as intestinal obstructions that require operations if they are to live. Sometimes, the parents and the doctor will decide not to operate, and let the infant die. Anthony Shaw describes what happens then:

> . . . When surgery is denied [the doctor] must try to keep the infant from suffering while natural forces sap the baby's life away. As a surgeon whose natural inclination is to use the scalpel to fight off death, standing by and watching a salvageable baby die is the most emotionally exhausting experience I know. It is easy at a conference, in a theoretical discussion, to decide that such infants should be allowed to die. It is altogether different to stand by in the nursery and watch as dehydration and infection wither a tiny being over hours and days. This is a terrible ordeal for me and the hospital staff—much more so than for the parents who never set foot in the nursery.[1]

I can understand why some people are opposed to all euthanasia, and insist that such infants must be allowed to live. I think I can also understand why other people favor destroying these babies quickly and painlessly. But why should anyone favor letting "dehydration and infection wither a tiny being over hours and days?" The doctrine that says that a baby may be allowed to dehydrate and wither, but may not be given an injection that would end its life without suffering, seems so patently cruel as to require no further refutation. The strong language is not intended to offend, but only to put the point in the clearest possible way.

My second argument is that the conventional doctrine leads to decisions concerning life and death made on irrelevant grounds. 5

Consider again the case of the infants with Down's syndrome who need operations for congenital defects unrelated to the syndrome to live. Sometimes, there is no operation, and the baby dies, but when there is no such defect, the baby lives on. Now, an operation such as that to remove an intestinal obstruction is not prohibitively difficult. The reason why such operations are not performed in these cases is, clearly, that the child 6

[1]A. Shaw, "Doctor, Do We Have a Choice?" *The New York Times Magazine*, January 30, 1972, p. 54.

has Down's syndrome and the parents and doctor judge that because of that fact it is better for the child to die.

But notice that this situation is absurd, no matter what view one takes of the lives and potentials of such babies. If the life of such an infant is worth preserving, what does it matter if it needs a simple operation? Or, if one thinks it better that such a baby should not live on, what difference does it make that it happens to have an unobstructed intestinal tract? In either case, the matter of life and death is being decided on irrelevant grounds. It is the Down's syndrome, and not the intestines, that is the issue. The matter should be decided, if at all, on that basis, and not be allowed to depend on the essentially irrelevant question of whether the intestinal tract is blocked. 7

What makes this situation possible, of course, is the idea that when there is an intestinal blockage, one can "let the baby die," but when there is no such defect there is nothing that can be done, for one must not "kill" it. The fact that this idea leads to such results as deciding life or death on irrelevant grounds is another good reason why the doctrine should be rejected. 8

One reason why so many people think that there is an important moral difference between active and passive euthanasia is that they think killing someone is morally worse than letting someone die. But is it? Is killing, in itself, worse than letting die? To investigate this issue, two cases may be considered that are exactly alike except that one involves killing whereas the other involves letting someone die. Then, it can be asked whether this difference makes any difference to the moral assessments. It is important that the cases be exactly alike, except for this one difference, since otherwise one cannot be confident that it is this difference and not some other that accounts for any variation in the assessments of the two cases. So, let us consider this pair of cases: 9

In the first, Smith stands to gain a large inheritance if anything should happen to his six-year-old cousin. One evening while the child is taking his bath, Smith sneaks into the bathroom and drowns the child, and then arranges things so that it will look like an accident. 10

In the second, Jones also stands to gain if anything should happen to his six-year-old cousin. Like Smith, Jones sneaks in planning to drown the child in his bath. However, just as he enters the bathroom Jones sees the child slip and hit his head, 11 and fall face down in the water. Jones is delighted; he stands by, ready to push the child's head back under if it is necessary, but it is not necessary. With only a little thrashing about, the child drowns all by himself, "accidentally," as Jones watches and does nothing.

Now Smith killed the child, whereas Jones "merely" let the 12
child die. That is the only difference between them. Did either man behave better, from a moral point of view? If the difference between killing and letting die were in itself a morally important matter, one should say that Jones's behavior was less reprehensible than Smith's. But does one really want to say that? I think not. In the first place, both men acted from the same motive, personal gain, and both had exactly the same end in view when they acted. It may be inferred from Smith's conduct that he is a bad man, although that judgment may be withdrawn or modified if certain further facts are learned about him—for example, that he is mentally deranged. But would not the very same thing be inferred about Jones from his conduct? And would not the same further considerations also be relevant to any modification of this judgment? Moreover, suppose Jones pleaded, in his own defense, "After all, I didn't do anything except just stand there and watch the child drown. I didn't kill him; I only let him die." Again, if letting die were in itself less bad than killing, this defense should have at least some weight. But it does not. Such a "defense" can only be regarded as a grotesque perversion of moral reasoning. Morally speaking, it is no defense at all.

Now, it may be pointed out, quite properly, that the cases of 13
euthanasia with which doctors are concerned are not like this at all. They do not involve personal gain or the destruction of normal healthy children. Doctors are concerned only with cases in which the patient's life is of no further use to him, or in which the patient's life has become or will soon become a terrible burden. However, the point is the same in these cases: the bare difference between killing and letting die does not, in itself, make a moral difference. If a doctor lets a patient die, for humane reasons, he is in the same moral position as if he had given the patient a lethal injection for humane reasons. If his decision was wrong—if, for example, the patient's illness was in fact curable—the decision would be equally regrettable no matter which method was used to carry it out. And if the doctor's decision was the right one, the method used is not in itself important.

The AMA policy statement isolates the crucial issue very well; the crucial issue is "the intentional termination of the life of one human being by another." But after identifying this issue, and forbidding "mercy killing," the statement goes on to deny that the cessation of treatment is the intentional termination of a life. This is where the mistake comes in, for what is the cessation of treatment, in these circumstances, if it is not "the intentional termination of the life of one human being by another"? Of course it is exactly that, and if it were not, there would be no point to it. 14

Many people will find this judgment hard to accept. One reason, I think, is that it is very easy to conflate the question of whether killing is, in itself, worse than letting die, with the very different question of whether most actual cases of killing are more reprehensible than most actual cases of letting die. Most actual cases of killing are clearly terrible (think, for example, of all the murders reported in the newspapers), and one hears of such cases every day. On the other hand, one hardly ever hears of a case of letting die, except for the actions of doctors who are motivated by humanitarian reasons. So one learns to think of killing in a much worse light than of letting die. But this does not mean that there is something about killing that makes it in itself worse than letting die, for it is not the bare difference between killing and letting die that makes the difference in these cases. Rather, the other factors—the murderer's motive of personal gain, for example, contrasted with the doctor's humanitarian motivation—account for different reactions to the different cases. 15

I have argued that killing is not in itself any worse than letting die; if my contention is right, it follows that active euthanasia is not any worse than passive euthanasia. What arguments can be given on the other side? The most common, I believe, is the following: 16

"The important difference between active and passive euthanasia is that, in passive euthanasia, the doctor does not do anything to bring about the patient's death. The doctor does nothing, and the patient dies of whatever ills already afflict him. In active euthanasia, however, the doctor does something to bring about the patient's death: he kills him. The doctor who 17 gives the patient with cancer a lethal injection has himself caused his patient's death; whereas if he merely ceases treatment, the cancer is the cause of the death."

A number of points need to be made here. The first is that it is not exactly correct to say that in passive euthanasia the doctor does nothing, for he does do one thing that is very important: he lets the patient die. "Letting someone die" is certainly different, in some respects, from other types of action—mainly in that it is a kind of action that one may perform by way of not performing certain other actions. For example, one may let a patient die by way of not giving medication, just as one may insult someone by way of not shaking his hand. But for any purpose of moral assessment, it is a type of action nonetheless. The decision to let a patient die is subject to moral appraisal in the same way that a decision to kill him would be subject to moral appraisal: it may be assessed as wise or unwise, compassionate or sadistic, right or wrong. If a doctor deliberately let a patient die who was suffering from a routinely curable illness, the doctor would certainly be to blame for what he had done, just as he would be to blame if he had needlessly killed the patient. Charges against him would then be appropriate. If so, it would be no defense at all for him to insist that he didn't "do anything." He would have done something very serious indeed, for he let his patient die. 18

Fixing the cause of death may be very important from a legal point of view, for it may determine whether criminal charges are brought against the doctor. But I do not think that this notion can be used to show a moral difference between active and passive euthanasia. The reason why it is considered bad to be the cause of someone's death is that death is regarded as a great evil—and so it is. However, if it has been decided that euthanasia—even passive euthanasia—is desirable in a given case, it has also been decided that in this instance death is no greater an evil than the patient's continued existence. And if this is true, the usual reason for not wanting to be the cause of someone's death simply does not apply. 19

Finally, doctors may think that all of this is only of academic interest—the sort of thing that philosophers may worry about but that has no practical bearing on their own work. After all, doctors must be concerned about the legal conse- 20 quences of what they do, and active euthanasia is clearly forbidden by the law. But even so, doctors should also be concerned with the fact that the law is forcing upon them a moral doctrine that may well be indefensible, and has a considerable effect on their practices. Of course, most doctors are not now in the position of being coerced in this matter, for they do not regard themselves as merely going along with what the law requires. Rather, in statements such as the AMA policy statement that I have quoted, they are endorsing this doctrine as a central point of medical ethics. In that statement, active euthanasia is condemned not merely as illegal but as "contrary to that for which the medical profession stands," whereas passive euthanasia is approved. However, the preceding considerations suggest that there is really no moral difference between the two, considered in themselves (there may be important moral differences in some cases in their *consequences*, but, as I pointed out, these differences may make active euthanasia, and not passive euthanasia, the morally preferable option). So, whereas doctors may have to discriminate between active and passive euthanasia to satisfy the law, they should not do any more than that. In particular, they should not give the distinction any added authority and weight by writing it into official statements of medical ethics.

THE THINKING PROCESS

STRUCTURE

1. The last two sentences of paragraph 1 set out Rachels' focus and purpose. What is the function of the sentences that lead up to those statements? Stated fully and in your own words, what is Rachels' thesis? At what point in the essay does the thesis become clear?

2. Example is probably the most frequently used pattern of organization, and Rachels uses examples to carry the main line of his argument. Which examples are explored in what paragraphs? For each example, write down the point it illustrates. How effectively do examples structure the essay?

3. One of the most frequently used argumentative techniques is acknowledging the arguments of the opposition and refuting them. Where in his essay does Rachels use this technique? Where does he show concern that his own argument may be difficult to accept? Given Rachels' consideration for his audience, what attitudes or views can you attribute to the readers of *The New England Journal of Medicine?*

STYLE

1. Although the topic is of general interest, Rachels' "Active and Passive Euthanasia" clearly addresses doctors. Reread the last paragraph. How does Rachels counter the view that his point "is only of academic interest"? What is the effect of including the parenthetical statement? What specific action is Rachels calling for? What other courses of action might be possible, ones that Rachels does not mention? Evaluate the effectiveness of the concluding paragraph.

2. A writer shapes his or her style to appeal to the reader's reason or emotions or a combination of the two. Examine Rachels' evidence. What sources does he use? To what extent do his examples rest upon an appeal to authority? To reason? To common sense? To humanitarian instincts? Would you classify his examples as logical or emotional appeals? Why? Considering the original audience, would the essay have been more effective or less so had Rachels depended upon extensive research and documentation?

3. To test the validity of his claim that killing is not morally worse than letting someone die. Rachels sets out two cases which he then develops in paragraphs 10 through 12. Are the cases valid examples? How or how not? In what sense can they be thought of as a false analogy to the doctor's situation? How and why does Rachels dispute that claim?

4. In paragraph 15, Rachels analyzes the connotations of "killing" and "letting die" to explain the "different reactions" to the terms. He argues that morally the two are the same but that people respond to them differently. How does he explain this difference? Is the explanation valid? How or how not? How does Rachels' discussion in the paragraph relate to his overall line of argument?

IDEAS FOR A FIRST DRAFT

Moral issues confront us daily: Can a nuclear war be justified? Can suicide be considered a moral act? Is plea bargaining morally sound? At what point should a juvenile be tried as an adult? None of these questions has a simple answer, and all of them demand research. Consider these questions and any others you would like to add to the list. Choose one, and then jot down the likely authorities whose views you should consider. If you are examining nuclear war, for instance, you will want to find out what various military and political leaders as well as scientists, theologians, and philosophers have to say; or if you are examining the issue of plea bargaining, you will want to know the views of attorneys for the defense and prosecution as well as those of noted jurists and civil liberties groups. The *Reader's Guide* as well as the *New York Times Index* provides good leads to this kind of information, as, of course, does the card catalogue.

As you conduct your research, divide your notes into pros and cons. You may have formed definite views on the issue before you started your research, but if you did not, the weight of the evidence should determine your stand. On a separate sheet of paper for each position, draw up a list of the major arguments. Once you have completed your lists, trim the arguments on your side to two or three to discuss in depth. On the sheet that lists the opposing points, mark those that counter yours and at least two others you must contend with.

Your introduction should present a brief history of the issue, a discussion of why it is of particular concern now, and a statement of your position. Since some of your readers probably disagree with your stand on the issue, you might begin the body of the paper by acknowledging and countering the opposition. Then introduce your least important point, advancing your argument to the most important.

You can place your discussion of the opposing views in the introduction or conclusion, or you can weave them into the body of your paper. No matter where you address them, handle them with respect, and refute them with evidence. For all you know, your readers hold these views, and while they may entertain an opposing opinion, your job is to persuade them to adopt your view, not to insult or condescend.

For your conclusion, you might spell out the actions that can and should be taken, relate a brief personal narrative that explains your interest, quote a telling statement or statistic, or summarize your argument forcefully. Your purpose is to persuade your readers to share your conviction or to take action, so the more effective your conclusion, the better your chances for success.

THE WRITING PROCESS

INVENTION

If you are working on a previous assignment in this chapter, you already have a rough draft and can move on to Organizing and Developing. If you are starting a new argumentative essay, however, you might want to address an immediate campus issue or a far broader philosophical concept. The assignments that follow outline the steps for both types of papers.

1. Some campus problems are perennial—the quality of food in the cafeteria, the lack of sufficient parking, the chaos of registration—and most people, particularly the people responsible, are tired of hearing about them. Instead, look for an issue few have discussed: more and more varied night classes; shorter, more concentrated summer sessions; a campus day-care center; a franchise-operated snack bar; a required computer literacy course; a drop-in tutoring service. Add your own ideas to the list.

To decide on which campus topic to pursue, conduct some preliminary research to find out which issue is of greatest student interest, which lends itself well to being researched, and who within the university administration is responsible for the change. Your sources will probably be past issues of campus newspapers, interviews with individuals, and the campus librarian, who will probably be able to suggest other materials. Select a topic, and as you conduct your research keep in mind the person who can effect the changes you desire, for that person will be your audience; a vice-president for business affairs, for instance, would be particularly interested in any line of argument that could save or generate money. Your topic may dictate specific headings for your information, but some general ones are standard: *problem, solution, objections to the solution, and counter-arguments for those objections.*

You can shape your paper as a private letter to the proper authority or as a public news story for the university community, one in which you urge the person in authority to make the change you support. Choose the format that better serves your purpose.

2. A more challenging and abstract topic centers on the phrase *pursuit of happiness.* The Declaration of Independence calls it an "unalienable right," along with life and liberty, but what does *the pursuit of happiness* mean in moral terms? Obviously, the concept must operate within the bounds of law, but within those bounds, can it be used to justify selfishness, what the journalist Tom Wolfe calls the excesses of the "Me decade"? Does the phrase lie as a principle behind our increasingly permissive attitudes toward sex, our soaring divorce rate, the extreme mobility that exists within our society? Exactly what does the "right to the pursuit of happiness" mean? How does it function within our society? How should it function?

Your instructor might focus a class discussion on the topic which will lead you to sources, and once you have established some tentative cause-and-effect relationships, you may find standard works helpful, such as the *Reader's Guide.* As you conduct your research, you will probably develop specific headings, but at the preliminary stage some general ones are in order: *historical definition, present interpretation, examples of effects, recommendations.*

ORGANIZING AND DEVELOPING

To get a clear sense of direction before you start writing your first draft, review your notes. Summarize them on a separate sheet that states your topic, thesis, audience, major points, and the most important arguments that can be used against yours. Under *audience*, note down any preconceptions or concerns your readers may have. If you are writing about the scheduling of classes and your audience is a department chairperson, odds are he or she must schedule classes after juggling student needs, faculty preferences, available space, and heating and cooling costs: these are considerations for you as well. On the other hand, you might address the paper on pursuit of happiness to young adults and note that many have not thought of the long-range future. That fact may call for an emotional and logical appeal to them as future parents, who for the good of their children, their society, and themselves need to examine what they mean by "happiness."

Keeping your summary sheet near by, begin your draft. Your introduction can have a multiple purpose: it can catch the reader's attention, establish you as someone who can speak with authority, alert the reader to the structure of the paper, define necessary terms, provide a background to your topic, state the thesis, and describe the problem.

The body of the paper will be structured according to the headings you have used together with the overriding principle of dramatic order. Perhaps begin with a less crucial point and build to the most important one. Along the way, you may find it helpful to include any necessary background and definitions. The paper on happiness, for instance, calls for at least two definitions: What is "happiness"? What is a "right"? Different periods of history and different cultural interpretations will reveal different answers.

You may find it best to weave the central opposing views into your own points or to group them by themselves. If the opposing points can be dealt with quickly but fairly, they can be included early in the body of the paper or worked into the conclusion.

Like the introduction, the conclusion can perform multiple functions, all of which reinforce your argument; it can summarize your points, state or restate your thesis, call for action, describe the beneficial effects of your proposal, reinforce your authority, cite an expert opinion, or warn of disaster if the situation continues. It must also provide a sense of closure, that is, the impression that the argument has concluded and that the prosecution rests.

FINDING A VOICE

In argument the writer's voice is a crucial technique of persuasion. The reader is far more inclined to believe a writer who projects fairness, honesty, and a concern for the public good than one who appears to be self-centered, biased, or hotheaded. One way to double-check your voice and tone is to put yourself in the shoes of a reader who holds an opposing view and then reread the draft from that perspective, annotating the margins with comments such as "So what?," "Let's hear it for apple pie," and "Yes, but . . . ." To write argument effectively, you must give the other side its due and respect the opinions of those who disagree with you.

The two most common traps for the argumentative essayist are ignoring the opposition altogether by writing to an audience that already believes the thesis or slighting the opposition and twisting their arguments and one's own. Logical fallacies are techniques that dishonest writers or sophists resort to:

attacking the person or group instead of the argument *(ad hominem, ad populem)*;
attacking a false issue (straw man) or a minor one (begging the question) instead of the real or major one;
setting out two extreme positions and implying there is no middle ground (either/or);
comparing two examples that are essentially dissimilar (false analogy);
reaching a conclusion without adequate evidence (hasty generalization);
ignoring the complexities of the issue (over-simplification);
citing an expert in one field as an expert in another (misusing authority);
claiming a causal relationship where it does not exist *(non sequitur)* or is temporal *(post hoc ergo propter hoc)*;
changing the terms of a definition (shift in definition);
raising a false and emotionally charged issue (red herring);
and encouraging the acceptance of an idea because "the majority believes it" (bandwagon).

All of these fallacies can be avoided if the writer is honest with the topic and with the reader. (For a more detailed discussion of logical fallacies, see the Glossary of Rhetorical Terms.)

POLISHING

Reread your paper to check the tone. You are addressing an audience who is part of the problem as well as part of the solution, but you don't want to be too heavy-handed or sanctimonious. Woo your audience; don't browbeat them. Then reread the paper again, tallying your different appeals to reason and to emotion. Does the tally correspond to your intentions? Have you cited a sufficient number of sources? Are they valid ones? In order for you to be credible, your appeals to reason should outnumber those to emotion.

Double-check the summary sheet you made earlier to insure you have included those points in your paper. Is your thesis clearly stated? Effectively placed? Have you dealt with your audience's preconceptions and concerns? Have you covered all your major points in sufficient depth? Have you countered the more important opposing arguments? If everything checks out, test your paper on a friend or classmate. If that person does not represent your intended audience, ask him or her to play the part after you have explained exactly what the role is. Read the paper aloud, and then ask your reader the following questions:

1. If you disagreed with the writer to begin with, did the paper change your mind? If not, did it make you rethink your position? If not, why not?

2. If you agreed with the writer to begin with, did the paper reinforce your conviction? If not, why not?

3. If you had not thought about the topic beforehand, do you now agree with the writer's position? If not, why not? Sometimes a person's beliefs are so set that nothing short of a brain transplant can change them, but if at the least you have forced such a person to stop and think again, that's success.

THINKING AHEAD

To sharpen your argumentative skills for future use as well as to make your use of evidence more flexible and your use of tone more varied, take the paper you have just written and rewrite it, reversing your position by supporting the opposition. In doing so, you should still be honest with your subject and continue to avoid logical fallacies. After you have completed the new paper, you may find that you have written yourself into the position you once argued against. Often the way to discover what you think about a topic is to write about both sides of it.

PART 5

THE WRITER AS SPEAKER

On a recent list of the ten things people most fear, public speaking ranks second, next to death. In ancient Greece, that juxtaposition was not as absurd as it is today. There, a person's life could depend on the ability to speak effectively because Athenian law dictated that citizens had to argue their own defense. Sometimes the speeches were written by others, and many an orator established a lucrative sideline in ghostwriting. A few were so persuasive they not only affected the everyday actions of the state, but they influenced the very fate of the nation and its culture. Alcibiades, the Athenian general and politician, is held personally accountable by many historians for initiating the downfall of the Athenian empire; in 427 B.C. it was he who persuaded the Senate to wage war with Syracuse, an ill-fated expedition on both military and moral grounds.

What Alcibiades said to the Athenians is lost to history, but more recent examples of political oratory saw the birth of a different kind of democracy. Patrick Henry, speaking to the Virginia Convention in 1775, urged a different kind of war:

> Is life so dear or peace so sweet as to be purchased at the price of chains and slavery? Forbid it, Almighty God. I know not what course others may take, but as for me, give me liberty or give me death!

No matter what the occasion or the times, the power to persuade, to provoke, to move the minds and hearts of an audience is electrifying.

The political speeches of the silver-tongued Daniel Webster resound with the same measured cadences, contrasts, and balanced phrases of his oratorical predecessors. "Liberty and Union, now and forever, one and inseparable," declared Webster, and in another speech he affirmed, "One country, one constitution, one destiny." Similar techniques reappear in Abraham Lincoln's speeches. On the brink of the Civil War, President Lincoln addressed a political meeting in New York: "Let us have faith that right makes might, and in that faith let us to the end dare to do our duty as we understand it." The forceful bonding of style, content, and persuasive purpose makes Lincoln an appropriate figure for Barbara Jordan to cite in her keynote address to the Democratic National Convention. Delivered in 1976, the year of the bicentennial, the address is reprinted in this section.

In addition to legal and political speeches, we have also inherited the third type of Greek oratory—the ceremonial speech. Whether for the Fourth of July, the christening of a ship, or a high-school graduation, speeches are delivered in honor of a particular occasion almost as frequently as they are given in the courts and in the political arena. Most are heard as the inevitable adjunct to ceremony, but sometimes the speeches reach far beyond the occasion to reassert common values, to establish a sense of shared humanity, to recognize a turning point in life or history. Thus William Faulkner, in a little-known address included in this section, uses the event of a high-school graduation to speak to broader issues; and Albert Einstein uses the Intellectuals' Conference for Peace as a forum to propose a solution to impending nuclear disaster.

Perhaps the best known of all ceremonial speeches is Lincoln's *Gettysburg Address.* Delivered at the dedication of the Civil War cemetery, the speech plays upon the word *dedicate* to rekindle the Union's cause so that "this nation, under God, shall have a new birth of freedom; and that government of the people, by the people, for the people, shall not perish from the earth." In its eloquence and effect, Lincoln's speech rivals the funeral oration of Pericles, delivered in the fifth century B.C. on a similar occasion, the honoring of soldiers killed in battle.

In the early Renaissance, the rise of Protestantism combined with scholasticism to popularize the sermon, a style of oratory that has a strong tradition in the United States. From the Puritan times of Jonathan Edwards' "Sinners in the Hands of an Angry God," to Aimee Semple McPherson's rousing evangelism, to Oral Roberts' and Billy Graham's religious campaigns of today, the sermon has a large following, particularly in the South where the rhythms of the Bible and of spirituals have led to a tradition in its own right, a tradition echoed in Barbara Jordan's address to the Democratic Convention.

Orators and preachers are public figures, the former associated with the affairs of the state, the latter with the church. Lecturers are public figures as well, but the scope of a lecturer is both narrower and broader than that of other speakers: narrower because the focus is on the particular; broader because all subjects fall within the province of a lecture. University classes are often referred to as lectures, whether they are or not, and the "lecturer" is an official academic position. Although some lectures have been collected and passed on in book form, as in the case of Sigmund Freud's *Introductory Lectures on Psychoanalysis*, the fame of a lecturer is apt to spread only as far as a university's alumni, and occasionally legends surround professors whose former students return year after year to attend an especially moving lecture.

Interviews, like lectures, call for research and preparation, but essentially they are prompted monologues or imbalanced dialogues whose focus stays squarely on the individual being interviewed. The interviewer steers the conversation, posing prepared and spontaneous questions to reveal the personality, opinions, and experience of the individual in the spotlight, whether it be a baseball player like Hank Aaron or a comedian like Mel Brooks. If the interview is to be published, editing skills also come into play as the interviewer-turned-writer refines and polishes the rougher edges of speech to accommodate the stricter requirements of print.

Speeches and sermons are primarily persuasive while lectures are primarily explanatory, but both rely on involving listeners, engaging them directly and indirectly, and both depend upon the spark of the speaker's presence. To use words effectively is to practice the art of rhetoric; to recast those words into effective speech is to practice the art of public speaking. And the difference between written and spoken discourse is considerable. Discourse that is to be heard, whether conversational, informal, or formal, differs from discourse to be read, in organization, syntax, diction, and voice.

A speech or lecture must set out its major points so clearly that they can be identified as the reader hears them; many of the subtleties of the personal essay's "tumbling progression" would be lost on listeners. So, too, crucial sentences in a speech or lecture should be memorable, and therefore they depend heavily on rhetorical devices such as repetition, alliteration, parallelism, and contrast. Diction must be vivid yet accessible, carrying sound, sense, and imagery. The connotations of the diction in the opening sentence of the *Gettysburg Address,* for instance—"our fathers *brought forth* . . . a *new* nation, *conceived* in *liberty*"—suggest the Union Army's purpose, underscored later in the speech: "that this nation, under God, shall have a *new birth* of *freedom.*" And of course the human voice—through modulation and pauses—controls and interprets words as no printed page ever can.

At its best, public speaking crosses the lines of genre, language, nationality, race, and religion to move and inspire us all. Pericles, Cicero, Elizabeth I, Robespierre, William Pitt, Edmund Burke, Susan B. Anthony, Winston Churchill, Golda Meir, all—like Martin Luther King—"had a dream" and were eloquent in its defense.

CHAPTER 10

THE INTERVIEWER

Interviewing is an art as old as conversation. But the modern technology of tape and video recorders and the media of radio and television have given the interview a new impact and prominence, showing it to be an effective way to convey facts, opinions, and personalities. Late night and early morning television shows abound with budding Johnny Carsons and Barbara Walterses, and the on-the-spot interview after the crucial game or shattering tragedy has become a standard broadcast format. Questions run the gamut from the thoughtful reporting of an Edward R. Murrow, talking to the citizen-on-the-street in London during the World War II blitz, to the school of tastelessness sometimes seen on the local news, "And how did you feel, Mrs. Jones, after you ran over your baby?" From the abrasiveness of Howard Cosell to the smoothness of Dick Cavett, interviewers' styles vary as widely as their subjects.

The same variety exists among printed interviews. Interviewers in *Playboy* pose questions to famous and sometimes infamous newsmakers in hopes of intellectual insight or the sort of revelations that put Jimmy Carter's lustful heart and born-again enthusiasm in the news, while interviewers for the *Paris Review* series "Writers at Work" probe the writing habits and processes of well-known authors. The techniques may differ, but the interviewers have similar purposes and guidelines.

Watching, reading, or listening to an interview is the next best thing to being there. An interviewer researches the interviewee's background and prepares a variety of questions that illuminate significant facts as well as the personality of the individual under scrutiny. Yet the questions are not railroad tracks along which the interview must run. The questioner must also be a good listener who pursues topics that arise in the dialogue, perhaps leading the conversation down unexpected paths.

The give and take of a successful interview, however, is only possible after the interviewer has established a relationship with the individual, and exactly how that relationship is established varies among interviewers and their subjects. An icebreaker—a compliment, a joke, an apology, a blunt question—usually sets the tone and encourages the interviewee to relax and perhaps confide or to resist and perhaps reveal a flash of temper. The tone set in the first few questions makes the difference between a "Sixty Minutes" Mike Wallace and a "Today's" Jane Pauley.

The interviewer cannot carry on a dialogue alone, however, and the conversation is made infinitely easier by a good subject who meets the questioner halfway. Someone who responds only "yes," "no," or "maybe" or who chooses to be boorish or flippant or garrulous is an interviewer's nightmare. The interviews included in this chapter illustrate the kind of rapport that leads to an effective dialogue. A National League baseball hero, Hank Aaron is accustomed to interviews, perhaps so much so that the interview itself could have been a carbon copy of a thousand others. But Lee Michael Katz probes, and Aaron, as he says, is direct, "I'm going to tell everybody what I think is right." Not one to dodge controversy, Aaron is not one to create it either, and it is Katz's questioning that reveals the painful underside of "what should have been a happy time," Hank Aaron's setting a new major league record.

Mel Brooks, on the other hand, gives a very different kind of interview, one in which the line between the man and the onstage comic character is hard to discern. Larry Siegel, who interviewed Brooks for *Playboy*, found his subject as unpredictable as comedy itself.

LEE MICHAEL KATZ

An Interview with Hank Aaron

Hank Aaron became a household name in 1974 when he broke Babe Ruth's record; by the time he retired he had hit 755 home runs. Born in Mobile, Alabama, in 1935, Aaron first played baseball in the old segregated Negro League but was soon discovered by the then Milwaukee Braves. In addition to his home run record, Aaron holds several others: extra-base hits, runs batted in, total bases, and games played. After playing 23 years of major-league baseball, Aaron retired in 1976; he was elected to the Hall of Fame in 1982 and now serves as director of player development for the Atlanta Braves. His achievements make him a natural subject for an interview, and Lee Michael Katz, a frequent contributor to the *Washington Post*, conducted the one that follows, which appeared on June 5, 1983.

Q. You think the people who said that you'd never defeat Babe Ruth's record, actually made you break Babe Ruth's record? 1

A: Oh yes. There's no question about it. They drove me to it. The fans and the people that wrote all those vicious letters to me. I thought they should have been writing encouraging letters. They were writing letters trying to tear me apart. I wanted to make people eat their words. 2

Q: Did you ever get letters with racial slurs? Letters threatening your life? 3

A: Oh yeah. Many of 'em. Many times. Not only me. My 4
daughter, my family. Got quite a few of them.

Q: What were the letters that bothered you the most? 5

A: Well, none of them bothered me as much as just finding 6
out what an awful lot of people think about a black person in this country. I was doing something that I thought was entertaining to every person in this country. Records are made to be broken. I'm hoping that some day some kid will come along and finally break my record. Who the hell cares? It just showed me how much bigotry we have in this country. How many little people in this country that we have. How many people still thought that blacks had no business in baseball. That was the thing I was most resentful of?

Q: Did you actually have guards? 7

A: The last two years I had somebody with me all the time. 8
In spring training. Every time I walked out of the clubhouse, someone was with me. Every time I went to the bank. If I went to Cincinatti there was someone there with me. I never could travel by myself. The sad part about the whole thing for 2½ years was I never had a chance to join my teammates. They would stay in one part of the hotel and I had to stay in another part. I would be registered in one room and stay in another room. Just to decoy people off.

Q: Threatening phone calls? 9

A: Letters, phone calls, just a little of everything. It was a 10
sad time in my career.

Q: In what should have been a happy time. 11

A: I should have been really enjoying myself. 12

Q: If you had been white do you think you would have 13
had to have had an Atlanta policeman with you all the time?

A: No, no way. I don't think Pete Rose did. They just 14
didn't want to see a black man surpass a white. I was not allowed to open letters that came to the ball park. The FBI first and then the police department.

Q: Did you feel like a prisoner to your status and your 15
race?

A: I was. I was. It was a fishbowl. 16

Q: Do you ever wish your name wasn't Hank Aaron? 17

A: I wish my son's name wasn't Hank Aaron. It doesn't 18 bother me as much as it bothers him. He had to live up to the things that I have accomplished.

Q: Did people judge him as having to be a great baseball player? 19

A: A great athlete. 20

Q: Has he been interested in it? 21

A: No. He played a little football and that was it. 22

Q: Do you think that's been very traumatic for him? 23

A: Yeah, it hurt him. He wasn't able to relax. At least he could have had the luxury of enjoying [sports] while he was a young kid in high school. The pleasure of doing just like the rest of the kids. 24

Q. Don't sometimes you run into a father who never made it to the major leagues who tries to channel all his energies into the sons? 25

A. I hate to say it but that's why you have so many terrible sportswriters. They're frustrated ex-athletes. They haven't been successful at anything. All of a sudden they see someone that the game came fairly easy to. They jump on him. He can't do anything right. You've got a lot of those bad sportswriters in this country. I hate to say that, but a lot of bad sportswriters. I do have a few that as far as I'm concerned are good friends of mine. But they are a few. 26

A lot of them are just downright vicious. They got too much power, sportswriters. I don't want it to be like Russia. But still newspaper people got too damn much power for me. They can say anything they want to say about me and I have no recourse at all. I can't carry it to court. I can't do anything. 27

Q: You don't feel that you could make your case for the media? 28

A: How could you do it? They always got the last pen. There's no way I can win that battle. So I just let 'em write and forget about it. But some of them are just very, very vicious when they write. 29

I had one here in Atlanta who I call an Archie Bunker, because that's exactly what he is. I was talking about the baseball game as being a game of racists. He jumped on me and started talking about my wife! Started talking about my whole family! He talked about my wife's ex-husband, who was deceased. He 30 was the Rev. Sammy Williams, the doctor of philosophy who taught at Morehouse College. A very brilliant man. He said some things about him. It was a vicious article. I had several lawyers wanted me to carry him to court but why? Why? Why? I just decided I was going to forget about it. But it was very upsetting.

Q: Did you come from an affluent family? 31

A: No, no, no. My father was just a common laborer. He 32
made ends meet from week to week. Sometimes he would work this week and the next two weeks he wouldn't work at all. My father was not educated, my mother was not educated. But they had a lot of mother and father in them and that beats education 10 times and over. You can understand and love other people.

Q: How many children in your family? 33

A: There were eight of us in the family. Four boys and four 34
girls. One of my brothers passed away as an infant.

Q: Did you feel you were poor? 35

A: Yes, we were poor, and I didn't have to feel it. I *know* we 36
were poor. There was three of us sleeping in the same bed. I don't see how much poorer you can get.

Q: You went to a segregated school? 37

A: Yes. 38

Q: Did you work before you played baseball profession- 39
ally?

A: I worked three jobs. I worked as an ice boy, I cut yards, 40
and I picked blackberries. Of course, it took like a week to put some dollars in my pocket.

Q: Are you financially secure? 41

A: I can get along, but I have to work in order to maintain 42
whatever I want. I got a nice home. Sixteen acres right in the city of Atlanta and I got a five-acre lake back there. If I want to go fishing, I'll go fishing.

Q: Now that you're relatively affluent do you ever try and 43
make up, with your own children, that you grew up in poverty?

A: I think that's the hard thing about growing up very, 44
very poor and then getting to the point where you do have little things. I know I'm a long ways from being rich. But if I wanted to leave out of this office today and go on a speaking engagement for a week I could make $10,000 or $15,000. And yes, I very much spoiled my kids by giving 'em too much instead of letting

'em know that the same hard work applies to them as applied to
me.

Q: Do you feel that your accomplishments, in breaking 45
Babe Ruth's record, have failed to receive proper recognition?

A: Probably will never receive the recognition that is due. 46

Q: Because you're black? 47

A: Right. 48

Q: Does that bother you? Is that something that you live 49
with every day?

A: No, no. It's nothing that bothers me. I'm going to be 50
black until the day I die. I've been black for 48 years and I won't
pretend not to be black. I've enjoyed my life. It's the problem
that they have to deal with, not me, I don't have to deal with it.
I hit the home run, they got to figure out how they going to continue to snub it.

Q: Have people found ways to snub it? 51

A: Oh yes, oh yes. S---, now they talk about the Japanese 52
ballplayer, Sadaharu Oh. He got 800 home runs. I'm the second
best—home runs. I saw some article saying, "It was Babe Ruth
and Hank Aaron and now it's Sadaharu Oh, Babe Ruth and
Hank Aaron."

Q: Sadaharu Oh has hit more home runs than you have, 53
but he's hit them in Japanese baseball. Do you think that com-
pares at all to your record?

A: No, I know damn well it doesn't. He's a great ballplayer, 54
but he did it in Japan. It's not professional baseball.

Q: Is it like the Great White Hope? 55

A: That's true. That's why ice hockey is so popular in parts 56
of America now. Because the average white fan don't have to
identify with black hockey players. If you talk to the average
black person in this country they don't know anything about ice
hockey. That is one reason why ice hockey in certain parts of
this country is so popular.

Q: How come you didn't do that many endorsements, 57
aside from the relatively unsuccessful $200,000 one for
Magnavox?

A: That was a million dollars for Magnavox, not $200,000. 58
But I don't know.

Q: You didn't get offers? My God, you're Hank Aaron. 59

A: I didn't get the offers. 60

Q: A sportswriter in this newspaper said that when you were conquering Babe Ruth's record that the fame sickened and soured you. That you received fame in almost terminal doses. Did you feel that way? 61

A: I was doing no more than I had done before. I was averaging 35 or 40 home runs a year. I was scoring a hundred and some runs. All of a sudden everybody starts focusing their attention upon me. 62

It came in doses, and to be very honest with you, it was frightening. If the white sportswriters in this country had had their druthers who they would rather have break the record—Willie Mays or Hank Aaron—they would have said Willie Mays. Willie's not going to be very controversial. I'm the one that tells people what I think. They want you to laugh and scratch your head. I'm going to tell everybody what I think is right. If you don't accept the fact, the hell with you. 63

Q: You think they couldn't accept intellect in a ballplayer, especially when he's breaking Babe Ruth's record? 64

A: They couldn't accept that in me because they didn't think about me at all as being the one that was most likely to break the record. They don't say it out loud but I can see the little bugs ringing in their ear. They say how the hell did he slip up and do it? For 14 years nobody interviewed Hank Aaron. 65

Q: Do you think no one ever really cared about what Hank Aaron has to say? 66

A: Oh, I'm sure they cared. I could say something that would make the news today. For example, about me making a statement about being the commissioner of baseball. Hell, I'm serious as a heart attack about that. I want to be the commissioner. Hell, why not? It's the best job in baseball. I don't see where it's going to be that complicated. They've had some guys in there that screwed it up already. I think that I could do a better job as some of the rest of the guys. I just think that things in baseball need to be discussed seriously. I think that there are some franchises in baseball that are in serious trouble. 67

Q: Which ones? 68

A: Cleveland, Minnesota to name two of 'em. And there may be one or two other ones. 69

Q: What would you do to save them as commissioner of baseball? 70

A: First of all—which may not be a very popular thing 71
with the players—you've got to put a cap on the salaries. Keep good ballplayers in these cities.

The second thing, try to have interleague play. In the last 72
part of the season, the Cubs are 20 games out and the White Sox are 20 games out, what would be wrong with having the Cubs and the White Sox play a series? Do you think it would draw?

Q: Sure. 73

A: Damn right it would. What would be wrong with hav- 74
ing the Mets and the Yankees play an interleague series? I'm talking about for real. I'm not talking about a charitable game. I'm talking about baseball.

Q: How does one get to be commissioner of baseball? How 75
do you lobby for it? Is it like the pope? Do they send smoke signals?

A: I've sent my smoke signal already. 76

Q: What do you think the odds are that Henry Aaron will 77
be the next commissioner of baseball?

A: Oh, I think it's very good. 78

Q: You think next month you'll be commissioner of base- 79
ball?

A: I just think my chances are as good as anybody else's. 80

Q: Even though you're black? 81

A: Yeah. I hope they don't hold that against me. 82

Q: Do you ever want to go into politics? 83

A: No, no, never did. 84

Q: Are any of the current presidential contenders trying to 85
get your endorsement?

A: I have had calls from Glenn, Mondale. I went to some 86
meetings when Glenn was here.

Q: Several people have written books about the traveling 87
and the godlike status of baseball players affecting marriages. How do you feel about that?

A: I say it's a piece of trash. People are looking for some- 88
thing to sell. Wives writing about ballplayers having girlfriends on the road. They marry these guys. There ain't nobody pushin' them. My wife, as much as I travel, she's never accused me of anything. And I've had opportunities to do most anything I wanted to do. I don't come back telling her anything. I just don't really understand why all of a sudden all these books on ball-

players have come out saying, well all I want to is just tell the truth.

Q: What did you do after the games when you were travel- 89
ing?

A: Went home and went to bed. 90

Q: You didn't go out with your teammates or anything like 91
that?

A: I went right to my hotel and went to bed. 92

Q: Are you a loner? 93

A: That's me. I am a loner. 94

Q: What do you? Watch TV? 95

A: I used to watch a lot of television and later on in my 96
career I started reading a lot.

Q: What sort of books? 97

A: Magazines. I started reading a lot of newspapers. I got 98
to be a fan of the soap operas before they were popular and were half an hour still.

Q: What was your favorite? 99

A: "As the World Turns." 100

Q: Are there things that you can't do because you're such 101
a celebrity?

A: I remember one time getting on a flight with Jane 102
Fonda. She took a blanket and put it over her head. She didn't take it off until she got to Los Angeles. Sometime you'll put your arm in a sling as though you had sprained your arm. Just get tired of signing autographs.

Q: A few years back you said you'd like to own a major- 103
league baseball club. Are you still interested?

A: Ha, ha, if I said that I must have been dreamin'. If I had 104
that kind of money I could think of a hell of a lot of ways that I could spin it around without owning a baseball club.

Q: Do you miss playing baseball? 105

A: Not at all. Not one bit. First of all I can't put on the uni- 106
form any more. It's too little. I'm a little bigger than that now.

Q: Don't you ever think about picking up the bat again, 107
once again hitting some runs in the stadium?

A: None whatsoever. I will never play baseball again. 108

THE THINKING PROCESS

STRUCTURE

1. One of the interviewer's techniques is to open with a subject that the interviewee expects, thereby getting the obvious out of the way while setting the person at ease with a familiar question. Katz, for instance, starts with Aaron's most notable feat, but the conversation quickly turns to racism. Where else in the interview does that topic come up? Note each of the instances, and figure out for each who brought up the subject. How does the theme of racism structure the interview?

2. In addition to racism, what other topics are covered in the interview? Which ones does Katz introduce? Which does Aaron raise?

3. Examine the interview as a whole. What major divisions can you discern? What reasons do you have for dividing the interview as you do?

4. Most published interviews are edited to remove unnecessary repetition and to tighten up what may have been an overly loose structure. The questions and the answers, however, must be true to what was said and its sequence. Reread paragraphs 1–6 and 105–108. How successfully do these paragraph blocks function as an introduction and a conclusion? Do they seem unedited, lightly edited, heavily edited? How so?

STYLE

1. An interviewer tries to ask all of the basic questions that readers might have. Does Katz succeed? To what extent does he function as a surrogate reader, following through with questions you would have wanted to ask? Does he pursue all of his questions? How or how not?

2. To keep the interviewee in the limelight, interviewers generally try to stay in the background, displaying little of their own personality. Katz, however, makes comments (11), asks some leading questions (15, 23), and presses Aaron (81). Is the interview less effective or more so for the part Katz takes in it? Explain.

3. The object of an interview is to elicit information and personality. How successful is Katz in showing the reader what sort of person Aaron is? How would you characterize Aaron? How does Katz bring out those traits?

4. Any interview is only as good as the interviewer's questions. Examine Katz's questions in detail. Do any cover more than one topic? Are any ambiguous? On the average, how long are they? Of all the questions Katz asks, how many would you classify as neutral? Leading? Abrasive? How many seem prepared in advance? On the whole, how would you evaluate the quality of Katz's questions?

IDEAS FOR AN INTERVIEW

Make a list of questions that you would like to be asked in an interview, and then turn to Ideas for an Interview on page 373, following the next section.

LARRY SIEGEL

An Interview with Mel Brooks

Playboy magazine published two interviews with Mel Brooks, the first in October 1966 and the second in February 1975. The first interview is reprinted below in its shortened version, as edited by G. Barry Golson in *The Playboy Interview* for Playboy Press in 1981. In 1966, Mel Brooks was just beginning his movie career as producer and director. He had cut an album, *The 2000-Year-Old-Man,* and had written the hit television series "Get Smart."

After his interview, Brooks went on to produce and direct popular films like *The Producers* (which includes the musical *Springtime for Hitler), Blazing Saddles,* and *Young Frankenstein. The Producers* was conceived, written, and directed by Brooks, who won the Academy Award for best screen play in 1968. His most recent film is *To Be or Not to Be,* a remake of the 1942 Jack Benny-Carole Lombard black comedy, focusing on Nazis in Poland in World War II and a theatrical troupe.

The interviewer Larry Siegel is a satirist himself. As you read the selection, see if you can analyze how the satire of both men flavors their conversation.

Playboy: Mel, we'd like to ask you— 1

Brooks: Who's *we?* I see one person in the room. Not counting me. 2

Playboy: By "we" we mean *Playboy.* 3

Brooks: In other words, you're asking questions for the 4
entire sexually liberated *Playboy* organization?

Playboy: Yes. 5

Brooks: By the way, how much are you paying me for 6
this?

Playboy: We don't pay our interview subjects. 7

Brooks: How about *you*, Mr. We? Do *you* get paid for this 8
thing?

Playboy: Well, yes. But that's because we're employed by 9
Playboy. With the help of the editors, we prepare the questions and conduct the interview.

Brooks: I'll tell you what. I'll ask *you* the questions. Let 10
them pay *me*.

Playboy: Mel, can we begin now? 11

Brooks: Fine, do you gavotte? 12

Playboy: Let's sit this one out. You've recently completed 13
a series of radio commercials as Ballantine Beer's "2500-year-old Brewmaster." It's a character quite similar to your famous 2000-year-old man, in that once again you jog satirically through the pages of history. But the big difference is: Now you're peddling beer. Why did you sell out to Madison Avenue, like they say?

Brooks: I decided that I had given enough of myself to 14
mankind. After all, my definitive 12-volume series on enlightened penology was completed; my staff and I had UNESCO running in apple-pie order; and of course I had just come up with the vaccine to wipe out cystic fibrosis. So I felt I could afford to allow myself a few monetary indulgences.

Playboy: Why Madison Avenue? 15

Brooks: Frankly, they made me the best offer. 16

Playboy: What were some of the other offers you re- 17
ceived?

Brooks: Well, Fifth Avenue offered me $4000 a week, Lex- 18
ington Avenue offered me $3500, and the Bowery's offer was insulting.

Playboy: The Brewmaster has a thick German accent. 19
The 2000-year-old man has a Jewish accent. Why do you use dialects when you perform?

Brooks: It's easier to hide behind accents. Once you're 20
playing a character you have more mobility, more freedom. I suppose it's also cowardice on my part. I can say anything I

want, and then if people question me, I say, "Don't blame me. Blame the old Jew. He's crazy."

Playboy: Aren't you a lot like your old boss, Sid Caesar, 21
in this respect?

Brooks: Yes. When I began working with Sid on *Your* 22
Show of Shows, I noticed that he always had trouble expressing himself as Sid Caesar. So I'd always try to provide him with an accent or a character to hide behind. Once in character, Sid is the funniest man in the world.

Playboy: What made you decide to give the 2000-year-old 23
man a Jewish accent?

Brooks: It's not a Jewish accent. It's an *American*-Jewish 24
accent. And in 50 years it will disappear. I think it'll be a great loss.

Playboy: You're obviously proud of being Jewish. 25

Brooks: Proud and scared. 26

Playboy: How do you feel about the current Jewish kick 27
in American humor?

Brooks: Unless Jews do Jews accurately, I consider the 28
whole thing to be in questionable taste.

Playboy: Then the character of the 2000-year-old man is 29
never in questionable taste?

Brooks: I don't think so. He may be pompous at times; he 30
may be a nut, but he's always honest and compelling. And the accent is always accurate.

Playboy: Why are so many top comedians and comedy 31
writers Jewish?

Brooks: When the tall, blond Teutons have been nipping 32
at your heels for thousands of years, you find it enervating to keep wailing. So you make jokes. If your enemy is laughing, how can he bludgeon you to death?

Playboy: Mel, you're co-creator of *Get Smart*. Since it vio- 33
lates every standard of tested TV comedy—a bumbling antihero, far-out satire, and so on—why is it so successful?

Brooks: I'd say because of a bumbling antihero, far-out 34
satire, and so on.

Playboy: What do you mean by "and so on"? 35

Brooks: What do *you* mean by "and so on"? 36

Playboy: Well, we meant that the public could identify 37
with, and yet feel superior to, a nitwit like Maxwell Smart.

Brooks: That's what *I* meant. 38

39 **Playboy:** How does a clod like Smart differ from the bird-brained protagonists in situation comedies such as *Ozzie and Harriet*?

40 **Brooks:** Guys like Ozzie Nelson are lovable boobs. There's nothing lovable about Don Adams' Max Smart. He's a dangerously earnest nitwit who deals in monumental goofs. He doesn't trip over skates; he loses whole *countries* to the Communists.

41 **Playboy:** And standard situation comedies, on the other hand, deal with dull people in petty situations?

42 **Brooks:** Right. And in their supposedly true-to-life little episodes, they avoid anything approaching reality. For years I've always wanted to see an honest family TV series—maybe something called *Half of Father Knows Best*. The other half of him was paralyzed by a stroke in 1942 when he suspected we might lose the War.

43 **Playboy:** Did you have any trouble selling the series to NBC?

44 **Brooks:** Plenty. ABC put up the original money to develop the thing, but when we took them our first script, they thought it was too wild. They wanted something more "warm and lovable."

45 **Playboy:** What did they mean by "warm and lovable"?

46 **Brooks:** Who knows? Maybe a nice mother in a print dress, with undulant fever.

47 **Playboy:** Did you make changes for them?

48 **Brooks:** Yes, we figured we'd try to make them happy. So we threw in a dog. But they didn't like it.

49 **Playboy:** Why not?

50 **Brooks:** The dog was asthmatic.

51 **Playboy:** Why did they object to that?

52 **Brooks:** I suppose they felt we might offend some important dogs.

53 **Playboy:** Do you think *Get Smart* will spawn wittier comedy series in the future?

54 **Brooks:** There's certainly an audience for them. Somewhere between those who sop up the gelatinous, brain-scrambling nonsense of *Petticoat Junction* and the intellectuals who catch *Basic Hungarian* at six A.M. is a vast segment of the population that wants intelligent entertainment. Without morals.

55 **Playboy:** You mean the public wants amoral TV?

Brooks: No, I mean they want TV without little sermons. 56
For years *The Danny Thomas Show* was doing the Ten Commandments. Every episode had a little message to deliver: Don't lie, don't kill your neighbor, don't covet your neighbor's wife, don't uncovet your neighbor's wife. . . .

Playboy: Living in New York, with a hit TV show being 57
filmed on the Coast, you must be doing a lot of traveling these days.

Brooks: I spend a lot of time in L.A. on business, but I 58
also travel for pleasure. I just got back from Europe.

Playboy: How did you like it? 59

Brooks: I love it. Europe is very near and dear to my 60
heart. Would you like to see a picture of it?

Playboy: You carry a picture of Europe? 61

Brooks: Sure, right here in my wallet. Here it is. 62

Playboy: It's very nice. 63

Brooks: Of course, Europe was a lot younger then. It's 64
really not a very good picture. Europe looks much better in person.

Playboy: It's a fine-looking continent. 65

Brooks: It gives me a good deal of pleasure, but it's always 66
fighting, fighting. I tell you, I'll be so happy when it finally settles down and gets married.

Playboy: Mel, there's a rumor going around that you in- 67
vented the popular expression "pussycat" on one of your records.

Brooks: I didn't invent it. It's an old Jewish-American ex- 68
pression. When anyone was dear and sweet, they would call him a pussycat. But I think I was the first one to use it in show business. In our first 2000-year-old man record, Carl asked me if I knew Shakespeare. I said, "What a pussycat he was! What a cute beard!"

Playboy: Have you thought up a new expression to re- 69
place "pussycat"?

Brooks: Yes, I have. "Water rat." "Look at him. What a 70
nice water rat!" You know something? It doesn't work as well as "pussycat."

Playboy: You're right. Can you think of any other funny 71
expressions?

Brooks: "Confusion to the French." 72

Playboy: What the hell is that? 73

Brooks: It was a toast that Horatio Hornblower used 74
aboard his flagship. It's always been one of my favorites. Good
old Horatio! What a water rat.

Playboy: Would you ever like to be a director of films? 75

Brooks: I'd love to be one. I think I'd be a great comedy 76
director. As a matter of fact, I have just finished a screenplay
called *Marriage Is a Dirty, Rotten Fraud.* I'd like very much to
direct it.

Playboy: Is it based on your own personal experience? 77

Brooks: No, it's based on a very important conversation I 78
overheard once while waiting for a bus at the Dixie Hotel terminal.

Playboy: What are the chances of a studio assigning you 79
to direct it?

Brooks: Very, very good. Well, let me amend that slight- 80
ly: None.

Playboy: What else are you working on? 81

Brooks: *Springtime for Hitler.* 82

Playboy: You're putting us on. 83

Brooks: No, it's the God's honest truth. It's going to be a 84
play within a play, or a play within a film—I haven't decided yet.
It's a romp with Adolf and Eva at Berchtesgaden. There was a
whole nice side of Hitler. He was a good dancer—no one knows
that. He loved a parakeet named Bob—no one knows that
either. It's all brought out in the play.

Playboy: What was the first funny thing you ever said? 85

Brooks: "Lieutenant Faversham's attentions to my wife 86
were of such a nature I was forced to deal him a lesson in manners."

Playboy: That's pretty funny. Do you recall to whom you 87
said that?

Brooks: Very vividly. It was an elderly Jewish woman car- 88
rying an oilcloth shopping bag on the Brighton Beach Express.

Playboy: What was her reaction to the remark? 89

Brooks: She immediately got up and gave me her seat. 90

Playboy: Who makes *you* laugh? 91

Brooks: It's very hard to get me to laugh at a comic. What 92
I want is something really funny. But how can I verbalize what I
think is really funny? Now, Harry Ritz of the Ritz Brothers—
there's someone who makes me laugh. To me he is the father of
modern American visual comedy. He sired Caesar, Berle, Lewis,

all of them. Jonathan Winters is another guy who can break me up.

Playboy: But he's a gentile. 93

Brooks: I love gentiles. In fact, one of my favorite activi- 94
ties is Protestant spotting.

Playboy: How do you do that? 95

Brooks: It's not difficult. First you look for a family, the 96
members of which address each other as "Mother" and "Dad." What I mean is, the father calls the mother "Mother" and the mother calls the father "Dad." Not just the kids.

Playboy: Are they easy to spot? 97

Brooks: Oh, yes, they're always in a white Ford station 98
wagon filled with hundreds of jars of mayonnaise and tons of white bread. Say, who's that guy that just walked into the room with a camera?

Playboy: That's one of our photographers. He's going to 99
take a few shots of you to run with the interview.

Brooks: Should I undress? 100

Playboy: It's not for the gatefold, Mel. You'll be shot fully 101
dressed. But while we're on the subject, do you think there's a sexual revolution going on in this country?

Brooks: Yes, I do think there's a sexual revolution going 102
on, and I think that with our current foreign policy, we'll probably be sending troops in there any minute to break it up.

Playboy: In where? 103

Brooks: How do I know? We always send in troops when 104
there's a revolution.

Playboy: We hate to get personal, but, speaking of sex, 105
why haven't you asked us to introduce you to a Playmate or a Bunny?

Brooks: Three reasons: It would be impolite; it would be 106
beneath my dignity; and besides, I'm a fag. Anyway, the trouble with Playmates and Bunnies is that they're too openly sexy and clean-cut. I've been taught ever since I was a kid that sex is filthy and forbidden, and that's the way I think it *should* be. The filthier and more forbidden it is, the more exciting it is.

Playboy: By those criteria, can you give us an example of 107
someone you consider sexy?

Brooks: To me *anyone* is sexy if they're not obvious about 108
it. A 71-year-old man in a fur collar and spats could be enormously sexy under the right circumstances.

Playboy: What would be the right circumstances? 109

Brooks: Well, if you're in the moonlight, if you're by a 110
lazy lagoon—and if you're a 71-year-old *woman* in a fur collar and spats.

Playboy: Is it true that you're always on? 111

Brooks: No, I'm only on when the people I'm with are 112
worth it. If they're superperceptive. Or if they're just good.

Playboy: Which would you rather do—perform or write? 113

Brooks: Performing is easier. Writing is more durable. 114

Playboy: We usually wind up our interviews with a ques- 115
tion like this one: What do you think will prove to be the most important legacy of our age?

Brooks: Carl Reiner once asked me a similar question on 116
one of our records, and in jocular fashion I said, Saran Wrap. But I've become a lot more mature since then. I suppose I've also grown with the times.

Playboy: So *now* what do you think will prove to be the 117
most important legacy of our age?

Brooks: Glad Bags. 118

Playboy: Well, Mel, thanks very much for taking the time 119
to talk to us.

Brooks: I would have been much happier gavotting. 120

THE THINKING PROCESS

STRUCTURE

1. Examine the interview as a whole. What major divisions can you distinguish? What reasons do you have for dividing the interview as you do? Who controls the interview, Siegel or Brooks?

2. A good interview, like a good essay, has a definite shape and sense of progression. Do Siegel's questions move from the particular to the general or from the general to the particular? How so?

3. To give the impression of natural conversation, inter- viewees must accept or ignore some of the conventions of an interview. What conventions does Brooks question? What effect does his recognition of the artificiality of the interview have?

STYLE

1. What evidence do you find that Siegel is well prepared for the interview? How familiar is he with the events in Brooks' life? With his work?

2. How would you characterize Brooks, the person? To what extent is Siegel responsible for bringing out elements of Brooks' personality? To what extent can you distinguish between Brooks the person and Brooks the comic?

3. Brooks' brand of humor comes out clearly in the interview. How would you characterize it? What techniques does Brooks employ to get a laugh?

4. An interview is only as good as the interviewer's questions. Examine the questions Siegel poses. On the average, how long are they? Are any ambiguous? How many would you classify as neutral? As leading? As abrasive? If you have answered question 4 in the section on Style for the interview with Aaron, how would you compare the quality of the two interviewers' questions?

IDEAS FOR AN INTERVIEW

For this assignment, you will interview one of your classmates for twenty to thirty minutes and then present the results of the interview in a ten-minute oral report to the class. Before you select a subject and begin, you need to devise some questions. If it is early in the semester, you will want to ask factual questions, but if your classmates already know one another, you may want to focus on more open-ended questions. Make a list of both varieties, and write down more questions than you will use; few moments are more awkward than those in which an interview stalls because the interviewer can't think of anything else to say.

Choose someone unfamiliar to interview so that you will be

in the same situation as most of your listeners and therefore more likely to ask the kinds of questions they might pose: "Where were you born?" "What's your intended major?" "Why did you decide on this college?" Questions like these are only starting points and need to be followed through. For instance, a student who decided to go to your college because it was close to home might be led into an interesting discussion of the importance of friends and family. Your purpose is twofold: to elicit the information your listeners want to know and to bring out the person's character.

Once you have selected an interviewee, review your notes to see which question you want to start with and in what sequence the others might follow. Also select one question for your conclusion and phrase it clearly as the final question. Review your questions: Does each one focus on one topic only? Are any "yes/no" questions? If so, do you follow with open-ended ones? Are any more than twenty-five words? If so, trim them. Do your questions have some variety—do some relate to facts, others to opinions? When you have finished editing your questions, put them on notecards so that you can use them unobtrusively. Use note paper for the responses.

Start the interview with an icebreaker, perhaps an obvious factual question to put the person at ease. As the interview progresses, feel free to ignore your notes and pursue any line of response that is interesting. You shouldn't feel bound to your notes; they are simply guides and prompts. Try to record the answers as accurately as possible and, if you can, use a tape recorder. Don't let the tape take the place of your notes, however; transcribing an interview is tedious and time-consuming.

To turn your notes into an oral report, review your questions and answers to determine which will provide essential information of interest to the class. You need not begin the report where the interview began nor end where it ended, but you should stay faithful to the sequence of the questions you plan to include. You will find the tape recording valuable after you have sketched out your oral report and want to supplement it with a quotation that carries the exact phrasing and intonation of the person you have interviewed. Rehearse your report to make sure your delivery is effective (see p. 430).

THE INTERVIEWING PROCESS

INVENTION

Consider the distinguished individuals on your campus or in your community. Perhaps a member of the faculty has recently received an award or had a book published or a student has received a distinctive fellowship; consider, too, outstanding athletes, from Ping-Pong to football. Within your community, look for people who have recently been appointed or elected to office or who have been honored by their profession, for instance, a medal for bravery given to a fire fighter or to a police officer, recognition given to a top salesperson, volunteer, business executive, artist, or philanthropist. Make a list of possibilities, and then select the individual you would most like to know. Keep an audience in mind for the interview, perhaps your classmates, your college or local newspaper, or if you are interviewing a celebrity, a national publication.

Call or write the person to set up the interview. You should explain who you are, that you have a writing assignment that calls for an interview, and why you have chosen that particular individual. You should also remember that the person is doing you a favor, and so the interview should be at his or her convenience, not yours. If you mention several of the topics you have in mind, you may set the person at ease, and if you want to tape the interview to flesh out your notes, ask permission to do so and offer to send a copy of the tape.

Do as much preliminary research as you can, discovering

the details of the individual's achievements and as much factual data as possible. Consult local or national newspaper files in your library to find out where the person was born and grew up, the schools he or she attended, and so on. Perhaps you will turn up a quotation or two that the individual can respond to. Put the results of your research on notecards, and then start thinking of questions you want to pose.

Your interview should bring out the significant details of the person's achievements and character. If you think first about your readers, you may have a better idea of what questions to ask, for you will be interviewing on their behalf. Your classmates, for example, may be action-oriented and therefore want to know about the physical side of, say, a football star's life—how many games, how many injuries, and so on. On the other hand, they may be more interested in questions about the emotional element of the wins and losses, how it feels to be booed by one's own fans or worshipped by children. Or maybe your readers are interested in the intellectual aspect of the game, the strategy behind the calls, the playbook.

Devise more questions than you will be able to use, and write them out on notecards. A long list will put you in an inquisitive frame of mind and will be available if you panic. Like speeches, interview questions are best not read off the page but asked as though part of a conversation; notecards can jog your memory.

ORGANIZING AND DEVELOPING

Sort through your questions to see how they can be categorized, trying different arrangements until you find the most suitable. Perhaps a simple categorization of primary and secondary questions will do, and if so, limit the crucial ones to three or four. Or try thinking of the questions in terms of past, present, and future, or as facts and opinions, or as they focus on key events in the individual's life.

Once you have an overall plan for the direction of the interview, review your questions again, and see which ones would work well to start and to finish the interview. Think of a way to open the conversation by establishing the tone you want to sustain for the rest of the session. Perhaps a compliment or a few words of thanks for taking the time to be interviewed would be a good way to establish a rapport with your subject. Often you can use a "thank you" to indicate the end of the interview as well, or perhaps ask the individual if he or she wants to add anything. Examine your ending questions to make sure that a key word or two will make it clear that the last question is just that.

The questions themselves should be short and to the point:

1. One item per question.
2. No question over 25 words.
3. All questions phrased clearly.
4. All questions couched in neutral diction.
5. A variety of questions.

Review your questions to see if any are leading ("Would you say you were disappointed?") or abrasive ("Was there any truth to your opponent's accusations?"). Some of these questions can be effective, but a little Mike Wallace goes a long way.

FINDING A VOICE

Write or call to confirm your interview, and when the time comes, dress as though you were going to appear on the local news; even if the person you are interviewing is your famous best friend, your apparel will set a formal, serious tone.

No matter whom you are interviewing, the person is apt to be busy, so without rushing, set the interview in motion as soon as you can, opening with the icebreaker you prepared beforehand. As you pose your questions, try to keep in the background, guiding the conversation but not forcing it. Be polite and friendly, and try to cover your nervousness or perhaps confess to it: unless you are interviewing a public figure, your interviewee may be more nervous than you are.

Remember that good interviewers are also good listeners, so allow the individual some latitude; the conversation that results might reveal more than your carefully prepared questions. After the interview is over, write a brief note of thanks and send along your final version of the written interview.

POLISHING

When you start writing the interview in final form, remember that you can and should edit, removing needless repetition and deleting unimportant responses. You must remain true to the questions and answers and to their sequence, but you may find that the first few did no more than initiate the interview, some in the middle were fillers, and others at the end trailed off into awkwardness. Begin and end the final version with the best opening and closing available to you.

Usually a person's character is conveyed in speech, so don't tidy up responses unless you find an obvious slip. If a person interjects "you know" or an occasional "hell" or "damn" or a colloquialism, don't eliminate it; if every other phrase is "you know," use your own judgment in editing and keep only the ones that contribute to the flavor of speech.

Identify the key parts of the interview and check your notes against the tape recording, if you made one, to insure accuracy. Then after you have finished your final editing and proofreading, write a brief introduction that identifies the person. If the interview were to be published, your introduction would preface the interview in italics.

THINKING AHEAD

The techniques interviewing requires will stand you in good stead when you are conducting library research, gathering opinions of experts or citizen-on-the-street responses, and, of course, when you yourself are being interviewed. Few meetings are more important than the job interview, and if you are an effective interviewer, chances are you'll be a successful interviewee.

Watch the experts—Barbara Walters, Dick Cavett, and the like—to see how they handle a difficult person, someone who is loquacious or taciturn. Spot the techniques they use to get an interview going, to redirect its focus, to nudge it along if it stalls, and to conclude it. Their methods are often subtle and all the more worthwhile noting because of their subtlety.

CHAPTER 11

THE LECTURER

The scene: a lecture hall. The time: forty minutes into the hour. The action: the speaker strides across the room, swivels on a heel, moves to the lectern, pauses, raises a hand as if invoking the gods, and startles you with an insight into your world.

An effective lecture is more than a monologue; it is a soliloquy—a dramatization of information. Successful lecturers carefully prepare beforehand and entertain or persuade as well as instruct. In addition to relying on facts and figures, they convey ideas, stimulate thought, and, at best, inspire.

Speaking with lively intelligence about a subject is a cultivated skill. Good lectures require hours of preparation spent researching the topic, estimating the audience's knowledge, organizing the material, devising new methods of presentation, clarifying main points and transitions, discovering suitable analogies, anecdotes, diagrams, and quotations. A good lecturer must develop the ability to gauge the audience, ask questions, field responses, isolate individual points, and integrate ideas. Some lecturers practice in front of mirrors, others use tape recorders, and still others enact the lecture in their minds. Some write out the full lecture, and others rely on brief notes.

To punctuate lectures, speakers cannot employ commas,

periods, and exclamation marks, so they use instead gesticulations and voice—moving hands, waving arms, making faces, even kicking feet, varying pitch, changing intonation, acting different roles—whatever emphasizes the point at hand. Headings on the chalkboard and handouts often emphasize the lecture's organization, signaling changes in ideas and taking the places of paragraphs. (Paragraphs, like punctuation, are a convention found only in writing.) Visual aids, gestures, voice modulation can make a potentially dry lecture come to life; lecturing in a monotone, hiding behind the lectern, shuffling papers, and reading anything other than a short quotation can turn even the most lively subject to stone.

Sometimes the drama is inherent in the relationship between the speaker and the audience. Although Freud, for instance, had to combat the biases of his listeners in his first introductory lecture on psychoanalysis, included later in this chapter, he also used his sense of his audience to raise objections, clarify points, and delineate his stand—all important elements of argument and persuasion. Nonetheless, Freud's lectures are predominantly expository, exemplifying how to lead an audience into an understanding of a subject: "I shall not tell it to you," he says to his listeners in a later lecture, "but shall insist on your discovering it for yourself."

The content of a lecture and the personality behind it also make it an easy target for parody as Jean Shepherd shows in an imaginary lecture on the Van Culture presented to an imaginary introductory sociology class. Though a parody, the piece is nevertheless true to the spirit of the lecture—instructive, entertaining, and provocative. As you read it, try to hear the lecturer's voice, its sarcasm and asides, and the intention behind it.

You won't often be asked to give a parody of a lecture, but you may well have to give the real thing or its first cousin—the oral report, a fundamental means of communication in almost any professional field. Research, organization, and presentation are just as important to an effective oral report as to a lecture, perhaps in the practical sense more so when the speaker is trying to sell a proposal—an important skill in business, engineering, architecture, and the like. The skills you develop as a lecturer will make you more aware of the complexity of the spoken word and better practiced in the intricacies of communication.

SIGMUND FREUD

Elementary Introduction to Psycho-Analysis

The father of psychoanalysis, Sigmund Freud (1856-1939) was born in Moravia and educated in Vienna, where in 1881 he received his degree in medicine. He collaborated with Josef Breuer on using hypnosis to treat hysteria, and the final paper that resulted in 1895 marks the beginning of psychoanalysis as we know it today. A few years later, Freud rejected hypnosis for the techniques of free association, and he split with Breuer over the psychic role of sexual energy. Freud initially earned the hostility of the medical profession with his emphasis on sexuality and his belief that the same sexual impulses that cause "nervous and mental diseases . . . also make contributions that must not be underestimated to the highest cultural, artistic, and social creations of the human spirit."

His major contributions to psychology and psychoanalysis are expressed in *The Interpretation of Dreams* (1900), *The Psychopathology of Everyday Life* (1904), *The Ego and the Id* (1923), and *Three Contributions to the Sexual Theory* (1925). Freud also explored applying psychoanalytic theory to cultural problems in *Totem and Taboo* (1913) and *Moses and Monotheism* (1939). When the Nazis occupied Austria in 1938, Freud fled to England where he died a year later.

A frequent speaker and lecturer, Freud is probably best known for his *Introductory Lectures on Psychoanalysis*, a series of twenty-eight lectures delivered to medical students at the

University of Vienna from 1915 to 1917. The lecture that follows began the series. It reflects the general skepticism directed toward psychoanalysis and the particular hostility aimed at those, like Freud, who practiced it (3). At the time Freud delivered the lecture, he had been on the faculty at the University of Vienna for thirty years, first as a lecturer and then as a professor. Freud comments that his lectures "were improvised and written out immediately afterwards," adding that he "possessed a phonographic memory." His lecture and concern for his audience reveal Freud the person—quiet, realistic, intelligent, perceptive, strong-willed—a psychoanalyst who believed that sexual symbolism had its limits and that there are times when "a cigar is just a cigar."

Ladies and Gentlemen,—I cannot tell how much knowledge about psycho-analysis each one of you has already acquired from what you have read or from hearsay. But the wording of my prospectus—'Elementary Introduction to Psycho-Analysis'—obliges me to treat you as though you knew nothing and stood in need of some preliminary information. 1

I can, however, assume this much—that you know that psycho-analysis is a procedure for the medical treatment of neurotic patients. And here I can at once give you an instance of how in this field a number of things take place in a different way—often, indeed, in an opposite way—from what they do elsewhere in medical practice. When elsewhere we introduce a patient to a medical technique which is new to him, we usually minimize its inconveniences and give him confident assurances of the success of the treatment. I think we are justified in this, since by doing so we are increasing the probability of success. But when we take a neurotic patient into psycho-analytic treatment, we act differently. We point out the difficulties of the method to him, its long duration, the efforts and sacrifices it calls for; and as regards its success, we tell him we cannot promise it with certainty, that it depends on his own conduct, his understanding, his adaptability and his perseverance. We have good reasons, of course, for such apparently wrongheaded behaviour, as you will perhaps come to appreciate later on. 2

Do not be annoyed, then, if I begin by treating you in the same way as these neurotic patients. I seriously advise you not to 3 join my audience a second time. To support this advice, I will explain to you how incomplete any instruction in psycho-analysis must necessarily be and what difficulties stand in the way of your forming a judgement of your own upon it. I will show you how the whole trend of your previous education and all your habits of thought are inevitably bound to make you into opponents of psycho-analysis, and how much you would have to overcome in yourselves in order to get the better of this instinctive opposition. I cannot, of course, foretell how much understanding of psycho-analysis you will obtain from the information I give you, but I can promise you this: that by listening to it you will not have learnt how to set about a psycho-analytic investigation or how to carry a treatment through. If, however, there should actually turn out to be one of you who did not feel satisfied by a fleeting acquaintance with psycho-analysis but was inclined to enter into a permanent relationship to it, I should not merely dissuade him from doing so but actively warn him against it. As things stand at present, such a choice of profession would ruin any chance he might have of success at a University, and, if he started in life as a practising physician, he would find himself in a society which did not understand his efforts, which regarded him with distrust and hostility, and unleashed upon him all the evil spirits lurking within it. And the phenomena accompanying the war that is now raging in Europe will perhaps give you some notion of what legions of these evil spirits there may be.

Nevertheless, there are quite a number of people for whom, 4
in spite of these inconveniences, something that promises to bring them a fresh piece of knowledge still has its attraction. If a few of you should be of this sort and in spite of my warnings appear here again for my next lecture, you will be welcome. All of you, however, have a right to learn the nature of the difficulties of psycho-analysis to which I have alluded.

I will begin with those connected with instruction, with 5
training in psycho-analysis. In medical training you are accustomed to *see* things. You see an anatomical preparation, the precipitate of a chemical reaction, the shortening of a muscle as a result of the stimulation of its nerves. Later on, patients are demonstrated before your senses—the symptoms of their illness, the products of the pathological process and even in many cases the agent of the disease in isolation. In the surgical departments

you are witnesses of the active measures taken to bring help to patients, and you may yourselves attempt to put them into effect. Even in psychiatry the demonstration of patients with their altered facial expressions, their mode of speech and their behaviour, affords you plenty of observations which leave a deep impression on you. Thus a medical teacher plays in the main the part of a leader and interpreter who accompanies you through a museum, while you gain a direct contact with the objects exhibited and feel yourselves convinced of the existence of the new facts through your own perception.

In psycho-analysis, alas, everything is different. Nothing 6
takes place in a psycho-analytic treatment but an interchange of words between the patient and the analyst. The patient talks, tells of his past experiences and present impressions, complains, confesses to his wishes and his emotional impulses. The doctor listens, tries to direct the patient's processes of thought, exhorts, forces his attention in certain directions, gives him explanations and observes the reactions of understanding or rejection which he in this way provokes in him. The uninstructed relatives of our patients, who are only impressed by visible and tangible things—preferably by actions of the sort that are to be witnessed at the cinema—never fail to express their doubts whether 'anything can be done about the illness by mere talking'. That, of course, is both a short-sighted and an inconsistent line of thought. These are the same people who are so certain that patients are 'simply imagining' their symptoms. Words were originally magic and to this day words have retained much of their ancient magical power. By words one person can make another blissfully happy or drive him to despair, by words the teacher conveys his knowledge to his pupils, by words the orator carries his audience with him and determines their judgements and decisions. Words provoke affects and are in general the means of mutual influence among men. Thus we shall not depreciate the use of words in psychotherapy and we shall be pleased if we can listen to the words that pass between the analyst and his patient.

But we cannot do that either. The talk of which psycho- 7
analytic treatment consists brooks no listener; it cannot be demonstrated. A neurasthenic or hysterical patient can of course, like any other, be introduced to students in a psychiatric lecture. He will give an account of his complaints and symptoms,

but of nothing else. The information required by analysis will be given by him only on condition of his having a special emotional attachment to the doctor; he would become silent as soon as he observed a single witness to whom he felt indifferent. For this information concerns what is most intimate in his mental life, everything that, as a socially independent person, he must conceal from other people, and, beyond that, everything that, as a homogeneous personality, he will not admit to himself.

Thus you cannot be present as an audience at a psycho- 8
analytic treatment. You can only be told about it; and, in the strictest sense of the word, it is only by hearsay that you will get to know psycho-analysis. As a result of receiving your instruction at second hand, as it were, you find yourselves under quite unusual conditions for forming a judgement. That will obviously depend for the most part on how much credence you can give to your informant.

Let us assume for a moment that you were attending a lec- 9
ture not on psychiatry but on history, and that the lecturer was telling you of the life and military deeds of Alexander the Great. What grounds would you have for believing in the truth of what he reported? At a first glance the position would seem to be even more unfavourable than in the case of psycho-analysis, for the Professor of History no more took part in Alexander's campaigns than you did. The psycho-analyst does at least report things in which he himself played a part. But in due course we come to the things that confirm what the historian has told you. He could refer you to the reports given by ancient writers, who were either themselves contemporary with the events under question or, at any rate, were comparatively close to them—he could refer you, that is to say, to the works of Diodorus, Plutarch, Arrian, and so on. He could put reproductions before you of coins and statues of the king which have survived and he could hand round to you a photograph of the Pompeian mosaic of the battle of Issus. Strictly speaking, however, all these documents only prove that earlier generations already believed in Alexander's existence and in the reality of his deeds, and your criticism might start afresh at that point. You would then discover that not all that has been reported about Alexander deserves credence or can be confirmed in its details; but nevertheless I cannot think that you would leave the lecture-room in doubts of the reality of Alexander the Great. Your decision

would be determined essentially by two considerations: first, that the lecturer had no conceivable motive for assuring you of the reality of something he himself did not think real, and secondly, that all the available history books describe the events in approximately similar terms. If you went on to examine the older sources, you would take the same factors into account—the possible motives of the informants and the conformity of the witnesses to one another. The outcome of your examination would undoubtedly be reassuring in the case of Alexander, but would probably be different where figures such as Moses or Nimrod were concerned. Later opportunities will bring to light clearly enough what doubts you may feel about the credibility of your psycho-analytic informant.

But you will have a right to ask another question. If there is 10
no objective verification of psycho-analysis, and no possibility of demonstrating it, how can one learn psycho-analysis at all, and convince oneself of the truth of its assertions? It is true that psycho-analysis cannot easily be learnt and there are not many people who have learnt it properly. But of course there is a practicable method none the less. One learns psycho-analysis on oneself, by studying one's own personality. This is not quite the same thing as what is called self-observation, but it can, if necessary, be subsumed under it. There are a whole number of very common and generally familiar mental phenomena which, after a little instruction in technique, can be made the subject of analysis upon oneself. In that way one acquires the desired sense of conviction of the reality of the processes described by analysis and of the correctness of its views. Nevertheless, there are definite limits to progress by this method. One advances much further if one is analysed oneself by a practised analyst and experiences the effects of analysis on one's own self, making use of the opportunity of picking up the subtler technique of the process from one's analyst. This excellent method is, of course, applicable only to a single person and never to a whole lecture-room of students together.

Psycho-analysis is not to be blamed for a second difficulty in 11
your relation to it; I must make you yourselves responsible for it, Ladies and Gentlemen, at least in so far as you have been students of medicine. Your earlier education has given a particular direction to your thinking, which leads far away from

psycho-analysis. You have been trained to find an anatomical basis for the functions of the organism and their disorders, to explain them chemically and physically and to view them biologically. But no portion of your interest has been directed to psychical life, in which, after all, the achievement of this marvelously complex organism reaches its peak. For that reason psychological modes of thought have remained foreign to you. You have grown accustomed to regarding them with suspicion, to denying them the attribute of being scientific, and to handing them over to laymen, poets, natural philosophers and mystics. This limitation is without doubt detrimental to your medical activity, since, as is the rule in all human relationships, your patients will begin by presenting you with their mental *façade*, and I fear that you will be obliged as a punishment to leave a part of the therapeutic influence they are seeking to the lay practitioners, nature curers and mystics whom you so much despise.

I am not unaware of the excuse that we have to accept for 12
this defect in your education. No philosophical auxiliary science exists which could be made of service for your medical purposes. Neither speculative philosophy, nor descriptive psychology, nor what is called experimental psychology (which is closely allied to the physiology of the sense-organs), as they are taught in the Universities, are in a position to tell you anything serviceable of the relation between body and mind or to provide you with the key to an understanding of possible disturbances of the mental functions. It is true that psychiatry, as a part of medicine, sets about describing the mental disorders it observes and collecting them into clinical entities; but at favourable moments the psychiatrists themselves have doubts of whether their purely descriptive hypotheses deserve the name of a science. Nothing is known of the origin, the mechanism or the mutual relations of the symptoms of which these clinical entities are composed; there are either *no* observable changes in the anatomical organ of the mind to correspond to them, or changes which throw no light upon them. These mental disorders are only accessible to therapeutic influence when they can be recognized as subsidiary effects of what is otherwise an organic illness.

This is the gap which psycho-analysis seeks to fill. It tries to 13
give psychiatry its missing psychological foundation. It hopes to discover the common ground on the basis of which the convergence of physical and mental disorder will become intelligible.

With this aim in view, psycho-analysis must keep itself free from any hypothesis that is alien to it, whether of an anatomical, chemical or physiological kind, and must operate entirely with purely psychological auxiliary ideas; and for that very reason, I fear, it will seem strange to you to begin with.

I shall not hold you, your education or your attitude of 14
mind responsible for the next difficulty. Two of the hypotheses of psycho-analysis are an insult to the entire world and have earned its dislike. One of them offends against an intellectual prejudice, the other against an aesthetic and moral one. We must not be too contemptuous of these prejudices; they are powerful things, precipitates of human developments that were useful and indeed essential. They are kept in existence by emotional forces and the struggle against them is hard.

The first of these unpopular assertions made by psycho- 15
analysis declares that mental processes are in themselves unconscious and that of all mental life it is only certain individual acts and portions that are conscious. You know that on the contrary we are in the habit of identifying what is psychical with what is conscious. We look upon consciousness as nothing more nor less than the *defining* characteristic of the psychical, and psychology as the study of the contents of consciousness. Indeed it seems to us so much a matter of course to equate them in this way that any contradiction of the idea strikes us as obvious nonsense. Yet psycho-analysis cannot avoid raising this contradiction; it cannot accept the identity of the conscious and the mental. It defines what is mental as processes such as feeling, thinking and willing, and it is obliged to maintain that there is unconscious thinking and unapprehended willing. In saying this it has from the start frivolously forfeited the sympathy of every friend of sober scientific thought, and laid itself open to the suspicion of being a fantastic esoteric doctrine eager to make mysteries and fish in troubled waters. But you, Ladies and Gentlemen, naturally cannot understand as yet what right I have to describe as a prejudice a statement of so abstract a nature as 'what is mental is conscious'. Nor can you guess what development can have led to a denial of the unconscious—should such a thing exist—and what advantage there may have been in that denial. The question whether we are to make the psychical coincide with the conscious or make it extend further

sounds like an empty dispute about words; yet I can assure you that the hypothesis of there being unconscious mental processes paves the way to a decisive new orientation in the world and in science.

You cannot have any notion, either, of what an intimate connection there is between this first piece of audacity on the part of psycho-analysis and the second one, which I must now tell you of. This second thesis, which psycho-analysis puts forward as one of its findings, is an assertion that instinctual impulses which can only be described as sexual, both in the narrower and wider sense of the word, play an extremely large and never hitherto appreciated part in the causation of nervous and mental diseases. It asserts further that these same sexual impulses also make contributions that must not be underestimated to the highest cultural, artistic and social creations of the human spirit. 16

In my experience antipathy to this outcome of psycho-analytic research is the most important source of resistance which it has met with. Would you like to hear how we explain that fact? We believe that civilization has been created under the pressure of the exigencies of life at the cost of satisfaction of the instincts; and we believe that civilization is to a large extent being constantly created anew, since each individual who makes a fresh entry into human society repeats this sacrifice of instinctual satisfaction for the benefit of the whole community. Among the instinctual forces which are put to this use the sexual impulses play an important part; in this process they are sublimated—that is to say, they are diverted from their sexual aims and directed to others that are socially higher and no longer sexual. But this arrangement is unstable; the sexual instincts are imperfectly tamed, and, in the case of every individual who is supposed to join in the work of civilization, there is a risk that his sexual instincts may refuse to be put to that use. Society believes that no greater threat to its civilization could arise than if the sexual instincts were to be liberated and returned to their original aims. For this reason society does not wish to be reminded of this precarious portion of its foundations. It has no interest in the recognition of the strength of the sexual instincts or in the demonstration of the importance of sexual life to the individual. On the contrary, with an educational aim in view, it has set about diverting attention from that whole field of ideas. That is 17 why it will not tolerate this outcome of psycho-analytic research and far prefers to stamp it as something aesthetically repulsive and morally reprehensible, or as something dangerous. But objections of this sort are ineffective against what claims to be an objective outcome of a piece of scientific work; if the contradiction is to come into the open it must be restated in intellectual terms. Now it is inherent in human nature to have an inclination to consider a thing untrue if one does not like it, and after that it is easy to find arguments against it. Thus society makes what is disagreeable into what is untrue. It disputes the truths of psycho-analysis with logical and factual arguments; but these arise from emotional sources and it maintains these objections as prejudices, against every attempt to counter them.

We, however, Ladies and Gentlemen, can claim that in asserting this controversial thesis we have had no tendentious aim in view. We have merely wished to give expression to a matter of fact which we believe we have established by our painstaking labours. We claim, too, the right to reject without qualification any interference by practical considerations in scientific work, even before we have enquired whether the fear which seeks to impose these considerations on us is justified or not. 18

Such, then, are a few of the difficulties that stand in the way of your interest in psycho-analysis. They are perhaps more than enough for a start. But if you are able to overcome the impression they make on you, we will proceed. 19

THE THINKING PROCESS

STRUCTURE

1. Paragraphs 1 through 4 introduce the lecture by establishing the relationship between Freud and his audience and by giving an overview of what Freud will cover. Analyze the relationship Freud sets up with his audience in the introduction. In which paragraphs does he set out what his lecture will cover? What is the purpose of paragraph 4?

2. Freud recognizes the attitudes of his audience by structuring his lecture around the difficulties involved in understanding psychoanalysis. What paragraphs deal with what difficulties? Why might Freud have presented them in the order that he does?

3. Like many writers and speakers, Freud draws upon a number of patterns of organization. In which paragraphs does he use definition? Comparison and contrast? Process analysis? Cause and effect? Which organizational mode predominates?

4. Paragraphs 18 and 19 conclude the lectures by summarizing, by taking a stand, and by looking ahead to the lectures that will follow. What are the "painstaking labours" referred to in paragraph 18? Why might Freud have felt it necessary to make the "claim" that he does? Does paragraph 19 provide adequate closure? Why or why not?

STYLE

1. Divisions within a lecture must be clear because the audience can detect them only by listening. What words does Freud use to indicate major shifts within the lecture? Are they satisfactory? How or how not?

2. The tone of a lecture is critical, for underrating the audience may seem condescending, overrating apologetic. How would you characterize Freud's assessment of his listeners? Does he respect them, distrust them, what? What evidence can you summon for your views? How would you describe Freud's tone?

3. Although Freud would like to change the attitude of his audience, his primary purpose is expository, to explain his subject. Explanations are usually marked by words indicating causal relationships *(thus, because, therefore)* and semantic relationships *(for instance, for example, but, nevertheless, first, next,* etc.). To what extent does Freud depend on words of this nature? How effectively does he set forth his explanation?

4. Select several key sentences from the lecture. What basis did you use to choose them? Aside from their meaning, what distinguishes the sentences? To what extent do they differ syntactically from the sentences surrounding them? What stylistic techniques does Freud use to emphasize the sentences?

IDEAS FOR A FIRST DRAFT

Working alone or as part of a group, think of a contemporary subject that you are an "expert" on, no matter how seemingly trivial it is (such as video games or Dungeons and Dragons, David Bowie or J. R. R. Tolkien). Then put yourself in Freud's position, facing an audience that not only isn't knowledgeable about your subject but one that regards it with skepticism, even hostility. Your purpose is primarily informative—to introduce and to explain your subject—but it is also persuasive in that you have to deal with your audience's negative attitudes and biases.

If punk rock is your current interest, think, for instance, of how it strikes the eyes and ears of a local PTA group or the Rotary Club or any group of adults over thirty. Consider the attitudes of your audience. What prejudices might they hold? What knowledge might they have? In what contexts are they operating? List these attitudes, prejudices, and references, and consider as well what points of contact you can make. The same audiences that might think video games a waste of time and money may have grown up to the bells and thumps of pinball machines; those who regard computers as alien objects probably take the typewriter and telephone for granted.

Like Freud, you can structure your lecture around the difficulties your audience needs to overcome in order to understand your subject, or you may want to organize your points less strictly, relating them to your audience's experience. No matter what organization you choose, you need to start by establishing a relationship with your audience, granting their doubts and working from there to set up the kind of tone you want. You will probably be relying on definition, but comparison and contrast can help make the unfamiliar familiar, historical exposition can clarify the development of your subject, and cause and effect can explain its functions and impact.

Keep in mind that you need to set out your lecture so that its major points can be clearly identified by listening. Similarly, pay close attention to the need for transitions and logical connections. To establish causal and semantic relationships, you might want to use the conventional words and phrases, discussed above in question 3 under Style.

JEAN SHEPHERD

The Van Culture

Jean Shepherd is the author of *In God We Trust: All Others Pay Cash*, *The Phantom of the Open Hearth*, and *A Fistful of Fig Newtons* (1981) from which the following excerpt was taken. Perhaps more familiar as a humorist and storyteller on radio and television, he has also published in *Playboy*, *Car and Driver*, and *The Whole Fun Catalog*.

"The Van Culture" is an imaginary lecture addressed to "Sociology 101," a hypothetical class. It is a parody—a take-off—that Shepherd himself introduces with "I imagined a future sociologist lecturing on various aspects of The Car to future classes." As you read the selection, see if it fulfills the aim, structure, and style of an effective lecture.

Today, class, we are going to take up the brief study of one of the true curiosities of late twentieth-century American life, a substrata of the population which I shall herein designate as The Van Culture. There has not been much written about this in literature; hence I feel strongly that it is time to put it down for the record, a whole way of life that has evolved, quietly, without notice of the more official sociologists and compulsive categorizers of the American scene. It revolves around that homely product of automotive technology known generically as The Van. 1

The Van Culture, loosely speaking, is an offshoot of an 2

earlier culture which I hereby designate the VW People. They bear little if any resemblance to The Camper Crowd, although there are some superficial, very superficial, points of resemblance. Obviously, their vehicles have some similarities, such as unwieldiness, bulk, and a marked tendency to flip in any crosswind hitting more than 20 mph in gusts. Also, both types of vehicle can be used for sleeping purposes and for lugging crowds over the landscape. After that, the resemblances cease.

The Winnebago or Camper Crowd tends to be dedicated family types, somewhat overweight, highly conservative politically, extremely fertile, and usually middle-aged, regardless of their chronological age. They read the *Reader's Digest, Field & Stream, The American Legion Monthly, TV Guide,* and can be heard any time of the day or night endlessly blabbing back and forth over their beloved CB radios, using such terms as "Code Seven," "Ten-Four," etc., picked up by watching "Adam 12" in reruns, one of their all-time favorite TV shows. 3

On the other hand, The Van People tend to be heavily bearded, dedicated lifetime subscribers to *Rolling Stone,* compulsive consumers of granola, and they often pride themselves on making their own yoghurt. Their social habits tend to a distinct aversion to marriage unless it is performed by a guru or a Navaho shaman standing knee-deep in the waters of Gitchee-Goomie while the assembled company bays in concert to the moon, evoking the Great Wolf God, which is guaranteed to bestow eternal happiness and good vibes forever. 4

In spite of the fact that a considerable number of them are now rapidly approaching their fifties, they remain forever nineteen. As for their political views, when they bother to vote at all they will cast their ballot for any black on the ticket, or, if no black is running, a woman. Their perfect candidate for any office would be a black woman, and ideally a black homosexual woman who once worked in the lettuce fields and has a strong dash of Cheyenne blood in her veins. 5

At this point, class, I feel it necessary to point out that I—personally—am making no value judgments, merely describing for the record some of the more significant movements of our time, the last quarter of the twentieth century. 6

Both groups, The Van Culture and The Camper Crowd, seem to enjoy plastering their respective vehicles with various bits of propaganda material designed to prove, apparently, to the world at large that the souls and hearts of the inmates of said 7 vehicle are in the right place. It is in the actual contents, philosophicaly speaking, of the messages that the sharp divergence of the two cultures can be seen. The Camper Crowd is forever proclaiming proudly its married togetherness: The Murchisons; Al & Frieda Bugleblast; Betty, Bob, Ronnie, Bonnie, Donnie, and Rover. This is often accompanied by a frank admission of their home base, regardless of how dismal it may be. Kalamazoo, Michigan, Jackson, Mississippi, Teaneck, New Jersey, Frankfurt, Indiana seem to be among the more popular locales. This is often accompanied in large block letters by the proud CB call sign: KFU 9768, apparently the assumption being that passing mobs of like persuasion would care to communicate, instantly, with Al and Frieda and presumably Bonnie Jean and Rover. They also enjoy proclaiming publicly their never-ending cheerfulness; displaying such bumper stickers as: Have a Good Day, Have You Tried Smiling? and often Christ Is the Answer or Honk If You Love Jesus.

On the political side, their stickers usually radiate suspicion 8
of the world at large and often downright paranoia: Fight Godless Communism, Gun Control Laws Mean Only Criminals Have Guns, People Kill; Not Guns, and that all-time favorite America—Love It or Leave It.

On the other hand, The Van People are fond of plastering 9
their equipment with such goodies as: Danger—I Brake for Animals (apparently on the assumption that the mean old Others are endlessly and maliciously bashing their cars into goats, pigs, elderly St. Bernards, draft horses, mud turtles, and other lowly creatures with which we share this planet), Have You Thanked a Green Plant Today? Boycott Lettuce (Grapes, California Tomatoes, Kohlrabi), War Is Bad for Children and Other Living Things, and No Nukes! They, like their Camper brethren, feel compelled to advertise their political views through the medium of decals and stickers: Anderson—the Only Choice, Ban Hand Guns, Third World Power (Woman Power, Gay Power, Indian Power, Chicano Power, Granola Power).

The Van Culture shares with The Camper Crowd a com- 10
pulsion to advertise its interpersonal relationships, although in a very different fashion. While The Camper Crowd seems to be very specific (Al & Frieda & the Kids), The Van Culture deals only in generalities (Love) (Peace), although just whom it loves or whom it is at peace with is never, ever specified (. . . I gotta keep my options open, baby).

The Van Culture appears to be, at least publicly, highly conscious of our environment. At any rate, that's what its signs say: Don't Pollute, Ecology Is for People and Dogs and Everybody, Honor Earth, Return the Earth to the People, No Nukes! These last seem to assume that vans don't pollute while Pintos do, and that the diet Dr. Pepper that The Van Culture is forever swilling comes in more ecologically compatible cans than the Pabst Blue Ribbon that The Camper Crowd tends to guzzle. 11

Both groups have one overwhelming trait in common—they share intense self-approval. If I were less kind I would use the word "smug," but since I'm a very kind person and am always considerate of the feelings of others and bear a total love for my fellow man (Naturally, I cannot use this word. Future social historians, I firmly believe, are going to study the various strata in our society and their significance to the time by standards other than the old-fashioned class divisions such as economic, educational, racial, and ethnic.), I should say fellow "person." 12

All these lines are blurring rapidly, while such new social divisions as The Camper Crowd and The Van Culture are becoming more sharply defined. Incidentally, there is a newly emergent subgroup under The Van Culture that could be called The Used School Bus Tribe. I wonder what would happen to the drug traffic here in the United States if all vans magically disappeared in one puff of smoke. It is a little-known but highly significant fact that a vast percentage of quick drug buys are made out of vans. It truly could be said that a pusher who drives a van is, in fact, a Wheeler Dealer. This twist that the van has taken is somewhat ironic, since back in the early days of this type of vehicle it was first touted to the public with ads showing cool, well-educated mommies, social science majors all, obviously well-heeled suburbanites, vanning a crowd of well-scrubbed kids, off to the Little League, or camp, or whatever. Daddy taught Economics at a local junior college, wore thick glasses, religiously read the *New Republic,* and cherished his membership in the Adlai Stevenson I'm Proud I'm an Egghead club. These same apple-cheeked kids grew up to push smack out of an identical van from a parking lot outside a shopping center in Fort Lauderdale. This has nice overtones of the Theater of the Absurd. 13

On the other hand, The Camper Crowd has seen its be- 14

loved conveyance put to other than clean-limbed, nature-loving purposes. For example, a notorious string of Mafia-controlled bordellos operated very successfully (and in fact still do) out of a string of true Recreational Vehicles, complete with red plush interiors, brass spittoons, and in at least one case, a four-channel tape deck specializing in Turn-of-the-Century Whorehouse Piano.

The driving styles of both sects are as opposed as their 15
philosophies. The Camper Crowd seems to be totally oblivious of any other machine on the road, ponderously rumbling with tanklike stolidity right down the exact middle of the turnpike. I have seen three hundred cars held up for hours by two or three strategically placed campers.

Naturally, there are exceptions in both groups and you'll 16
occasionally see a lunatic Winnebago driver careening along at eighty-five plus, reminding you of nothing so much as a runaway Cape Cod house on wheels with a baboon at the tiller, but generally The Camper Crowd's driving style is as conservative as its politics.

In contrast, The Van Culture mostly drives its badly sprung, 17
unstable, underbraked, high center of gravity, overloaded hulks as though they were so many Porsches. In fact, recently in a Howard Johnson on the Jersey Turnpike I got into a rap about vans that love to tailgate with a Jersey state cop who spends the days of his life patrolling the infamous NJP. . . .

It was after this discussion that I got to thinking about the 18
whole new Van Culture and all the good things it's brought to America; a new sense of togetherness for one. By the very nature of the van it tends to create crowds, and this can have, ultimately, a profound effect on our social structure, perhaps bringing together human beings after the splintering of the family group during the latter days of the seventies.

In fact, it's already happening. The Charles Manson family 19
was carted around over the landscape by its guru in a succession of vans, stolen and otherwise. The old Spahn ranch was never without a half-dozen vans liberally larded with *Peace* signs and *Love* stickers, all gassed up and ready to go out on another exciting hit. In fact, several of the murders attributed to the Family were over disputed ownership of vans. Manson also utilized a used school bus, seats removed, carpeted with old rugs, to house

his bevy of love-conscious females before they finally settled down to good solid family life at the ranch. In one sense, Manson was a true social innovator.

So there you have it, class. Today's discussion of The Van 20
Culture. I don't find it necessary to remind you that questions about this subject will appear on the blue book exam at the end of this semester.

THE THINKING PROCESS

STRUCTURE

1. "The Van Culture: Sociology 101" is an essay written as a lecture. What are the functions of paragraphs 1, 6, 12, 20? Do you find them effective?

2. As in all lectures, the central purpose of "Sociology 101" is to inform. What basic pattern of organization does Shepherd use to structure his lecture? To what extent does Shepherd employ definition and classification? Briefly list the categories that differentiate between the Van and Camper Cultures.

3. Although the basic purpose of lecturers is to instruct, they must entertain in order to keep their audience's attention and they must stimulate thought not rote memory. In which passages is Shepherd entertaining his audience? In which is he trying to make his audience think? Does he ever attempt both at once?

STYLE

1. Lecturers must be aware of the ages, interests, backgrounds, and experiences of their audiences to avoid speaking above or beneath them. Shepherd is delivering a lecture to an introductory sociology class. What diction does he use that belongs to the technical language of sociology?

2. Shepherd includes colloquial language in his lecture. Find several examples. What are their functions? Do you find the variations in diction effective, erratic, what?

3. Because speech cannot use the conventions of the paragraph, lecturers must clearly signal changes of topic so that their audience can easily follow them. List the opening phrases and clauses of Shepherd's paragraphs. Explain whether or not they adequately signal the new units of information.

IDEAS FOR A FIRST DRAFT

You are going to write or present a parody of a lecture. Select a lecturer, subject, and lesson that lend themselves well to parody. Observe the person closely during a lecture. Does he or she have pet phrases or gestures? Write them down. Does the person have a set way of sequencing a lecture, ending it, asking or answering questions? What about writing on the board or moving about the room? Also note any idiosyncratic characteristics of voice. Perhaps the person has an unusually pitched voice or phrases sentences with an odd intonation or uses nothing but multisyllabic words. Take your list of characteristics and categorize them according to the headings that seem logical; speech habits, movements, and patterns of organizing material are common ones.

Then think about the subject itself and the primary aim of a lecture: to inform. What diction and elements seem ready-made for humor? The sciences, for instance, are always inventing terms ("black hole," "quark") so you might invent your own vocabulary; the humanities are always scrutinizing minute details, finding meaning everywhere, so you might accentuate that propensity. Or, like Shepherd, you might choose a subject to parody for a Sociology 101 class: cinema-types, ice cream experts, baseball as an art form, fitness freaks, the archetypal college preppy, junk-food junkies.

Once you have determined what to parody and how, begin writing your draft. If you are going to deliver the paper orally, keep it to ten to twenty minutes or else you might strain its humor; if the parody is an essay, use first person and perhaps build in parenthetical stage directions. To check your tone, read your draft aloud or give it to a friend who is familiar with the lecturer. You want to exaggerate but within the bounds of taste: you can be barbed but not cruel.

THE LECTURING PROCESS

INVENTION

If you are presently working on an assignment in this chapter, skip to Organizing and Developing; if not, imagine that you have been assigned to give a lecture on the subject of your choice. If you have written a report in part 2, you have a wealth of information to draw upon. If not, select a subject of interest to you; it may be one that you know well or one that you want to know more about, but whatever the case, you will need to do some research. You want to gather the facts and the opinions of the experts, and you want to draw your own conclusions as well. As you collect your materials, look for photographs, illustrations, or diagrams that you can use as visual aids to supplement your presentation.

ORGANIZING AND DEVELOPING

Astronomy to zoology, Archimedes to Zoroaster, aardvark to zeugma—whatever your subject—you need to create a structure for your lecture. If your subject is abstract or complex like nuclear fusion, begin with a concrete analogy or with the familiar. If you are dealing with a process, like etching, perhaps begin with some background information and then conduct a step-by-step explanation. If cause and effect is the best mode for your topic, as it might be for an analysis of the Viet Nam War, make the chain of causes and subsequent effects clear. Or you may choose a dramatic organization for your lecture, leading up to startling events or essential discoveries. Your classmates are your audience so your information will have to be complex enough to interest them yet simple enough to be comprehensible.

Once you have gathered your information and have determined a basic pattern of organization, write down the central points you want to make. In a fifty-minute lecture, four major points are sufficient. Don't try to compress too much information in the time you have. Under your major points you should make subheads, and then note examples, descriptions, quotations, anecdotes, and essential facts that you want to relate. Make sure that your examples and analogies are vivid and lively; sustaining your audience's interest is essential.

You may want to see if you have any information that you could work into a handout for the class—an outline of the most important points or supplementary material like a bibliography, figures, or graphs. Also make sure that you're prepared to use the chalkboard during your lecture. Define and spell any terms that might be unfamiliar; identify people and places as well. If you are presenting your lecture orally, write out your points on a sheet of paper or notecards; include any pertinent definitions, quotations, or facts that you intend using for illustration. If you are writing a lecture as a paper assignment, begin writing as if you were directly addressing a class. Keep in mind your audience and the fact that you are performing. Remember at the end of the lecture to summarize your basic points briefly.

FINDING A VOICE

If your lecture is a written assignment, read it aloud. Does it sound as if an authority is speaking naturally? Does the speaker project a distinct personality? Do you consciously address the audience? You can expect to use first person singular and plural as well as second person. Include any diagrams or handouts with your paper. If you are writing a parody, you might want to indicate gestures and the like in parentheses; exaggeration is fine as long as it's not excessive.

If your lecture is to be delivered orally, try finding a tone you think appropriate for your audience, perhaps a mixture of formal and informal diction, reserving formal language for the technical aspects of the subject and informal for your explanations, illustrations, and anecdotes. Think of points you can dramatize and underscore with gestures. You want control over your subject matter, yet you want your audience to be able to interrupt with questions.

POLISHING

If your lecture is to be submitted as an essay, try to find a volunteer to read it aloud. Is your information informative? Entertaining? Are there are any passages that seem unnatural? Are all of your points clear? Are your transitions from one point to the next readily apparent? Are the major sections in the lecture marked clearly enough so that your listeners can hear them? Are you addressing the class directly? Are you conscious of being on stage? Are you concluding with a reassertion of your essential points? If your paper is a parody of a particular lecturer, ask some other students who share classes with you to see if they can recognize the instructor by your essay alone. If not, ask for suggestions.

If your lecture is to be oral, don't write it out completely; instead, practice delivering it from your notes until you feel comfortable with the material, and make sure that you emphasize transitions and logical connections so that they can be recognized by the ear. During your presentation, feel free to refer to your notes, but nothing is more deadly than reading to your audience. (For further discussion, see "How to Make a Speech" on p. 430.)

Everyone has a different style of lecturing, so try to determine which style is best for you. Body movement can underscore your remarks, so move around the room freely, gesticulate, write on the board, do whatever feels comfortable, but don't stay glued to one spot crouching behind the lectern. Be flexible enough to answer questions of clarification during your lecture, and save time for substantive questions at the end.

THINKING AHEAD

Lecturing is good practice for any public speaking because it accustoms you to performing in front of an audience without having to focus solely on persuading or entertaining—two more difficult modes. Note any problems you encountered either in your research or in your lecture. Did you use all of your information? If not, why not? If so, did you try to include too much? Did you have a thorough knowledge of your material without relying too frequently on your notes? Were you entertaining as well as informative? Did you have any distracting gestures or expressions? Ask for anonymous, written evaluations from your instructor and classmates so that you can perfect your speaking style.

CHAPTER 12

THE ORATOR

An orator is a skilled, eloquent public speaker, somewhat of a rarity in the twentieth century perhaps, but certainly a dominant figure in ancient Greece. The Greeks divided oratory into three types—legal, political, and ceremonial and had speakers who excelled in each—Lycurgus, Demosthenes, and Pericles. In 429 B.C., Cleon was so inspiring that he convinced the Athenian Assembly to send an expedition to massacre every adult male in Lesbos; but Diodotos was so persuasive that the Assembly rescinded its edict and sent its swiftest ship to turn back the navy.

Today few orators prevent wars, and addresses to the courts are left to lawyers, but political and ceremonial speeches flourish as do a more modern form of oratory, religious sermons.

Memorable speeches must instruct, entertain, inspire, and persuade. Relying more on emotional appeal than on specific information, effective speeches are also distinguished from argumentative essays by inspiration. The immediacy of speakers speaking and audiences listening, the modulations of the voice from stage whispers to shouts, the gesticulations from arm waving to table thumping, the emotional tension of responses both individual and communal, from cheers or boos to tears and laughter—all create a dramatic scene that the written word alone can never achieve.

Consider the great political orators of our century—Winston Churchill, Franklin Delano Roosevelt, Adolf Hitler, Charles de Gaulle, Martin Luther King, Jr.—individuals whose speeches alone have determined the course of history. To understand the magnetism and inspiration of Hitler's speeches, you needn't know German; simply listen to a recording or view a film clip, and note the intensity of the voice and the fury of the gestures that inflame mob hysteria.

In June of 1941, six months before the United States entered World War II, F. D. R. assured the English:

> We, too, born to freedom, and believing in freedom, are willing to fight to maintain freedom. We, and all others who believe as deeply as we do, would rather die on our feet than live on our knees.

The force of the excerpt comes from the parallel structure of the phrases and sentences, the repetition of "we," "believe," and "freedom," the further emphasis of the long *e* in "deeply," "feet," "knees," the vivid imagery and juxtaposition of the final clauses, the emotive words, and the cadences of the phrasing.

But the greatest orator of the age was Winston Churchill, of whom the reporter Edward R. Murrow said, "He mobilized the English language and sent it to battle." A telling example is that renowned passage from Churchill's speech on Dunkirk:

> We shall not flag or fail. We shall go on to the end. We shall fight in France, we shall fight on the seas and oceans, we shall fight with growing confidence and growing strength in the air, we shall defend our island, whatever the cost may be, we shall fight on the beaches, we shall fight on the landing grounds, we shall fight in the fields and in the streets, we shall fight in the hills; we shall never surrender.

The incantation, the repetition, the parallelism, the all-encompassing imagery, the patriotism, and the indomitable will all articulate the battle cry.

A battle cry of a different sort was iterated in 1961 by John F. Kennedy in his inaugural address. Here President Kennedy relies on wordplay, on the metaphor of battle, on balance and repetition:

> Now the trumpet summons us again—not as a call to bear arms, though arms we need—not as a call to battle, though embattled we are—but a call to bear the burden of a long twilight struggle, year in and year out, "rejoicing in hope, patient in tribulation,"—a struggle against the common enemies of man: tyranny, poverty, disease and war itself.

Oration extends beyond the realm of politics. Samuel Clemens (Mark Twain) was one of the most popular, entertaining, and renowned of nineteenth-century American speakers. Banquets, dinners, luncheons, political meetings, benefits, fund-raisers, clubs, churches, schools, congress—all echo with Mark Twain speaking. In "On Speech-Making Reform" in 1885, Clemens set down some rules for effective speaking:

> The best and most telling speech is not the actual impromptu one, but the counterfeit of it; . . . that speech is most worth listening to which has been carefully prepared in private and tried on a plaster cast, or an empty chair, or any other appreciative object that will keep quiet, until the speaker has got his matter and his delivery limbered up so that they will seem impromptu to an audience.

With that introduction, Clemens describes the performance of the best speaker:

> And that man will soar along, in the most beautiful way, on the wings of a practiced memory; heaving in a little decayed grammar here, and a little wise tautology there, and a little neatly counterfeited embarrassment yonder, and a little finely acted stumbling and stammering for a word—rejecting this word and that, and finally getting the right one, and fetching it out with ripping effect, . . . and at last, with supreme art, he will catch himself, when in the very act of sitting down, and lean over the table and fire a parting rocket, in the way of an afterthought, which makes everybody stretch his mouth as it goes up, and dims the very stars in heaven when it explodes. And yet that man has been practicing that afterthought and that attitude for about a week.

And if his listeners aren't impressed by a positive model of the prepared speaker, Clemens plays on the fear that we all have of public embarrassment as he describes the genuinely impromptu speaker who "goes waddling and warbling along, just as if he thought it wasn't any harm to commit a crime so long as it wasn't premeditated."

The speeches included in this chapter range from a graduation address by William Faulkner, to an appeal for world peace by Albert Einstein, to a political address by Barbara Jordan. Each in its own way incorporates the conventional devices of repetition and charged language; each demonstrates a keen sense of purpose and audience; each informs, entertains, and persuades; each inspires. As you read the speeches aloud, try to imagine the immediacy of the speaker facing the audience, the actions and reactions, the mounting tensions, and the final applause.

Shakespeare's Mark Antony declares himself "no orator," confessing in his eulogy for Julius Caesar that he has "neither wit, nor words, nor worth, / Action, nor utterance, nor the power of speech, / To stir men's blood." "I only speak right on," he declares, and then using every technique in the book of oratory—appealing to sentiment, to reason, to anger, and to his audience's values—he stirs the blood of all who hear him through the ages. The well-delivered speech is writing dramatized.

WILLIAM FAULKNER

Address to the Graduating Class, University High School

In May of 1951, some seven months after he received the Nobel Prize for Literature, William Faulkner addressed the graduating class of the University High School in Oxford, Mississippi, the home of the University of Mississippi and the town in which Faulkner spent much of his life. Oxford is also the prototype of Faulkner's "Jefferson," the seat of his legendary Yoknapatawpha County, the fictional site of his most celebrated novels, *The Sound and the Fury* (1929), *As I Lay Dying* (1930), *Absalom, Absalom!* (1936), and *The Reivers* (1962), for which he won the Pulitzer Prize. Read aloud the speech that follows so that you can hear its cadences and let your ear guide you through Faulkner's syntax. The "wise Frenchman" to whom Faulkner refers is Henri Estienne, a sixteenth-century writer and publisher.

Years ago, before any of you were born, a wise Frenchman said, 'If youth knew; if age could.' We all know what he meant: that when you are young, you have the power to do anything, but you don't know what to do. Then, when you have got old and experience and observation have taught you answers, you are tired, frightened; you don't care, you want to be left alone as long as you yourself are safe; you no longer have the capacity or the will to grieve over any wrongs but your own. 1

So you young men and women in this room tonight, and in 2
thousands of other rooms like this one about the earth today,

have the power to change the world, rid it forever of war and injustice and suffering, provided you know how, know what to do. And so according to the old Frenchman, since you can't know what to do because you are young, then anyone standing here with a head full of white hair, should be able to tell you.

But maybe this one is not as old and wise as his white hairs 3
pretend or claim. Because he can't give you a glib answer or pattern either. But he can tell you this, because he believes this. What threatens us today is fear. Not the atom bomb, nor even fear of it, because if the bomb fell on Oxford tonight, all it could do would be to kill us, which is nothing, since in doing that, it will have robbed itself of its only power over us: which is fear of it, the being afraid of it. Our danger is not that. Our danger is the forces in the world today which are trying to use man's fear to rob him of his individuality, his soul, trying to reduce him to an unthinking mass by fear and bribery—giving him free food which he has not earned, easy and valueless money which he has not worked for;—the economies or ideologies or political systems, communist or socialist or democratic, whatever they wish to call themselves, the tyrants and the politicians, American or European or Asiatic, whatever they call themselves, who would reduce man to one obedient mass for their own aggrandizement and power, or because they themselves are baffled and afraid, afraid of, or incapable of, believing in man's capacity for courage and endurance and sacrifice.

That is what we must resist, if we are to change the world 4
for man's peace and security. It is not men in the mass who can and will save Man. It is Man himself, created in the image of God so that he shall have the power and the will to choose right from wrong, and so be able to save himself because he is worth saving;—Man, the individual, men and women, who will refuse always to be tricked or frightened or bribed into surrendering, not just the right but the duty too, to choose between justice and injustice, courage and cowardice, sacrifice and greed, pity and self;—who will believe always not only in the right of man to be free of injustice and rapacity and deception, but the duty and responsibility of man to see that justice and truth and pity and compassion are done.

So, never be afraid. Never be afraid to raise your voice for 5
honesty and truth and compassion, against injustice and lying and greed. If you, not just you in this room tonight, but in all

the thousands of other rooms like this one about the world today and tomorrow and next week, will do this, not as a class or classes, but as individuals, men and women, you will change the earth. In one generation all the Napoleons and Hitlers and Caesars and Mussolinis and Stalins and all the other tyrants who want power and aggrandizement, and the simple politicians and time-servers who themselves are merely baffled or ignorant or afraid, who have used, or are using, or hope to use, man's fear and greed for man's enslavement, will have vanished from the face of it.

THE THINKING PROCESS

STRUCTURE

1. Speakers as well as writers often arrange their ideas using one or more patterns of organization. Faulkner, for instance, uses definition together with cause and effect to express his central idea. How does he define *fear?* What does Faulkner say are the effects of fear?

2. Speakers must develop an acute sense of the audience they address and establish a relationship with that audience from the start. What paragraph or paragraphs provide the introduction to Faulkner's speech? What words or phrases in the introduction relate specifically to the audience he addresses? In what wider context(s) does he place his audience? Why might he have chosen to do so?

3. What audience does Faulkner address in the first sentence of his concluding paragraph? Does his focus stay on that audience for the rest of the paragraph? Explain. What action does Faulkner want his audience to take? Why might he have urged individual rather than collective action?

4. In sermons, speakers often take a quotation as their text and expound upon it to urge the audience to moral action. In a sense, Faulkner's speech is like a sermon. To what extent is his choice of quotation appropriate to the occasion of the speech? To its structure?

STYLE

1. Speakers have an advantage over writers because they can address their audience directly. Examine Faulkner's pronouns. Is his choice of second person effective? How or how not? Why might he have chosen to refer to himself in the third person? Does he use first person singular? Plural? What overall effect does Faulkner achieve through his use of point of view?

2. Most speakers vary the length and structure of their sentences, and Faulkner does so to an extreme. How long is the speech's shortest sentence? Longest? Rewrite one of the longer sentences, breaking it into two or more. What is gained? Lost?

3. Repetition, alliteration, and parallel structures all lend sentences cadence and rhythm as well as emphasis. In what sentences does Faulkner draw upon these techniques? How do the techniques reinforce meaning?

4. Often unskilled writers are warned against beginning a sentence with a conjunction for fear that they may end up with an unsuccessful fragment. Faulkner, however, begins the first three sentences of paragraph 3 with conjunctions. Are the sentences fragments? Why or why not? What effect does Faulkner achieve by beginning with conjunctions? Where else in the essay does he use the same technique? Does it have the same effect? How or how not?

IDEAS FOR A FIRST DRAFT

Imagine that you have been asked to address the senior class of your high school a week before their graduation or that you have been invited to address the incoming high-school freshmen. You have accepted an invitation, and now must compose a speech. Try to second-guess your audience's interests. High-school freshmen are probably feeling lost and know relatively little of what may await them; high-school seniors probably feel much the same way about going on to college or joining the work force. Try to deduce what they may want to hear; their concerns are probably much the same as yours were at that age. Make a short list of what is apt to be on their minds when you address them; then make another list of what you want to say to this audience. Looking for connections, review the two lists, and select a subject.

After you have chosen a subject, list the points you want to make. If you examine them side by side with your audience's concerns, you will probably be able to make some connections that will sustain the students' interest; for instance, you could tie their anxiety over what to expect in college to your broader point about the challenges of education; their mixed feelings about ending one phase in their lives and beginning another to your ideas on the importance of taking risks.

Look up the key word or words of your topic in *Bartlett's Familiar Quotations* to find a text that will serve as an effective opening or one you can use to structure your speech. Perhaps write down three or four quotations that seem apt. To judge which works best, you may want to compose the introduction after you have written the body of your speech.

Ask yourself how you want to affect your audience. Do you want to inspire, persuade, entertain, inform? Some combination? To achieve your purpose, look at the list of points you want to make and determine what pattern(s) of organization will work well: definition, example, description, classification, narrative, cause and effect, comparison and contrast, process analysis. Do you need to define any of your key terms? Would first person singular or plural be more effective? Is second person appropriate?

Start writing the body of your speech, using the pattern(s) of organization inherent in what you have to say. You will probably find that you want to focus your paragraphs on separate points and use vocabulary and allusions that are readily understandable.

After you have sketched out the body of the paper, work on your introduction and conclusion. You might want to begin with one of the appropriate quotations from *Bartlett's* and close with an echoing allusion or an adaptation of it. You may also find your introduction a good place to define any important terms, just as your conclusion is ideal for a summary and a call to action.

When you reread your draft, pay particular attention to your tone and character as your speech reveals them. You want to seem neither aloof nor familiar.

ALBERT EINSTEIN

A Message to Intellectuals

Albert Einstein (1879–1955) was a world-famous theoretical physicist, known for formulating the special and general theories of relativity as well as contributing to unified field and quantum theories. Born a German Jew, Einstein became a United States citizen in 1940, having left Europe after his property was confiscated by the Nazis.

During his career, he held various prestigious posts and positions, including those at the University of Zurich, the German University in Prague, the Federal Institute of Technology in Zurich, the Prussian Academy of Sciences in Berlin, the Kaiser Wilhelm Institute in Berlin, and the Institute for Advanced Studies at Princeton.

Einstein's publications include *Relativity: The Special and the General Theory* (1918), *The Meaning of Relativity* (1921), *The World As I See It* (1934), *Out of My Later Years* (1950), and *Ideas and Opinions* (1954). For his work on the photoelectric effect—the emission of electrons when light falls on surfaces—he won the Nobel Prize in Physics in 1921.

A great lover of the arts and an amateur violinist, Einstein was also an ardent pacifist, active in the cause of world peace. As his message to an international meeting in Wroclav, Poland, shows, Einstein was passionate about the danger of mass destruction through nuclear arms, a possibility that his theories had inadvertently helped to bring about.

The Organizing Committee of Intellectuals' Conference for Peace objected to the address, and thus it was never delivered but released instead to the press on 29 August 1948. As you read Einstein's message, see if you can deduce what the committee's objections might have been.

We meet today, as intellectuals and scholars of many nationalities, with a deep and historic responsibility placed upon us. We have every reason to be grateful to our French and Polish colleagues whose initiative has assembled us here for a momentous objective: to use the influence of wise men in promoting peace and security throughout the world. This is the age-old problem with which Plato, as one of the first, struggled so hard: to apply reason and prudence to the solution of man's problems instead of yielding to atavist instincts and passions. 1

By painful experience we have learnt that rational thinking does not suffice to solve the problems of our social life. Penetrating research and keen scientific work have often had tragic implications for mankind, producing, on the one hand, inventions which liberated man from exhausting physical labor, making his life easier and richer; but on the other hand, introducing a grave restlessness into his life, making him a slave to his technological environment, and—most catastrophic of all—creating the means for his own mass destruction. This, indeed, is a tragedy of overwhelming poignancy! 2

However poignant that tragedy is, it is perhaps even more tragic that, while mankind has produced many scholars so extremely successful in the field of science and technology, we have been for a long time so inefficient in finding adequate solutions to the many political conflicts and economic tensions which beset us. No doubt, the antagonism of economic interests within and among nations is largely responsible to a great extent for the dangerous and threatening condition in the world today. Man has not succeeded in developing political and economic forms of organization which would guarantee the peaceful coexistence of the nations of the world. He has not succeeded in building the kind of system which would eliminate the possibility of war and banish forever the murderous instruments of mass destruction. 3

We scientists, whose tragic destination has been to help in making the methods of annihilation more gruesome and more effective, must consider it our solemn and transcendent duty to do all in our power in preventing these weapons from being used for the brutal purpose for which they were invented. What task could possibly be more important for us? What social aim could be closer to our hearts? That is why this Congress has such a vital mission. We are here to take counsel with each other. We must build spiritual and scientific bridges linking the nations of the world. We must overcome the horrible obstacles of national frontiers. 4

In the smaller entities of community life, man has made some progress toward breaking down anti-social sovereignties. This is true, for example, of life within cities and, to a certain degree, even of society within individual states. In such communities tradition and education have had a moderating influence and have brought about tolerable relations among the peoples living within those confines. But in relations among separate states complete anarchy still prevails. I do not believe that we have made any genuine advance in this area during the last few thousand years. All too frequently conflicts among nations are still being decided by brutal power, by war. The unlimited desire for ever greater power seeks to become active and aggressive wherever and whenever the physical possibility offers itself. 5

Throughout the ages, this state of anarchy in international affairs has inflicted indescribable suffering and destruction upon mankind; again and again it has depraved the development of men, their souls and their well-being. For given time it has almost annihiliated whole areas. 6

However, the desire of nations to be constantly prepared for warfare has, however, still other repercussions upon the lives of men. The power of every state over its citizens has grown steadily during the last few hundred years, no less in countries where the power of the state has been exercised wisely, than in those where it has been used for brutal tyranny. The function of the state to maintain peaceful and ordered relations among and between its citizens has become increasingly complicated and extensive largely because of the concentration and centralization of the modern industrial apparatus. In order to protect its citizens from attacks from without a modern state requires a for- 7 midable, expanding military establishment. In addition, the state considers it necessary to educate its citizens for the possibilities of war, an "education" not only corrupting to the soul and spirit of the young, but also adversely affecting the mentality of adults. No country can avoid this corruption. It pervades the citizenry even in countries which do not harbor outspoken aggressive tendencies. The state has thus become a modern idol whose suggestive power few men are able to escape.

Education for war, however, is a delusion. The technological developments of the last few years have created a completely new military situation. Horrible weapons have been invented, capable of destroying in a few seconds huge masses of human beings and tremendous areas of territory. Since science has not yet found protection from these weapons, the modern state is no longer in a position to prepare adequately for the safety of its citizens. 8

How, then, shall we be saved? 9

Mankind can only gain protection against the danger of unimaginable destruction and wanton annihilation if a supranational organization has alone the authority to produce or possess these weapons. It is unthinkable, however, that nations under existing conditions would hand over such authority to a supranational organization unless the organization would have the legal right and duty to solve all the conflicts which in the past have led to war. The functions of individual states would be to concentrate more or less upon internal affairs; in their relation with other states they would deal only with issues and problems which are in no way conducive to endangering international security. 10

Unfortunately, there are no indications that governments yet realize that the situation in which mankind finds itself makes the adoption of revolutionary measures a compelling necessity. Our situation is not comparable to anything in the past. It is impossible, therefore, to apply methods and measures which at an earlier age might have been sufficient. We must revolutionize our thinking, revolutionize our actions, and must have the courage to revolutionize relations among the nations of the world. Clichés of yesterday will no longer do today, and will, no doubt, be hopelessly out of date tomorrow. To bring this home to men all over the world is the most important and most fateful social 11 function intellectuals have ever had to shoulder. Will they have enough courage to overcome their own national ties to the extent that is necessary to induce the peoples of the world to change their deep-rooted national traditions in a most radical fashion?

A tremendous effort is indispensable. If it fails now, the supranational organization will be built later, but then it will have to be built upon the ruins of a large part of the now existing world. Let us hope that the abolition of the existing international anarchy will not need to be bought by a self-inflicted world catastrophe the dimensions of which none of us can possibly imagine. The time is terribly short. We must act now if we are to act at all. 12

THE THINKING PROCESS

STRUCTURE

1. In their opening statements, speakers are usually most concerned with matters of audience, tone, and purpose. How does Einstein's opening paragraph address these concerns?

2. What is the thesis of Einstein's speech? Where in the essay does he place it? Why do you think he waits as long as he does to present it?

3. Oral discourse can be shaped in ways similar to written discourse—as personal essays, reports, analyses, reviews, argumentative essays. Which form does Einstein draw on in his speech? How does the structure of his speech compare to the written discourse it parallels? How does it differ?

4. Why is paragraph 9 composed of only a single sentence? Because listeners, as opposed to readers, are not aware of paragraphs, why do you think that Einstein set off this sentence? What verbal clues to indicate shifts and emphasis do you think that he would have provided during his speech?

5. Examine the message's concluding paragraph. What elements does Einstein include to make it an effective closing? Why do you think that he introduces his conclusion by a question (11)?

STYLE

1. Throughout his speech, Einstein switches from first person plural *we* (1) to third person singular *man* (2, 3) to first person singular *I* (5). Review his speech, examining the various changes in person. Why do you think that Einstein uses *we* in paragraphs 1 and 12? Why does he switch to *I* in 5? Why does he distance himself and the group he addresses from mankind in 2 and 10? Do you find the changes in person effective? Why or why not?

2. Einstein uses vivid adjectives and adverbs to enhance his description of the problem of nuclear war—"catastrophic," "overwhelming" (2); "poignant," "tragic," "murderous" (3); "gruesome," "brutal" (4). Examine these adjectives in context. Do you find them overstated, understated, accurate, what? Try substituting your own sets of adjectives in these sentences; first use sets weaker than Einstein's and then stronger. What are the differences in effect? Which do you prefer and why?

3. In the last six sentences of paragraph 4, Einstein uses a rhetorical technique common to speeches—a series of questions and answers. Parallel elements (similar grammatical structure and phrasing) make the sentences particularly effective for listeners. What parallel elements do you see in the questions? In the answers?

4. In the written version of the address, Einstein has put "education" in quotation marks (7). Why? How would he convey his idea in oral communication?

5. One way of making a point is by emphasizing the negative. Examine paragraph 11. Which sentences are negative? What techniques does Einstein use to counter this pessimism? Are they effective? Why do you think that Einstein uses negation?

IDEAS FOR A FIRST DRAFT

You have been asked to raise money for a particular cause: perhaps for a charity like the American Heart Fund, the National Cancer Association, the American Red Cross, United Way, the Sickle Cell Anemia Fund; or perhaps for a political party or lobby, a college or university, a church, an ecological, political, or preservation group, or a symphony orchestra. Whatever topic you select, make sure you learn about the organization in detail by conducting the necessary research.

After the appropriate research, you are now ready to write a speech asking for contributions to your cause. Your audience will be generally sympathetic or they wouldn't be in attendance, yet few people are particularly eager to donate vast sums of money, so you will still need to inform, but most of all to entertain, inspire, and persuade.

Your speech should consist of three parts—the introduction, body, and summation. For an introduction, think of a way to lead into your subject gradually. Like Einstein, you might start by invoking a common purpose, or perhaps try humor or a shock that is particularly effective. In the body of your speech, briefly explain the purpose, and then concentrate on the aims of your organization and/or fund-raising drive. To persuade the audience to give money, you may want to use charged language, vivid description, and repetition to drive home your points. Perhaps, like Einstein, you should concentrate on the gravity of the problem your fund-raising will solve, or maybe a lighter tone is in order—a personal narrative, whether serious or humorous. You may want to structure your speech with cause and effect or process analysis, making sure your major points are clearly discernible to the ear. For your conclusion, you'll want to stress the seriousness of the subject at hand and make a final pitch to achieve your persuasive goal.

BARBARA JORDAN

Who Then Will Speak for the Common Good?

The Democratic National Convention that led to the nomination of Jimmy Carter, who subsequently defeated incumbent President Gerald Ford, was held in July of 1976, eight days after the nationwide celebration of the bicentennial. The five years prior to the convention had been turbulent: the Democratic Party suffered from its association with the Viet Nam War, the Republicans from the Watergate scandals; the country's international image had been tarnished by the revelations of overseas CIA activities and bribery involving U.S. business operating abroad. At home, the public was still reeling from the Patty Hearst kidnapping case and two assassination attempts on the life of President Ford; and the country's two top officials were in office by default, Rockefeller through the resignation of Agnew, Ford through the resignation of Nixon. The United States in 1976 seemed to have strayed far from the ideals set down in the Declaration of Independence and the Constitution.

Against this background, Barbara Jordan rose to give the opening address. A congresswoman from Texas, Jordan represented what the *New York Times* labeled the "classic American success story": born black and poor, bright and ambitious, she attended the segregated schools of Texas and went on to earn a law degree at Boston University; shortly thereafter she entered politics, first as a state senator and then as a representative to Congress, where she served on the House Judiciary Committee. On that committee, Jordan made a lasting public impression with her judicious opening statement on the impeachment of President Nixon. Accustomed since childhood to the cadences and delivery of black preachers, and trained in traditional oratory and debate as well as in law, Barbara Jordan delivers memorable speeches; the Philadelphia *Evening Bulletin* notes that "getting on the same podium with Miss Jordan is like trying to sing-along with Marian Anderson."

At present, Barbara Jordan has retired from office and holds the Lyndon Baines Johnson public service professorship in the LBJ School of Public Affairs at the University of Texas at Austin.

One hundred and forty-four years ago, members of the Democratic Party first met in convention to select a Presidential candidate. Since that time, Democrats have continued to convene once every four years and draft a party platform and nominate a Presidential candidate. And our meeting this week is a continuation of that tradition. 1

But there is something different about tonight. There is something special about tonight. What is different? What is special? I, Barbara Jordan, am a keynote speaker. 2

A lot of years passed since 1832, and during that time it would have been most unusual for any national political party to ask that a Barbara Jordan deliver a keynote address . . . but tonight here I am. And I feel that notwithstanding the past that my presence here is one additional bit of evidence that the American Dream need not forever be deferred. 3

Now that I have this grand distinction what in the world am I supposed to say? 4

I could easily spend this time praising the accomplishments of this party and attacking the Republicans but I don't choose to do that. 5

I could list the many problems which Americans have. I could list the problems which cause people to feel cynical, angry, 6 frustrated: problems which include lack of integrity in government; the feeling that the individual no longer counts; the reality of material and spiritual poverty; the feeling that the grand American experiment is falling or has failed. I could recite these problems and then I could sit down and offer no solutions. But I don't choose to do that either.

The citizens of America expect more. They deserve and they 7
want more than a recital of problems.

We are a people in a quandary about the present. We are a 8
people in search of our future. We are a people in search of a national community.

We are a people trying not only to solve the problems of the 9
present: unemployment, inflation . . . but we are attempting on a larger scale to fulfill the promise of America. We are attempting to fulfill our national purpose; to create and sustain a society in which all of us are equal.

Throughout our history, when people have looked for new 10
ways to solve their problems, and to uphold the principles of this nation, many times they have turned to political parties. They have often turned to the Democratic Party.

What is it, what is it about the Democratic Party that makes 11
it the instrument that people use when they search for ways to shape their future? Well I believe the answer to that question lies in our concept of governing. Our concept of governing is derived from our view of people. It is a concept deeply rooted in a set of beliefs firmly etched in the national conscience, of all of us.

Now what are these beliefs? 12

First, we believe in equality for all and privileges for none. 13
This is a belief that each American regardless of background has equal standing in the public forum, all of us. Because we believe this idea so firmly, we are an inclusive rather than an exclusive party. Let everybody come.

I think it no accident that most of those emigrating to 14
America in the 19th century identified with the Democratic Party. We are a heterogeneous party made up of Americans of diverse backgrounds.

We believe that the people are the source of all govern- 15
mental power; that the authority of the people is to be extended, not restricted. This can be accomplished only by providing each citizen with every opportunity to participate in the management of the government. They must have that.

We believe that the government which represents the au- 16
thority of all the people, not just one interest group, but all the people; has an obligation to actively underscore, actively seek to remove those obstacles which would block individual achievement . . . obstacles emanating from race, sex, economic condition. The government must seek to remove them.

We are a party of innovation. We do not reject our tradi- 17
tions, but we are willing to adapt to changing circumstances, when change we must. We are willing to suffer the discomfort of change in order to achieve a better future.

We have a positive vision of the future founded on the belief 18
that the gap between the promise and reality of America can one day be finally closed. We believe that.

This my friends, is the bedrock of our concept of governing. 19
This is a part of the reason why Americans have turned to the Democratic Party. These are the foundations upon which a national community can be built.

Let's all understand that these guiding principles cannot be 20
discarded for short-term political gains. They represent what this country is all about. They are indigenous to the American idea. And these are principles which are not negotiable.

In other times, I could stand here and give this kind of expo- 21
sition on the beliefs of the Democratic Party and that would be enough. But today that is not enough. People want more. That is not sufficient reason for the majority of the people of this country to vote Democratic. We have made mistakes. In our haste to do all things for all people, we did not foresee the full consequences of our actions. And when the people raised their voices, we didn't hear. But our deafness was only a temporary condition, and not an irreversible condition.

Even as I stand here and admit that we have made mistakes 22
I still believe that as the people of America sit in judgment on each party, they will recognize that our mistakes were mistakes of the heart. They'll recognize that.

And now we must look to the future. Let us heed the voice 23
of the people and recognize their common sense. If we do not, we not only blaspheme our political heritage, we ignore the common ties that bind all Americans.

Many fear the future. Many are distrustful of their leaders, 24
and believe that their voices are never heard. Many seek only to satisfy their private work wants. To satisfy private interests.

But this is the great danger America faces. That we will 25
cease to be one nation and become instead a collection of interest groups: city against suburb, region against region, individual against individual. Each seeking to satisfy private wants.

If that happens, who then will speak for America? 26

Who then will speak for the common good? 27

This is the question which must be answered in 1976. 28

Are we to be one people bound together by common spirit 29
sharing in a common endeavor or will we become a divided nation?

For all of its uncertainty, we cannot flee the future. We 30
must not become the new puritans and reject our society. We must address and master the future together. It can be done if we restore the belief that we share a sense of national community, that we share a common national endeavor. It can be done.

There is no executive order; there is no law that can require 31
the American people to form a national community. This we must do as individuals and if we do it as individuals, there is no President of the United States who can veto that decision.

As a first step, we must restore our belief in ourselves. We 32
are a generous people so why can't we be generous with each other? We need to take to heart the words spoken by Thomas Jefferson:

"Let us restore to social intercourse that harmony and that 33
affection without which liberty and even life are but dreary things."

A nation is formed by the willingness of each of us to share 34
in the responsibility for upholding the common good.

A government is invigorated when each of us is willing to 35
participate in shaping the future of this nation.

In this election year we must define the common good and 36
begin again to shape a common good and begin again to shape a common future. Let each person do his or her part. If one citizen is unwilling to participate, all of us are going to suffer. For the American idea, though it is shared by all of us, is realized in each one of us.

And now, what are those of us who are elected public offi- 37
cials supposed to do? We call ourselves public servants but I'll tell

you this: we as public servants must set an example for the rest of the nation. It is hypocritical for the public official to admonish and exhort the people to uphold the common good if we are derelict in upholding the common good. More is required of public officials than slogans and handshakes and press releases. More is required. We must hold ourselves strictly accountable. We must provide the people with a vision of the future.

If we promise as public officials, we must deliver. If we as 38 public officials propose, we must produce. If we say to the American people it is time for you to be sacrificial; sacrifice. If the public official says that, we (public officials) must be the first to give. We must be. And again, if we make mistakes, we must be willing to admit them. We have to do that. What we have to do is strike a balance between the idea that government should do everything and the idea, the belief, that government ought to do nothing. Strike a balance.

Let there be no illusions about the difficulty of forming 39 this kind of a national community. It's tough, difficult, not easy. But a spirit of harmony will survive in America only if each of us remembers that we share a common destiny. If each of us remembers when self-interest and bitterness seem to prevail, that we share a common destiny.

I have confidence that we can form this kind of national 40 community.

I have confidence that the Democratic Party can lead the 41 way. I have that confidence. We cannot improve on the system of government handed down to us by the founders of the Republic, there is no way to improve upon that. But what we can do is to find new ways to implement that system and realize our destiny.

Now, I began this speech by commenting to you on the 42 uniqueness of a Barbara Jordan making the keynote address. Well I am going to close my speech by quoting a Republican President and I ask you that as you listen to these words of Abraham Lincoln, relate them to the concept of a national community in which every last one of us participates: "As I would not be a slave, so I would not be a master. This expresses my idea of Democracy. Whatever differs from this, to the extent of the difference is no Democracy."

THE THINKING PROCESS

STRUCTURE

1. Memorable speeches are apt to be those addressed not only to a particular audience but to a more general one as well. Though Barbara Jordan is speaking specifically to the delegates at the Democratic Convention, she is also addressing other groups. Identify her other audiences. What evidence can you find to support your ideas?

2. What is Jordan's purpose for including each of the audiences you have identified in question 1? Is she trying to persuade, entertain, inspire, inform? How so? Given the temper of the times, evaluate the appropriateness of her purposes.

3. What actions does Jordan ask for? Who is to take them? Where in the speech does she propose them? What reasons can you find for their sequence?

4. Speeches or papers that have multiple purposes addressed to multiple audiences must be carefully structured to be clear. What major divisions can you find in Jordan's speech? What reasons can you deduce for those divisions and their sequence? Are there any subdivisions of note? If so, what and why?

5. Almost every paragraph has a topic sentence which it expands and develops into a logical unit that contributes to the overall development of the piece. Less frequently, a paragraph serves a transitional or rhetorical function instead, signaling a change in direction or dramatically emphasizing a point. What examples can you find of these latter two functions? How effective are they?

STYLE

1. Persuasion enlists appeals to reason and emotion. Which predominates in Jordan's speech? How do her allusions further her appeals to emotion or to reason?

2. One way to make a short sentence even shorter is to lead into it with a long one. Where does Jordan use short sentences? Are they well placed? Rewrite several, joining them to other sentences. What is gained? Lost?

3. The repetition of words and phrases can add to the cadence and rhythm of prose as well as reinforce terms crucial to meaning. Where does Jordan use repetition? Parallelism? Read these sentences out loud. Which words are you forced to stress? How crucial are they to the meaning of the sentence? To its rhythm?

4. Metaphorical language reinforces meaning by evoking an image in the listener's mind, thus making an abstract idea more concrete. In paragraph 19, for example, Jordan uses the words "bedrock" and "foundations" to express the concept of the Democratic Party as a tangible, solid structure. Where else does Jordan use metaphoric language? To what end? How effective is the technique?

IDEAS FOR A FIRST DRAFT

Cast yourself first in the role of an attorney, and look through your local newspaper to find a story about a person arrested for a crime. You will probably find several possibilities ranging from burglary to murder. Your job will be to play the part of the attorney for the defense or for the prosecution and to make a summary speech to the jury. The facts you have to work with are the ones reported in the paper though you are free to add anything that is plausible. The news account, for instance, may give only the name, age, and address of the accused, but you could add occupation (or lack of one), family, and any relevant character traits although any added material should be kept to a minimum.

If your instructor wishes, you can turn the presentation into a group assignment, two people to a story, each of whom argues the opposite side of the case before the class as a whole—the jury. To turn the project into more of a group assignment, work up teams for the prosecution and the defense. Both sides, however, should agree to the additional "facts" of the case.

Before you start drafting your appeal to the jury, write down the charges, the facts, and the plea. Expand each one of these topics so that you have a thorough understanding of the basics of the case. Then on another sheet of paper, note which characteristics of the jury you might appeal to in your summation as well as those elements of the case that you can best use to your advantage. For example, if you are defending a teenager accused of murder, you might take the ages of the jury into account. The same holds true for race, sex, economic level, and values.

Your speech begins with the traditional "Ladies and gentlemen of the jury," but where it goes from there is up to you. Perhaps discuss the evidence chronologically or dramatically. Remember that you must account for all the facts of the case. Your appeal to the jury should stress emotion but not at the expense of reason. Evidence, whether in the form of mitigating circumstances or a smoking revolver, should form the backbone of your summation.

The tougher you make your case for yourself, the better your summation is apt to be. Open and shut cases rarely involve any of the techniques of persuasion that you want to exemplify.

After you have written your appeal to the jury, put yourself into the mind of the defendant and create a dramatic situation where he or she is speaking aloud, perhaps a monologue, perhaps a confession to a priest, a phone call home to mother, an exchange with a fellow prisoner. These paragraphs can be as colloquial as you like, depending upon the prisoner's economic, social, and educational background and upon the person addressed. Writing this discourse will give you practice in the different rhythms and levels of diction we all use.

Thus your essay will consist of two parts: a lawyer's formal speech to the jury and an alleged criminal's informal and colloquial monologue or dialogue. The two taken together will demonstrate a variety of purpose and tone.

THE SPEAKING PROCESS

If you are currently working on an assignment in this chapter, skip to the paragraph below; if not, select a topic related to your major, hobby, or chosen profession, one about which you can write a speech to deliver to your classmates. Your speech should persuade your audience to try your hobby or to consider your major or profession. You audience is one you know well—composed of students similar to yourself in age and in general interests perhaps, but one that probably differs widely in majors and in specific interests.

How to select a topic, how to compose, organize, and deliver a speech are set out by George Plimpton in "How to Make a Speech," the essay that follows. Plimpton, made famous by Intellevision commercials, is also well known as the editor of the *Paris Review* and author of *Paper Lion* and other you-are-there sports books. If you follow the speaking process that Plimpton outlines and use rhetorical principles judiciously, your resulting speech will be a success.

GEORGE PLIMPTON

How to Make a Speech

One of life's terrors for the uninitiated is to be asked to make a speech. 1

"Why me?" will probably be your first reaction. "I don't have anything to say." It should be reassuring (though it rarely is) that since you were asked, somebody must think you do. The fact is that each one of us has a store of material which should be of interest to others. There is no reason why it should not be adapted to a speech. 2

Why know how to speak? Scary as it is, it's important for anyone to be able to speak in front of others, whether twenty around a conference table or a hall filled with a thousand faces. 3

Being able to speak can mean better grades in any class. It can mean talking the town council out of increasing your property taxes. It can mean talking top management into buying your plan. 4

How to pick a topic. You were probably asked to speak in the first place in the hope that you would be able to articulate a topic that you know something about. Still, it helps to find out about your audience first. Who are they? Why are they there? What are they interested in? How much do they already know about your subject? One kind of talk would be appropriate for 5 the Women's Club of Columbus, Ohio, and quite another for the guests at the Vince Lombardi dinner.

How to plan what to say. Here is where you must do 6
your homework.

The more you sweat in advance, the less you'll have to 7
sweat once you appear on stage. Research your topic thoroughly. Check the library for facts, quotes, books and timely magazine and newspaper articles on your subject. Get in touch with experts. Write to them, make phone calls, get interviews to help round out your material.

In short, gather—and learn—far more than you'll ever use. 8
You can't imagine how much confidence that knowledge will inspire.

Now start organizing and writing. Most authorities sug- 9
gest that a good speech breaks down into three basic parts—an introduction, the body of the speech, and the summation.

Introduction: An audience makes up its mind very quickly. 10
Once the mood of an audience is set, it is difficult to change it, which is why introductions are important. If the speech is to be lighthearted in tone, the speaker can start off by telling a good-natured story about the subject or himself.

But be careful of jokes, especially the shaggy-dog variety. 11
For some reason, the joke that convulses guests in a living room tends to suffer as it emerges through the amplifying system into a public gathering place.

Main body: There are four main intents in the body of the 12
well-made speech. These are 1) to entertain, which is probably the hardest; 2) to instruct, which is the easiest if the speaker has done the research and knows the subject; 3) to persuade, which one does at a sales presentation, a political rally, or a town meeting; and finally, 4) to inspire, which is what the speaker emphasizes at a sales meeting, in a sermon, or at a pep rally. (Hurry-Up Yost, the onetime Michigan football coach, gave such an inspiration-filled half-time talk that he got carried away and at the final exhortation led his team on the run through the wrong locker-room door into the swimming pool.)

Summation: This is where you should "ask for the order." 13
An ending should probably incorporate a sentence or two which sounds like an ending—a short summary of the main points of the speech, perhaps, or the repeat of a phrase that most em-

bodies what the speaker has hoped to convey. It is valuable to think of the last sentence or two as something which might produce applause. Phrases which are perfectly appropriate to signal this are: "In closing . . ." or "I have one last thing to say . . ."

Once done—fully written, or the main points set down on 3″ × 5″ index cards—the next problem is the actual presentation of the speech. Ideally, a speech should not be read. At least it should never appear or sound as if you are reading it. An audience is dismayed to see a speaker peering down at a thick sheaf of papers on the lectern, wetting his thumb to turn to the next page. 14

How to sound spontaneous. The best speakers are those who make their words sound spontaneous even if memorized. I've found it's best to learn a speech point by point, not word for word. Careful preparation and a great deal of practicing are required to make it come together smoothly and easily. Mark Twain once said, "It takes three weeks to prepare a good ad-lib speech." 15

Don't be fooled when you rehearse. It takes longer to deliver a speech than to read it. Most speakers peg along at about 100 words a minute. 16

Brevity is an asset. A sensible plan, if you have been asked to speak to an exact limit, is to talk your speech into a mirror and stop at your allotted time; then cut the speech accordingly. The more familiar you become with your speech, the more confidently you can deliver it. 17

As anyone who listens to speeches knows, brevity is an asset. Twenty minutes are ideal. An hour is the limit an audience can listen comfortably. 18

In mentioning brevity, it is worth mentioning that the shortest inaugural address was George Washington's—just 135 words. The longest was William Henry Harrison's in 1841. He delivered a two-hour 9,000-word speech into the teeth of a freezing northeast wind. He came down with a cold the following day, and a month later he died of pneumonia. 19

Check your grammar. Consult a dictionary for proper meanings and pronunciations. Your audience won't know if you're a bad speller, but they will know if you use or pronounce 20 a word improperly. In my first remarks on the dais, I used to thank people for their "fulsome introduction," until I discovered to my dismay that "fulsome" means *offensive* and *insincere.*

On the podium. It helps one's nerves to pick out three or four people in the audience—preferably in different sectors so that the speaker is apparently giving his attention to the entire room—on whom to focus. Pick out people who seem to be having a good time. 21

How questions help. A question period at the end of a speech is a good notion. One would not ask questions following a tribute to the company treasurer on his retirement, say, but a technical talk or an informative speech can be enlivened with a question period. 22

The crowd. The larger the crowd, the easier it is to speak, because the response is multiplied and increased. Most people do not believe this. They peek out from behind the curtain and if the auditorium is filled to the rafters they begin to moan softly in the back of their throats. 23

What about stage fright? Very few speakers escape the so-called "butterflies." There does not seem to be any cure for them, except to realize that they are beneficial rather than harmful, and never fatal. The tension usually means that the speaker, being keyed up, will do a better job. Edward R. Murrow called stage fright "the sweat of perfection." Mark Twain once comforted a fright-frozen friend about to speak: "Just remember they don't expect much." My own feeling is that with thought, preparation and faith in your ideas, *you* can go out there and expect a pleasant surprise. 24

And what a sensation it is—to hear applause. Invariably after it dies away, the speaker searches out the program chairman—just to make it known that he's available for next month's meeting. 25

P A R T 6

THE WRITER IN MULTIPLE ROLES

FURTHER READINGS

As varied as the writer's repertoire is, the roles frequently overlap, and the writings in this section exemplify the writer in multiple roles. "Oops! How's That Again?" is a historical study of the Freudian slip, a study which includes exposition as well as psychological, literary, and political analysis. Roger Rosenblatt, the author, is a senior editor of *Time*, where this essay first appeared.

Personal history is the basis of "An Evening at the Waldorf' by Jean and Bud Ince, an autobiographical sketch that contains six styles of writing—a young man's story, a young woman's story, a letter from a hotel manager, a letter from a famous chef, and the couple's views thirty years later. *Gourmet*, the magazine in which the essay was published, has over a half million readers and is "edited for those interested in the various aspects of 'good living'—i.e., the preparation of fine foods, wine, dining out, sports and travel."

Even public speakers can assume multiple roles. The inaugural address of John F. Kennedy in January, 1961, is not simply a speech, but a persuasive declaration of a policy, a promise, and a presentation of oral and written style that political and literary analysts will enjoy. So too, Edward R. Murrow combines the roles of speaker and writer. He wrote "March 9, 1941" as a radio script for his wartime broadcast on CBS. Millions listened to the observations and evaluations that represented his impression of England girding for the German spring offensive.

Expository prose is so pervasive that it is found everywhere and anywhere. Exposition also undergirds Pauline Kael's review of *Superman*, "The Package." Her focus, however, remains evaluative, and the standards she applies in the film review are similar to those of her audience, the readers of the *New Yorker*, where the Apple ad (see chapter 8) also appeared.

Evaluation provides the background to Russell Baker's "Little Red Riding Hood Revisited," for to parody sociologists, lawyers, politicans and the like, Baker must first analyze their language before he shows its hollowness. His essay appeared in his regular column, "Sunday Observer," in the *New York Times* Sunday magazine section.

Along with columns, editorials—short persuasive pieces about current mores, policies, and events—are featured in magazines and newspapers. "Absence of Moral Teaching" is from the *Daily Oklahoman*, a small newspaper with a circulation of 169,000, established in 1894 and published in Oklahoma City. "Justice: A Cynical View" was published in the *(free) Weekly Newspaper*, a throwaway whose distribution covers Colorado's Roaring Fork Valley, from the sophisticated resort of Aspen to the rough-and-ready shale towns of Rifle and Silt. The editorials exemplify the extremes of the genre's style and subject matter and incorporate elements of evaluation as well.

But of all the roles in the writer's repertoire, the personal essayist's is probably the most popular and unique, for here writers express their private thoughts. An associate editor of *Field and Stream*, Gene Hill in "The Waiting Game" describes the concerns and motivations of the fly fisherman and does so using techniques of evaluation and exposition as well. The magazine where the essay appeared has a circulation of slightly over two million and since 1895 has been "devoted to the outdoors—fishing, hunting, camping, boating, and conservation." Hill's collected articles appear in *Hill Country*, *Mostly Tailfeathers*, and *A Hunter's Fireside Book*. In contrast the magazine of the National Audubon Society, *Audubon*—published bimonthly since 1899—has a much more modest circulation of 300,000 and is "devoted to significant reading on nature and to attaining the conservation goals of the society." One feature is the "Essay," where Peter Steinhart's "Leave the Dead" appeared, a meditation on life and death in nature and humanity that ends on a persuasive note. Steinhart, who teaches writing at Stanford University, has also published articles in *Harper's* and *National Wildlife*. Jan Halvorsen, now assistant editor of the *Twin Cities Courier* of St. Paul, Minnesota, writes in contrast to such universal themes. In *Newsweek*'s "My Turn," she relives the personal trauma of losing her job and combines her observations with exposition and evaluation.

As you read the selections that follow, consider the writer's roles, audience, style, and purpose. And enjoy the essays.

PETER STEINHART

Leave the Dead

Three years ago, the drought and my own horticultural ignorance got together to kill a tree. It was a fine twenty-foot toyon that some passing bird had seeded beside my house long before my arrival. Its dark leaves had lent shade to forty dry California summers, and its bright-red winter berries had fed forty generations of robins and waxwings. It is still standing, a hoary skeleton of brittle gray branches that claws at my rooftop on winter nights. My neighbors think it is a disgrace, a smudge on the neighborhood's otherwise tidy record of punctilious hedges and unblemished lawns. They ask when I'll cut it down and plant something else.

But I won't cut it. It works for my garden and for my mind. I have come to admire the dignity of its death, its unwillingness to melt away in defeat, its hospitality to new kinds of bird and insect. I'm on the side of the forest, and this tree links me to a larger cause. We need a few dead trees around—here and everywhere.

I have tried to explain to my neighbors. A dead tree stays standing long after its sap has dried and its arboreal hopes have turned to heart rot. It doesn't shrink from death as if apologizing for some defect of form. In death, it still lives. It urges you to think about the relationships between the living and the nonliving. Dead trees are natural monuments, and without them, we'd probably have to put up more statues of General Sherman.

But my neighbors grow uneasy and change the subject. The dead thing in my yard gnaws at them. A dead tree, they think, ought to be whisked away, just as a deceased patient is wheeled discreetly from the hospital ward. Death, even in trees, is a sting we like to put out of our minds.

We protest death in odd ways. Last summer, an anguished young lady rushed into a veterinarian's office in Redmond, Oregon. She held the patient, a decapitated ant, up to the face of the startled veterinarian and begged him to save its life. The vet, more worried about the lady than the insect, told her that he was very sorry, but without the ant's head there was nothing he could do. The lady left in tears.

Gilbert Grosvenor, president of the National Geographic Society and formerly editor of its magazine, reports that a dramatic photograph of cheetahs eating a still-live impala on the plains of Africa brought the magazine more angry letters than any photograph it had ever published. The letters complained that the editors ought not to have shown nature so red and cruel.

Complaints like that are the pleas of a war-weary people. The images of human death and suffering hang over us like autumn smoke. Moments after sneaking idealogues blow up a bus in Beirut, we are treated to crisp pictures of the carnage in our living rooms. Our radios and newspapers recite homicides as if they were commodity prices. The weight of media gore suggests that the world has gone insane and that the corpses could easily be our own. We try to numb the terror by watching more and more of it, hoping to grow calluses against the touch of fear.

And then we fight the tide. We feel a responsibility to keep the meanness from seeping so deep into our nature that it redefines us all as brutes and ends all hope of a better world. We begin by denying age and death. We leave our elders rocking on the porches of small towns in the Midwest and move to Colorado. We worship youth and make heroes of men and women whose faces are unlined by experience or care. We do not witness death; when death approaches we send the body to a hospital and turn our faces to the wall. We do not slaughter our own food. We do not eat cows or sheep or pigs, but something that comes from a freezer, cold, bloodless, and wrapped in plastic.

We also try to weed death out of nature. We shoot and poison predators, arguing that predation is cruel and wasteful.

We dump herbicides on plants so that we don't have to strangle them with our own hands. We spray pesticides to stop insects from inflicting death on our blameless apples and corn. Until recently, we regarded forest fires as nature's way of stealing timber.

Our denial of death is nowhere as extreme as it is in our forest policy. The nation's first forester, Gifford Pinchot, wrote in 1900: "The wood of a tree which dies in the forest is wholly wasted. Not only is the old tree lost, but ever since its maturity, it has done little more than intercept light which would have otherwise given vitality to a valuable crop of younger trees. It is only when the ripe wood is harvested properly and in time that the forest attains its highest usefulness."

We have always cut out the dead trees in our forests, and Ronald Reagan has urged us to cut more, "since we have permitted a lot of dead trees to accumulate which are harmful to the woodland ecology." The U.S. Forest Service declares that 35 percent of the forests of the West consist of merchantable dead timber. And increasing demands for fuel have accelerated the cutting. Robert Radtke of the Forest Service declares, "Near the eastern cities, energy-conscious people are just clearing the woods of dead trees." At least two electrical generating plants are now burning wood, and there are proposals to turn whole forests into alcohol factories.

On private lands, which constitute 70 percent of our forests, most of the old and dead trees already have been cut. The Forest Service estimates that all the virgin timber on private lands will be gone by the year 2000. When the old trees have been cleared, they will be replaced with uniform, even-aged, genetically engineered stock. While the virgin woods took up to two centuries to produce harvestable trees, the cloned replants may be cut in forty years. In such places, there will be no old or dead trees.

Such stands will no longer be forests. For, in a true forest, more than a third of the trees may be dead or dying. And thousands of creatures, from wood-loving fungi to chipmunks and owls, have adapted to this fact of mortality. One third of the birds and mammals that dwell in the forest need dead trees for nesting, feeding, and roosting. Evolution has so polished the relationship between birds and snags that cavity-nesting species such as bluebirds, flycatchers, and swallows are more polygamous, nest earlier, have larger clutches, and fledge more young than noncavity-nesting birds.

Cavity-nesters fight for the trees. A single Nuttall's woodpecker has been seen defending its nest against downy woodpeckers, violet-green swallows, western bluebirds, ash-throated flycatchers, and house wrens. Shortages can make strange bedfellows: A single cavity once yielded the eggs of a hooded merganser, a golden-eye, and a barred owl.

Where old trees have been removed, wildlife vanishes. In the Great Lakes states, logging eliminated the fisher and the pine marten. In the South, the ivory-billed woodpecker retired with the old trees it needed for feeding and nesting. Cutting of dead trees in Yosemite Valley in the 1930s displaced acorn woodpeckers and flickers. A recent Arizona study showed that cutting dead ponderosa pines reduced populations of cavity-nesting birds 50 percent. Swallows dropped 90 percent, and one species of woodpecker vanished. In Louisiana, the scarcity of large old pines subject to a particular kind of decay clouds the future of the red-cockaded woodpecker. In Washington, wildlife officials fear the mountain bluebird is on the decline.

Where snag-dependent species go, the braid of consequence keeps on unraveling. Cavity-nesting birds help regulate insect populations. Studies in Colorado have shown that woodpeckers consume up to 98 percent of the spruce beetles and migrate into areas of insect epidemic. In European forests, after massive and expensive installation of nesting boxes brought back small populations of cavity-nesters, insect plagues were much reduced. And studies by Chris Maser of the Bureau of Land Management have shown that chipmunks, salamanders, mice, and other creatures which burrow under roots and logs are instrumental in dispersing the spores of mycorrhizal fungi. The fungi attach to the roots of all conifers. Without them, the trees cannot break up soil substances and absorb nutrients. Maser believes that without wood rats, flying squirrels, and other lovers of dead wood the forest itself might perish.

The U.S. Forest Service has been attempting to retain old trees. The rule in its Missouri subregion, for example, calls for the retention of 10 percent of the forest in old growth. But state and private forests, which account for 79 percent of the American woods, do not generally have such policies. Some states still require logging crews to remove dead trees to make their working place safe, and where the states have tried to amend the rules, federal worker-safety regulations calling for the removal of snags to protect logging crews prevent the change. And as more private lands turn into suburbs, shopping centers, and industrial parks, the old growth is fast disappearing.

Foresters will argue that it is more efficient to rely upon aerial sprays and chemical fertilizers than to trust woodpeckers and downed wood. They feel good about the change because they have eliminated not only nature's economic inefficiencies but death itself.

But it is arrogance to think that we can bend all of nature to our human shyness of the subject of death. We can turn ecological landscapes into economic landscapes, make them quieter and less varied. But we cannot beat the death sentence. Our previous efforts have had unhappy consequences. Predator control led to flurries of malignant population growth among deer and rabbits, and the animals stripped the woods and died of starvation. Profligate use of pesticides nearly exterminated ospreys and pelicans while ruining the natural insect controls that were already in the fields. Forest-fire prevention guaranteed that the inevitable fires would be hotter and more destructive.

Our ignorance of death is that we see it as a social loss rather than as an ecological fact. And by bringing that social interpretation to nature, we have made some bad mistakes. Allowing death to remain an ecological event is going to be one of the struggles of our time. Says Marshall White, research associate at the University of California, "Understanding death is going to be *the* wildlife problem of the remainder of the century. The public is going to have to find out that when you harvest, you really mean killing things. They are going to have to find out that a large amount of death is natural in the forest."

If we cannot accept death in nature, we shall never live with it gracefully in society. As our ignorance of death grows, we find ourselves pondering problems our ancestors may not have found so difficult: Where do we put our old people? How do we admit that we are beyond the opportunities we once dreamed? How much youth must we abandon to be good parents? How do we keep our sense of purpose in a ledger-ruled world? How can we face our own inevitable endings?

I do not know the answers to such questions. But the dead tree in my yard is one way of keeping the questions in front of me. The tree is part of the skein of mystery and the braid of consequence. It takes me beyond the enigma of dying, into the fact of death. It is too small to house a wren, and I could not begin to name the lightless molds and faceless insects that are quietly dismantling it. But I know that they are there, along with the sparrows and scrub jays that feed on them. A mockingbird drops by now and then to watch the consternation of my neighbors. In its own way, the tree sings to me. In the end, I hope gravity will take it.

EDWARD R. MURROW

March 9, 1941

Soon it will be spring in England. Already there are flowers in the park, although the parks aren't quite as well kept as they were this time last year. But there's good fighting weather ahead. In four days' time the moon will be full again and there's a feeling in the air that big things will happen soon.

The winter that is ending has been hard, but Londoners have many reasons for satisfaction. There have been no serious epidemics. The casualties from air bombardments have been less than expected. And London meets this spring with as much courage, though less complacency, than at this time last year.

Many ancient buildings have been destroyed. Acts of individual heroism have been commonplace. More damage has been done by fire than by high explosives. The things cast down by the Germans out of the night skies have made hundreds of thousands of people homeless. I've seen them standing cruel cold of a winter morning with tears frozen on their faces looking at the little pile of rubble that was their homes and saying over and over again in a toneless unbelieving way, "What have we done to deserve this?"

But the winter has brought some improved conditions in the underground shelters. It has brought, too, reduced rations; repeated warnings of the imminence of invasion; shorter restrictions upon the freedom of the individual and organizations.

When spring last came to England the country was drifting and almost dozing through a war that seemed fairly remote. Not much had been done to give manpower and machinery to the demands of modern war. The story of the spring, summer, and fall is well known to all of you. For the British it was a record of one disaster after another—until those warm, cloudless days of August and September when the young men of the Royal Air Force beat back the greatest air fleet ever assembled by any nation. Those were the days and nights and even weeks when time seemed to stand still. At the beginning they fought over the English Channel, then over the coast of Kent, and when the German bombers smashed the advance fighter bases along the coast the battle moved inland. Night after night the obscene glare of hundreds of fires reddened the bellies of the big, awkward barrage balloons over London, transforming them into queer animals with grace and beauty. Finally the threat was beaten off. Both sides settled down to delivering heavy blows in the dark. Britain received more than she gave. All through the winter it went on. Finally there came bits of good news from the western desert. But even Tobruk and Bengazi seemed far away. Victories over the Italians are taken for granted here. Even the children know that the real enemy is Germany.

It hasn't been victories in the Middle East or promises of American aid that have sustained the people of this island during the winter. They know that next winter, when it comes, it will probably be worse, that their sufferings and privations will increase. Their greatest strength has been and is something that is talked about a great deal in Germany but never mentioned here—the concept of a master race.

The average Englishman thinks it's just plain silly for the Germans to talk about a master race. He's quietly sure in his own mind that there is only one master race. That's a characteristic that caused him to adopt an attitude of rather bored tolerance toward all foreigners and made him thoroughly disliked by many of them. But it's the thing that has closed his mind to the possibilities that Britain may be defeated.

The habit of victory is strong here. Other habits are strong, too. The old way of doing things is considered best. That's why it has taken more than a year and a half to mobilize Britain's potential strength and the job is not yet finished.

The other day, watching a farmer trying to fill in a twenty-foot-deep bomb crater in the middle of his field, I wondered what would happen before he harvested the next crop from that bomb-torn soil. I suppose that many more bombs will fall. There will be much talk about equality of sacrifice which doesn't exist. Many proud ships will perish in the western approaches. There will be further restrictions on clothes and food. Probably a few profiteers will make their profits.

No one knows whether invasion will come, but there are those who fear it will not. I believe that a public-opinion poll on the question "Would you like the Germans to attempt an invasion?" would be answered overwhelmingly in the affirmative. Most people, believing that it must be attempted eventually, would be willing to have it come soon. They think that in no other way can the Germans win this war, and they will not change their minds until they hear their children say, "We are hungry."

So long as Winston Churchill is Prime Minister, the House of Commons will be given an opportunity to defend its traditions and to determine the character of the government that is to rule this country. The Prime Minister will continue to be criticized in private for being too much interested in strategy and too little concerned with the great social and economic problems that clamor for solution.

British propaganda aimed at occupied countries will continue to fight without its heavy artillery, until some sort of statement on war aims or, if you prefer, peace aims has been published.

And in the future, as in the past, one of the strangest sensations for me will be that produced by radio. Sometime someone will write the story of the technical and military uses to which this new weapon has been put; but no one, I think, will ever describe adequately just what it feels like to sit in London with German bombs ripping in the air, shaking the buildings, and causing the lights to flicker, while you listen to the German radio broadcasting Wagner or Bavarian folk music. A twist of the dial gives you Tokyo talking about dangerous thoughts; an American Senator discussing hemisphere defense; the clipped, precise accent of a British announcer describing the proper method of photographing elephants; Moscow boasting of the prospects of the wheat harvest in the Ukraine; each nation speaking almost any language save its own, until, finally, you switch off the receiving set in order that the sounds from the four corners of the earth will not interfere with the sound of the German bombs that come close enough to cause you to dive under the desk.

The bombs this spring will be bigger and there'll be more of them, probably dropped from a greater height than ever before. Berlin and London will continue to claim that their bombs hit the military targets while the enemy's strike mainly churches, schools, hospitals, and private dwellings.

The opening engagement of the spring campaign is now being fought in the Atlantic. The Admiralty has taken over control of the shipyards in an effort to speed up production and repairs. Merchant sinkings will probably reach alarming proportions, but there will always be men to take ships out. The outcome of the battle in the Atlantic will be decisive. This island lives by its ships, and the ships will be carrying supplies from America.

There was no dancing in the streets here when the "lend-lease" bill was passed, for the British know from their own experience that the gap between legislation and realization can be very wide. They remember being told that their frontier was on the Rhine, and they know now that their government did very little to keep it there.

The course of Anglo-American relations will be smooth on the surface, but many people over here will express regret because they believe America is making the same mistakes that Britain made. For you must understand that the idea of America being of more help as a nonbelligerent than as a fighting ally has been discarded, even by those who advanced it originally. Maybe we shall do some frank, forthright talk across the Atlantic instead of rhetoric, but I doubt it. One thing that is not to be doubted is that the decisions taken in Washington between now and the time the crops are harvested will determine the pattern of events for a long time to come. British statesmen are fond of repeating that Britain stands alone as the defender of democracy and decency, but General Headquarters is now on Pennsylvania Avenue in Washington, D.C. Many Britishers realize that. Not all of them are happy about it, for the policies of Washington have not always been the policies of the Tory party, which still rules this country. Presumably, the decisions of Washington will be taken in the full light of publicity and debate, and no mere radio reporter has the right to use the weight of monopolized opportunity in an effort to influence those decisions. We can only deliver to you an occasional wheelbarrowload of stuff, tell you where it comes from, and what sort of air-raid shelter or bastion you build with it is a matter for free men to decide, but since part of reporting must necessarily be personal, I'd like to end this with my own impression of Britain on the verge of spring and big events.

There's still a sense of humor in the country; the old feeling of superiority over all other peoples remains. So does class distinction. There is great courage and a blind belief that Britain will survive. The British aren't all heroes; they know the feeling of fear; I've shared it with them. They try to avoid thinking deeply about political and social problems. They'll stand any amount of government inefficiency and muddle. They're slow to anger, and they die with great dignity. They will cheer Winston Churchill when he walks through block after block of smashed houses and offices as though he'd brought them a great victory. During a blinding raid when the streets are filled with smoke and the sound of the roaring guns, they'll say to you: "Do you think we're really brave, or just lacking in imagination?"

Well, they've come through the winter, and they've been warned that the testing days are ahead. Of the past months, they may well say: "We've lived a life, not an apology." And of the future, I think most of them would say: "We shall live hard, but we shall live."

from the DAILY OKLAHOMAN

Absence of Moral Teaching

Complaints of poor pupil discipline in the public schools are nothing new. But incidents related by a group of Oklahoma City teachers at a hearing this week focus new attention on a problem that cries out for solution.

The chilling reports of molestation, assaults, gun-carrying, stabbings, strong-arm robbery, an attempted hanging, pot-smoking and the availability of alcohol and drugs demonstrate that the infamous "blackboard jungle" doesn't exist only in places like New York or Chicago or Los Angeles.

But even more disconcerting is the allegation that enforcement of normal rules of behavior is lax, inconsistent or non-existent. That is a terrible indictment of the school administration. It should be answered, and, of course, the administration has the right to air its case, too.

The fact that the special hearing at which the allegations were made was conducted by the Oklahoma City Federation of Teachers might give rise to a suspicion the union was baiting the administration, perhaps in preparation for the annual contract talks.

That is too simple an explanation, in view of persistent and widespread reports of disciplinary failures not only here but throughout the nation. Indeed, the teachers' group has performed a service to the patrons and the school district by going public with a problem that has been hinted at repeatedly but seldom dealt with openly.

The teachers, stymied on the one hand by lack of backing

from administrators who don't want to roil the waters and by parents threatening to sue, are understandably frustrated. But in a sense they, or at least the profession to which they belong, have brought the trouble on themselves by adherence to a philosophy that might be called moral neutrality.

Recurrent in the teachers' testimony is the twin theme of defiance of authority and absence of moral responsibility in the students. The usual disclaimer that a few students cause most of the problems wasn't made. Even if it were, it would not mitigate their seriousness.

What seems clear is that the well-publicized decline in academic performance in the past two decades can be equated with the breakdown in classroom discipline. This can be attributed to several factors: crosstown busing that takes youngsters out of familiar neighborhoods and circle of friends, lack of parental support for teachers' disciplinary measures (a far cry from the old days when a kid punished at school could expect an even tougher reception at home) and the current emphasis on students' "rights" fostered by court rulings.

A California educator, Paul Copperman, has written that a classroom teacher must be an "authority figure." A decline in student achievement shows a breakdown in that authority, which he says is caused be a permissive educational ideology now dominating the schools and by bureaucratic and judicial interference.

Others characterize the problem as the absence in young people of a basic morality, the result of teaching that nothing is right or wrong. Thus, when a student learns that all choices are equally valid, he becomes skeptical about morality and this leads him into wrong actions.

Until the teaching of values of integrity, truth, personal accountability and respect for others' rights is restored to the curriculum, classroom discipline can only get worse.

GENE HILL

The Waiting Game

A drake mallard on the opposite bank watched me false casting. He would stand on one foot every so often and he looked like he was wearing orange baby mittens. He had a disapproving attitude, which I attributed to my casting stroke. I don't much care for it either.

I've often remarked, and often to the wrong people, that I thought much of the so-called mystique of fly fishing was nonsense. Not that I think it's easy, but it isn't neurosurgery either. It's just that I think too many people are taking the fun out of it by over-Latinizing, over-nomenclature, and over-everything.

One example: I was fishing the "fabled" Test a couple of years ago and my young English river-keeper was adamant about casting only to rising fish, upstream, with a dry fly. Fine, but at this period of the day there weren't any rising fish, so we were sitting on the bank telling each other lies. I took out my fly box and he asked if he could look through it. With more than a little disdain, he held up one of my favorite flies—a small Gray Ghost streamer.

"You actually use this?" he asked.

I told him that I'd caught more fish, including a few Atlantic salmon, on that pattern than any other. He smiled a bit condescendingly and said: "I rather think that our trout are a bit too sophisticated to go for that." Since nothing else was happening, I asked him if I could tie it on and make a couple of casts. "Why not," he said. I made three casts and caught three browns, the last one about 4 pounds. To my everlasting credit, I refrained from a little speech about big fish eating big flies, but we didn't get along very well after that.

My mallard kept following on the off-bank as I waded downstream. My guess is that some fisherman had been throwing bread crumbs in the water and the mallard was waiting for a handout from me. Trout fishing is not a spectator sport unless you're the mate of an osprey.

I am not a good judge of the quality of a trout fly, I can name only a few patterns, and I don't tie flies. I'm content with my tying friends' rejects and the few flies I buy in tackle stores. Nor am I an expert on the finer points of fly tackle. I do have a handful of bamboo rods. I absolutely cannot cast with one of them despite its famous name. There are four or five others, all from different makers, that I will never part with. My trout rods are all bamboo, and I use space-age-material rods for salmon and tarpon. But I can't rate any of my fly rods, just as I wouldn't attempt to grade a Boss shotgun against a Purdey or a Holland. No doubt I could use one better than the others for some indefinable reason of fit or balance, but they're all fine. It wouldn't be dollar snobbery either, because one of my "best" rods is an old Heddon, worth about half what I had to pay for my waders.

I just like to fly fish, even if I am ignorant, clumsy, and stubborn. I don't go for the vocabulary or the finer points of the art. If they won't take anything as big as a size 18, I leave the fishing to my betters and sit and smoke a pipe, or else I go off somewhere by myself and practice my casting, which is always rusty and not likely to get much better.

I like the dream within a dream in fly fishing—the quarry in one distant world probed best by the mind's eye, and you in another, acting as much the predator as the otter or the merganser, or at least trying to. I regard most of my catches as happy accidents and stand in pure awe of the skills I have seen exhibited by truly fine fishermen. But I don't envy them. I don't want to tie up a few cress bugs with my streamside outfit. I don't want to use an 8X tippet; I can't even see 8X. I will stay with my Adams, my Gray Ghost, and my Joe's Hopper, and the only thing I have to clean when I get home is my language.

I like watching my mallard, and I think he's enjoying watching me. I wonder if ducks get bored, or curious? Why not? Maybe he's a philosopher and will share with his wife a couple of laughs about my dress and what I was doing with a stick and some orange-colored string.

I wondered for quite a while about the fascination of fly fishing. Why is it that I can wade into a stream at 10 in the morning, look at my watch in a "couple" of hours, and find out that it's late afternoon. I really think it's like dreaming, only in reverse, where you have this long involved thing happening to you and you wake up and discover you've only been asleep a few minutes. It's like watching a water snake. The small boy in you says "throw a rock at him!" The growing-older man says "don't do that, it's waiting for something." You know that everyone and everything is waiting for something to happen; we just don't know quite what or quite when. I imagine that the snake likes the feel of the warm rock on his belly and the soothing touch of the water on his tail. And so do I. We both like it here and we're both fishing for something—when we get around to it.

I like fly fishing, I guess, as a nice way to pass time; waiting. It is a respectable thing to do as opposed to being purely idle, stretched out in a hammock, or taking a nap on the couch. You at least look serious—and industrious—a vest full of instruments, polarized glasses, wading staff and net, perhaps a small canvas creel, and the busy little hum of the fly line slicking through the rod guides. "There," you say, "is a serious man," if you should see me poised like a heron in some stream. Far from it. There you see an idler in costume, a man wondering where the time went. Not the past hour or so while exchanging nods with a duck or mulling a two-penny philosophy about a mud-colored snake, but the past five or ten years. He is thinking about his work that has been left undone, his loves unknown, and that just yesterday he was only a boy.

To paraphrase a favorite silliness, I often think that life is fly fishing in miniature. Standing still in a current that is running past you, carrying with it the things you can only see for a flash of time. You keep casting and then, when you least expect it, everything goes just right. And, suddenly, without much having happened, the day is almost over. It is getting dark and the duck and the snake have gone to their mysterious resting places. The thin light of a summer moon seems cold and the night calls of the owl and the bittern sound hostile. It seems as if the whole world has something more important to do and the fisherman is in the way. With half regret and half relief the fisherman stands free from the water, cumbersome in his heavy waders on the land. He will come back tomorrow. Tonight, he will dream about what it was he was waiting to have happen.

JEAN AND BUD INCE

An Evening at the Waldorf

This is a true story about a young couple in love and the most glamorous hotel in the world. We are telling the story together because it is so indelibly a part of both of our lives that neither of us could tell it alone.

One rainy October evening, thirty years ago, I sat in my room at the Naval Academy in Annapolis, staring at a navigation lesson and thinking of Jean. I had met her the previous August in Chicago, just before my summer leave expired, and I had fallen in love with her. Three days later I was back in Annapolis, surrounded by rules and regulations, while she was a thousand miles away, surrounded by eligible bachelors. Things looked bleak indeed.

There was one bright spot on the horizon. Jean had promised to come east to Philadelphia for the Army-Navy football game in November. We had been invited to spend the weekend as houseguests of my uncle and aunt in New York. If there was going to be any hope at all for me, that weekend was going to have to be the one that she would never forget. I shoved my books aside and wrote the following letter:

Room 5455, Bancroft Hall
U.S. Naval Academy
Annapolis, Maryland
15 October 1948

The Manager
The Waldorf-Astoria
New York City, New York

Dear Sir:

On Saturday afternoon, November 27th, I expect to pick my way across the prostrate bodies of the West Point football team to a seat in Memorial Stadium where a girl will be waiting—a very special girl who I hope will some day follow me from port to port on the "Far China Station." We will hie away by taxi to the railroad station where we will entrain for New York. Once there we will again take a taxi, this time to your hotel—and that, dear sir, is where you and The Waldorf-Astoria come in.

I am very much in love with this young lady, but she has not yet admitted to an equivalent love for me. Trapped as I am in this military monastery, the chances I have to press my suit are rare indeed. Therefore this evening must be the most marvelous of all possible evenings, for I intend to ask her to be my wife.

I would like a perfect table—neither too close to nor too far from the orchestra. There should be candlelight, gleaming silver, and snowy linen. There should be wine and a dinner that will be the culmination of the chef's career. Then, at precisely midnight, I would like the orchestra to play "Navy Blue and Gold" very softly, and I intend to propose.

I would appreciate it very much if you could confirm this plan and also tell me approximately what the bill will be. I am admittedly not getting rich on thirteen dollars a month, but I have put a little aside. So please give me your estimate of the cost—and I'll bet it will be plenty!

Very truly yours,
E. S. Ince
Midshipman, U.S.N.

I sealed the envelope and, before I could lose my nerve, stuffed it into the mailbox. The minute it was gone I regretted having sent it. It seemed to me that it was callow and smart-alecky and, above all, presumptuous. The manager of the most famous hotel in the world was certainly not going to be interested in the love life of an obscure midshipman. The letter would be thrown into the wastebasket where it belonged.

One week went by and then another. I forgot about the letter and tried frantically to think of some other way that I could convince Jean in thirty-six hours that she should spend the rest of her life with me. Then one morning I found on my desk an envelope upon which was engraved "The Waldorf-Astoria." I almost tore it to shreds in my eagerness to open it, and read:

Dear Midshipman Ince:

Your very nice letter has been receiving some attention from our staff here. Just for fun I am going to attach the reply from our Maitre d', the famous Rene Black.

Frankly, unless you have private resources, I think it is entirely unnecessary to spend so much money. I would be happy to make a reservation for you in the Wedgwood Room and will see to it that you have a very nice table, the best of attention, flowers—and you and your girl order directly from the menu whatever intrigues you. You certainly can have a couple of cocktails and very nice dinners and a bottle of champagne for one third of what Rene Black suggests. However you are the only one who can make the decision so let me know how you would like to have us arrange your little party.

Best wishes.

Cordially yours,
Henry B. Williams
Manager

P.S.: I think your delightful letter *inspired* our Mr. Black!

Needless to say, I hastily unfolded the piece of yellow paper on which Rene Black had typed his reply. Here is what it said:

When Lucullus dined with Lucullus, his gastronomic accoutrements were planned as you now do, every detail in presentation of the festivity. Times and manners have changed but little the unobtrusive elegance and distinctive "savoir faire" of amphytrionic distinction—to include Hors d'oeuvre de luxe;

the Potage generally omitted by ladies (and not to be forced on her); the traditional fish course to be presented as an entr'acte of surprise; the resistance of the menu to show the bird being caught in the nest (which will help your philology in carrying the battle of the nuptials), or as we say in French "la poulanie," and like Talleyrand, will highly praise the artisan of the casserole as having been the Cagliostro of your machinations.

The price of this manoeuvre, including wines, gratuities, flowers, and everything named, will be in the vicinity of one hundred dollars, with which we hope your little cache is fortified for complete victory. Following is a description of your menu—

Black pearls of the Sturgeon from the Caspian Sea, stuffed into the claws of lobsters, and eulogizing the God of the Oceans.

The Filet of Pompano known as the Demoiselle of the Atlantic, placed in a paper bag with the nomenclature "Greetings from the Poseidon."

The Breast of Chicken served in a little nest to represent the safety of the ketch, with its escort of vegetables and green salad.

An excellent dessert bearing the nomenclature "Ritorna vincitor" from Aïda, and little galettes. A sweet liqueur to seal the anticipation.

Wines in small quantities but of choice bracket, of lip-smacking delectability. Pink Champagne. Flowers. Candles, music, etc. All this will blossom with those hundred dollars that you were so provident to save.

I was thunderstruck with excitement and full of gratitude to the two busy men who had taken time to write, but I was also dismayed. I didn't have even close to one hundred dollars saved. With my November paycheck included, I would have a grand total of sixty-six dollars and twenty-five cents when I met Jean after the game, and there were train fares and other expenses to consider. Regretfully I wrote Mr. Williams that he had made a much closer estimate of my resources than had Mr. Black, and I would appreciate it if he would reserve a table for me.

I heard nothing further from The Waldorf. The days went by with no confirmation of my reservation—nothing. I was sure that my letter had never reached Mr. Williams, or that the whole thing had been taken as a joke. Finally it was the weekend of November twenty-seventh. The Brigade of Midshipmen went to Philadelphia and watched their inspired team hold highly favored Army to a 21-21 tie in one of the most thrilling football games ever played. After the game I rushed to meet Jean, and she was just as pretty and wonderful as I had remembered her.

On the train to New York I blurted out the whole story and showed Jean the letters from Mr. Black and Mr. Williams. I told her that I wasn't sure that we had a reservation at all, and I questioned whether we should even go to The Waldorf. We decided that we should, and that, even if we didn't have a reservation, we would at least see the famous hotel. So we got into a taxi at Pennsylvania Station, and I said the enchanted words, "Waldorf-Astoria," trying to sound as though I said them every day. In minutes we were at the door.

We walked into the lobby. To the right, at the top of a short flight of steps, was the Wedgwood Room. There was a velvet rope at the bottom of the steps, and another at the top, with a majordomo posted at both places. A crowd of fashionably dressed couples was patiently waiting for admittance. They all looked fabulously rich. Jean and I were wide-eyed as we stared at the magnificence of the lobby. I looked at her, and she looked at me. Finally I gulped, "Here goes," and went fearfully up to the major-domo at the foot of the stairs. I felt like Oliver Twist when I said, "Sir, I am Midshipman Ince, and I wonder if you by any chance might happen to have a reservation for me."

Like magic he swept away the rope! "Indeed we do," he said, and suddenly we saw the headwaiter at the top of the steps smiling and saying, "Midshipman Ince?" "Yes sir," I managed. "Right this way," he said, and snapped his fingers. A captain popped up out of nowhere like a genie from a lamp and led us across the room toward a beautiful table. Two waiters were leaning over it, lighting tall white candles. . . .

Walking ahead of Bud, I looked in amazement at the table. Centered between the candles in a low white vase were flowers—white stephanotis and pink sweetheart roses. When the red-coated waiter seated me I found a box at my place. Tucked under its ribbon was a card that read, "With the compliments of The Waldorf-Astoria." Catching my breath, I opened it and found a corsage of white baby orchids. A menu, unlike any I had ever seen, lay on the table in front of the centerpiece.

The menu was hand-painted in watercolor. A gray navy ship

steamed toward the upper right-hand corner, and highlighted on the left was a sketch of a girl's head with blue lovebirds in her hair. Printed with a flair in French, it read:

MENU

Le Fruit Ninon
La Volaille Bergerac
Legumes Testida
La Salade Pigier
La Friande Agrippina
Mayan en Tasse

Wedgwood Room Nov. 27, 1948

At the very moment when our excitement over the flowers, the table, and the menu had subsided to a point admitting of intrusion, our waiter said to Bud, "I have just one question to ask you."

(I was sure he was going to ask me if I could pay for all this!)

"Would you like a cocktail?"

We agreed that we would like a Manhattan, *and that was indeed the only question we were asked all evening.*

The dinner began. Silver sparkled and crystal glistened in the candlelight. Eddie Duchin and his orchestra played in the background. Service was constant, attentive, and unobtrusive. We never felt a waiter near us. Everything simply happened as if by sorcery. Wines we had never tasted, "in small quantities but of choice bracket, of lip-smacking delectability," appeared with each course. The Fruit Ninon *was splendid.* La Volaille Bergerac *was sealed in parchment, which the waiter slit to release its steaming aroma. The* Legumes Testida *never dreamed that under other circumstances one could think them beans. The* Salade *was perfection. Everything was perfection. Each course was more lovely than the one that came before it, and every taste and flavor would have thrilled the most meticulous epicure.*

About halfway through our dinner a distinguished gentleman with silvery-gray hair and a large Gallic nose approached our table with a smile and said, "I am Rene Black. I just came over to make sure that you were not angry with me." Bud leaped to his feet, and I beamed as we poured out our thanks to the man who had planned this evening. He drew up a chair and sat down and talked, delighting us with anecdotes of his continuing love affair with his wife, the origin of omelets, and a wonderful tale of a dinner party he gave his regiment in France during World War I. When we asked him if he had painted the menu he smiled, turned it over, and quickly sketched the head of a chef with his pen. Under it he wrote, "Si l'amour ne demande que des baisers à quoi bon la gloire de cuisinier." *(If love requires only kisses, what is the use of the fame of the cook?)*

After Mr. Black left our table, I looked at Bud. I had made plans to come to see the Army-Navy game and to spend the weekend with him, and the plans had been exciting. I had finished college and was trying my wings as a "career girl," but as I fell asleep on the Pullman on the way to Philadelphia, I wondered how I would feel about the dashing midshipman I had met so briefly last summer.

Here we were in The Waldorf-Astoria hotel in New York. I had seen it from the street before and had listened to conversation about Peacock Alley and the Starlight Roof, but now we were really there! We had just talked with the famous Rene Black; we had been served a dinner to delight royalty and were sipping wine together. How wonderful. How wonderful. How wonderful!

A photographer came up to us and said, "Mr. Black has asked me to take your photograph with the compliments of The Waldorf." The flash caught us, raising our glasses to each other, in perhaps the happiest instant ever recorded on film.

A few moments later Eddie Duchin left his bandstand and came to our table. The already legendary orchestra leader was warm and friendly as he talked about the great game Navy had played that afternoon. "I was cheering too," he said, and went on to tell us about his own service in the navy during World War II. When Jean's attention was distracted for a moment, Mr. Duchin leaned over to me and whispered, " 'Navy Blue and Gold' at midnight. Good luck!" He rose, grinning, and walked back to his piano.

He had hardly left when there was a stir and a buzz of conversation on the other side of the room. Jean and I looked for the source of the excitement, and then we saw it! Our dessert, *La Friande Agrippina,* carried triumphantly aloft across the dining room in a rainbow of colored spotlights. Great clouds of vapor billowed from silver cups filled with dry ice at each corner of the silver serving dish. In the center was a nest of ice cream within which rested two meringue lovebirds.

We had finished the delicious confection and were sipping a liqueur when the waiter told me that there was a telephone call for me in the lobby. I excused myself and followed him, wondering who in the world could be calling me, only to find the headwaiter waiting just outside the door. He handed me the bill and said, "We thought you might prefer not to have this brought to your table." I turned the slip of paper over fearfully and looked at the total. It was thirty-three dollars—exactly one third of Mr. Black's one hundred, and exactly what I had written Mr. Williams I could afford. It was clear to me that this amount couldn't even begin to cover the cost of the evening to The Waldorf, and equally clear that the reason the bill was presented with such exquisite finesse was to save me embarrassment had I not had thirty-three dollars. I looked at the headwaiter in amazement and gratitude, and he smiled and said, "Everyone on the staff hopes that all goes well for you."

Bud came back to the table gleaming, and, in answer to my curiosity about the telephone call, said, "It was nothing important. Shall we dance?" I felt his hand on my arm, guiding me gently to the floor.

Other couples danced about us chatting and, it seemed to me, smiling on us as they glided past. I saw only Bud. We were living a fairy-tale evening, and it was all real. Bud was real, the midshipman who had charmed me during the two evenings we had spent together last August and who had existed since only through letters. I had spun dreams about him during those three months of paper and ink, and now I looked into his face as we danced. "I'm in love!" I thought, "How wonderful. I'm in love."

At five minutes till midnight we were sitting at our table in a glow of happiness. Suddenly the wine steward appeared at my side with a small bottle of chilled Champagne. He opened it with a subdued "pop" and filled two crystal goblets with the sparkling golden wine. I raised my glass to Jean, and at that moment the orchestra drummer ruffled his drums softly, as if in a command for silence. Eddie Duchin turned toward us, smiled, and bowed. He raised his hand and brought it down, and suddenly we heard the melody of that most beautiful and sentimental of all college alma maters. " . . . For sailormen in battle fair since fighting days of old have proved the sailor's right to wear the Navy Blue and Gold." It was the magic moment to which every other moment of the evening had led. I looked at Jean, my wonderful Jean, and with a lump in my throat said, "Will you marry me?"

Bud and I were married the following June. Now, thirty years later, with our five children grown and establishing their own lives and the Midshipman a Rear Admiral, we sometimes turn the pages of the lovely wedding gift we received from Mr. Williams—a handsomely bound limited edition of the history of The Waldorf-Astoria. In it one can read of the princes and potentates, presidents and kings, who have been guests of that glamorous hotel. But there is one evening that is not included there—an evening in which kind, warm-hearted, gently romantic men opened a door of happiness for a young couple in love. That evening is ours, and its testimony is Mr. Black's wedding gift. Framed and displayed in a place of honor on our dining room wall, it is a watercolor sketch of a little chef tending his spit in an ancient kitchen. Printed in his familiar hand across the top he has repeated the words

Si l'amour
ne demande que des baisers
à quoi bon
la gloire de cuisinier.

from the (free) WEEKLY NEWSPAPER

Justice: A Cynical View

If any of us needed any further examples that old dame Justice is not only blind these days, but also deaf, crippled and downright senile, then events around the West last week should have settled the matter once and for all.

First, there was the incident in Yellowstone National Park in which some tourists "provoked" (the official term) a bull buffalo until he charged them. The tourists weren't hurt too bad, but the buffalo would be destroyed, park officials said. Remember that the tourists were at fault.

Next, a 14-year-old Bayfield kid who admitted stabbing to death a 13-year-old neighbor girl and her 9-year-old sister, was sentenced—without benefit of trial, so nobody will ever know why he did it—to serve two years in a state juvenile home.

And finally, of course, there was the Denver judge who sentenced a man who was described as "clean, steady, employed, quiet and conscientious" to spend the next two years working at his job during the day but sleeping in jail. The fact that the man had admitted killing his wife by shooting her five times in the face didn't seem to matter as much as his personal bathing habits.

Something is terribly, terribly wrong with a system that advocates killing a poor, dumb animal which is only reacting to improper provocation; while, at the same time, apparently puts a two-year price tag on a human life.

The fact of the matter is that all the available evidence points to our judicial system as being rife with incompetent judges who are almost impossible to remove from office because of an entangled web of bureaucracy.

Instead of being a stalwart blindfolded lady with a sword, Justice has become, in many cases, a truly blind octogenarian with the mind and whims of a malicious child, driving a Sherman tank.

This may sound like the words of a professional cynic, but the best advice we can give folks is to stay out of her way.

Unless you plan on killing somebody, of course.

Then you're probably home free. After two years, anyway.

PAULINE KAEL

The Package

Christopher Reeve, the young actor chosen to play the lead in *Superman,* is the best reason to see the movie. He has an open-faced, deadpan style that's just right for a windup hero. Reeve plays innocent but not dumb, and the combination of his Pop jawline and physique with his unassuming manner makes him immediately likable. In this role, Reeve comes close to being a living equivalent of comic-strip art—that slang form of simplified storytelling in which the visual and verbal meanings can be totally absorbed at a glance. But *Superman,* one of the two or three most expensive movies ever made, and with the biggest *event* promotion yet, is a cheesy-looking film, with a John Williams "epic" score that transcends self-parody—cosmic fanfares keep coming when there's nothing to celebrate. The sound piercing your head tells you that you should remember each name in the euphoric opening credits. That's where the peak emotion in the film is: in the package.

Superman gives the impression of having been made in panic—in fear that "too much" imagination might endanger the film's appeal to the literal-minded. With astronomic sums of money involved (though not in ways perceptible to viewers), the producers and the director, Richard Donner, must have been afraid even of style—afraid that it would function satirically, as a point of view (as it does in the James Bond pictures). Style, to them, probably meant the risk of camp, which might endanger the film's appeal to the widest audience. Several modern directors (most notably Godard) have been influenced by the visual boldness of comic-strip art—by the primary colors, unfurnished environments, and crisp, posterish sophistication—and the Pop artists who did blowups of comic-strip frames made us conscious of the formal intelligence in those cartoons, but *Superman* hasn't been designed in terms of the conventions of Pop. It has no controlling vision; there's so little consistency that each sequence might have had a different director and been color-processed in a different lab. Visually, it's not much more than a 70-mm. version of a kiddie-matinee serial. *Superman* carries a dedication to its cinematographer, Geoffrey Unsworth, who died a few months ago, but this poorly lighted and, for the most part, indifferently composed film is not a fitting tribute to the man who shot *Cabaret.*

The immediacy of comic strips has a magical effect on kids. The plot is socked to them, with exclamation points. And we go to *Superman* hoping for that kind of disreputable energy. But it isn't there, and you can feel the anticipatory elation in the theatre draining out. Donner doesn't draw us in and hold on to us; we're with him only in brief patches—a few seconds each. The plotting is so hit or miss that the movie never seems to get started. It should, because there's a marvellous, simplistic fantasy in the story of Superman: a superior being from another planet who is so strong that he can take care of the problems afflicting ours with his bare hands, but who must not reveal himself, and so goes among us in disguise as Clark Kent, a timid, clumsy, bespectacled reporter. Jerry Siegel and Joe Shuster, the Cleveland teen-agers who developed the idea and began trying to market the strip in 1933 and finally succeeded in 1938, provided a metaphor for the troubles and conflicts of boy dreamers: hidden inside the fumbling, fear-ridden adolescent is the all-competent giant. The divided hero is both a ninety-seven-pound weakling and Charles Atlas, but, unlike human beings, with their hope that the clown will grow into the hero, Superman is split forever. He can perform miracles, but he remains frustrated: as Clark Kent, this lonely stranger cannot win the woman he loves—the girl reporter Lois Lane—because she is in love with Superman. (Like the Scarlet Pimpernel and a number of other mass-culture heroes, he is his own rival.) This tragicomic figure might have provided a great central character for a space-adventure picture—a supremely human non-human hero—if only the moviemakers had trusted the idea of Superman.

The story has been updated from the thirties to the seventies, but not modernized, not rethought—just plunked down in the seventies. In the era of Al Pacino, Dustin Hoffman, and Woody Allen—a time when people acknowledge the humor and good sense in cowardice—might not the girl reporter (Margot Kidder) find herself drawn to Clark Kent's unsureness and feel some conflict in her swooning response to Superman? (She might even prefer Clark Kent.) And, in an era in which urban corruption and decay are deep and widespread, Superman's confident identification with the forces of law and order, and his thinking that he's cleaning up Metropolis (New York City) when he claps some burglars and thieves in jail, might be treated with a little irony. (It would be more fun to see him putting out a fire while kids threw stones at him, or arresting a mugger and being surrounded by an angry, booing crowd, or tackling the garbage problem.) The Superman who announces "I'm here to fight for truth, justice, and the American way" needs a little ribbing. But the film doesn't bring any ambiguity into this portrait of an outsize F.B.I man from space. It doesn't risk new sources of comedy. It sticks to dumb jokes about spelling, and low-comedy scenes between Lex Luthor (Gene Hackman), the criminal mastermind who makes his home under Grand Central Station, and his bungling helper (Ned Beatty), with Luthor's floozy (Valerie Perrine) looking on. You can see that Hackman likes the idea of dressing up in what must be Liberace's castoffs and playing a funny maniac, and when he has a halfway good line he scores his laugh. But he's strenuously frivolous, like a guest villain on a late-sixties "Batman" show. Most of the time, he and Beatty are doing deliberately corny material—a kiddies' version of the kind of burlesque routines that Roy Kinnear does in Richard Lester movies—and the director can't seem to get the timing right.

Probably the moviemakers thought that the picture would sell on its special effects—Superman's flying, and his rescues, and the disasters and cataclysms. The special effects are far from wizardly, though, and the editing often seems hurried and jerky just at the crucial moments. The biggest effects (such as Superman's zipping up the San Andreas fault) are truncated—a couple of quick shots and out. In the early scenes, on the planet Krypton, where the infant Superman lives, we're acutely conscious of the lack of elegance in the design, because Krypton, which is supposed to be more advanced than Earth by thousands of years, has plastic chandelier décor, like a Vegas lobby. There is only one truly elegant trick effect in the Krypton footage: three revolutionary "traitors" who are expelled from the planet become reflections trapped in a fifth-dimensional object that suggests a flying mirror. The conversation of the advanced beings on Krypton isn't very stimulating, either. Mostly, it's just the infant's father, Jor-El (Marlon Brando), delivering ponderosities. Brando has begun to look like an Indian chief, and he confers a distinguished presence on his scenes. His magnificent head is topped with white hair, and he does a straightforward God the Father performance, with perhaps a trace of Claude Rains in his intonations. Jor-El packs his plump, bright-eyed infant off to Earth, in a little star-shaped spaceship, just before Krypton is destroyed. It's a husky three-year-old with an impish expression who lands in a farming area, in a sequence of considerable charm. Glenn Ford is an inspired choice for Pa Kent, the farmer, who, with Ma Kent (Phyllis Thaxter), adopts the boy—Ford's resources as an actor having contracted to the point where he has become a comic-strip version of the simple good American. Photographically, this farmland section, with almost motionless clouds hovering over wheat fields that stretch to infinity, and one or two looming figures, has a look that's related to Pop enlargements, but it's the enlargement of Andrew Wyeth or Peter Hurd. It doesn't have the stylish crude strength of cartoons—its strength is softer, more genteel. Though visually striking, this section is weakened by a choice that makes almost no sense: instead of going directly from the child actor to Christopher Reeve and letting him play the eighteen-year-old Superman, the film introduces another actor (Jeff East), who doesn't look like the little boy or like Reeve. This intermediate figure is very inexpressive, and something about him seems all wrong—is it just his pompadour, or is he wearing a false nose?

Part of the appeal that has made Superman last so long is surely in the quasi-religious feelings that children develop about him: he's the savior myth of their very own subculture. Although this film tries to supply an element of mysticism (the box-office lesson of *Star Wars* and The Force has been learned), it's Superman in the form of the joyless interim actor who goes to the North Pole to commune with his psychically still alive father. Jor-El informs him of his mystical mission to serve "collective humanity," and Brando shows a gleam of amusement as he instructs the youth in the capacity for goodness of the people on Earth, and says, "For this reason above all—their capacity for good—I have sent them you, my only son." The sequence takes place at the Fortress of Solitude, which constitutes itself out of the ice for Superman. This should be the magical heart of the film, and surely a building that materializes out of ice might do so with occult symmetry? But the mystic fortress looks like a crystal wigwam that is being put up by a stoned backpacker.

The film rallies when Reeve takes over—especially when he gets out of the drably staged scenes at the offices of the *Daily Planet*, gets into his red cape and blue tights, flies over Metropolis, and performs a string of miracles. Yet after the first graceful feat, in which he saves Lois Lane, who has fallen from a helicopter that crashed on a skyscraper, and then steadies the falling chopper (with the injured pilot inside) and gently lifts it to safety, the other miracles don't have enough tension to be memorable: each one wipes out our memory of the one before. And the insufferable shimmering metallic music—as congratulatory as a laugh track—smudges them together. When Superman takes his beloved up for a joyride in the sky, the cutting works against the soaring romanticism that we're meant to feel, and, with Lois reciting Leslie Bricusse lyrics to convey her poetic emotions, even the magic of two lovers flying hand in hand over New York City is banalized. Lois Lane has always been one of the more boring figures in popular mythology: she exists to get into trouble. Margot Kidder tries to do something with this thankless part, but she's harsh-voiced, and comes across as nervous and jumpy; she seems all wrong in relation to Reeve, who outclasses her. He's so gentlemanly that her lewdness makes one cringe. (We aren't given a clue to what our hero sees in Lois Lane. It might have been more modern fun if he hadn't been particularly struck by her until she'd rejected his cowardly Clark Kent side for his Superman side—if like any other poor cluck, he wanted to be loved for his weakness.)

Superman doesn't have enough conviction or courage to be solidly square and dumb; it keeps pushing smarmy big emotions at us—but half-heartedly. It has a sour, scared undertone. And you can't help being aware that this is the sort of movie that increases the cynicism and sense of futility among actors. In order to sell the film as star-studded, a great many famous performers were signed up and then stuck in among the plastic bric-a-brac of Krypton; performers who get solo screen credits, with the full blast of trumpets and timpani, turn out to have walk-ons. Susannah York is up there as the infant Superman's mother, but, though Krypton is very advanced, this mother seems to have no part in the decision to send her baby to Earth. York has no part of any kind; she stares at the camera and moves her mouth as if she'd got a bit of food stuck in a back tooth. Of all the actors gathered here—all acting in different styles—she, maybe, by her placid distaste, communicates with us most directly.

RUSSELL BAKER

Little Red Riding Hood Revisited

In an effort to make the classics accessible to contemporary readers, I am translating them into the modern American language. Here is the translation of "Little Red Riding Hood":

Once upon a point in time, a small person named Little Red Riding Hood initiated plans for the preparation, delivery and transportation of foodstuffs to her grandmother, a senior citizen residing at a place of residence in a forest of indeterminate dimension.

In the process of implementing this program, her incursion into the forest was in mid-transportation process when it attained interface with an alleged perpetrator. This individual, a wolf, made inquiry as to the whereabouts of Little Red Riding Hood's goal as well as inferring that he was desirous of ascertaining the contents of Little Red Riding Hood's foodstuffs basket, and all that.

"It would be inappropriate to lie to me," the wolf said, displaying his huge jaw capability. Sensing that he was a mass of repressed hostility intertwined with acute alienation, she indicated.

"I see you indicating," the wolf said, "but what I don't see is whatever it is you're indicating at, you dig?"

Little Red Riding Hood indicated more fully, making one thing perfectly clear—to wit, that it was to her grandmother's residence and with a consignment of foodstuffs that her mission consisted of taking her to and with.

At this point in time the wolf moderated his rhetoric and proceeded to grandmother's residence. The elderly person was then subjected to the disadvantages of total consumption and transferred to residence in the perpetrator's stomach.

"That will raise the old woman's consciousness," the wolf said to himself. He was not a bad wolf, but only a victim of an oppressive society, a society that not only denied wolves' rights, but actually boasted of its capacity for keeping the wolf from the door. An interior malaise made itself manifest inside the wolf.

"Is that the national malaise I sense within my digestive tract?" wondered the wolf. "Or is it the old person seeking to retaliate for her consumption by telling wolf jokes to my duodenum?" It was time to make a judgment. The time was now, the hour had struck, the body lupine cried out for decision. The wolf was up to the challenge. He took two stomach powders right away and got into bed.

The wolf had adopted the abdominal-distress recovery posture when Little Red Riding Hood achieved his presence.

"Grandmother," she said, "your ocular implements are of an extraordinary order of magnitude."

"The purpose of this enlarged viewing capability," said the wolf, "is to enable your image to register a more precise impression upon my sight systems."

"In reference to your ears," said Little Red Riding Hood, "it is noted with the deepest respect that far from being underprivileged, their elongation and enlargement appear to qualify you for unparalleled distinction."

"I hear you loud and clear, kid," said the wolf, "but what about these new choppers?"

"If it is not inappropriate," said Little Red Riding Hood, "it might be observed that with your new miracle masticating products you may even be able to chew taffy again."

This observation was followed by the adoption of an aggressive posture on the part of the wolf and the assertion that it was also possible for him, due to the high efficiency ratio of his jaw, to consume little persons, plus, as he stated, his firm determination to do so at once without delay and with all due process and propriety, notwithstanding the fact that the ingestion of one entire grandmother had already provided twice his daily recommended cholesterol intake.

There ensued flight by Little Red Riding Hood accompanied

by pursuit in respect to the wolf and a subsequent intervention on the part of a third party, heretofore unnoted in the record.

Due to the firmness of the intervention, the wolf's stomach underwent ax-assisted aperture with the result that Red Riding Hood's grandmother was enabled to be removed with only minor discomfort.

The wolf's indigestion was immediately alleviated with such effectiveness that he signed a contract with the intervening third party to perform with grandmother in a television commercial demonstrating the swiftness of this dramatic relief for stomach discontent.

"I'm going to be on television," cried grandmother.

And they all joined her happily in crying, "What a phenomena!"

JAN HALVORSEN

How It Feels to Be Out of Work

Layoffs, unemployment and recession have always affected Walter Cronkite's tone of voice and the editorial page. And maybe they affected a neighborhood business or a friend's uncle. But these terms have always been just words, affecting someone else's world, like a passing ambulance. At least they were until a few weeks ago, when the ambulance came for me.

Even as I sat staring blankly at my supervisor, hearing, "I've got bad news: we're going to have to let you go," it all still seemed no more applicable to my daily life than a "60 Minutes" exposé. I kept waiting for the alternative—"but you can come back after a couple of months," or "you could take a salary cut, a different position," or even, "April fool." But none of these came. This was final. There was no mistake and no alternative.

You find yourself going back over it in your idle moments. There wasn't so much as a "Thank you" for the long nights working alone, the "Sure, no problem, I'll have it tomorrow," the "Let me know if I can help," the "I just went ahead and did it this weekend" and, especially, for the "You forgot to tell me it changed? Oh, that's all right, I'll just do it over. No big deal."

No big deal. How it all echoes through your evenings and awakens you in the morning. The mornings are probably the worst—waking up with the habitual jar, for the first two weeks, thinking, "I'm late!" Late for what? The dull ache in your lower stomach reminds you: late for nothing.

Again, you face the terms. "Loss of self-esteem and security, fear of the future, stress, depression." You wonder dully if eating a dozen chocolate-chip cookies, wearing a bathrobe until 4, combing your hair at 5, cleaning behind the stove (twice) and crying in an employment-agency parking lot qualify as symptoms of stress or maybe loss of self-esteem. Fighting with your spouse/boyfriend? Aha—tension in personal relationships.

The loss of a job is rejection, resulting in the same hurt feelings as if a friend had told you to "bug off." Only this "friend" filled up 40 to 60 (or more) hours of your week. Constant references to the staff as "family" only accentuate the feeling of desertion and deception. You picture yourself going home to your parents or spouse and being informed. "Your services as our daughter/my wife are no longer required. Pick up your baby pictures as you leave."

Each new affirmation of unemployment renews the pain: the first trip to the employment agency, the first friend you tell, the first interview and, most dreaded of all, the first trip to the unemployment office.

Standing in line at the unemployment office makes you feel very much the same as you did the first time you ever flunked a class or a test—as if you had a big red "F" for "Failure" printed across your forehead. I fantasize myself standing at the end of the line in a crisp and efficient blue suit, chin up, neat and straight as a corporate executive. As I move down the line I start to come unglued and a half hour later, when I finally reach the desk clerk, I am slouching and sallow in torn jeans, tennis shoes and a jacket from the Salvation Army, carrying my worldly belongings in a shopping bag and unable to speak.

You do eventually become accustomed to being unemployed, in the way you might accept a bad limp. And you gradually quit beating yourself for not having been somehow indispensable—or for not having become an accountant. You tire of straining your memory for possible infractions. You recover some of the confidence that always told you how good you were at your job and accept what the supervisor said: "This doesn't reflect on your job performance; sales are down 30 per cent this month."

But each time you recover that hallowed self-esteem, you renew a fight to maintain it. Each time you go to a job interview and give them your best and they hire someone else, you go another round with yourself and your self-esteem. Your unemployment seems to drag on beyond all justification. You start to glimpse a stranger in your rearview mirror. The stranger suddenly looks like a bum. You look at her with clinical curiosity. Hmmm. Obviously into the chronic stages. Definitely not employable.

We unemployed share a social stigma similar to that of the rape victim. Whether consciously or subconsciously, much of the work-ethic-driven public feels that you've somehow "asked for it," secretly wanted to lose your job and "flirted" with unemployment through your attitude—probably dressed in a way to invite it (left the vest unbuttoned on your three-piece suit).

But the worst of it isn't society's work-ethic morality; it's your own, which you never knew you had. You find out how much self-satisfaction was gained from even the most simple work-related task: a well-worded letter, a well-handled phone call—even a clean file. Being useful to yourself isn't enough.

But then almost everyone has heard about the need to be a useful member of society. What you didn't know about was the loneliness. You've spent your life almost constantly surrounded by people, in classes, in dorms and at work. To suddenly find yourself with only your cat to talk to all day distorts your sense of reality. You begin to worry that flights of fancy might become one way.

But you always were, and still are, stronger than that. You maintain balance and perspective, mainly through resorting frequently to sarcasm and irreverence. Although something going wrong in any aspect of your life now seems to push you into temporary despair much more easily than before, you have some very important things to hang on to—people who care, your sense of humor, your talents, your cat and your hopes.

And beyond that, you've gained something—a little more knowledge and a lot more compassion. You've learned the value of the routine you scorned and the importance of the job you took for granted. But most of all, you've learned what a "7.6 per cent unemployment rate" really means.

ROGER ROSENBLATT

Oops! How's That Again?

At a royal luncheon in Glasgow last month, Businessman Peter Balfour turned to the just-engaged Prince Charles and wished him long life and conjugal happiness with Lady Jane. The effect of the sentiment was compromised both by the fact that the Prince's betrothed is Lady Diana (Spencer) and that Lady Jane (Wellesley) is one of his former flames. "I feel a perfect fool," said Balfour, who was unnecessarily contrite. Slips of the tongue occur all the time. In Chicago recently, Governor James Thompson was introduced as "the mayor of Illinois," which was a step down from the time he was introduced as "the Governor of the United States." Not all such fluffs are so easy to take, however. During the primaries, Nancy Reagan telephoned her husband as her audience listened in, to say how delighted she was to be looking at all "the beautiful white people." And France's Prime Minister Raymond Barre, who has a reputation for putting his *pied* in his *bouche*, described last October's bombing of a Paris synagogue as "this odious attack that was aimed at Jews and that struck at innocent Frenchmen"—a crack that not only implied Jews were neither innocent nor French but also suggested that the attack would have been less odious had it been more limited.

One hesitates to call Barre sinister, but the fact is that verbal errors can have a devastating effect on those who hear them and on those who make them as well. Jimmy Carter never fully recovered from his reference to Polish lusts for the future in a mistranslated speech in 1977, nor was Chicago's Mayor Daley ever quite the same after assuring the public that "The policeman isn't there to create disorder; the policeman is there to preserve disorder." Dwight Eisenhower, John Kennedy, Spiro Agnew, Gerald Ford, all made terrible gaffes, with Ford perhaps making the most unusual ("Whenever I can I always watch the Detroit Tigers on radio"). Yet this is no modern phenomenon. The term *faux pas* goes back at least as far as the 17th century, having originally referred to a woman's lapse from virtue. Not that women lapse more than men in this regard. Even Marie Antoinette's fatal remark about cake and the public, if true, was due to a poor translation.

In fact, mistranslation accounts for a great share of verbal errors. The slogan "Come Alive with Pepsi" failed understandably in German when it was translated: "Come Alive Out of the Grave with Pepsi." Elsewhere it was translated with more precision: "Pepsi Brings Your Ancestors Back from the Grave." In 1965, prior to a reception for Queen Elizabeth II outside Bonn, Germany's President Heinrich Lübke, attempting an English translation of "*Gleich geht es los*" (It will soon begin), told the Queen: "Equal goes it loose." The Queen took the news well, but no better than the President of India, who was greeted at an airport in 1962 by Lübke, who, intending to ask, "How are you?" instead said: "Who are you?" To which his guest answered responsibly: "I am the President of India."

The most prodigious collector of modern slips was Kermit Schafer, whose "blooper" records of mistakes made on radio and television consisted largely of toilet jokes, but were nonetheless a great hit in the 1950s. Schafer was an avid self-promoter and something of a blooper himself, but he did have an ear for such things as the introduction by Radio Announcer Harry Von Zell of President "Hoobert Heever," as well as the interesting message: "This portion of *Woman on the Run* is brought to you by Phillips' Milk of Magnesia." Bloopers are the lowlife of verbal error, but spoonerisms are a different fettle of kitsch. In the early 1900s the Rev. William Archibald Spooner caused a stir at New College, Oxford, with his famous spoonerisms, most of which were either deliberate or apocryphal. But a real one—his giving out a hymn in chapel as "Kinquering Kongs Their Titles Take"—is said to have brought down the house of worship, and to have kicked off the genre. After that, spoonerisms got quite elaborate. Spooner once reportedly chided a student: "You have hissed all my mystery lectures. In fact, you have tasted the whole worm, and must leave by the first town drain."

Such missteps, while often howlingly funny to ignorami like us, are deadly serious concerns to psychologists and linguists. Victoria Fromkin of the linguistics department at U.C.L.A. regards slips of the tongue as clues to how the brain stores and articulates language. She believes that thought is placed by the brain into a grammatical framework before it is expressed—this in spite of the fact that she works with college students. A grammatical framework was part of Walter Annenberg's trouble when, as the newly appointed U.S. Ambassador to Britain, he was asked by the Queen how he was settling in to his London residence. Annenberg admitted to "some discomfiture as a result of a need for elements of refurbishing." Either he was overwhelmed by the circumstances or he was losing his mind.

When you get to that sort of error, you are nearing a psychological abyss. It was Freud who first removed the element of accident from language with his explanation of "slips," but lately others have extended his theories. Psychiatrist Richard Yazmajian, for example, suggests that there are some incorrect words that exist in associative chains with the correct ones for which they are substituted, implying a kind of "dream pair" of elements in the speaker's psyche. The nun who poured tea for the Irish bishop and asked, "How many lords, my lump?" might therefore have been asking a profound theological question.

On another front, Psychoanalyst Ludwig Eidelberg made Freud's work seem childishly simple when he suggested that a slip of the tongue involves the entire network of id, ego and superego. He offers the case of the young man who entered a restaurant with his girlfriend and ordered a room instead of a table. You probably think that you understand that error. But just listen to Eidelberg: "All the wishes connected with the word 'room' represented a countercathexis mobilized as a defense. The word 'table' had to be omitted, because it would have been used for infantile gratification of a repressed oral, aggressive and scopophilic wish connected with identification with the preoedipal mother." Clearly, this is no laughing matter.

Why then do we hoot at these mistakes? For one thing, it may be that we simply find conventional discourse so predictable and boring that any deviation comes as a delightful relief.

In his deeply unfunny *Essay on Laughter* the philosopher Henri Bergson theorized that the act of laughter is caused by any interruption of normal human fluidity or momentum (a pie in the face, a mask, a pun). Slips of the tongue, therefore, are like slips on banana peels; we crave their occurrence if only to break the monotonies. The monotonies run to substance. When that announcer introduced Hoobert Heever, he may also have been saying that the nation had had enough of Herbert Hoover.

Then too there is the element of pure meanness in such laughter, both the meanness of enjoyment in watching an embarrassed misspeaker's eyes roll upward as if in prayer—his hue turn magenta, his hands like homing larks fluttering to his mouth—and the mean joy of discovering his hidden base motives and critical intent. At the 1980 Democratic National Convention, Jimmy Carter took a lot of heat for referring to Hubert Humphrey as Hubert Horatio Hornblower because it was instantly recognized that Carter thought Humphrey a windbag. David Hartman of *Good Morning America* left little doubt about his feelings for a sponsor when he announced: "We'll be right back after this word from General Fools." At a conference in Berlin in 1954, France's Foreign Minister Georges Bidault was hailed as "that fine little French tiger, Georges Bidet," thus belittling the tiger by the tail. When we laugh at such stuff, it is the harsh and bitter laugh, the laugh at the disclosure of inner condemning truth.

Yet there is also a more kindly laugh that occurs when a blunderer does not reveal his worst inner thoughts, but his most charitable or optimistic. Gerald Ford's famous error in the 1976 presidential debate, in which he said that Poland was not under Soviet domination, for instance. In a way, that turned out to contain a grain of truth, thanks to Lech Walesa and the strikes; in any case it was a nice thing to wish. As was U.N. Ambassador Warren Austin's suggestion in 1948 that Jews and Arabs resolve their differences "in a true Christian spirit." Similarly, Nebraska's former Senator Kenneth Wherry might have been thinking dreamily when, in an hour-long speech on a country in Southeast Asia, he referred throughout to "Indigo-China." One has to be in the mood for such a speech.

Of course, the most interesting laugh is the one elicited by the truly bizarre mistake, because such a mistake seems to disclose a whole new world of logic and possibility, a deranged double for the life that is. What Lewis Carroll displayed through the looking-glass, verbal error also often displays by conjuring up ideas so supremely nutty that the laughter it evokes is sublime. The idea that Pepsi might actually bring one back from the grave encourages an entirely new view of experience. In such a view it is perfectly possible to lust after the Polish future, to watch the Tigers on the radio, to say "Equal goes it loose" with resounding clarity.

Still, beyond all this is another laugh entirely, that neither condemns, praises, ridicules nor conspires, but sees into the essential nature of a slip of the tongue and consequently sympathizes. After all, most human endeavor results in a slip of the something—the best-laid plans gone suddenly haywire by natural blunder: the chair, cake or painting that turns out not exactly as one imagined; the kiss or party that falls flat; the life that is not quite what one had in mind. Nothing is ever as dreamed.

So we laugh at each other, perfect fools all, flustered by the mistake of our mortality.

JOHN F. KENNEDY

Inaugural Address

My Fellow Citizens:

We observe today not a victory of party but a celebration of freedom—symbolizing an end as well as a beginning—signifying renewal as well as change. For I have sworn before you and Almighty God the same solemn oath our forebears prescribed nearly a century and three quarters ago.

The world is very different now. For man holds in his mortal hands the power to abolish all form of human poverty and to abolish all form of human life. And yet the same revolutionary beliefs for which our forebears fought are still at issue around the globe—the belief that the rights of man come not from the generosity of the state but from the hand of God.

We dare not forget today that we are the heirs of that first revolution. Let the word go forth from this time and place, to friend and foe alike, that the torch has been passed to a new generation of Americans—born in this century, tempered by war, disciplined by a cold and bitter peace, proud of our ancient heritage—and unwilling to witness or permit the slow undoing of those human rights to which this nation has always been committed, and to which we are committed today.

Let every nation know, whether it wish us well or ill, that we shall pay any price, bear any burden, meet any hardship, support any friend or oppose any foe in order to assure the survival and success of liberty.

This much we pledge—and more.

To those old allies whose cultural and spiritual origins we share, we pledge the loyalty of faithful friends. United, there is little we cannot do in a host of new cooperative ventures. Divided, there is little we can do—for we dare not meet a powerful challenge at odds and split asunder.

To those new states whom we now welcome to the ranks of the free, we pledge our word that one form of colonial control shall not have passed merely to be replaced by a far more iron tyranny. We shall not always expect to find them supporting our every view. But we shall always hope to find them strongly supporting their own freedom—and to remember that, in the past, those who foolishly sought to find power by riding on the tiger's back inevitably ended up inside.

To those people in the huts and villages of half the globe struggling to break the bonds of mass misery, we pledge our best efforts to help them help themselves, for whatever period is required—not because the communists are doing it, not because we seek their votes, but because it is right. If the free society cannot help the many who are poor, it can never save the few who are rich.

To our sister republics south of our border, we offer a special pledge—to convert our good words into good deeds—in a new alliance for progress—to assist free men and free governments in casting off the chains of poverty. But this peaceful revolution of hope cannot become the prey of hostile powers. Let all our neighbors know that we shall join with them to oppose aggression or subversion anywhere in the Americas. And let every other power know that this Hemisphere intends to remain the master of its own house.

To that world assembly of sovereign states, the United Nations, our last best hope in an age where the instruments of war have far outpaced the instruments of peace, we renew our pledge of support—to prevent its becoming merely a forum for invective—to strengthen its shield of the new and the weak—and to enlarge the area to which its writ may run.

Finally, to those nations who would make themselves our adversary, we offer not a pledge but a request: that both sides begin anew the quest for peace, before the dark powers of destruction unleashed by science engulf all humanity in planned or accidental self-destruction.

We dare not tempt them with weakness. For only when our

arms are sufficient beyond doubt can we be certain beyond doubt that they will never be employed.

But neither can two great and powerful groups of nations take comfort from their present course—both sides overburdened by the cost of modern weapons, both rightly alarmed by the steady spread of the deadly atom, yet both racing to alter that uncertain balance of terror that stays the hand of mankind's final war.

So let us begin anew—remembering on both sides that civility is not a sign of weakness, and sincerity is always subject to proof. Let us never negotiate out of fear. But let us never fear to negotiate.

Let both sides explore what problems unite us instead of belaboring the problems that divide us.

Let both sides, for the first time, formulate serious and precise proposals for the inspection and control of arms—and bring the absolute power to destroy other nations under the absolute control of all nations.

Let both sides join to invoke the wonders of science instead of its terrors. Together let us explore the stars, conquer the deserts, eradicate disease, tap the ocean depths and encourage the arts and commerce.

Let both sides unite to heed in all corners of the earth the command of Isaiah—to "undo the heavy burdens . . . (and) let the oppressed go free."

And if a beach-head of cooperation can be made in the jungles of suspicion, let both sides join in the next task: creating, not a new balance of power, but a new world of law, where the strong are just and the weak secure and the peace preserved forever.

All this will not be finished in the first one hundred days. Nor will it be finished in the first one thousand days, nor in the life of this Administration, nor even perhaps in our lifetime on this planet. But let us begin.

In your hands, my fellow citizens, more than in mine, will rest the final success or failure of our course. Since this country was founded, each generation has been summoned to give testimony to its national loyalty. The graves of young Americans who answered that call encircle the globe.

Now the trumpet summons us again—not as a call to bear

arms, though arms we need—not as a call to battle, though embattled we are—but a call to bear the burden of a long twilight struggle, year in and year out, "rejoicing in hope, patient in tribulation"—a struggle against the common enemies of man: tyranny, poverty, disease and war itself.

Can we forge against these enemies a grand and global alliance, North and South, East and West, that can assure a more fruitful life for all mankind? Will you join in that historic effort?

In the long history of the world, only a few generations have been granted the role of defending freedom in its hour of maximum danger. I do not shrink from this responsibility—I welcome it. I do not believe that any of us would exchange places with any other people or any other generation. The energy, the faith and the devotion which we bring to this endeavor will light our country and all who serve it—and the glow from that fire can truly light the world.

And so, my fellow Americans: ask not what your country will do for you—ask what you can do for your country.

My fellow citizens of the world: ask not what America will do for you, but what together we can do for the freedom of man.

Finally, whether you are citizens of America or of the world, ask of us the same high standards of strength and sacrifice that we shall ask of you. With a good conscience our only sure reward, with history the final judge of our deeds, let us go forth to lead the land we love, asking His blessing and His help, but knowing that here on earth God's work must truly be our own.

ACKNOWLEDGMENTS

INTRODUCTION

"Coke's Big Marketing Blitz." *Business Week*, May 30, 1983, p. 58.

"Lunar Tunes" from *New York Day by Day* by Clyde Haserman and Laurie Johnston in *The New York Times*, July 7, 1982. Copyright © 1982 by The New York Times Company. Reprinted by permission.

From *In Search of Light: The Broadcasts of Edward R. Murrow*, 1938–1961, edited with an introduction by Edward Bliss, Jr. Copyright © 1967 by the Estate of Edward R. Murrow. Reprinted by permission of Alfred A. Knopf, Inc.

PART 1

From "Howling Back at the Wolves." Geoffrey Wolff, ed., *The Edward Hoagland Reader.* New York: Random House, 1968, p. 8.

Mark Twain, *Roughing It.* Berkeley: University of California Press, 1972, pp. 66–67.

CHAPTER 1

From *The Personal Notebooks of Thomas Hardy*, edited by Richard H. Taylor. Copyright © 1979 by Richard H. Taylor. Reprinted by permission of Columbia University Press.

Michael Faraday, *Faraday's Diary—Vol. I*, Sept. 1820–June 11, 1832. London: G. Bell and Sons, Ltd., 1932.

Excerpts from *The Diary of Virginia Woolf, Volume One*. Copyright © 1977 by Quentin Bell and Angelica Garnett. Reprinted by permission of Harcourt Brace Jovanovich, Inc., the Author's Literary Estate and The Hogarth Press.

"September 15th" Reprinted from *Journal of a Solitude* by May Sarton, by permission of W. W. Norton & Company, Inc. Copyright © 1973 by May Sarton.

Reprinted from *The Journals and Papers of Gerard Manley Hopkins* edited by Humphry House (1959) by permission of The Oxford University Press. © The Society of Jesus 1959.

CHAPTER 2

Frederick Douglass, *My Bondage and My Freedom*, 1855.

From *The Autobiography of Charles Darwin* 1809–1882. Copyright © 1958 by Nora Barlow. Reprinted by permission of Harcourt Brace Jovanovich, Inc. and A. D. Peters & Co., Ltd.

Specified excerpts (pp. 109–116 and "Author's Note" on page 192) from *Mark Twain's Autobiography, Volume I*, by Mark Twain. Copyright 1924, by Clara Gabrilowitsch; renewed, 1952, by Clara Clemens Samossoud. Reprinted by permission of Harper & Row, Publishers, Inc.

"When the Other Dancer Is the Self" Copyright © 1983 by Alice Walker. Reprinted from her volume *In Search of Our Mothers' Gardens* by permission of Harcourt Brace Jovanovich, Inc.

CHAPTER 3

Edward Hoagland, *Tugman's Passage*. New York: Random House, 1982.

"Grace In Motion" by Gary Esolen from *Gambit*, September 25–October 1, 1982, Vol. 3, No. 38. Reprinted by permission.

"A Love That Transcends Sadness" by Willie Morris. Copyright © 1981 by Willie Morris. First appeared in *Parade*. Reprinted by permission of The Sterling Lord Agency, Inc.

"The Eyes of Fear" by Laurence Shames from *Esquire*, September 1982. Copyright © 1982 Esquire Associates. Reprinted by permission.

Specified excerpt from "Foreword" and "Bedfellows" from *Essays of E. B. White*. "Bedfellows" originally appeared in *The New Yorker*. Copyright 1956, © 1977 by E. B. White. Reprinted by permission of Harper & Row, Publishers, Inc.

PART 2, CHAPTER 4

Bertrand Russell, "On History" from *Basic Writings of Bertrand Russell*, 1904.

"Eli Whitney" from *Concise Dictionary of American Biography*. Copyright © 1980 Charles Scribner's Sons. Reprinted with the permission of Charles Scribner's Sons.

"Eli Whiteney" from *The New Encyclopaedia Britannica*, Volume 19. Chicago: Encyclopaedia Britannica Inc., 1982.

"The Black Reaction to *Gone With The Wind*" by John D. Stevens from *Journal of Popular Film*, Fall 1973. Copyright © 1973 by Sam L. Grogg, Jr., Michael T. Marsden, and John G. Nachbar. Reprinted by permission.

"If You've Got an Ounce of Feeling, Hallmark Has a Ton of Sentiment" by James McKinley. Copyright © 1982 American Heritage Publishing Co., Inc. Reprinted by permission from *American Heritage*, December 1982.

"Curtain Raiser" from *The Armada* by Garrett Mattingly. Copyright © 1959 by Garrett Mattingly. Reprinted by permission of Houghton Mifflin Company.

CHAPTER 5

Lewis Thomas, "Are We Fit to Fit in?" *Sierra*, March/April 1982.

From "Black Holes 'n' You" by Alex Heard from *The New York Times*, April 2, 1983. Copyright © 1983 by The New York Times Company. Reprinted by permission.

T. H. Huxley, "We Are All Scientists" from *New Treasury of Science* by Harlow Shapley, Samuel Rapport, and Helen Wright. New York: Harper & Row, 1965.

"Useful and Surprising Facts About Eggs" by Mark Mikolas in *The (Old) Farmers Almanac*, 1983. Reprinted by permission of the author.

From *The Fate of the Earth*, by Jonathan Schell. Copyright © 1982 by Jonathan Schell. Reprinted by permission of Alfred A. Knopf, Inc. Originally appeared in *The New Yorker*.

"On Being the Right Size" from *Possible Worlds and Other Papers* by J. B. S. Haldane. Copyright, 1928, by Harper & Row, Publishers, Inc.; renewed, 1956, by J. B. S. Haldane. Reprinted by permission of Harper & Row, Publishers, Inc., the author's Literary Estate and Chatto & Windus.

PART 3

Evelyn Waugh, *A Handful of Dust*. New York: Dell, 1934, p. 41.

CHAPTER 6

"An Informal Tour of Europe as a State of Mind" by John E. Pluenneke. Reprinted from the June 20, 1983 issue of *Business Week* by special permission, © 1983 by McGraw-Hill, Inc.

"E.T. The Extra-Terrestrial" by Peter Rainer from *Mademoiselle*, September 1982. Copyright © 1982 by the Condé Nast Publications Inc. Reprinted by permission of the author.

"Very High Sci-Fi" by Tom O'Brien from *Commonweal*, August 13, 1982. Copyright © 1982 by Commonweal Publishing Co. Reprinted by permission.

"Food matches elegant decor" by John V. R. Bull from *The Philadelphia Inquirer*, June 19, 1983. Reprinted by permission.

CHAPTER 7

"Cake Mixes" Copyright © 1982 by Consumers Union of United States, Inc., Mount Vernon, NY 10553. Excerpted by permission from *Consumer Reports*, March 1982.

From *To Read Poetry* by Donald Hall. Copyright © 1982 by CBS College Publishing. Reprinted by permission of CBS College Publishing.

"Stopping by Woods on a Snowy Evening" from *The Poetry of Robert Frost* edited by Edward Connery Lathem. Copyright 1923, © 1969 by Holt, Rinehart and Winston. Copyright 1951 by Robert Frost. Reprinted by permission of Holt, Rinehart and Winston, Publishers.

Excerpts from "The Confrontation of the Two Americas" from *Time*, October 2, 1972. Copyright © 1972 Time Inc. All rights reserved. Reprinted by permission.

PART 4

From "Aids Anxiety" by Michael Daly in *New York* Magazine, June 20, 1983. Copyright © 1983 by Michael Daly. Reprinted by permission of The Sterling Lord Agency, Inc.

From *Madame Bovary*, by Gustave Flaubert, translated by Francis Steegmuller. Copyright © 1957 by Francis Steegmuller. Reprinted by permission of Random House, Inc.

CHAPTER 8

"Timeless Beauty Under Gorgeous Skies" by Tricia Hurst from *Guestlife*, 1982. Copyright © 1982 Desert Publications, Inc. Reprinted by permission.

CHAPTER 9

"On the Need for Asylums" from *Late Night Thoughts on Listening to Mahler's Ninth Symphony* by Lewis Thomas. Copyright © 1981 by Lewis Thomas. Reprinted by permission of Viking Penguin Inc.

"Cheating on Campus: Who's Really to Blame?" by Gary Pavela from *The Chronicle of Higher Education*, February 9, 1981. Copyright © 1981 by The Chronicle of Higher Education. Reprinted with permission.

"Active and Passive Euthanasia" by James Rachels from *The New England Journal of Medicine*, January 9, 1975, Vol. 292, No. 2. Reprinted by permission of the author.

PART 5, CHAPTER 10

"Baseball Was a Nasty Business for a Black Man: Hank Aaron, Home-Run Hitting King, Talks to Lee Michael Katz" from *The Washington Post*, June 5, 1983. Reprinted by permission of Lee Michael Katz.

CHAPTER 11

"Lecture I" reprinted from *Complete Introductory Lectures on Psychoanalysis* by Sigmund Freud. Translated and Edited by James Strachey, by permission of W. W. Norton & Company, Inc. Copyright © 1966 by W. W. Norton & Company, Inc. Copyright © 1965, 1964, 1963 by James Strachey. Copyright 1933 by Sigmund Freud. Copyright renewed 1961 by W. J. H. Sprott. Copyright 1920, 1935 by Edward L. Bernays.

Excerpt from *A Fistful of Fig Newtons* by Jean Shepherd. Copyright © 1981 by Snow Pond Productions, Inc. Reprinted by permission of Doubleday & Company, Inc.

CHAPTER 12

Copyright 1951 by Estelle Faulkner and Jill Faulkner Summers. Reprinted from *Essays, Speeches and Public Letters*, by William Faulkner, edited by James B. Meriwether, by permission of Random House, Inc.

"A Message to Intellectuals" from *Out of My Later Years* by Albert Einstein. Copyright 1950 by The Philosophical Library, Inc. Reprinted by permission.

"Who Then Will Speak for the Common Good?" by Barbara Jordan from *Vital Speeches of the Day*, Vol. 42, No. 21, August 15, 1976, pp. 645–46. Reprinted by permission.

"Power of the Printed Word" advertisement, "How to Make a Speech" by George Plimpton. Reprinted by permission of International Paper Company.

PART 6

"Leave the Dead" by Peter Steinhart from *Audubon*, January 1981. Reprinted by permission of the author.

Edward R. Murrow, March 9, 1941 broadcast, *This Is London* (New York: Simon & Schuster). Reprinted with the permission of the Edward R. Murrow Estate.

"Absence of Moral Teaching" from *The Daily Oklahoman*, May 1983. Reprinted by permission.

"The Waiting Game" by Gene Hill from *Field & Stream*, June 1983. Copyright © 1983 CBS Publications, the Consumer Publishing Division of CBS Inc. Reprinted by permission.

"An Evening at the Waldorf" by Jean and Bud Ince from *Gourmet*, December 1978. Reprinted by permission of the authors.

"Justice: A Cynical View" by James L. Files from *The (Free) Weekly Newspaper*, June 29, 1983. Reprinted by permission.

"The Package" from *When the Lights Go Down* by Pauline Kael. Copyright © 1975, 1976, 1977, 1978, 1979, 1980 by Pauline Kael. Reprinted by permission of Holt, Rinehart and Winston, Publishers.

"Little Red Riding Hood Revisited" by Russell Baker from *The New York Times*, January 13, 1980. Copyright © 1980 by The New York Times Company. Reprinted by permission.

"Oops! How's That Again?" by Roger Rosenblatt from *Time*, March 30, 1981. Copyright © 1981 Time Inc. All rights reserved. Reprinted by permission.

John F. Kennedy, "Inaugural Address," 1961.

GLOSSARY OF RHETORICAL TERMS

Active voice See *Voice.*

Ad hominem A logical fallacy in which the argument is directed at the person, not the view held by the person. Name-calling.

Ad populem A logical fallacy in which the argument is directed at the group the opponent belongs to, not the views held by the opponent. Name-calling.

Aim See *Purpose.*

Allusion A reference to a real or fictitious person, place, or thing. An allusion is a concise form of association that carries the meaning of the thing alluded to and uses it to enhance the writer's own meaning.

Analogy One of the patterns used to develop an idea. Analogy examines a topic by comparing it point by point to something seemingly unlike but more commonplace and less intricate. Analogy extends a metaphor, concentrating on one subject; comparison and contrast explores the similarities and differences of two or more subjects within the same class.

Antithesis The use of opposite words or phrases to emphasize contrasting ideas that are usually stated in balanced or parallel terms.

Argumentative appeals The three classical appeals central to argument: *logos,* the appeal to reason; *pathos,* to emotion; and *ethos,* to the writer or speaker's persona. For a fuller discussion, see part 4 and chapter 9.

Argumentative writing One of the four major purposes of writing, Argument attempts to move the reader to action or to adopting the writer's conviction. Many teachers distinguish between argumentative and persuasive writing: argumentative writing appealing primarily to reason, persuasive writing to emotion.

Assertion Sometimes the author's major assertion appears in the essay's title (Peter Steinhart, "Leave the Dead"), sometimes in a key sentence. Often, however, the reader deduces the writer's assertion by considering the essay's most important statements, most of which appear as topic sentences.

Audience The intended readership for a given work. The audience can be general, as in Lewis Thomas' "On the Need for Asylums," specific as in James Rachels' "Active and Passive Euthanasia," or multiple, as in Francine Klagsbrun's "Hooray for Jewish Mothers!" No matter what the audience, a writer should keep in mind A. D. Van Nostrand's summary of the "Common Reader": a person who does not know the thesis, is impatient, shares the writer's level of maturity and education, and knows something about the subject.

Balanced sentence See *Sentence.*

Begging the question A logical fallacy in which the major line of argument is dodged and a lesser line taken up instead.

Cause and effect One of the patterns used to develop an idea. Cause and effect examines the topic to discover, explain, or argue why a particular action, event, situation, or condition occurred.

Chronological organization See *Organization.*

Classification One of the patterns used to develop an idea. Classification examines a class of things according to shared characteristics, grouping the things according to a similar feature.

Coherence Literally the quality of sticking together. To communicate ideas clearly to the reader, the writer must present material in a logically integrated, understandable, and consistent manner; in short, words, phrases, clauses, sentences, and paragraphs must cohere. Coherence can be achieved by using appropriate transitions, logical sequences, and interlocking ideas.

Comparison and contrast One of the patterns used to develop an idea. Comparison and contrast examines two or more subjects by exploring their similarities and differences. Similarities are usually developed through literal and logical comparisons within similar categories: small cars such as VW and Honda, popular music such as rock and disco. Figurative comparisons usually come under analogy. In contrasting subjects, differences fall into two categories: differences in kind, such as Yale has a football team and the University of Chicago does not; or differences in degree, such as the University of Michigan has a better football team than the University of Texas.

Conflict An element essential to narrative. Conflict involves pitting one force against another: Mary, Queen of Scots against Elizabeth I, Catholicism against the Church of England, and France and Spain against England, all in Garrett Mattingly's "Curtain Raising."

Complex sentence See *Sentence.*
Compound-complex sentence See *Sentence.*
Connotation The meanings associated with and suggested by a word that augment its explicit denotative or dictionary definition. The words *home* and *domicile* have a similar denotative value, but they differ radically in their connotations.
Cumulative sentence See *Sentence.*

Deductive reasoning The method of argument whereby the author first gives the assertion and then explores the reasoning behind it. "Cheating on Campus: Who's Really to Blame?" and "TV Violence: The Shocking New Evidence" are both organized deductively.
Definition One of the patterns used to develop an idea. Definition examines a word or phrase by exploring its meaning, determining its essence. Simple definition employs synonyms, antonyms, and etymology; extended definition may use classification, comparison, description, and example as well as other patterns in order to expand upon the connotations of a word or phrase.
Denotation See *Connotation.*
Description One of the patterns used to develop an idea. Description explores the subject by breaking it down into parts in order to better understand the whole. It draws upon the senses to paint vivid images usually set in time and space, employing repetition, enumeration, spatial development, perspective, and imagery. Description can be classified according to what is described, a person, place, or thing, or according to how it is described, subjectively or objectively.
Detail A precise description—"quaking aspens" instead of "trees," for example.
Diction The writer's choice of words. The level of diction (colloquial, slang, informal, technical, formal) along with denotation, connotation, and sound determine the writer's judgment of a word's appropriateness to the work's audience and the writer's purpose.
Division Usually associated with classification. First a subject is divided into groups, then examples can be sorted out—classified—into the groups or categories.
Dramatic organization See *Organization.*

Either/or reasoning A logical fallacy in which the central term is claimed to be either one thing or another, omitting any possibility of middle ground. A writer who argues that a person must believe in either democracy or communism is guilty of either/or thinking.

Ethos See *Argumentative appeals.*

Example One of the patterns used to develop an idea. Example explores an assertion by illustrating it, showing how the assertion applies in particular instances. Example is used to provide evidence to support generalizations.

Expository writing See *Purpose.*

Expressive writing One of the four major purposes of writing. Expressive writing emphasizes the author's feelings or attitudes toward the subject.

Fallacy See *Logical fallacies.*

False analogy A logical fallacy in which the analogy does not hold true. James Rachels, for instance, equates a murder with a doctor's letting a patient die, and he points out the false analogy.

Hasty generalization A logical fallacy in which a conclusion is reached on the basis of inadequate examples or sampling. If Eugene H. Methvin had rested his assertion on one or two examples, he would have been guilty of hasty generalization.

Imperative mood See *Mood.*

Imperative sentence See *Sentence.*

Indicative mood See *Mood.*

Inductive reasoning The method of argument whereby the author first presents information and then moves from explanation and evidence to a logical conclusion. Alice Walker, Francine Klagsbrun, and Sigmund Freud all use inductive reasoning in their essays.

Information writing One of the four major purposes of writing. Informative writing attempts to further the reader's understanding about the topic.

Interrogative sentence See *Sentence.*

Irony A statement or action in which the intended meaning or occurrence is the opposite of the surface one. The very notion of mass-producing personal sentiment ("If You've Got an Ounce of Feeling, Hallmark Has a Ton of Sentiment") is ironic.

Journalistic questions The traditional questions: who, what, where, when, why, and how.

Logical fallacies Errors in reasoning. See *Ad hominem, Ad populem, Begging the question, Either/or reasoning, False analogy, Hasty generalization, Misusing authority, Non sequitur, Post hoc, Propter hoc, Shift in definition, Straw man.*

Logos See *Argumentative appeals.*

Loose sentence See *Sentence.*

Metaphor An implied but direct comparison in which the primary term is made more vivid by associating it with a quite dissimilar term. Virginia Woolf, for instance, likens her journal-writing to a "haphazard gallop."

Middle premise See *Syllogism.*

Misusing authority A logical fallacy in which a person's skill or knowledge in one area is assumed to exist in another. A successful baseball player may be a valid authority on makes of baseball gloves, for instance, but not on after-shave lotion.

Modes Common patterns of thought used to explore, develop, and organize a topic. The various modes or patterns can be classified according to their function: those that sequence information are narration, process, and cause and effect; those that compare are analogy and comparison and contrast; and those that divide are classification, description, definition, and example.

Mood An aspect of the verb that reveals the attitude of the writer. The indicative mood states fact or asks a question; the subjunctive mood states a matter of possibility, desire, contradiction, or uncertainty; the imperative mood states a command or request.

Name-calling See *Ad hominem* and *Ad populem.*

Narration One of the patterns used to develop an idea. Narration explores a topic by presenting a story or account of an experience bounded by time and space. Whereas cause and effect emphasizes *why*, and process emphasizes *how*, narration emphasizes *what*. Narration can be factual, grounded in an actual event, or fictional, grounded in the imagination.

Non sequitur A logical fallacy in which the causal relationship claimed does not follow: "The essay was published in *The New York Times*, so it must be accurate."

Organization The manner in which a paragraph or essay is put together. Essays are usually organized by several principles: the various modes, and chronological, dramatic, or spatial order. Chronological order is determined by time, dramatic order by emotional effect, and spatial order by physical location.

Paradox A statement that appears to be contradictory yet may in fact be true; an apparent contradiction.

Paragraph A cohesive unit of thought or emphasis set off by indention. Most paragraphs develop a controlling assertion or topic sentence, explicit or implied, and therefore run to 150 words or so; other shorter paragraphs function as transitions or as rhetorical devices.

Paragraph block A group of paragraphs that taken together develop a controlling assertion or topic sentence. E. B. White's "Bedfellows" illustrates how paragraph blocks can help guide the reader through an essay.

Parallelism The repetition of words or grammatically similar phrases, clauses, or sentences to emphasize coherence.

Parody An exaggerated imitation that treats a serious subject in an absurd manner, ridiculing both form and content. Jean Shepherd's "Van Culture" parodies a college lecture.

Passive voice See *Voice.*

Pathos See *Argumentative appeals.*

Patterns of organization Common patterns of thought used to explore, develop, and organize a topic. The various patterns can be classified according to their function. Those that sequence material are cause and effect, process, and narration; those that compare are analogy and comparison and contrast; those that divide are classification, description, definition, and example. Patterns of organization are also called modes.

Persona The mask or character assumed by the writer to engage the intended audience. While the most obvious persona is an ironic one (as in the case of Jean Shepherd), to achieve credibility, focus, and emphasis, all writers assume personas to greater or lesser degrees.

Periodic sentence See *Sentence.*

Persuasive writing See *Argumentative writing* and *Purpose.*

Point of view The perspective from which the work is related. In nonfiction, point of view usually refers to the writer's use of personal pronouns (*I, you, he, she, we, they*, etc.); in fiction, point of view is usually further divided into first person, limited omniscient, omniscient, and objective.

Post hoc, propter hoc A logical fallacy in which a temporal relationship is mistaken for a causal one; if all your lights went out just as you plugged in your new television set and you then assume you are the cause of the power failure, you may be in a *post hoc* trap.

Process One of the patterns used to develop an idea. Process examines the topic to discover the series of steps or acts that brought or will bring about a particular result. Whereas cause and effect emphasizes why, and depends primarily on analysis, process emphasizes how and depends primarily on classification. For example, the topic "leaving the teaching profession" can be developed by cause and effect, explaining *why* by providing an analysis of the various reasons that lay behind the decision, or by process, explaining *how* by showing the steps that were involved, steps that may be put in categories such as first doubts, the brink of decision, and tidying up. Process can be further divided into historical, practical, and scientific: historical process deals with topics such as how the United States will carry out foreign policy or how Mary, Queen of Scots, met her end; practical process deals with topics such as how to avoid a hangover; scientific process deals with topics such as how animals achieve an ideal size.

Purpose Most written work can be classified into one of four categories according to its purpose: expressive writing, such as journal entries and diaries that analyze, record, relate the writer's feelings and ideas; informative or expository writing, such as explanations and analyses that further the reader's understanding about the topic; persuasive or argumentative writing, such as narratives, descriptions, and analyses that try to move the reader to action or to share the writer's conviction; and literary writing, such as poems, plays, short stories, and novels that create fictional worlds out of the interplay of language. In general, expressive writing emphasizes the writer, informative writing the subject, persuasive writing the reader, and literary writing the language itself.

Sarcasm A caustic or sneering remark or tone that is usually ironic as well.

Satire The use of wit, sarcasm, irony, and parody to ridicule or expose some folly or evil.

Sequence See *Organization*.

Sensory detail Detail relating to one or more senses. See *Detail*.

Sentence In grammar, sentences can be classified as simple, compound, and compound-complex. A simple sentence has one main clause and no subordinate clauses; a complex sentence has a main clause and a subordinate clause; a compound sentence has two or more main clauses and no subordinate clause; and a compound-complex sentence has two or more main clauses and one or more subordinate clauses.

In rhetoric, sentences can be classified as declarative, stating facts; as interrogative, asking questions; as imperative, giving commands; and as exclamatory, expressing feeling.

Also in rhetoric, certain types of sentences achieve certain effects; the cumulative or loose sentence, in which the main clause comes first, occurs most frequently and allows for modification without sacrificing clarity; the less used periodic sentence, in which the main clause comes last, achieves dramatic tension; and the balanced sentence, in which phrases are parallel, usually emphasizes contrast.

Shift in definition A logical fallacy in which the meaning of a term central to the argument is changed. A person who shifts the definition of lying from intention to deceive to the far narrower meaning of verbal untruth is guilty of a shift in definition, a form of *begging the question.*

Simile A stated but removed comparison in which the primary term is made vivid by associating it with a quite dissimilar one. Simile differs from metaphor in that simile uses a term of comparison such as "like" or "as," as in Thomas Hardy's "Rain: like a banner of gauze waved in folds across the scene."

Simple sentence See *Sentence.*

Spatial organization See *Organization.*

Straw man A logical fallacy in which the argument is shifted to an insignificant or unrelated point, which is then attacked and destroyed in hopes that some of the destruction will carry over to the main point. The use of an extreme example is a popular form of straw man argument.

Subjunctive mood See *Mood.*

Syllogism A form of deductive reasoning composed of a major premise, a minor or middle premise, and a conclusion: All Labrador retrievers are gentle; Beartrap is a Labrador retriever; therefore Beartrap is gentle. Note that a syllogism can be logical but false, as above.

Syntax The way in which words are put together to form phrases, clauses, and sentences; the grammatical relationship between the words.

Thesis A statement about a subject that accounts for the relevant information about it; a statement or assertion of the subject's significance. An essay's thesis is its umbrella statement, the assertion at the highest level of generality under which all the essay's other assertions fit.

Tone A writer's attitude toward the subject and the audience. An author's tone can be contemplative (Willie Morris), enthusiastic (Peter Rainer), tongue-in-cheek (Francine Klagsbrun), and so on.

Topic sentence A topic sentence is to the paragraph what the thesis is to the essay. It states the topic and an assertion about the topic. Whether implicit or explicit, the topic sentence is the paragraph's controlling idea.

Transition A word, phrase, sentence, or paragraph can serve as a transition, carrying the reader smoothly from point A to point B. Some transitions, such as time markers and semantic guideposts—*therefore, however, but,* etc.—are overt; others are more subtle—a repeated word or phrase, a synonym for a key term, a shift in tense. All, however, provide coherence and unity.

Voice In grammar, the term refers to forms of the verb. If the subject performs the action, the verb is in the active voice; if the subject is acted upon, the verb is in the passive voice: "I bit the dog" versus "The dog was bitten by me."

In rhetoric and composition, voice refers to the reader's sense of the writer as a real person. A writer's voice is a combination of tone and persona.

Wordplay A clever phrasing of words, a pun.

INDEX